Crabgrass Crucible

Christopher C. Sellers

Crabgrass 🌿 Crucible

Suburban Nature and the Rise of Environmentalism in Twentieth-Century America

The University of North Carolina Press　Chapel Hill

Publication of this book was supported in part by a generous gift from Mary Coker Joslin in memory of William C. Coker.

Designed by Michelle Coppedge. Set in Sabon with ITC American Typewriter display by Rebecca Evans. Manufactured in the United States of America.

The paper in this book meets the guidelines for permanence and durability of the Committee on Production Guidelines for Book Longevity of the Council on Library Resources.

The University of North Carolina Press has been a member of the Green Press Initiative since 2003.

Library of Congress Cataloging-in-Publication Data
Sellers, Christopher C.
Crabgrass crucible : suburban nature and the rise of environmentalism in twentieth-century America / Christopher Sellers.
p. cm.
Includes bibliographical references and index.
ISBN 978-0-8078-3543-2 (cloth : alk. paper)
1. Environmentalism—United States—History—20th century. 2. Suburbs—United States—History—20th century. 3. Environmental policy—United States—History—20th century. 4. United States—Environmental conditions. I. Title.
GE197.S4 2012
304.20973'091733—dc23
2011044466

16 15 14 13 12   5 4 3 2 1

To suburban journeyers far and wide,

but especially **Nancy & Annie**

Contents

Illustrations, Maps, and Figures

Figures

Green's Suburban Provenance

This book's most formative moment came in 1994, when I became a suburbanite. That year, my wife and I bought a house on Long Island, New York, by local lights "the nation's first suburb."[1] Seeking shelter on Long Island seemed about as far as you could get from anyone's idea of a nature quest. Driving around, my overriding impression was how, as if in archetype, its endless subdivisions, malls, and traffic matched my preconceptions of what a suburb was. To the realtor, we must have seemed just as true to type: first-time home buyers, looking for a place in between our jobs to raise our seven-month-old. After two months of house touring and haggling, we agreed to buy a three-bedroom Cape. Trading away decades of salary, but eager to end our bit part as buyers, we signed the papers for a tiny piece of the New York metropolis.

At least, that side of the place seemed easiest to see. Later, I grew to realize there was more to our new home than that.

I found it difficult to disentangle my initial, favorable impression of the house we had bought from its trees. Reaching perhaps seventy feet up, far above the roof, an oak and a linden, thick in trunk, framed our view of the house from the front the moment we first drove up. They had in all likelihood been planted, but many years back, before the house itself arose. After we had tucked away our title papers and settled into familial and workaday routines, those trees kept gaining in girth and leaf span, sprouting and shedding with the seasons, nourished by the rain. As the act of home buying faded into memory, they and other plants and creatures close by crept further into our consciousness. Around the house, they were hardest to miss when they spurred work or worry: the grass, when begging for the mower or sprinkler hose; some field mice, after wriggling their way into our kitchen; an ant colony that tracked from the linden tree's roots into our basement walls. In idle moments, as well, our minds could shutter open to how profuse a life lay near at hand. One summer at dusk, as my wife sat out on the deck, three raccoons walked in single file across the back fence. Another afternoon, staring out from my upstairs study in a moment of reverie, I realized that all hint of a house or fence or road had vanished, papered over by the bright, bobbing greenery of new leaves. From the right angle, in the right light, even in this seemingly most built of places, the natural world began to loom closer.

"Back to nature"—the very phrase connotes the importance of memory to popular notions of what is natural and wild. Those many-lobed leaves and scampering creatures, I was not just seeing them but *recognizing* them. What clicked was perhaps some trace of ancestral memory, no doubt filtered through what I had read by nature writers and scientists. I also could not mistake the echoes of my own early years in a small town in the western North Carolina mountains. Back then, of course, what I had seen, like the Long Island yard ogled by our toddling child, had come less filtered through adult understanding. What struck me as well, in comparing these two places in the present, via regular returns to where my parents still lived, was how much of the built side of Long Island was overtaking Hendersonville, North Carolina.

The avalanche of new construction followed a pattern so familiar to early twenty-first-century Americans as to be ingrained in their bones. Roads added lanes, traffic, and strips of chain stores. Out next to the interstate, the first mall appeared, followed by the first Wal-Mart and a host of other big-box stores. All around the town edges, the apple orchards shrank back, ridges shed their trees, hillsides grew spotted with subdivisions. Accelerating especially over the 1990s real estate boom, the changes literally hit home in the neighborhood where the house of my childhood lay. An old sandpit where we had dug our make-believe forts filled in with split-levels. The creek we had dammed and trolled for crayfish turned trashier and smellier. Those same memories that cued my eye motes to Long Island's oaks, rhododendrons, and robins magnified my disquiet over this many-fronted assault on where they had been born.

This book is about how, through similar moments and memories, the grass roots of what we now call "environmentalism" first stirred. The formal research for this book began just after my Long Island move, as I looked into a band of litigants whose activism had helped inspire Rachel Carson's *Silent Spring*. Five years before that celebrated publication, in 1957, this group—suburbanites all—launched the first public trial against the pesticide DDT. Through this trial, they sought articulation and outlet for a much greater breadth of anxieties ever more widely shared. This book tells how urbanization, as it proceeded along the edges of many American cities after World War II, produced its own characteristic form of alienation.[2] This estrangement, at the heart of what were among the world's freest and most financially lubricated land markets, pivoted around the home rather than the workplace. The alienated were owners of smaller lots, not those dispossessed of land. This alienation had historic consequences. Among them, a new movement calling itself environmentalism arose, at once sweeping and self-abnegating in vision, to become its most powerful and lasting political expression. My chief argument is this: Those ideologies and coalitions that made this movement a popular force after World War II were born in those places touched most and earliest by postwar sprawl.

Sprawl, in its broadest sense, is far from new.[3] Since antiquity, cities have grown through the spreading out of traditionally urban functions—housing, marketing, and manufacturing—to mix among lands devoted to agriculture, logging, or mining and other classically rural uses. Most important for my story is that around the largest and fastest growing of America's post–World War II metropolises, this process achieved a recognizable pattern and reached a certain threshold. As decentralization accelerated, courtesy of cars, trucks, and freeways, the edges of cities such as New York and Los Angeles bore the early brunt of a new dispersion of industry, also of an epochal shift in home ownership. In the three decades after 1940, the proportion of families holding title to their own roofs hiked upward from 43.6 percent to 62.9 percent of American households.[4] The edges of America's greatest and wealthiest cities were the first to become overwhelmed by a suburban development that has since transformed the edges of towns across the United States, even across the rural South. Internationally as well, similar versions of sprawl have overtaken cities throughout the developed world, especially as a nation's urbanites have acquired automobiles.[5]

Sprawl's ubiquity has made it easier for many of us to empathize with how, where it crystallized earliest, a local environmentalism could also stir. Los Angeles as well as New York, among the first to acquire a freeway scale of dispersion, also played host to forerunning environmental mobilizations, significantly prior to the first Earth Day in 1970. Elsewhere—for instance, around Atlanta, which I also researched in depth—sprawl's later arrival stirred a local environmentalism, but via delayed dynamics that provided a study in contrasts. I have now reserved that history for another book. If the histories of Los Angeles and New York proved far easier to intermesh into a single tale, it was not because differences of timing and region were unimportant. Long Island's slightly earlier sprawl stemmed from the fact that New York was already the nation's largest city and also from the features it shared with smaller cities in the Northeast and Midwest. Their cores were older and denser, thanks to long-standing roles as regional seats of the nation's manufacturing. That younger Los Angeles sprawled so rapidly during and just after the World War II period also owed much to regional trajectories it shared with neighboring cities. Its rise, to become the nation's second largest city, reflected the passage of jobs and people to the Western Sunbelt. Especially for readers who live in neither of these metropolises, I stress how their individual stories more or less reflect those of other cities in their regions, as well as experiences shared, whether sooner or later, in other urbanizing corners of the nation.[6]

The earliness of the sprawl in Long Island and Los Angeles accorded them an additional historical distinctiveness. They became cultural icons, expressive of the troubles that dawned with a new, increasingly more dispersive style of city building. Exemplars from these places first dramatized the arrival of a suburbia so large-scale and packed as to be called "mass." They supplied much of the imagery whereby "urban sprawl" morphed from description into slur. By the time the first Earth Day rolled around, the gathering afflictions of these suburbanizing metropolises, not least their pollution, had sealed their notoriety as this nation's canaries in the mine. That their ills could serve as such harbingers was not merely due to their accessibility to the nation's media, much of which headquartered in their downtowns. It also stemmed, not so paradoxically, from local *political* innovations: how their suburban residents became among America's first to forge popular new ways of invoking nature to mobilize a citizenry.

This postwar reputation of Greater New York City and Greater Los Angeles as dying canaries has long obscured the nature that their urban edges continued to harbor, as well as the path-breaking ways residents rallied on its behalf. Adam Rome's *Bulldozer in the Countryside* offers a case in point.[7] Deftly unpacking the problems associated with postwar suburbs that made them major targets for environmentalists, he simply rules out the possibility of nature in suburbs, much less any authentic nature seeking. Ecological awareness, he suggests, could only have originated from the outside, among professional ecologists, federal officials, and public-minded elites. Rome thereby echoes the assumptions of a long-standing choir of others, from urban and environmental historians, to city and regional planners, to many a contemporary environmentalist. But the truth of the matter, I have found, is quite the opposite. Through shared experiences, knowledge, and politics first forged *within* America's most dynamic postwar urban edges, suburb dwellers deserve much of the credit for inventing modern environmentalism. Among their innovations, in particular, were new ways of thinking about a nature under threat: not as distant resources in need of conservation, but as "the environment."

Sprawl, after all, was not just about the building of subdivisions or malls; into the midst of its churning transformations it ushered a growing population whose expectations ran otherwise. Ever more unmistakably over the twentieth century, the outward expansion of American cities has been spearheaded by quests for more natural surroundings, whether from greenery or privacy or small-town comfort or countryside.[8] Consequently, folded within the many additions to the nation's metropolitan areas since 1900 are not just people and their edifices but new, historically and geographically specific patterns of nonhuman life. Think for a moment about an older downtown you know, a Manhattan or a San Francisco; compare it with just about any American suburb with which you are familiar. Like the Long Island where I live, our suburban versions of the city leave much more space for plants and animals. Whether expressly imported, or arriving (or remaining) independent of human intent, their flora and fauna comprise a characteristically *suburban nature*. This book, as it now stands, pivots not so much around "suburbia" or "sprawl" themselves as around this ecological substrate, at once built and biological. If my subject is suburban, it is so in an older, strictly geographic sense: like "urban edge" or "periphery," about those places lying more or less beyond a downtown.

Attending closely to suburban nature, this book seeks to flip long-standing generalizations about "suburbia" on their heads. The term evokes a visual monotony; yet suburban uniformity did not come so easily. To create it, in places as different as Long Island and Los Angeles, regional contrasts in topography, flora, and aridity, among others, had to be overcome. Nor was the suburban confined to the tamest and most subdivided of landscapes. Defined as a location rather than as a place stereotype, the suburban names a continuum of places, all of them hybridizing city with country, but in differing measure: from the most densely built and domesticated of subdivisions all the way out to where farms and forests predominate. Bringing the wilder reaches of the urban edge into the picture, in particular, helps illuminate a diversity of suburban places that is every bit as ecological as it is social, even if we are more accustomed to speaking about it in terms of class and race.

Nassau County's Greenbelt Trail, a twenty-two-mile path blazed in the 1980s, slips through the historic heartland of this diversity, Long Island's postwar suburban landscape. Starting at a trailhead not far from the Southern State Parkway, you can walk a more or less continuous thread of secluded patches of woodland and meadow across the island, along a thirty-mile radius out from Manhattan, from south to north. Throughout its southerly length, the trail stays within a strip of state park at most a quarter mile wide, sandwiched between a Scylla and Charybdis of stereotypical suburban development. To its east is Levittown, a massive subdivision whose trees have matured but whose lawns remain little changed from when the town, then all-white and middle-to–working class, served as mass suburbia's prototype. West of the trail, meanwhile, lies North Amityville, a postwar suburban haven for blacks banished from Levittown. There, amid still smaller lawns and lesser trees, any rural surrounds have long since been lost. Among their replacements, unseen by trail walkers, more than a handful of Superfund sites lie within a mile, a long-neglected industrial legacy of Long Island suburbanizing. Once the path crosses the island's central axis, however, and especially to the north of Jericho Turnpike, more fulsome woods and greenery flourish. On both sides, forest preserves abound, courtesy of the county, the township of Oyster Bay, and the Nature Conservancy. A tree cover more dense and extensive than sixty years ago envelopes villages like Upper Brookville and Cold Spring Harbor; nurseries and farms thrive. There, New York's wealthy continue to find suburban landscapes suitable to their pocketbooks and their liking.

This diversity among suburbs, at once socioeconomic, racial, and ecological, is far from new. In places such as Long Island and Los Angeles, we cannot understand the making of post–World War II suburban environmentalism without acknowledging its earlier versions and their consequences. Much early striving after nature's protection arose in the suburbs of the better off. Disturbed by, among other things, the arrival of a lower class of suburbanite, they began organizing on behalf of the preservation of wilder urban-edge lands, around or like their own neighborhoods. "Conservation," they called it, part of a movement then over half a century old, devoted to protecting the nation's natural resources. Soon, however, talk of a local nature's defense began to spill out of these mostly elite neighborhoods. Less well-off suburbanites, as well, rallied against threats to their own surroundings. These were harder to imagine in the conservation-ist mold, as on behalf of a nature that was unspoiled. Among the rising worries, as well, new contaminants of air and water impended, no matter how wide or manicured or wild one's backyard. As agendas widened to encompass these worries, of more as well as less modest suburban vintage, coalition building ensued. At the same time, a long-term reshuffle of the very vocabulary by which Americans talked about suburbs as well as na-ture, charted in the figures of this book's Appendix, was culminating. Out of these many metamorphoses and convergences, a compelling new object of defense came to be imagined: the environment. Later on, the laws and agencies that became this movement's legacy themselves would stand ac-cused of environmental injustice, of an indifference toward the dilemmas of working-class and minority neighborhoods.[9] But suburban environmen-talism, at the moment of its making, was itself a movement toward envi-ronmental justice.

For the sake of clarity, let me spell out this book's working definition of "environmentalism." Three features distinguished it from the earlier con-servation movement, as well as from a mostly urban and earlier movement for public health, whose dealings with pollution it would also challenge. *First*, it united concerns that the state and its professionals, in response to these earlier movements, had rent asunder. Most significantly, against the grain of much reigning expertise and officialdom, it welded together the cause of preserving natural lands with worries about contamination and pollution. At its ideological core lay a new postsanitary naturalism. It was forged in opposition to established expertise in public health as well as conservation. Arguably, it was more deeply ecological even than the pe-riod's formal science of "ecology," for how it posited threats to nonhuman nature and to human bodies side by side, as interwoven or even one and the same. *Second*, the new environmentalism stressed participatory democ-racy, rather than control by an expert or enlightened few. *Third*, it mobi-lized millions. By the mid-1960s out from New York and Los Angeles, this set of issues would yoke together coalitions of thousands of participants. Among its further achievements was the first Earth Day in 1970, the big-gest mass protest in America to that time, still in some respects the high–watermark of popular environmental activism in the United States.

If a closer look at a place like today's Long Island yields strong traces of the surprising suburban roots of environmentalism, on one front it does not: pollution. Echoes do still resonate of those concerns that, in the 1950s and 1960s, made industrial contaminants such a powerful and unifying issue. Modern movements around breast cancer and endocrine disrupters reprise those worries about manufactured chemicals that stirred in Carson's time. So does the booming trade in organic foods and an episodic opposition to mosquito sprays. But for many of us, the sentinel presence of the Environmental Protection Agency, and decades-long development of the law and science of pollution, quell any more visceral and immediate sense of dread. Stepping back to how suburban Long Islanders or Angelenos experienced pollution in the years just after World War II requires an imaginative leap.

Theirs was a time when metropoliswide currents of air as well as water were just being discovered, alongside the new, exotic, and often noxious chemicals they turned out to carry. The discoverers were not just scientists; laypeople's eyes burned and their throats stung. It was a time when the foremost authorities of the day sought to reassure, but also when today's ways of detecting pollutants, of discerning their wider and longer-term impacts, were only just being born. Heightening the stakes, gruesome yet poorly understood diseases like cancer were on the rise, spurring heated debates about whether pollutants were to blame. It is small wonder that among the exposed, confidence in existing experts waned. Faith in boundaries formerly considered secure and protective, of neighborhoods and also of human skin, crumbled. The pathological possibilities wafting into their homes and tissues only seemed to be magnified by the difficulties of knowing for certain either what people's exposures were or what effects these might have.[10] Postwar suburbanites—scientists and laypeople alike—gravitated toward new ecological ways of thinking, in which the porosity and vulnerability of their very bodies became far more difficult to deny.

Motivated and steered by the Long Island legal fight, Rachel Carson's *Silent Spring* (1962) expressed their fears with harrowing eloquence, to become the new movement's chief manifesto. "Once," she wrote in her opening fable, "there was a town in the heart of America where all life seemed to live in harmony with its surroundings." In these places, harmony stood visible in the parallel flourishing of human and nonhuman lives: in the beauty of laurel and wildflowers along its roadsides, in the deer and fox that "silently crossed the fields," in the trout-filled streams that flowed "clear and cold out of the hills," in the "abundance and variety of bird life."[11] This indeed was the suburban dream that so many had sought, a reassuring contact with the countryside and its nature that made cities seem far away. Loss of this abundance and harmony came at the hands not of sprawl itself, but of a "white granular powder," what her readers instantly recognized as a pesticide. Through it, people and trees, birds and foxes all faced the prospect of sickness and death, of a spring when life itself could no longer be heard. Those powerful and pervasive concerns about humans' own biological fate that Carson expressed were not just hers. Already by 1962, a host of others around Long Island and Los Angeles had been enunciating a similar, chemically conceived naturalism, using it to yoke perils to people with those to fellow creatures. The contribution of *Silent Spring*, along with a slew of other popular volumes that are less remembered, was to render this message more sweeping and portable, to tote it to readers across the rest of the nation and world.

So it was that a modern popular form of environmentalism first appeared in the United States, of all the nations of the industrialized West. Understanding why requires serious attention to the nostalgia that sprawl's impacts have stirred in so many of us, but also to those urban and industrial forces that held out these dreams to so many, then collided idyll with reality. Inside what were arguably the world's least regulated and most frenzied housing markets, that nature people actually knew best, around their own homes and neighborhoods, became unsettling ground. The changes that followed were far-reaching and manifold. A new "commons" ideology gained purchase, of a shared air, water, or land that needed protecting; with it, a vocabulary that was historically new. "Nature" may still be, as Raymond Williams proclaimed some years back, the most complex word in the English language.[12] But since the midsixties, the term "environment" has made a run on nature's crown.

Today's activists can take inspiration from where as well as how this movement was hatched. What made smog or open space or pesticides so galvanizing in these places was neither scientific study, nor existing laws, nor the sheer scale of threat, though all of these played a role. This era's issues motivated a movement primarily by reaching into lay experiences, by striking nerves across neighborhoods. What this history does show is that at its beginnings, environmentalism was about "citizen story-telling": how ordinary people joined together to "turn the narrative of 'more' into a more positive story."[13]

 **Chapter 1**

Suburban Country Life

The prospect that the expanding city may permanently
overflow into village forms and contain cattle as well as men is
one of the most heartening evangels of future civilization.
—HARLAN DOUGLASS, *The Suburban Trend* (1925)

The literary advent of suburbia in America issued from the pen of a
nature seeker. Henry Bunner, a reporter and playwright who worked
in New York City but resided in New Jersey, in 1896 wrote *The
Suburban Sage*, a book-length, partly fictional paean to his life there. He
himself was an avid walker who spent "many good golden hours . . . in
well-tracked woodland ways and in narrow foot-lanes through the windswept meadow grass." His enthusiasm traced back to a childhood in the
upper reaches of Manhattan, where "streets and houses were as yet too
few to frighten away that kindly old Dame Nature." There, he remembered
drinking up, "in great, big, liberal, whacking drafts," "my inheritance in
the sky and the woods and the fields, in the sun and the snow and the rain
and the wind." "Everyday's weather" brought "delight" "to a healthful
body and heart." Then, as thirty years later, particular landscapes nourished his experiences: those "of comfortable farm-houses and substantial
old-fashioned mansions standing in spacious grounds of woodland and
meadow." Such places and possibilities were very much on the minds of
those characters in Bunner's sketches who moved suburbward. They did
so, generally, because they "liked country life."[1]

Most historians of environmentalism have located the wombs of modern American "nature love" in places far from the suburban house lot.
From disciplines that are among the environmental movement's legacies,
those seeking its origins have offered three main currents of explanation.
First, some scholars have wheeled out universal species characteristics,
a human nature that stands, in important ways, outside the eyeblink of

recorded history.[2] These theories, though capturing facets of what environmentalism is, and was, pose more questions than they answer about its timing or geography. A second set of explicators, highlighting heroic leaders, situates environmentalism far more in particular moments. Led by the dueling Gifford Pinchot and John Muir, many have argued, a turn-of-the-century movement for conservation laid the foundations. Then along came Rachel Carson, and suddenly post–World War II environmentalism was born. Among the difficulties with this approach, it splices together two movements whose constituencies and agendas could hardly have been more different. And its top-down focus tends to obscure or downplay just what the more pervasive and popular roots of any environmental movement might have been.[3]

A third vein of scholarship has moved closer to an experience such as Bunner's, by homing in on environmentalism's more collective origins. From its role in the advent of a "risk" or "light-green" society, to its reflection of rising demands among consumers for a higher "quality of life," to its constitution as a "new social movement," many of these explanations nevertheless do not reach back much before World War II.[4] That they make so little reference not just to suburbs but to geography per se reflects the multiplicity of places and pathways that have led the industrialized West toward environmentalism. This book makes no pretense to encompass them all. Rather, by *placing* some of the most important of these origins in suburban locales, by demonstrating how such places catalyzed environmentalism in the United States, I show how these competing explanations may be rendered more compatible.

Between a risk society or postmaterialism described by European theorists and American scholars' insistence on the importance of consumerism, as well as between earlier popular constituencies for conservation and later ones for environmentalism, there lay a hidden connection. In the United States, even from Bunner's time, what nourished the nature love of the more and less scientifically qualified alike was a shared suburban experience. It was one not so much of home buying as home owning. Nor was it reducible to suburban dwellers' relationship with "the land," however fraught. What finally secured the breadth of environmentalism's appeal was how nature love itself had become ever more suffused with anxieties about human health.

For this last reason, we cannot understand the prominence of some suburbs in environmentalism's making without also situating them, and the movement itself, within a much longer and more unexpected history.

Almost entirely neglected by established explanations of environmentalism are its roots in legacies of health and medical thought. Stretching back
to classical times, identified largely with the Greek author Hippocrates, a
sturdy intellectual tradition had tied the prevalence of disease or health
to the natural features of places. Ubiquitous for centuries across Europe,
this vein of thinking underwent a revival in the nineteenth-century United
States. Settlers assessed the "salubrity" of frontier lands; victims of illness left their homes for spas, sea journeys, and health resorts; midcentury
physicians sought to measure the bodily impacts of climate or topography,
as their generation's version of scientific medicine. The ways of thinking
about health that proliferated now seem, at least to some historians, to
have been proto-ecological, anticipating that commingling of concerns
about ecology and human health that in the later twentieth century became
fundamental to environmentalism.[5]

One locus of this proto-ecological way of thinking has gone less explored. Long before Carson ever sat down to write *Silent Spring*, an in-
tertwined pursuit of nature and of physical vitality had already acquired
its own collective habitat in the United States. That landscape, shared by
millions after World War II, where nature could be sought and vim and
vigor sustained on a daily basis, was the urban edge.

Suburbs, of course, have their own historians, who routinely note the
centrality of natural settings to a suburban ideal. But they have been as
reluctant as their environmental conferees to consider its health-preserving
promises; nor have they accorded any longer or larger significance to suburban nature seeking.[6] A few historians of earlier suburbs do offer more
useful starting points, precisely by stepping outside of notions about
suburbs and suburbia that evolved after World War II. Resuscitating a
nineteenth-century term, John Stilgoe characterized that era's suburbs as a
"borderland" on the threshold of countryside.[7] The very word hints at just
how differently Americans of a hundred and fifty years ago viewed such
places. Theirs was a way of seeing and categorizing landscapes in which
our modern ideas of "suburbs," much less "suburbia," hardly figured in.
Before, and to a dwindling extent during, the long period over which modern ideas and actualities of an American suburbia congealed, nature's and
health's defining roles for other types of places remained far more familiar
and established. The city was where both seemed harder to find. In the
country, on the other hand, they stayed far easier to discover.

By the time Bunner pursued his nature love, even into the 1920s and
1930s, the notion of urban edges as borderlands was not yet dead. Another

intermediate category prevailed as well. Nature was so easy to see and love there, and health was so readily fostered, in part because he and his contemporaries could still view such places as "suburban countryside."

Through the early twentieth century, the rims of America's largest cities yielded to this as well as other characterizations precisely because of how up-for-grabs they had become. As the United States caught up to the most developed and industrialized European nations, a new turbulence had dawned in the land usage around its cities. Stirring the new pinnacle of diversity and dynamism was the arrival of factories and industry, as well as new residences. But what enabled so persistent a talk about this land as countryside was the expanding variety of agricultural uses. By the 1920s, the range of urban-edge dwellers who grew their own food, and the flourishing of market farms among them, garnered considerable attention in America's first nonfiction, book-length survey of *The Suburban Trend* (1925). Its author, Harlan Douglass, was so impressed with the prevalence of agriculture along urban rims that he speculated how, far into the future, suburbs would contain not just "village forms," but "cattle as well as men."[8]

Half a century of further changes would prove him less right, but into the 1930s Depression his projection was more spot-on. Urban-edge land itself and the categories that guided how so many Americans looked at it were a far cry from the perspective of their post–World War II counterparts. True, the subdivisions were accumulating, and authors of books and mass magazines were well on their way toward crafting a more specifically suburban sense of place. But even as industrial and commercial land users vied with residential developers and home buyers for urban-edge properties, in many suburbs the presence, look, and labor of the farm persisted. Moreover, impressions endured that nature as well as health might be met with there, between or among suburban house lots.

Seeking Nature and Health in a Suburban Countryside

Understanding why necessitates that we situate this era within a longer-term trajectory of change in urban-edge land use. Since classical times and before, the typically urban uses of land—for homes, shops, and work-places—had dropped off rapidly just beyond city edges. There, only hinterland or rural demands prevailed, in which the land's produce provided livelihoods: farms that grew crops or woodlots that yielded timber. Transitional zones between the rural and the urban remained thin, diverse, and difficult to characterize. They included poorer residents or racial minorities seeking more affordable land, noxious industries, and less reputable trades; farther out or in scenic corners, country homes of the wealthy might arise. But starting in Britain during the Industrial Revolution, and beginning around the edges of the largest and wealthiest U.S. cities some decades later, more citylike demands came to be imposed on urban-edge land. Starting even before Bunner was born, but much more dramatically by the time he wandered back to his childhood haunt, railroads and then streetcars facilitated an erosion of the clarity and discreteness of the boundaries separating America's largest and wealthiest cities from their surrounding countryside. While most suburban historians have concentrated on the suburbward spread of housing, urban edges over the latter half of the nineteenth into the twentieth century also drew entire factory-centered cities: Brooklyn outside Manhattan; Gary, Indiana, outside Chicago; Scottdale outside Atlanta.[9] What especially helped make this era's urban edges less conducive to a later, exclusively residential idea of suburbia, and more so to the notion of a suburban countryside, were the many new possibilities that arose for more traditionally rural and hinterlandish land uses.

Into the early twentieth century, what kept urban-edge farms prosperous even in the East were the many, ever-growing advantages accruing from their proximity to the largest city markets. Intensifying rail connections around cities like New York, Chicago, and Los Angeles enabled a regional agriculture in vegetables, fruits, and dairy products that expanded as these cities grew.[10] And while many of America's first "wilderness" parks appeared during this same late nineteenth-century period in more distant locations, the beaches and woods closer to urban peripheries drew larger shares of visitors. Around the biggest cities, a tourist trade took shape as hotels and restaurants sprang up. The better-off could join hunting clubs that maintained their own private reserves, or golf and sailing clubs, often with their own dining rooms and lodgings. More cheaply, room and board also became available "in private families, either in the towns or in nearby farms, at from $4.00 and up," or in "rented cabins," "with the meat and fish obtained near at hand."[11] That urban edges remained such flourishing sites both for farmers and for those seeking a more natural, wilder outdoors bolstered contemporary convictions that a suburban countryside could be found there.

The new residents who arrived on the urban edges of this period remained socioeconomically so diverse as to defy stereotyping—yet by and large they shared a reliance on cultivated fruits of the local land. A spectacularly visible nature particularly drew those who profited most from the

pooling of capital in these cities, often captains of the huge new corporations who sought second (or third or fourth) homes along more picturesque waterfronts or hillsides. Concentrated especially outside the biggest
and fastest growing cities, clusters of "country seats" merged into "Gold
Coasts." On Long Island, their owners joined farmers in prizing soil fertil-
ity and a long growing season. Also drawn by the hilly glacial moraine, they
were willing to pay as much as six thousand dollars an acre to delighted
farmers. Investing in the services of architects, landscapers, foresters, and
gardeners, they cultivated a local "nature" for its scenic value, while introducing a more urban valuation of their property. At the same time, most
estates included their own farmland, flocks, and herds. Cities large and
small acquired wealth belts or pockets: around Los Angeles, Pasadena's
Orange Grove Avenue, and Bel Air; and out from Atlanta, the homes of
Coca-Cola and textile owners and executives. "Picturesque enclaves" targeting the families of a new upper middle class of professionals and corporate managers multiplied, especially around the most capital-attractive
American cities. From Long Island's Garden City to Los Angeles's Palos
Verdes to Chicago's Riverside, they featured an elaborate landscape of
trees, lawns, shrubs, and parks, and plenty of room for gardens.[12]

Even around the richest cities, these enclaves were far and away the
exceptions in urban-edge development. For every one of these lavishly endowed, upper-end projects, scores of other developers bought and subdivided urban-edge lands and sold them with fewer urban provisions and
less artful or ornate foliage. Housing clusters and entire towns suddenly
appeared over the 1880s and 1890s and were sold to "working" families
of modest income. Already, subdivisions and developments could indeed
be large, yet customers often had to more or less fend for themselves. They
dug their own wells and cesspools, planted their own trees and shrubs,
and either hired their own builders or raised a roof with their own hands.
Buyers and builders in these brackets became chief customers of a new
factory-style production of building materials as well as mail-order homes.
Even in the most massive suburban developments, middle-class homeowners often acquired versions of what became known as the "homestead" lot.
With narrow urban fronts but with depths of two hundred or more feet,
homestead lots allowed for extensive gardens, as well as stables, barns, and
chicken coops behind the houses.[13]

For the suburban poor, mail-order kits themselves seemed a luxury. Into
the first decades of the twentieth century, a great many of those occupying
the least certain footholds in a city's cash economy also turned to urban-

edge land. Their settlements were well known for a partiality to backyard gardens and farm animals, in kinship to the shantytowns and favelas that would spring up around late twentieth-century megacities of the developing world. Bunner had covered one such colony in northern Manhattan for a New York newspaper in 1880. This "gypsy camp of superfluous poor" was about to be pushed out by brownstone and tenement houses. Many of these shanty dwellers were Irish and German immigrants who worked as day laborers or junk men or ragpickers in the city, or who kept their own "market gardens" and "stockyards." Tethered outside many houses, goats rivaled dogs as "the typical animal of the colony," joined by pigs, geese, rats, and some cows.[14]

Suburban migrants who sought this and other more cut-rate housing often had the strongest incentives to use their surrounding land in more hinterlandish ways—not just for shelter, but for the growing of food and the gathering of supplies such as firewood. The urban-edge poor thereby joined those in Gold Coast estates who grew their own sizable crops and kept their own beef and dairy herds, and those in middle- or working-class subdivisions who tilled homestead lots and kept cows or chickens. These food-producing promises of suburban living, more than any other, provided the linchpin for a new literature that wove residential and agricultural uses of urban-edge land together as "suburban country life."[15]

By the start of the twentieth century, a long tradition elaborating what later historians would term a "suburban" ideal regularly tied it to a place their readers knew fondly and well: the "country." From the moment those domestic visions that would increasingly be recognized as suburban first began appearing on this side of the Atlantic in the mid-nineteenth century, their most famous articulators, such as Andrew Jackson Downing, pointedly identified the houses and landscapes they designed as "country" ones.[16] The starting premise of Frank Scott's 1872 treatise was that "all the finer pleasures of rural life" could be taken on "from a half acre to four or five acres" of suburban ground "as a famishing man should take food." For these writers, suburban residence only served as a gateway to the satisfaction of a deeper, more meaningful hunger—for a country way of life.[17] By the time a 1910 federal commission sought to promote a "country life" movement, a slew of books and magazines devoted special attention to just how and why the edges of America's largest and fastest-growing cities were blurring. The country proximate to the largest and wealthiest cities seemed especially ripe for many of their aspirations, for they sought country life not so much as it actually was, but as it should be, as "ideal."

After a century in which lawns, leafy greenery, and houses like those depicted by Downing and Scott conjure up their own stereotypically suburban way of living, it has become difficult to recapture how differently Americans of 1900 made sense of them. For promoters of a suburban country life, the significance was broadly imaginative and connective, not just to neighboring, rural land uses but to meanings both larger and more personal. American variants of the country owed a heavy debt to British predecessors, the "country seats" of that nation's aristocracy and merchant elite, but the adoption of this ideal across the Atlantic brought less elite connotations. Country ideals also found taproots in what supposedly had long made the United States more democratic than its transatlantic forebears, a yeoman farmer-citizenry.

This tradition was under siege. In 1890 the U.S. Census had declared, and Frederick Jackson Turner famously elaborated, that the frontier for homesteading was now closed. The organized clout of farmers, newly asserted through Populism and Williams Jennings Bryan, had met with a resounding political defeat. The status of rural areas was eroding due to the vigor of industrial centers, and prominent and urbane commentators such as Liberty Hyde Bailey came to see farms and farmers as in dire need of improvement. Bailey himself grasped at the urban-edge migrations as a new and hopeful sign, pointing to an awakening pastoralism that could spur rural revival. As he noted, drawing on the 1900 census, "more than half the people of North America live in the country." Though many had left or were leaving, by 1901 many urban dwellers were contemplating a kind of return.[18] It was then that Bailey, confident of a potential readership in both camps, launched *Country Life* magazine. Giving name to what soon became known as a national movement, the periodical was published in Garden City, the Long Island picturesque enclave.

Contrary to the prevailing assumptions that America's future lay cityward, observers such as Bailey heralded an "outflux to the country [that] is greater and farther reaching" every year. Spearheading this movement, joining a long-standing "summer exodus country-ward," there had burst forth a "growth of suburbanism." "It was not many years ago that people lived in the suburbs as a matter of economy," explained Bailey. "Now they live in these parts because higher ideals may often be attained here." Lavish illustrations, high-toned topics, and florid language abounded in *Country Life*. It thereby aimed to uplift the "permanent country resident" to "a broader and closer intimacy with what he has," as well as to strengthen this suburbanizing outflux. Bailey and his publishers were joined by others.

The editors of a Boston-based competitor concurred that there was "probably no field which is more attractive to . . . publishers and which promises any larger returns than this same field of country life."[19]

Tellingly, those who sought to profit from the new suburbanism by talking only of the "suburban," without mentioning its "country" complement, risked losing their audience. Only in the wake of a lawsuit from Bailey's publisher in 1905 did the Bostonians' *Suburban Country Life* drop the "country" from its title, to become *Suburban Life*. It begged readers' forbearance: "While the word 'country' disappears from the title, it will be found omnipresent in the character of the articles and illustrations that appear in the magazine itself."[20] More broadly, aside from hints like Bunner's testimonial, those editing, writing, or reading these mass magazines left little evidence that the "suburbs" had much place in anyone's life stories, their personal sense of passage. Whether they had left the farm or stayed on it, remained in the downtown of a place like Chicago or New York or moved to its outskirts, most everyone, including Bunner himself, thought of their movement as between city and country. Suburbs themselves could be conceived, by and large, only as places in between.

At the same time, suburban country magazine writers joined Henry Bunner and other fellow realists and naturalists, such as W. D. Howells, sometime editor of the Boston-based *Atlantic* magazine, in fleshing out suburban settings with a character and interest of their own. Inaugurating a strand of American letters that, after World War II, would blossom into full-blown literature of "suburbia," these pioneer portraitists had few distinctly suburban traditions or experiences on which to draw. They too leaned heavily on the far richer tradition of "the inspiration and the peaceful joys of the country."[21] Its meanings were due, in no small measure, to the ways these places were inhabited. The "country" meant, first of all, lack of "congestion," fewer people. While some emphasized only the privacy they had found, Bunner described an "exercise of certain gentle sympathies, that thrive as poorly in the town's crowded life as the country wild-flowers thrive in the flower-boxes of tenement windows." Out from the city, people dealt with one another in a more humane and natural fashion, in a "spirit of helpful, homely, kindly neighborliness."[22]

As many scholars have emphasized, an ideology of domesticity underlay many of these visions. Describing this migration as one of the "city man" countryward, as many promoters did, took the husband's perspective on what was, ultimately, a familial choice. Grace Fanon, the coeditor of *Suburban Life*, tried to leverage the different perspective of a female readership by inviting women contributors and devoting articles to the decoration and upkeep of home interiors. By contrast, Bunner and other men often glossed over the considerable work that was required to keep up the blissful home they celebrated. They emphasized the country's full-time "advantages of pure air and a healthful, outdoor life" for wives but especially for children, who would thereby "grow to be strong, normal-minded men and women."[23]

In such differences, we can see a rather willful effort to naturalize contemporary gender roles, but also something more. Promoters of suburban country were tapping into long-standing ways of understanding landscapes in terms of their bodily impacts—in particular, their healthiness. The countryside, especially if high and dry or well cultivated, had long been considered healthier than cities. From the great waves of the wealthy who departed America's downtowns during nineteenth-century cholera epidemics to those many tuberculosis and asthma sufferers who left eastern cities to head to the Adirondacks or out West, certain kinds of rural places had long been thought not just to prevent disease but to cure existing ailments.[24] While the rise of germ theory eventually challenged such convictions, into the early twentieth century ideas about the healthiness of rural living persisted, forthrightly enticing migrations to the suburbs.

The presumed power of urban-edge nature to heal helped draw some of the era's most prominent therapeutic establishments. Tuberculosis sanitoriums offering "fresh air" cures abounded around the elevated outskirts of Los Angeles, New York, and other cities. New York State, at least, chose Long Island for some of its largest mental institutions, where nerve-wracked or "neurasthenic" patients, among others, could revive from the overstimulation and exhaustion of modern urban life. The health benefits of country living, suburban or otherwise, continued to find wide dissemination. In real estate ads through the early years of the century, resort homes were pitched for a "climate unsurpassed for lung and bronchial troubles." Suburban real estate, even around New York, was regularly touted for its "dry, healthy location," "pure air," and "pure and healthful water." The restorative potential of the suburban countryside also figured into the writings of America's "suburban sage." Henry Bunner's play "The Evolution of a Suburbanite" features a city dweller, "Mr. Citt," who visits the home of a suburb-dwelling friend. Mentioning that his wife has taken ill, he promises to bring her along when he comes again. "I can't tell you how relieved I shall be when I get Nellie and the baby out here in the fresh air and quiet! She can't help getting back her strength here; don't you think so?" Soon afterward, Mr. Citt and his family themselves turn suburbanite and set about recruiting a "Mr. Next."[25]

The suburban country not only cultivated healthy families, it exposed them to lives other than the human. Bunner himself was ill-disposed to look for nature inside the city; he opined the fate of "country wildflowers" in tenement window boxes and had little to say about a place such as Central Park. In the plants and animals of the countryside, by contrast, nature seemed at once more recognizable and more real. Here was another virtue of country life; if properly lived, it "open[ed] eyes" to the natural world. A young man of "dulled" senses from "years of city life" who then moves suburbward "cannot fail to be astonished and thrilled, and perhaps a little bit awed at the wonder of that green awakening" during his first spring. Self-consciously tapping into a turn-of-the-century "growth of literature pertaining to . . . the out-of-doors," *Country Life* featured articles on trees, birds, and other wildlife, as well as camping, hiking, and "wheeling" or "motoring." Not to be outdone, *Suburban Life* in 1907 absorbed the Chicago-based *Birds and Nature Magazine* into its fold, whose writers then supplied it with similar pieces.[26]

Crucially, if more emphatically for Liberty Hyde Bailey than for Henry Bunner, the country also meant "agriculture"—"the fundamental thing in a self-sustaining country life." For Bailey, suburban soil needed cultivating for economic and productive reasons; a self-described "countryman," he wanted to promote "self-sustaining" farms. Bunner, on the other hand, wrote of the "human longing to make a garden" as a "natural" biological instinct—"really, although we treat it lightly, a sort of humble first-cousin to the love of children." As suburban characters in Bunner's stories devoted weekends to gardening because it gratified, so Bailey urged a "nature love" among farmers, for instance, through a sensual and aesthetic appreciation of the "smell of the soil." Bailey's competing editors at *Suburban Life* targeted more pragmatic tillers, a "great class of well-to-do who love the country but are not millionaires." Contributors told how backyard agriculture—a poultry business, a family cow, or a vegetable garden—could supplement salaries.[27] Among this era's writers, lawn care, later the crux of suburban horticulture, took a decided backseat to gardening, whether of ornamentals or edibles.

If countrylike work enhanced adults' appreciation of the nature in and around their suburban residences, children discovered the nature of the suburban countryside more through play. Not just confined to their parents' house and land, they could safely and pleasurably roam on properties beyond. Bunner's recollections captured this ideal of an open countryside where, even if from a family of modest income and property, "children may watch the development of nature's wonderful forces as represented in plant, animal and insect." Neighbors, in "comfortable farm-houses and substantial old-fashioned mansions," scarcely noticed wandering children such as himself—except for a widowed mansion owner who invited him in for tea. Spotty surveillance by rural landowners in this era made property lines seem porous, even invisible. Roaming unimpeded through forests and meadows, fully exposed to the vagaries of weather, the young Bunner, but especially the older Bunner remembering back, felt these natural surroundings to belong, in important senses, to himself: "my inheritance."[28]

Bailey converged on this same point from another angle: In the "out-of-doors," "men are free." His rhetoric recalled Turner's freedom-loving frontiersmen, yet it also applied, in important ways, to the suburban country landscape.[29] So accessible was it to the casual walker that celebrants worried little about trespassing. The countryside could also become a site for what these magazines also touted for adults: "camping." Seeking out any "remote or neglected corner of the country," the camper strolled freely through it and pitched a tent in its midst. Should he or she run out of the food brought in, "there were fish in the streams, animals in the woods, and berries in the glades." *Suburban Life*'s camping guide recommended campsites near a "farmstead," "to replenish your larder." Eggs and milk were not just for the taking, of course; they were to be purchased at the farmhouse doorstep; property was "always to be respected." But warnings about not "felling trees" or "'cooning' corn and melons and milk" only applied to visibly "occupied land." Away from "the cities and towns" and the "fashionable resorts," even immediately beyond "the outskirts of a settlement," according to magazine writers, owners of "country" land often allowed camping, hunting, and fishing on their premises.[30]

Here, tucked within roseate memories and lofty rhetoric, was a notion of the suburban country as a "commons." Writers did not use this word; its broadening application would come much later. The historical land use pattern on which commons theorists would draw was nonetheless centuries old: the English and New England town greens, where everyone could graze their livestock.[31] As an informal commons, the suburban country's promised freedom was not just from surveyors' lines and title deeds, or from trespassing prosecutions. The meanings here were richer if more diffuse. That the out-of-doors should be so "free," that "the sky and the woods and the fields" remained a shared "inheritance," invoked an ideal of human liberation with deep resonance in American culture. Over the next century, nowhere more so than in suburban places, these precepts would echo and resound.

For even its most fervent spokespeople, however, the suburban country had its drawbacks. One should not expect "to find all the conveniences which are supplied in city homes." "Clayey" roads, which turned into "a mass of sticky clay mud every time the rain falls," could "take some of the fun out of suburban life." Residents might be "cut off from their friends and forced to miss many of the pleasures which they have enjoyed." A telephone provided some remedy, but "it is obviously impossible to play a game of whist or conduct a dinner party over the wire." Bunner's *Suburban Sage* chuckled over other difficulties faced by new arrivals: the frustrations of moving furniture, the head scratching over furnaces and other unfamiliar household equipment, the amiable annoyance of the "suburban dog."[32] Partly these and other difficulties were due to its being too isolated and rustic, of not including "something of the social and intellectual advantages and physical comforts of the city." Among these comforts were sanitary perquisites like flush toilets, as well as electric lights and telephones and the new, faster means of getting around. Many of these conveniences, suburban dwellers would welcome in; others proved more controversial.[33]

Already by the 1890s, those locating nature in a suburban countryside defined it not just positively, but through intimations of its vanishing. So it was with Henry Bunner; America's first self-declared *Suburban Sage* also penned its first narrative of a *suburban* nature lost. When he returned to his "old playground" of upper Manhattan sometime in the 1890s, Bunner found that the woodlands and meadows had been driven out by "those twain demons of encroachment, Taxes and Assessments." Now "checkered and gridironed with pavement and electric lights," the land had nary a hint of the nature into which he had earlier plunged. Instead of woodlands and meadows, there were distinctly lower-class residences: "Smug, mean little house[s], tricked out with machine-made scroll-work," as well as "squalid shant[ies]" of poor squatters.[34]

A place where nature could authentically be sought, the suburban countryside differed from other rural areas precisely in this vulnerability to jarring invasion. For Bunner, as for a host of others who would follow in his footsteps, the arrival of the city had impacts more far-reaching than the construction of new roads and houses. The erasure of his childhood haunts stirred him to idealize what he remembered about the nature there. An all-encompassing immersion in it, the utter freedom and well-being it fed—all these became easier to imagine in a place that no longer existed as he remembered it. The disgust and dismay that attended his nostalgia were also riven by a class prejudice that would become a familiar refrain of anti-suburban screeds. But at this 1890s moment, Henry Bunner voiced it to decry how an ideal suburbs with countryside had been wiped out by a "demoralised suburbs," a "cheap, tawdry, slipshod imitation of the real city." When these sentiments resurfaced half a century later, they would be rekindled by the intrusion of suburbia itself, a place whose own distinctively nonrural features had come increasingly into focus.

The Fate of the Suburban Country: Corrosion and Continuance

Before suburbia could be seen as invasive, many more Americans had to arrive at a clearer idea about what it was, and in ways that more decisively distinguished it from countryside. My explanation as to how they did so requires a starting acknowledgment: then as now, urban edges have invariably mixed the rural with the urban. This was so even in the late nineteenth and early twentieth centuries, when suburban residents, in stark contrast to later, remained more inclined to see and celebrate the countryside around them. Over the first decades of the twentieth century, however, this inclination slowly became harder to sustain.

Partly, the changes were material in character, involving urban-edge ground itself. More and more of the newcomers were not farmers. They became less dependent on their own land for food, and their living quarters hewed ever more so to the same pattern of single-family homes in subdivisions. Change also came in the realm of perceptions. As depictions of urban-edge living assumed a more exclusively residential cast, the urban-edge search for nature gained priority over any romance of the soil. New state and profession building contributed by instituting further differences between suburban and rural lands, as well as by divvying duties of public health and nature protection into more separate and expert jurisdictions. For all these reasons, the notion of a suburban countryside began to wither over the interwar years, especially around the largest and fastest-growing American cities. Nevertheless, especially in realms of popular culture and practice, links persisted between the urban-edge pursuits of health and of nature. (For ways these changes were reflected in popular media, see Figures 2 and 3 in the Appendix.) Visitors and residents alike continued to seek both, albeit in shifting ways, and in surroundings that stayed more countrylike, as well as those that became less so.

Over the early twentieth century, as barriers to larger-scale suburban home ownership began to crumble, home building along urban edges gained new impetus. An antiborrowing ethic that had long bolstered urban middle-class families' reluctance to buy homes came under assault during the early decades of the twentieth century. The assailants were not just advertisers, realtors, builders, and mortgage lenders but upper-level government officials. Campaigns encouraging home ownership by the 1920s reached all the way up to Commerce Secretary Herbert Hoover, who believed that borrowing to buy a home of one's own contributed to the greater good of American citizenship. Echoing the old Jeffersonian rhetoric about the yeoman farmer, the new exponents of home ownership downplayed the debts often incurred, even as the improving terms of the typical mortgage enabled more speculative and long-term borrowing.[35] With the growth in financing for home building, especially around cities like New York and Los Angeles, came a reordering of the business of real estate and construction that has been well recounted by its historians. Realtors professionalized and more speculative builders entered the scene, combining land acquisition, construction, and sales into a single firm. In mass magazines, the mounting attention to home building along urban edges had by the 1920s yielded a new way of discussing their growth: as "suburban development."[36]

Gradually, instead of being seen as comprising a jumble of land uses, the "suburban" was becoming more associated with a single, dominant one for residential housing. Nature itself still could be found there, nearly as much so as in Bunner's time. But the ways and means of its discovery were changing. Contacts with nature became an aspiration of more and more, but less and less via the pursuit of farming or cultivation.

Among those private initiatives that contributed to this tipping balance, especially in the more urban and wealthier regions of the nation, was the arrival of many more food stores that sought customers among the new suburban dwellers. A host of small, specialized distributors came into being—meat, poultry, fruit and vegetable stores—as more comprehensive grocery stores opened in the larger outlying towns. Early stores proved a boon to local farmers as well. Few of them were part of any national chain, so many sought out local suppliers. Some farmers offered another alternative to suburban migrants, a more direct trade that was pursued at the farmhouse doorstep.

The cost of food nevertheless remained high: from 45 to 60 percent of a working family's budget. Hence, out from the best-off subdivisions, especially in smaller cities and agricultural regions, but also wherever grocery stories were distant or nonexistent, urban-edge dwellers still grew extensive gardens. Over 40 percent of those in Middletown, Indiana, relied on backyard produce—probably at least as great a proportion as among those who lived in the remoter edges of the largest cities. But in the 1910s and 1920s, even the wealthiest suburban towns remained remarkably tolerant of inhabitants who wished to grow their own fruits and vegetables less out of necessity than as a hobby. Outside Los Angeles or New York, well-off, exclusive enclaves such as Pasadena and Garden City allowed chicken coops and stables; only hogs were seen as fit for banning.[37]

As for full-time commercial farmers, they continued to find advantages in cityward locations. Nearer the downtown markets that were most lucrative, they also benefited from an ease and cheapness of transportation there. Moreover, refrigeration had as yet done little to undermine their competitiveness in markets for most perishable fruits and vegetables. Cooling technology had not yet been "so perfected as to bring any of these products over journeys of several days . . . and deliver them to the consumer in as attractive condition as the home-grown."[38] But whatever market niches it enjoyed, commercial farming around America's urban peripheries was moving in directions that, for many Anglo Americans, eroded its romantic appeal. Commercial farms in the outer suburban rings of coastal New York and Los Angeles differed most markedly from those around many inland and smaller cities, including the midwestern "Middletown," in the racioethnic heterogeneity of their owners and workers. By 1920, a full third of farmers in Long Island counties were "foreign-born white." So were over a third in Los Angeles County, where the rest of the non-natives were either African American or Asian, primarily Japanese.[39]

This burgeoning diversity of land uses and users at America's urban edges by the 1920s, recently rediscovered by suburban historians, was not lost on Harlan Douglass.[40] His book-length treatise on *The Suburban Trend* recognized how commercial farming itself enabled a new upward mobility for minority groups who found fewer economic footholds inside the city. Shantytowns continued to surround the nation's cities, providing housing for farm as well as industrial workers. Douglass noted, "The heaviest concentrations of foreign-born populations in the United States are not urban but suburban." More so than Bunner with his Goatvilles, Douglass in the 1920s found it easier to distinguish urban-edge commercial farming and "rural suburbs" from those "industrial" types, which he found still less appealing. All told, a "veritable suburban hegira of the very poor," from "foreign" or "Negro suburbs" to "tin-can colonies" had, for Douglass, kept "genuinely frontier life along the margins of cities . . . a grim reality."[41]

Tightly clustered shacks lacking sanitation and harboring a "degenerate" social development were hard to square with any suburban country idyll. Yet Douglass was able to affirm the health- and nature-seeking of this older vision by explicitly confining his discussion of such quests only to the most white and best-off inhabitants. Among the many sorts of urban-edge residents, those of "upper middle class" communities constituted the most quintessential "suburbanites." They could most easily afford the larger acreage that made lots look farmlike; they also tended to hire out the more mundane varieties of land upkeep, like lawn mowing. Among them—himself included—he delineated a "suburban society" and a "distinct suburban psychology" that added up to a "genuine" suburban life. This suburban psychology still had its agrarian moments: many residents thought of and treated their properties in well-nigh agrarian terms, becoming "farmer[s] on a diminutive scale." But more so than for Bailey or Bunner, for Douglass's authentic "suburbanite," the work of cultivation now served as a way station to another, more overriding goal: the recovery of a primordial "nature." "Simple and subtle appeals," of the "sky and landscape, unobstructed," of wild birds and pets, reawakened "old virtues and kindnesses." Inexorably, the "inner man" became alive to those most ancient sentiments that had "evolved when men and animals were house-mates in some prehistoric cave." Douglass's authentic "suburbanite" became, even if he would scorn or deny the rubric, a "lover of nature." If primitivist nostalgia was fundamental to this love, it also could be cultivated in the younger generation. "With no more of nature than the suburban house lot affords," children found "not merely space for play but a certain environmental content and feeling for life." Among the benefits of this "environmental content" was not just nature appreciation but physical vitality, and not only for children. Leaf-raking mothers, too, gained picturesquely "flushed cheeks."[42]

Even as Douglass and others still affirmed these countrylike appeals, at least in "genuine" suburban living, public health experts and officials had launched major challenges to long-standing ways of linking healthiness to the countryside—or to any natural features of the land. While the cities of this period retained reputations for ill health, they also gave birth to the new laboratory-based science of bacteriology, a discipline that offered powerful new explanations for how infectious diseases got transmit-

ted: via tiny organisms called "germs." Older theories attributing disease
to miasmatic emanations of the land were overturned, even if some of
the connections they had made still held up. For instance, the new understanding of malaria as a germ spread by mosquitoes that bred in stagnant
water showed why low-lying wetland could cause fevers, whereas high, dry
land did not. As officials found ways of eradicating the dreaded *Anopheles*
mosquito, by draining wetlands and coating standing water with oil, their
engineering successes undermined long-standing beliefs that these, or any
other areas, might be naturally unhealthy. Especially as health scientists
and officials grew more confident in their own preventive abilities, convictions mounted in a "new public health" that could become universal and
essentially place-neutral. Laboratories had now demonstrated that germs
caused disease, and their presence in the environment had become more or
less easily detectable. So at least for leading health experts, considerations
of topography, climate, or flora no longer seemed to matter as much as previously. Whether working in city, suburb, or countryside, health experts
only needed to ensure certain sanitary requisites that kept disease germs
at bay: safe water supplies, sewer systems, swamp drainage, and perhaps
other health-related controls and oversight.

The result was a subtle yet decisive alteration in how health officialdom
viewed the human organism, a switch toward conceptions styled by recent
scholarship as a "modern body."[43] Unlike earlier, practitioners came to
suspect far less human vulnerability to other external causes of disease
beyond germs. Aside from infections, the human body was assumed to
be mostly sealed off from its surroundings, ecologically impervious. As
the hopes for vaccinations as well as personal hygiene also grew, Hibbert Hill in 1913 influentially characterized the evolution of a "new public
health." Compared to their predecessors, forward-looking health officials
were shifting their sites from the "environment"—"seeking the sources of
infectious disease in the surroundings of man"—toward the "individual"—
"find[ing] them in man himself."[44] Place-neutral as this new public health
seemed to proponents like Hill at the time, it remained far more persuasive
inside cities than beyond them. Within the metropolises of America's most
prosperous regions was where public health experts and officials had first
acquired early twentieth-century authority and influence. There as well,
they had installed the fullest array of germ-targeting infrastructure and
oversight—what made possible Hill's dismissal of environmental factors.
Along urban edges, however, these same public health protections and
programs arrived more slowly.

The lagging pace was not due to the lack of trying among public health advocates and experts. Over the first decades of the twentieth century, around New York and Los Angeles, state health departments and the governments of a smattering of suburban towns and counties set out to quell or tame the circulation of disease-bearing microorganisms. They turned their sites especially to germ-spreading organisms besides people: rats and mosquitoes, but also horses, cows, fowl, and other farm animals, creatures that the urban edges of New York, Los Angeles, and other U.S. cities still harbored in abundance. Public health and allied officials thereby confronted and sought to regulate suburban practices that many Americans continued to associate with the countryside, from outhouses and individual wells, to the backyard keeping of fowl and animals, to farmhouse sales of milk and produce. Their success on these and other fronts, from the first suburban building codes to new infrastructure projects for water supplies and sewers, helped transform many a suburb, making it appear to be less like what numerous Americans still thought of as countrylike.[45].

Yet many suburban residents, having been drawn to their more rural surroundings by a belief in the naturally restorative power of the countryside, saw little need for these importations. They even shunned them as too citylike. Over the 1920s and into the 1930s, an urban-edge politics of resistance often took public health officials by surprise. Rejection of the latest sanitary rules and provisions could be found among the suburban poor, but it erupted most visibly and effectively in richer, established enclaves. Some villages along Long Island's North Shore incorporated just to keep sewers out, along with the apartments and urban newcomers they surmised would follow.[46] It was about keeping down taxes, but more besides. Urban-edge dwellers, especially if they could afford their own cesspools and private garbage disposal methods, regarded city-forged public health and other measures as a threat to their own suburban country idyll. The more urban style of public health was unnecessary; rural lands and ways remained protection enough.

Many of these same suburban enclaves were, however, far more disposed to another regulatory tool first adopted by urban public health advocates: land-use zoning. Originating in German cities of the late nineteenth century, zoning asserted systematic public control over the demands that could be made on private property by legally restricting usage of that property—that is, its economic function. In the earliest American campaigns for zoning, waged in California cities and New York City in 1907, advocates leaned heavily on zoning's purported powers of disease prevention, how it could stymie disease transmission by discouraging slumlike human density and congestion. By the 1920s, zoning increasingly appealed to those in suburban enclaves where urban-style governance was just being hatched. Especially out from the largest and richest cities, zoning shed much of its health rationale. One reason was that zoning and planning were acquiring their own experts, with legal and scientific jurisdictions ever more distinct from those of sanitary counterparts. Their work became, more baldly, a way of shielding better-off residential districts from intrusions of just the sort that had troubled Bunner and other of the suburban countryside's celebrants: "Smug, mean little house[s]" and "squalid shant[ies]."[47] At the same time, the new zoning and planning officials reinforced the growing impact of the new public health on another front by helping to undermine the suburban coexistence of subdivisions and farms.

While some planners in British and European cities sought to protect a local metropolitan agriculture, American counterparts did not. Those devising the New York Regional Plan by 1929 downplayed the economic advantages of local, as opposed to imported, produce, emphasizing instead how pressures from Bunner's "twain demons, . . . Taxes and Assessments," worked against metropolitan-area agriculturalists. Recognizing the substantial benefits of "bring[ing] city and country into frequent juxtaposition," they nevertheless bowed to the prevailing sense that city-area farming was "an anachronism." Recommending a hands-off policy toward the conversion of farmland into subdivisions, New York's regional planners ensured this process could continue apace. A comparable initiative undertaken around the same time in Los Angeles took a similar approach. The 1930 Olmsted-Bartholomew Plan for the Los Angeles region also confined itself to espousing the preservation of land as public "parks, playgrounds and beaches."[48]

What the Olmsted-Bartholomew and other plans did register by the end of the decade was the growing number of people flocking to America's urban edges in search of an outdoor nature uncoupled from agrarian romance. Many frequented what Douglass termed "large-scale organization[s] for recreation," the private golf courses and "country clubs" enjoyed by well-to-do men. As if not more ubiquitous were the garden clubs dominated by women. A few private hunt clubs provided wilder exceptions, yet there as well, game attractants were artfully sown, drawing in ducks or birds to replace those felled by the shot of a gun. Boys and girls had their scouting and "campfire" clubs, whose nature studies and outings also demanded wilder settings. Adult groups sought a similar style of "tramping," from the burgeoning trails and walking clubs in eastern cities to the Sierra Club chapters sprouting in California's younger metropolises. By the 1920s both the Audubon Society, based in New York, and the Sierra Club of Southern California had launched what would become a century of political advocacy. But both remained as yet regionally concentrated, only small eddies in a flood of new groups that ventured into the outdoors together. The first *New York Walk Book*, issued by an American Geographic Society in 1923, listed Audubon as just one of some sixty-one "outing clubs" active in the New York City region. They ranged from church and company groups to athletic clubs, from the Appalachian Mountain Club to the Torrey Botanical Club to an "All Tramp Soviet."[49]

Promotions of walking exemplified some subtle but remarkable changes in this era's popular pursuit of an urban-edge nature. A host of nineteenth-century American tourist guides had simply assumed their readers would be pedestrians; the *New York Walk Book*, arriving in the era of the automobile, became among the first to promote "walk" in its title. Others preferred what was then a newfangled term, "hike." Whatever the name, its proponents kept alive earlier ideals of the suburban countryside, only with some strategic alterations.

Even as the natural environment was being declared irrelevant to public health and medicine, strains of environmental therapeutics underwrote the growing popularity of seeking nature on foot. Popular authors, like Angeleno L. C. Marr, assured his readers that it would lead to fewer "cases of 'nerves.'" Physicians, as well, wrote about the new fashion, in some cases keeping alive sweeping talk of nature's curative powers. The lead author of the *Walk Book*, a "medical man" named Robert Dickinson, promised boons from walking that echoed the health assurances of Douglass's "genuine suburbanite" experience. "The magic of the moccasin," he insisted, "still makes good medicine." Unlike the health that the countryside had been thought to foster in the mid-nineteenth century, this medicine did not work through the physical influence of places traversed, but through a kind of interior awakening. A primordial humanity was revived, at once psychological, visceral, and ancient, a "strain in the blood of us, all of us, of cave man and tree man . . . this call of the earth."[50] For Dickinson, the balm conjured through walking now lay mostly inside the body of the walker. Like the "suburban psychology" of Douglass, it was partly psychosomatic, if also including the physical exertion soon known as "exercise."

And yet for Dickinson and like-minded others, walking's boons nevertheless seemed to come easiest in places where nature was easiest to see.

Significantly, walkers of this era could still appreciate nature's presence in places that were recognizably worked or even built. By dint of the *Walk Book* and other guides, those locales to be most studiously avoided were the denser suburbs, macadamized roads, and particularly factories. Though guides might acknowledge most trampers to be "country-minded," they did not entirely shun urban or especially suburban landscapes. The New York guide argued briefly for nature-seeking ventures along New York City sidewalks, following old Indian paths now themselves "below the hard concrete." Los Angeles guide L. C. Marr suggested a "most delightful tramp" through an urban-rural patchwork: from the city's Griffith Park up over Mount Hollywood into Universal City, where you might catch "some real action" of moviemaking. Most journeys, however, began with a train or streetcar ride out into the countryside, a mixture of farms, country estates, and apparently unused land. Long Island walks coursed along remaining stretches of "old Dutch farmland" and, farther out on the island, along beaches and marshes, "country" or "farm roads," as well as bridle paths and trails. Among the "many adorable trips in the vicinity of Los Angeles" were the "many charming canyons nestled in the foothills" accessible through Hollywood or Pasadena. Trampers could not now expect to hunt or fish or pick from orchards; they had to bring their own food. If they were careful, guides suggested, barriers to accessing private lands remained few. More threatening to nature-seeking pedestrians was the "ever increasing automobile traffic on highways and secondary roads which . . . has spoiled many fine country walks."[51]

In these same mixed landscapes where walkers chased after health and nature, officials and experts associated with the conservation movement were moving to limit the mixture of activities by restricting many of those considered traditionally rural. In the name of protecting natural resources, those corners of the urban edge that stayed wilder became subject to game laws. State and federal officials took up new jobs of chasing poachers, tree-cutting trespassers, and squatters off public lands. Governments also exerted new legal controls over fishing and hunting even on private lands: time limits or "seasons" and, in the case of Long Island deer, a 1928 ban on the hunt.[52] Public forest reserves, created by the early twentieth century, more or less set aside certain lands for nature's protection and "wise" state-regulated use. Long Island gained only a tiny slice, but Los Angeles County, with the San Gabriel National Forest, received a much larger share.[53] Curtailing what many still saw as countrylike freedoms, the new conservationist officialdom further contributed to the demise of a suburban country ideal by securing rural lands where farms could not be found, but nature could.

So did another development on the urban edges of America's largest and wealthiest cities: the arrival of intentionally "mass" models for public recreation. From the 1920s into the 1930s, new kinds of parks recast nature on the edges of New York and Los Angeles in another, similarly de-agriculturalized mold. Bond issues for public parks on Long Island, as around Los Angeles, then led to a new park style, accessible to millions of car-driving city dwellers. Both the Jones Beach State Park on Long Island and Huntington Beach outside Los Angeles had their antinature foils— recreational spaces where rides, concession stands, and other human-built structures seemed utterly predominant. For the Long Island State Park Commission, it was Brooklyn's Coney Island; for California park designers, it was privately run "urban pleasure grounds." The more nature-rich parks they designed were heavily engineered, largely to make comfortable room for massive numbers of visitors. At Jones Beach, the alterations were unmistakable: dousing concrete over seventy-eight acres for parking lots and erecting a skyscraping "ornamental" water tower. However contrived their dunes and inland areas, park architects figured the places would still offer more for nature seekers than did Coney Island. Day travelers from New York City need only turn around to feast their eyes on the ocean and its waves.[54]

That ideals of the suburban countryside hung on into the 1920s, despite these developments, is also to say that for urban-edge visitors as well as residents, nature remained relatively easy to find nearby. That it might still bear so many visible human imprints did not spoil their ability to see it as "nature." So long as the main places where Americans knew nature were still classified and experienced as countryside, their notions of nature were not confined to the wildest and most preserved of places. Remarkably, even around the largest and wealthiest U.S. cities, many could seek and find nature in suburbs and through suburban cultivation. Nevertheless, those changes were already well under way that, after World War II, would make what Americans thought of as "nature" far more difficult to find there. The changes began with how, as more and more Americans moved to the suburbs, urban edges were acquiring new density—and not just of people and buildings. Culturally speaking, they were becoming harder to conceive of only as portals to the rural. They were, instead, acquiring a place character of their own, as suburbia. The rise of urban provisions and health oversight in many suburban places, as well as shifts in urban-edge agriculture, meant that this character, as it crystallized, was gradually folding more urban appearances and meanings into its definition.

Some forty years later, this generation's recreational parks, in particular, would catalyze a new nature politics by epitomizing the kind of preservation environmentalists did not want. But in the early thirties, as the Depression deepened, approximately 140,000 people visited Jones Beach on a single summer day, and a new edition of the *Walk Book* remained muted in its criticism of this state preserve. Jones Beach was "one of the finest and most populous beach resorts in the world," it declared. It then went on to quietly direct ramblers to nearby beaches that were "not much developed," such as Fire Island, a few miles farther east.[55] If the informal commons along America's most restive urban edges was being developed, by park officials as by others, in ways that some already found less than natural, the bigger threats to it, for all concerned, loomed from the Depression itself.

Economic desperation further corroded the viability of suburban country ideals along urban edges by the new varieties of agriculture it stirred. Depression-era migrations as well as agricultural change threatened a peaceful coexistence between upper-to-middle-class suburbia and the farm. In the early thirties, so-called jungles and homeless colonies expanded to "unbelievable proportions" outside many American cities.[56] Poor transients without a job or a roof over their heads were only the most destitute of the new arrivals. A "back to the land" movement propelled many others who were better off not so much to a distant and isolated countryside as to less settled parts of the urban edge. The widest impact of this movement came through a blossoming of subsistence production of vegetables and livestock across suburban areas as well as in smaller cities and towns.[57] Along urban edges, market farming flourished anew. Between 1930 and 1935 the number of commercial farms rose 6 percent in New York's Nassau County and 7 percent in Los Angeles County; farms' acreage and actual production in these counties hit historic peaks. Commercial goat and cattle herds returned even to Queens and Brooklyn. Especially around cities that drew more migrants from afar, the larger operations consolidated labor forces that were increasingly racialized, from the Polish, African, and Native Americans who worked Long Island's crops, to the Mexican and Japanese immigrants, joined by "Okies," the Dust-Bowl refugees, in Los Angeles–area fields and orchards.[58] Along these urban edges, even as more crops were cultivated, agricultural work became more indelibly associated with the period's deprivation and racial taint.

At the same time, reinforcing the racial line drawing were the very federal programs put in place to combat the Depression, through support of exclusively residential suburbanizing. As historians such as Kenneth Jackson have shown, New Deal housing programs over the postwar decades would help bring home ownership to a majority of American families. As the federal government began guaranteeing home mortgages up to thirty years, most of its decisions about housing only bolstered gathering convictions that "suburban" and "country" ideals were largely incompatible. Much has been made, for instance, of how government "red-lining" surveys of mortgage risks heavily favored the most "restrictive" and protected communities—the A-rated were almost uniformly well-to-do, suburban, and white—over inner cities. Less noted, these same surveys frowned upon the most countrylike uses of land. Places with too many "sustenance homesteads" could also be classified as poor credit risks. Most horrifying (and D-rated) of all were *not* downtowns, but places that were all too rural and backward as well as nonwhite, such as one corner of Los Angeles's rural fringe that was hopelessly abandoned to an "infiltration of goats, rabbits and dark-skinned babies."[59]

Federal assessors of mortgage risk were thereby observing that very diversity of urban-edge communities that Douglass had commented on fifteen years earlier. Up to this point, private markets had been largely responsible for the segregation that existed between such different corners of the urban edges, the medium by which racial prejudice and the stigma of being too countrylike reinforced one another. But the assessments joined with other New Deal initiatives to incorporate prevailing prejudices of both sorts into federal policy. Washington itself was now giving official sanction to the extraction of the countryside and the suburban from one another.[60]

As prosperity returned after World War II, new home buyers migrated to urban-edge places en masse, in what now came to be cast as the relocation of an entire American middle class. By the lights of many of the period's journalists and social scientists, notions of a "suburban country" had no relevance to where so many people were moving. But remnants of the suburban country persisted and not just on the urban-edge ground, where housing continued to cut into farmland. The suburban country lingered on in the memories and aspirations of those who became the next generation of suburban migrants. Even around the nation's largest and richest cities, many who moved there, even into the newest and most massive subdivisions, were seeking a kind of countryside home, where good health could be had and a semblance of nature could be found.

Part I
New York

 **Chapter 2**

Nature's Suburbia

S uddenly, around 1950, the nation's suburbs surged into the headlines. It began as a story about builders heroically stepping up their
projects just outside New York and other cities to relieve a postwar housing shortage. Strapped for affordable living space, returning veterans and their families had been living in cramped apartments or even
chicken coops. Now, huge low-cost developments like Levittown in Nassau County offered them the chance to own their own roof. Coverage
of suburban mass building quickly evolved into something more—it was
about an entirely new slice of the world where a youthful middle class was
moving (see Figure 4 in the Appendix). Business media led in the discovery
of these places. Other reporters, novelists, and social scientists soon joined
the throng, fleshing out these suburbs' uniqueness as a social milieu, as
exhibit A in the arrival of a new "mass consumer" society.

This story about what happened along America's postwar urban edges,
first formulated by its contemporaries, continues to be told and retold by
historians. Less remarked in this tale of mass suburbia's rise, from then
until now, is the shift in perspective and emphasis that accompanied it.
Among those who wrote about America's urban edges, a new angle of
vision was consolidating, one that marked a radical departure from how
urban edges were portrayed half a century earlier.

In the first flush of its coverage of the suburban exodus in 1950, *U.S.
News* could still speculate on how it stemmed from the "idea of a home
in the country—an acre of land, a garden, flowers [that have] always . . .
been popular with millions of Americans." But once coverage of suburbs
and suburbia took off, media and social scientific observers looking out
from the traditional downtown became far more inclined to see, instead, a
"mass suburbia." Dominated by houses and the human hand, it harbored
only the most meager of rural reminders, like the "little sapling outside the

picture window." The new demographic and observational tools becoming available bolstered the tacit commitment of many mass-suburbia portraitists to write the countryside or nearby nature out of what they saw.

Coverage drew, for instance, on the U.S. Census's first adoption of "suburbs" as a working category in 1950. For the census takers, suburbs were essentially urban places: though outside the city limits, they were still part of a metropolitan area. Suburbs' registered population gains of some 33 percent since 1940 (as opposed to a 9 percent gain inside the city limits) thus counted as the growth of metropolitan—as opposed to rural—America. Aerial photography, just coming into its own in the news magazines of the 1940s and 1950s, bolstered this more exclusively urban categorization of suburbs. Taken from several thousand feet up, its bird's-eye views obscured many details. Differences in houses, the faces or even bodies of those who lived there, the more isolated trees and forest patches, and street-level landscapes of shrubs and lawns: all these vanished when seen from on high. What stood out were the larger patterns crafted by developers: the similar house sizes and placement, the squared off, uniform grids that underlay most neighborhoods. Coverage of the lives of mass suburbia's residents imposed other, parallel biases. Journalists' localized, sociological preoccupations often confirmed that the new suburbanites *were* excessively social and, like their houses, conformist in bent. Thereby, most observers steered away from any nature-related questions.[1]

Media and other coverage of this new suburbia lost track of what earlier in the twentieth century had been easier to remember: that suburban migrants often sought the countryside. As mass-produced suburbs came to be portrayed in such stark departure from the suburban country idea, those seeking to explain the suburbs' demographic gains gravitated toward "push" over "pull" factors: Why suburban migrants were fleeing the city, rather than what might have drawn them away. The older, positive aspirations of suburban migrants, whether for health or nature, now rarely figured in. Suburbanites were "city folk" who pointedly did not seek surroundings that were essentially rural so much as where cities and buildings were absent: "Where there is more open space."[2]

The very word "suburbs" was undergoing an attendant shift in significance. No longer did it denote a mere location, still less a way station to the countryside. Rather, "suburbs" became nearly synonymous with "suburbia," the way of life of an entire "rising" middle class. In becoming journalistic staples and household words, suburbs and suburbia in the postwar period came to mean something quite different from what they had signified in Henry Bunner's time. By 1960, they named places where countryside as well as nature were hardly to be found.

This and the ensuing chapters seek to restore what these ways of seeing postwar suburbanization missed. In so doing, I do not mean to say that contemporary observers were entirely wrong. As historians' own perpetual debates attest, the same historical development, especially one so complex and multifaceted as urban growth, can yield multiple narratives of what happened, all of which may fit the known facts.[3] Nevertheless, especially to understand how critical suburban landscapes were to the making of a postwar environmental movement, we need to situate this long-standing narrative alongside other nature-attentive ones, more as well as less at odds with it.

Broadly speaking, it is useful to distinguish between three ways of narrating the history of suburbanizing. The most established one—favored not just by mass suburbia's early explicators but by most urban or regional planners, and by subsequent urban as well as suburban historians—sees suburbanizing as *city building*. Hence, to follow its history is to trace the spread of built environments outward from the urban cores where they are presumed to have originated. Among its virtues, this narrative yields important insights into how on-the-ground suburbanizing embodied larger dynamics of metropolitan growth. Suburbs arose and spread, for instance, via the new people, capital, and industries that flocked to an entire urban region, even as builders of the resultant housing, stores, and factories themselves favored previously undeveloped land. But as we shall see, the neglect of any nature or countryside at stake sparked a second narrative, starting in the 1950s: suburbanizing as *nature erasing*. Originating among self-declared conservationists, this narrative highlighted precisely those more natural lands and features that mass suburbs, especially, utterly destroyed. This same narrative, sweeping in its condemnations and reassuring in its rectitude, continues to dominate the thinking of many environmentalists today. Yet it too has its blind spots. It remains inattentive to the class and racial privilege in which it has so often been grounded, and it is dismissive of places and experiences that less well-off suburbanites have considered natural. As such, it has leaned on a narrow, restricted definition of what nature is. A central premise of this study is that such definitions have long stood in the way of any deeper understanding of the suburban roots of American environmentalism itself.

In this book I pursue a third kind of narrative, one that aims to set the origins and strengths of this nature-erasing tale within a broader, more *ecological* framing of the nature at stake.[4] Here, the point is to examine how, even as the countryside was being erased, it was also being steadily dangled before suburban migrants' eyes and, in a variety of ways, sustained or even folded into the resulting suburban fabric. By this ecological narrative, suburbanizing in the America of this period, as before, meant less an erasure of nature than its more or less artful *rearrangement*.

After all, builders and developers, as well as purchasers, of suburban housing still attended closely to the unbuilt particulars of urban-edge land. Preexisting terrain, topography, and flora, as well as planned grading and horticulture, all could play an important role in house construction, as well as in many a home purchase. Nor was the resulting landscape easily confined to a single ecological type, despite the emblematic role played by the most homogenous "mass suburbs" in press coverage. As a recent wave of social historians has emphasized, postwar suburbs were highly fragmented: while the range of neighborhoods was diverse, each was generally confined to certain racial, ethnic, and socioeconomic groups.[5] The concrete currency of these differences was also, in an important sense, ecological. Between neighborhoods, just as the houses might be bigger or smaller, so could the yards, plantings, and other unbuilt surroundings diverge widely, in ways that could matter a great deal.

In seeking to take these differences seriously, a more ecological narrative of postwar suburbanizing must begin with the actual changes wrought not just by a single builder but by multiple types of builders, across an entire suburbanizing region. Of all the housing developments that sprang up along the edges of U.S. cities, journalists and social scientists harbored a special fascination for the largest: along with the Levittowns, Park Forest outside of Chicago and Lakewood outside of Los Angeles. This fixation entailed a further confinement: to the nation's largest or fastest-growing cities, in its wealthiest regions. Of all U.S. cities, Greater New York City was far and away the most frequently mentioned; among mass suburbs, that honor fell to the first Levittown.[6] I begin with Long Island, where it lay, along the roiling edge of the nation's largest metropolis. Like the rims of other cities in America's northeastern and north central regions, the collective arrival of new suburbanites on postwar Long Island best fits journalists' and social scientists' stories of a "move to suburbia." Here as elsewhere in these regions, the trajectory of most suburban migrants was more uniformly as this contemporary tale would have it: out from a core downtown. Postwar construction on Long Island, as around the cities of Chicago or Boston or Detroit, also followed those geographic patterns

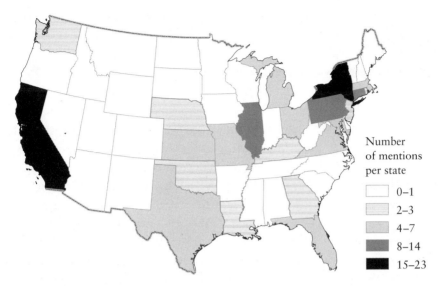

Geographic focus of post–World War II "suburbia" coverage. (Data compiled from
A Reader's Guide to Periodical Literature, *1955–57)*

that contemporaries would consider most characteristic. It rolled out, with
some leapfrogging, from an urban core that was clearly distinguishable,
established through earlier decades of industrializing. The transformation
of the Long Island edge of New York, more or less representative of urban
edges across the northern Atlantic and Great Lakes areas, offers the best
assessment of what the mass-suburbia story got right about the ecology of
urban-edge change in this era, but also a first exploration of how much it
missed.

   Not least of what Long Island shared with other urban edges in these
regions, but unnoted by observers of "mass suburbia," was its temper-
ate and seasonally varied climate. It also sported much waterfront and an
interspersed blend of hills and flats, forests and meadows. In Levittown
and beyond, natural-seeming features, whether cultivated or more inadvertent "gifts of the land," found their way into the plans and aspirations
of all manner of developers and home buyers. Those many microenvironments involved in Long Island's postwar suburbanizing ranged far beyond
a place such as Levittown itself. Among them were more customized subdivisions; farms and factories continuing to vie for urban-edge properties;
and suburban migrants who were not so much like Levittowners, whether
because they were considerably richer or poorer or because their skin was
not white. Among postwar builders as well as their early customers, both

ideas and many realities of the suburban countryside hung on along the Long Island ground, even in places that best fit the mass-suburbia tale.

The Hidden Natures of Mass Home Building

Nearly lost in the media coverage of Levittown's mass-produced birth was how the developer's advertisements featured a nature sell. Levittown promotions touted "beautifully landscaped" or "lawned, landscaped, and shrubbed grounds" at or near the top of these homes' most appealing features. "Even fruit trees have been planted!," the copy exclaimed. This pitch bore the imprint of Abraham Levitt, patriarchal namesake of the famous building firm. In 1947, in an opening article for the town newspaper, Levitt articulated high hopes not so much for the new town's houses or shopping centers as for its enveloping nature. He did so through an allegory: "Once upon a time," he wrote, "a clergyman was sent to lend 'spiritual guidance' to a 'bleak, desolate island.' . . . 'This place must attract birds,' said he. 'It must have the color of flowers.' He planted 'small seedlings all over the isle, and nursed and tended them. . . . Some years later, the trees grew to immense proportions, the shrubs gave forth fruits and berries, and flowers contributed their gay colors all over the isle. Then the birds came.'"[7] Levittown, too, Father Abraham predicted, had a future as an "isle of nightingales."

He thereby articulated aspirations for America's post–World War II urban edges that would soon be lost in an exploding literature about mass suburbia. An avid gardener and a devotee of Ernst Haeckel, the German who first coined the term "Ecologie," Abraham was a firm believer in uplift through greenery. "A person who lacks appreciation of" a "beautiful landscape," he wrote, "loses those great inner satisfactions which bread and glamour can not provide."[8] So vital did he consider Levittown's flora to its future that after retiring from the building operation itself, Abraham remained at the helm of the firm's landscaping department. However, the planted side of the Levittown project, and the man who directed it, received short shift in *Time*'s otherwise fawning coverage. In the magazine's 1950 cover story on the building firm and its project, Abraham's role was mentioned only at the end of the piece. As though to confirm his marginality, a small photograph of Levitt holding a tree was tucked at the bottom of the page and labeled "For father, grass seed."[9]

The face of his younger son William Levitt, on the other hand, was exalted by placement on the magazine's cover. Heading the firm's promotions, William developed a spin on the project that was far more in tune with contemporary media expectations. A pitchman par excellence, William sallied forth as the public face of the Levitt operation by pitching it as a canny adoption of "mass production" and "assembly-line" processes for home building. William's vision, far more than Abraham's, gained traction in the media from the late 1940s onward, as home ownership began soaring, soon to include a majority of American householders. Contemporaries were more impressed by all the new houses than by any plantings and small wonder. The tide of home construction that engulfed Long Island and other urban edges, especially around the nation's largest and richest cities, was truly phenomenal. As the clamor for housing was joined by calls for factories and malls, roads and highways and stores, urbanizing conversions overwhelmed vast stretches of Long Island's rural land. The arrival of Levittown itself, with its seventeen thousand homes, came to be seen as the first stirring of this tumult, one that had ushered in a scale of home-building projects altogether new to the American experience. Yet this, as other suburban housing arising on postwar Long Island, contended with a preexisting topography that was a natural as well as a historical product.

Starting just across the East River from Manhattan, Long Island juts out into the Atlantic some ninety miles due west. It is engulfed on the north by the Long Island Sound and on the south by a string of barrier islands, bays, and inlets. Its topography, like that of many parts of New England and the northern United States, dates back to the retreat of glaciers from the last Ice Age beginning about twenty thousand years ago. Departing ice sheets left two converging strings of hilly deposits, one along Long Island's hilly northern edge and another running toward the southeast, to point up its south fork.[10] The woods along its northerly spine then sprouted stands of oak, hickory, beech, walnut, and chestnut, like those across other parts of the Northeast. Razed for agriculture over the eighteenth and nineteenth centuries, trees had begun to return early in the twentieth, as farmland lay fallow or was turned into estates or upper-end subdivisions. The same could not be said of some hundred square miles of grassland that covered the island's interior into central Nassau County. Known as the Hempstead Plains, it gained distinction among early twentieth-century naturalists as the only native prairie east of the Alleghenies. Used as common pasture into the late nineteenth century, it was then converted, some of it into the ornamental landscaping of Alexander Stewart's Garden City, but mostly into potato farms. By 1940, only 1 percent of the original prairie remained

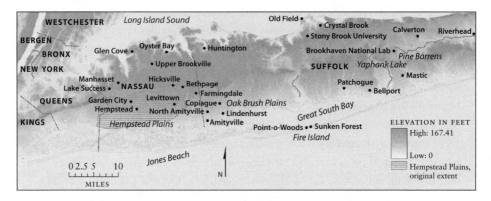

Long Island terrain and places. (Based on information from U.S. Geological Survey, and John Cryan, "Major Vegetation of Long Island," Heath Hen 1 [1981]: 41)

intact.[11] While postwar suburbanizing would bring more housing and residents to the shoreline settlements, former Hempstead prairie lands would shoulder the biggest early brunt, as the location of Levittown itself.

Until the end of World War II, with farming dominant across the island's interior, the vast majority of Long Islanders had still lived in and around shore towns. Begun as centers of fishing and shipping, these had then developed beaches and hotels for the tourist trade, along with upper-end suburban enclaves. Robert Moses's limited-access parkways had begun to open up the interiors to fast and easy automobile traffic in the 1930s. Combined with growing car and truck ownership as well as an expanding network of other paved roads, the new ease of transportation enticed many more potential users of inland acreage.

Nevertheless, land purchases by would-be builders of houses or factories hinged heavily on existing owners' willingness to sell. By the 1940s, many estate owners were finding it difficult to hang onto their large acreage. As businesses went downhill or as advancing age forced questions among mansion title-holders about how to pass properties down to multiple children, they increasingly confronted Bunner's "twain demons" of rising taxes and assessments. Postwar farmers faced similar travails. Growers in both Nassau and Suffolk Counties had long been aware of the encroaching suburban edge; they bore its risks in exchange for easy access to urban markets, at least up to a point. After the war, as their taxes mounted, the many additional, steadier jobs becoming available in construction, factories, and sales siphoned off their supply of farmworkers. Farmers chose to sell as potential tenants or laborers became scarcer, and as the profits from intensifying production near city markets failed to make up for what they owed the local government. So long as they could afford to pay the higher taxes, agriculturalists here and elsewhere might choose neither to farm nor to sell. In anticipation of further rises in land values, they thereby engaged in a speculative practice later termed "idling," most common among those farmers with the least productive soils.[12]

In the shorter run, Nassau and Suffolk farmers faced other postwar troubles. Potato prices were falling, and local Long Island governments often continued to ratchet up land use controls in ways that discouraged commercial dairying and livestock raising. Public health rules for selling food and milk locally also tightened, helping to drive out occasional or small producers.[13] By 1950 Levitt and Sons had become the largest home-building firm in the nation, thanks in part to a still further problem: a non-human migrant that turned up in the 1940s on Nassau County's modernizing potato farms. Growers' shift to potato monoculture had inadvertently invited the North American arrival of a new insect pest from Europe: the golden nematode. The most intensely infected farmland lay at the heart of the huge swathe that Levitt and Sons purchased for its record-breaking housing development. Enjoying a buyers' market, Levitt and Sons was able to buy approximately three thousand contiguous acres between 1946 and 1950 from fifty-five farmers.[14]

For many Nassau County farmers, the tipping point came once they realized how much more money they could make from selling their land than from farming it. Some with sufficient capital and a steadfast "love of farming," like Robert Rowehl, began again on land farther out in Suffolk County. Far from dying out, the farms in eastern Suffolk prospered over the postwar years, as did those few remaining in Nassau that found niches in the suburbanizing local economy.[15] It was the larger-scale, more commercially minded producers who mostly stuck with farming, to specialize in potatoes or milk or vegetables. Smaller-scale or more sporadic operators, who were also more dependent on local crop sales, were more likely to seek other livelihoods. By the same token, those who continued to farm were also more likely to ship to markets beyond Long Island. Early on, the island's farmer cooperatives sought to keep a foothold in the new consumer markets: for instance, through a new Nassau County potato-washing plant, which promised that "no longer will housewives need to expect dirt-encrusted and grimy potatoes."[16] Overall, however, local farms supplied a dwindling share of what went on the dinner tables of those many Long Islanders who were just arriving.

Missing from depictions of Long Island's new "mass suburbia" was the arrival of factories and commercial enterprises—starting with wartime aircraft plants—that offered more lucrative and abundant jobs for suburban migrants.[17] Not surprisingly, employment in commerce burgeoned, as retailers and wholesalers also bought up Long Island properties. The many new shopping centers and especially the ubiquitous supermarket further severed the long-standing dependence of suburban residents on the productivity of local land. Supplied by regional and national chains, supermarkets spurned many of these local products on which smaller, independent grocers had long relied.[18] From the late 1940s into the 1950s, however, the biggest new demands on Long Island land came from the builders of neither factories nor stores, but of housing.

Their dispersion of residences out from New York City would establish Long Island's reputation as the "birthplace" of modern, mass suburbia. What made so much owner-occupied habitation possible so early on Long Island, prior to much growth in paychecks, was the new influx of private capital into home building. New Deal mortgage guarantees and other programs, including one for returning veterans, helped catalyze considerable growth along the lower end of the housing market. Nowhere was the impact more intense than around New York City, on Long Island in particular. Between 1940 and 1970, housing units in Levittown's Nassau County rose 332 percent, nearly double the growth in the next-door New York City borough of Queens. The vast majority of these new units were single-family homes owned by their occupant.[19]

One cumulative effect of all this postwar home building was to erase the long-standing confinement of Long Island's housing to its shorelines. The built-up areas along its northern and southern shores still gained residents, but the main frontiers of housing construction veered inland, through what sprawl's critics would soon term "leapfrogging." Land purchases out from established towns meant cheaper land; moreover, the resulting subdivisions would be surrounded by unbuilt "natural" land—at least for a time. Along the southerly half of the interior, this informal commons consisted of a few second-growth forest patches, but mainly treeless farmland. Out from the village of Hempstead, the first Levittown itself marked a new milestone in inland leapfrogging. It soon served as the nucleus for additional waves of home building, as builders felt increasingly less constrained by considerations of swampy or shoreline land. As a result, postwar housing splayed in an ever more even pattern across Nassau and eastern Suffolk Counties.

This evenness itself belied the continued importance of natural or countrylike surroundings to post–World War II builders and realtors. On Long Island as elsewhere, they had long been aware of how such features, as well as importations of plants, improved property values. "Turning to Mother Nature for help," some called it. After the war, a survey by the *National Real Estate and Building Journal* indicated that a modest 6 percent of development costs went to landscaping. Yet two in five thought landscaping added "100% to sales value," and nearly two-thirds believed that the completed house should include it.[20] Not just deliberate planting but nearby natural features enhanced the marketing of suburban properties, nowhere more so than in the case of single-family homes. Preexisting topography and flora, as well as what builders themselves put in the ground, helped to differentiate or "class" the homes and neighborhoods in postwar housing markets. They were an especially important determinant of values for properties in the upper reaches of the market.

Though left out of much media coverage, a small but significant fraction of postwar suburban housing targeted the "truly 'luxury' ranges" of customers—those who could pay from $20,000 upward. On Long Island, most of these residences lay along a hilly North Shore that had originally harbored the island's densest woodlands. By the late forties, this area featured many second-growth forest patches and beaches, as well as numerous mansions from the Gold Coast era, many of which were being sold and converted to smaller lots. Neighboring villages and towns—Long Island's wealthiest—experienced an extraordinary surge of home building and population growth. A visible nature and countryside played important roles in the sales pitches for housing there. In *New York Times* ads for Nassau or Suffolk homes in April 1952, those touting the "landscaping," whether "beautiful" or "full" or "extravagant," averaged an asking price of $23,427, well within the luxury range. Those announcing "waterfront" or "canal" locations or "water views" went for $27,341. But the biggest premium came among those mentioning "tree-studded" or "wooded" lots, which averaged $34,700.[21]

One such example was Lake Success village, the site of new facilities for the United Nations, in northeastern Nassau. Between 1940 and 1960 it grew from 203 to 2,954 people (including newly annexed areas). Among the developments that sprang up was one containing five hundred homes costing between $21,000 and $33,000, begun in 1948 with the purchase of a 26-acre farm by developers Newell and Daniel.[22] Local flora, topography, and other outdoor features figured prominently not just in ads for this

The upper-end nature sell. New York Times *advertisement for Newell and Daniel housing development in Lake Success. (*New York Times, *August 15, 1948)*

upper-end housing but in its very design. Advertising copy foregrounded the "large and lavishly landscaped grounds" of one-third to two acres, as well as the privilege of using a communal space, "the Village Green." This central parklike area included "swimming pools and tennis courts," "recreation center and playgrounds," and even "a public school." Surrounding their "distinctive *new* country homes," near Nassau's boundary with Queens, the developers promised a veritable suburban countryside: a "beautiful quiet country atmosphere" in the "wooded hills of Lake Success."[23] Porter O. Daniel, the firm's architect, had long sought to meet "the public preference for homes that look as if they 'grew on the land.'" Like other upper-end developers, he and his partner Leroy Newell, made a point of "retain[ing], as far as possible" preestablished trees. Among these were the "fruit orchards and groves of old lindens" from the old estate that they were converting into smaller lots. They fitted their low-slung and sprawling "ranch-type homes" carefully to the sloping North Shore topography, enabling views of Little Neck Bay that strongly fortified their sales pitch.[24]

Reprising a vision of the suburban countryside, builders like Newell and Daniel nevertheless helped to modernize upper-end home construction. Abandoning an entirely customized process, they turned instead to semi-customized methods characteristic of the operative builder, along with the latter's integration of land purchases with building and sales. Escalating the number of homes they erected annually into the hundreds, they joined many others in jarring home construction out of a state that *Fortune* magazine in 1947 memorably described as a business "capitalism [had] forgot." It quickly evolved into what contemporaries recognized as a modern, organized endeavor. Nowhere was the impact of operative building greater than around the nation's largest metropolis, New York City.[25] In size and "modernity," however, the impact of operative builders on middle- to upper-end developments paled in comparison to their accomplishments in the lowest brackets. Over the late forties and early fifties, the Levitts helped lead the way in cut-rate prices for new single-family homes on Long Island, to below $8,000. They thereby opened an avenue into the wallets of potential home buyers about which housing analysts could only dream: "the production worker in manufacturing and other industrial lines."[26] Its clientele, as well as the sheer size of its new development, helped Levitt and Sons draw far more attention than any upper-end builder among journalists searching for a suburbia that had been "mass-produced."

What distinguished the Levitts' first such operation from the many others that would arise in these "affordable" housing brackets, locally and across the country, was a combination of scale and timing. The nation's other largest cities, Los Angeles and Chicago, acquired housing developments of seventeen thousand plus houses only in the early 1950s. By then, the first Levittown was nearly half a decade old. The Levitts' initial penetration of the lower-end housing market owed much to the pent-up demand and government programs of this historical moment. Famously, the company adapted Henry Ford's mass production methods for cars to house building. Folding into the operation of its own supply chains for building materials, through purchases such as that of a California lumber mill, the Levitts also borrowed techniques of the assembly line to bring down costs. They splintered the work involved to ensure "the most minute breakdown of operations" and relied heavily on machines to simplify and automate tasks. As a result, they could hire a cheaper workforce than competitors, with only 20 percent of it skilled and most of it nonunionized.[27] Moreover, those directly employed by Levitt and Sons were surprisingly few, only about four hundred at the operation's peak. Instead, it subcontracted the bulk of the hands-on work. Contemporary allusion aside, for the latter two reasons, the Levitts' innovations actually had greater kinship with what economists of the 1980s would term "flexible specialization" than with Ford's assembly line at River Rouge, Michigan.[28]

Also deemphasized in the news coverage was the contribution of the local terrain to the firm's factory-style production of houses. A massive development like this one required level, treeless land like that of the Hempstead Plains, most of whose hedgerows, as well, had been cleared away by its farmers. This terrain eased the building of roads and the maneuvering of trucks and work teams. Its limited variation allowed work on each foundation, house, and neighborhood to be just as similar, fulfilling the Levitts' plans. And lingering exceptions to the land's flatness were made to conform. Where hillocks or hedgerows or "Island Trees" (the original name for the area) remained, the developers had them bulldozed, literally to smooth the way for the building crews.[29] The same flatness, however, imposed additional considerations in this central part of the island, as opposed to hillier land to the north. If the builders did not grade the land, drainage could become a serious problem. Water pooled more easily on flat lands, and new networks of roads, houses, and lawns would shed rainwater quicker than the preexisting woods, meadows, or farms. Drainage could prove especially problematic where, as in Levittown, builders relied on cesspools, which leached into the local ground, rather than sewers or septic tanks, which were more expensive. To prevent pooling that might bring sewage to the surface during storms, the development's engineers directed bulldozer drivers to grade the site ever so slightly. They also reserved some plots as community sumps to capture the rainwater washing off roofs, roads, and lawns and allow it to seep into the ground.[30]

Unlike in upper-end developments that retained established foliage, housing constructed by the Levitts in central Nassau really did start with a treeless slate, naturally sustained through prairie ecology, then further shorn by the potato farmers. Developers' bulldozers brought a final clearance to the land that Abraham Levitt promised would become an "isle of nightingales." His trees, shrubs, and lawns went in only after the grading was done and the houses were finished. Nevertheless, the sheer amount of what they planted was formidable. Abraham's landscaping team dispensed 340 tons of grass seed and installed an estimated 75,000 fruit trees—four on each lot. These as well as the 50,000 shade trees they put in were only small saplings, so they favored fast-growing varieties such as willow. For the immediate landscaping effects around the houses, they relied on a quarter-million flowering shrubs and a like number of evergreens. The larger, slow-growing, and more expensive trees, such as oaks—the mainstay of upper-end foliage and the original forests to the north—only went into Levittown's "village greens."[31] Whatever corners they cut and however many houses they built, considerably more trees soon grew on this land than before thanks to their handiwork.

The media preference for projects on the scale of Levittown missed how atypical it was compared to other housing developments. The vast majority then under way even in the same county—not to mention in a host of other suburbanizing areas—were nowhere near as big. The three thousand houses built by Levitt and Sons in 1949 made up only about 16 percent of the total single-family dwelling units built in Nassau County that year and still less of the thirty thousand constructed in the peak year of 1950.[32] While many of these targeted home buyers were wealthier than Levit-towners, the lower reaches of the housing market also expanded. Other builders, with operations much smaller and less capitalized than those of Levitt and Sons, extended suburban home building, among other directions, southeastward into Suffolk County. There, land was cheaper, the water tables were higher, and trees were more common but scattered, comprising what became known as oak brush plains.

In 1950, after Levittown had ballooned to nearly full size, another family construction firm, the Romano brothers, purchased farmland a few miles farther east. Building about five hundred houses, they, too, folded all stages of suburban conversion into a single operation, to offer a final price of $6,990, which was slightly cheaper than Levittown houses. What distinguished their development, Ronek Park, from that of the Levitts and most others in the same price bracket was that most of its customers were black. African Americans, kept out of Long Island subdivisions via restrictive covenants up to 1948, continued to face more informal "steering" by realtors that kept the color line in housing alive and well. Across the nation, the rate of black home ownership nevertheless rose dramatically. Though starting at 20 percent in 1940 (a much lower rate than for whites), home ownership among African Americans had doubled by 1960. On Long Island, as in other suburban areas where they moved, the new black migrants could buy houses in only a few locations. There, the natural features, like other amenities, were generally less remarkable than in comparable developments for whites.[33]

Though hailed by the Federal Housing Administration (FHA) on the opening of their development in 1950, the Romanos showed less consideration to their customers than did Levitt and Sons. Because they mis-gauged the depth of the water table, some of the Romanos' lots were prone to flooding. The smaller size of individual lots—50' x 90' to 100' in Ronek Park versus 60' x 100' in Levittown—could exacerbate the drainage prob-lem. The Levitt plantings, especially around each lot, were lavish compared with those in Ronek Park. The Romano brothers only put in front and side lawns and planted but one tree in each home lot. Also, in contrast to Levittown's fully planted and provisioned "Village Greens," with their ball fields, swimming pools, and shopping centers, development of public spaces in Ronek Park was merely "contemplated."[34]

These differences actually made Ronek Park more typical than Levit-town of developments that targeted the less well-off of either race, whether white or African American. Advertising pitches for both of these groups made far less mention of natural amenities than did those for upper-end customers. In early April 1952, listings for "Long Island" in the *New Am-sterdam Times*, serving Harlem's black community, included not just single but two- and three-family homes. With an average price of $10,175, none alluded to woods or trees on the property; only two, to nearby water; and a handful, to the "landscaping"—with a slightly higher asking price. The chief reference to house exteriors was a "big backyard."[35] In all these respects, ads for this African American market were little different from those in *Newsday* for the middle and lower ends of the white suburban housing market.[36] Compared to the picturesque nature appearing in the real estate section of the *New York Times*, they depicted the land that came with houses as raw and shorn, reduced to pure commodity. Of course, such differences said far more about how realtors generally imagined these "consumers" than about how buyers themselves grasped the meaning of their home purchase. But in this context, the nature sell offered by Levitt and Sons does stand out as unique, especially for the income bracket of the home buyers it targeted. By installing and pitching "lawned, landscaped, and shrubbed grounds," Levitt promised a home much closer to that of Newell and Daniels, even when lot size and location kept them from deliv-ering as much.

As for the cumulative effects of home builders on the larger landscape, these examples alone—of Lake Success by Newell and Daniel, Levittown by the Levitts, and Ronek Park by the Romano brothers—confirm that many thousands of trees were being razed on Long Island. But they also point to some surprising conclusions about where the greater portion of woods were cut. Ronek Park's and Levittown's developers certainly sheared away any remaining trees, yet their building sites, whether former prairies or oak brush plains, harbored fewer trees to begin with. Many of them had already been felled by farmers. The hills around Lake Success and other North Shore communities, on the other hand, had long sprouted a denser variety of forest. On much of this land, where former nineteenth-century farms had become estates of the wealthy, the hardwoods had already begun growing back. House for house, perhaps even in sum, a great deal more trees were felled to make room for houses in Long Island's richer brackets—ironically, where the nature sell was most exercised.

These three examples also suggest a conclusion that runs counter to the stories about suburban migration prevailing in the media over this period. The "suburbia" to which so many were moving was not a single type of place. Ecologically speaking, the postwar landscape where suburbanizing occurred was actually a mosaic of microenvironments, varying hugely by neighborhood or development. Along the postwar edges of cities like New York, private developers worked to swell outward a patchwork of neighborhood ecologies whose city-country mixtures were far from uniform. It included neighborhoods in which nature could be more as well as less visible, where its presence might be positively but also negatively valued. In this period, as in that dominated by talk of the "suburban countryside," urban-edge contacts with land and nature *were* still possible. Whether they were more or less apparent, or more appealing than annoying, depended on the color of your skin and what kind of neighborhood you could afford.

Protecting the Public in the Private

For all the differences in how they dealt with natural amenities around the homes and neighborhoods they sold, postwar builders across Long Island were keenly aware of how vulnerable any subdivision was to the whims of its neighbors. That home lots and their surroundings remained almost entirely in private hands left the door open to all manner of neighborhood affronts, from gas stations to factories to unkempt lawns. Among the feared intrusions, the specter of urban-edge slums that had troubled the "suburban country" vision continued to haunt Long Island developers of this era. In response, builders and residents alike devised a growing assortment of tools to shield what they often agreed was a public interest in the private usage of properties in and around suburban towns. At stake was the stability, at once socioeconomic and ecological, of those microenvironments they sought to sell or called home.

Most pivotal to postwar efforts to contain the new turbulence in urban-edge land markets out from New York, as around many other American cities, was land-use zoning. Justified initially under public health law, zoning codes regulated private development by divvying up lands into "zones," each of which had its allowed uses, whether "residential," "industrial," or "commercial." Hardly ever did zoning advocates speak of protecting a natural feature nearby, yet the perspective of ecology illuminates the tacit import of greenery and terrain to many places they sought to shield. Local elites hoped to "stabilize" existing configurations of land use especially in the better-off neighborhoods, precisely where landscaping and waterfront views figured most robustly into real estate and home sales. Small, wealthy towns and villages like Lake Success and Old Field zoned most or all of their land into "residential A" districts. Over the 1940s and 1950s, as overarching townships and even counties gained the authority to zone, more and more zoning boards were established, and new expertise increasingly attempted to ally zoning with planning. Zoning codes evolved ever more elaborate grades and classifications of land use, often attenuating their implications for neighborhood preservation or public health.[37] Some residential neighborhoods were able to muster increasingly restrictive public controls for their own local ecology, natural and otherwise. Others were not. Developers there, the Levitts among them, were forced to fall back on older, private methods for ensuring some permanence to their suburban landscape.

In the northeastern and north central regions of the nation, the most aggressively restrictive zoning occurred in townships or incorporated villages like those on Long Island's North Shore, where wealthy New York–based businessmen and their families had settled in previous decades. By 1940, both Lake Success village in Nassau County and Old Field in Suffolk County already had "rigidly" enforced codes requiring plots to be at least ten thousand square feet, and building footprints to cover no more than a quarter of that area. Old Field, overlooking the Long Island Sound, had zoned itself exclusively for residence soon after incorporating during the 1920s. In 1948, "after long deliberation with a planning expert," its board of trustees decided to increase its minimum lot size ninefold—to two acres. Old Field residents fretted about the intrusion of developments with "a lot of small houses" or "a bunch of shacks," which threatened to "lower the property values." Moreover, "the class of people that comes in with a bunch of shacks doesn't add to the community welfare." Yet at least as pervasive a rationale, given at a village public hearing held in October 1948 in a mansion owned by shoe magnate Ward Melville, had less to do with people or houses than with the less built part of the landscape. Residents spoke out "to keep Old Field as near a rural community as is possible . . . we don't want a suburban community." Precisely through such efforts, the rustic ambience of Old Field was sustained, keeping the "nature" it had easier to see.[38]

Old Field's action signaled the birth of a trend. Large-lot zoning had a tremendous impact in northeastern states over the early postwar decades, nowhere more so than around New York. Whereas in the late 1940s, the Urban Land Institute found zoning for lot sizes bigger than one acre extremely rare, by 1960 more than half the land within fifty miles of Times Square was zoned for single-family lots of a full acre or more. In North Shore townships like Oyster Bay, the entire northerly third outside incorporated villages was zoned for two-acre home lots, just as in tiny Old Field. These measures did arouse some local opposition. At a public hearing in Old Field in October 1948, the main, unsuccessful voices had come from locals who did "not have sufficient property to comply," as well as others, including outside investors in local property, who announced their intention to "sell and develop land." In the courts, though, zoning by lot size quickly emerged as a court-sanctioned tool for controlling the pace and "character" of local development, after alternatives such as zoning by minimum floor space were struck down. In these years, courts largely failed to uphold that any larger, regional public interest might be at stake, conceding instead to the "public interest" that tiny and exclusive municipalities like Old Field claimed to represent.[39]

Across most other parts of suburbanizing Long Island after World War II, zoning officials pursued the "balanced" development advised by many experts and federal officials. They devised rules that were considerably less restrictive, with no protections for still-rural land. For instance, whereas the town of Oyster Bay set two-acre minimums in northerly residential areas, it allowed industrial and commercial development as well as cheaper multifamily and rental housing to the south, along the island's central spine. Similarly, long-established villages like Corona in Queens and Hempstead Village and Roosevelt in southerly Nassau zoned for these denser forms of residence in their downtown, helping to make them major destinations for black suburban migrants. Outside village or city limits, zoning requirements in central and southern Long Island remained not only less stringent but also less rigorously enforced. The southerly township of Hempstead, for example, had designated "A" and "B" residential districts in the areas where Levitt and Sons planned its "mass" subdivision.

Yet the project needed only a single zoning exemption for approval, for concrete slab foundations rather than basements. The Levitts easily secured it by packing the public hearing with homeless veterans. Farther out in Suffolk County, North Amityville, the Romanos' Ronek Park project faced still fewer zoning barriers. The unincorporated North Amityville had first been zoned by the township of Babylon as a "B" residential area, loosely collared by industrial zones. Its zoning status remained unchanged during the building of Ronek Park as well as after, when Babylon Township stepped up efforts to attract tax-paying industries. The results would make nearby, undeveloped patches ever more difficult to find.[40]

An important determinant of the current and future neighborhood ecologies across Long Island's expanding mosaic of landscapes, zoning provided far more protections for some builders and new home buyers than for others.[41] Lake Success's zoning codes helped to reassure buyers about Newell and Daniel's luxury development. The lesser standards of zoning faced by the Levitts or the Romanos made the land cheaper and freed up their own decision making, but it also opened doors to surrounding developments that could clash with their own schemes and promises. Here, Levittown in particular had the advantage of size. By acquiring all properties inside its town's huge radius, Levitt and Sons would gain a unique level of control over the surroundings of most houses they sold. So "we tried very hard," declared Abraham, "to buy up every farm and small acreage surrounding Levittown in order to eliminate objectionable spots."[42]

What worried the elderly Levitt, what spurred his targeting of farms especially, was the prospect of more of the urban-edge "Goatvilles" he remembered from early twentieth-century New York. Manhattan's last farm may have closed in 1940, but similar settlements had continued to arise farther out, including one Danteville, along Levittown's northern border.[43] To protect its budding subdivisions, Levitt and Sons leaned on an older tool of control: the restrictive covenant. Sweeping covenants banned all farm animals and fowl, only allowing "household pets." They required horticultural upkeep, from weeding to weekly lawn mowing, and banned fences, "whether fabricated or growing." Abraham thereby sought to protect the "public" dimensions of private lots in the new development, what, through field of vision if not legal title, belonged to all the inhabitants. "You will see fences only in neighborhoods 'down at the heel,'" he averred, "in 'shanty towns,' and in 'goatville' communities."[44]

While Old Field residents enacted public measures to secure the "rural character" of their neighborhood, keeping the vision of a "suburban country" alive, Abraham Levitt remained fearful of its flip side. Though the Levitts themselves lived within walking distance of cows in the North Shore's Great Neck, though Old Field estate owners still kept horse stables, Abraham worried about farm animals and fowl in his low-end customers' yards. To obviate the need for any backyard menagerie, the Levitts secured chain groceries rather than department stores as anchors for their shopping centers. They provided a refrigerator with each house they sold.[45] Abraham's concern stemmed in part from how the new Levittown was welcoming in those very ethnic groups that his own prewar developments had barred—with Italian or Jewish surnames (like the Levitts' own), akin to the residents of prewar Goatvilles. Even as they prodded and cajoled their new homeowners into the right kind of outdoor housekeeping, they found another target for similar exclusions: African Americans.[46]

Before and after the war, blacks heading straight from the more rural American Southeast to New York converged not just on Harlem but, in smaller numbers, on urban fringes like Long Island. Percentagewise, gains by blacks in Nassau County nearly equaled those of whites over this period, and, in Suffolk, outstripped the pace of white migration. Yet the exclusion of African Americans from more lucrative jobs, as well as prevailing perceptions not just of black but of mixed residential districts, dampened many builders' enthusiasm for this emergent African American market. The Romano brothers' experience with Ronek Park illustrates the difficulties faced by those who sought to build in and around "black" areas.

Buying up farms immediately north of Amityville village, the Romano brothers undoubtedly realized how close their development lay to neighborhoods that were already largely black. The area had been occupied by pre–World War II arrivals as well as a few Native American families who were racially excluded from home ownership inside the village. Migrants had been drawn, as well, by the "peaceful," "green" landscape of oak brush plains and farms, the cheapness of land prices, and the proximity of agricultural work. In buying up farmland in this area around 1950, the Romanos did not have the capital to accumulate nearly as much property as the Levitts had. Buying out the mixed neighborhood of African and Native American owners along Broadway and Albany Avenue was not an option. Instead, they decided on a "non-racial" policy of home sales for their new Ronek Park development. Effectively soliciting black customers rather than excluding them, they sought to make a virtue of what, given the neighborhoods next door, was a necessity. On announcing this policy, they received lavish praise from both the FHA and the National Association for the Advancement of Colored People, a telling indication of just how unusual this line of action was.[47]

Although the houses they sold were brand new, and the families moving into them were similar to Levittowners in age and occupation, the arrival of so many more blacks in North Amityville sparked allegations that on postwar Long Island, a dark-skinned version of Goatville was in the making. Edward Green, a local realtor, ranted before the Babylon town board in 1953 that the unincorporated areas north of Amityville had become a "shanty town" where people "live like pigs." "We're going into the housing conditions of the share-croppers," he warned. Green did not have to say the residents were black; tying "conditions" he could see "from the train window" to the southern system of tenant farming was hint enough.[48]

Green's tirade, together with these other examples, suggests some important determinants of whether the rural characteristics of a neighborhood on postwar Long Island were seen as favorable or distasteful. Rural reputation depended less on how much farmland surrounded a neighborhood than on how big were its houses, how manicured its landscaping, and how fully "sanitary" its provisions. In comfortable, elite (and white) enclaves like Old Field, sanitation seemed a given, farm animals were assumed to be easily controllable, and crops were grown more as a hobby than a livelihood. There, the rural look of the land remained highly prized. But in urban-edge haunts of the less well off, where the threat of the Goatville hovered, a more rural appearance and ambience could seem threatening. Especially along these lower reaches of suburban housing, the ethnicity or race of homeowners added to the coding. White outsiders like Edward Green had little trouble reading the new African American arrivals in Ronek Park as triggering rural degradation and poverty. The Levitts, with many more resources at their disposal, were able to engineer a quite different reputation for the first Levittown. Its many new residents, by and large descended from those same Southern and Eastern European immigrants who had peopled the Goatvilles, lived in what became widely recognized as an exemplar of the new suburbia.

DESPITE THE ACTUAL VARIETY of suburbs that arose in a place like Long Island, contemporary media blurred all these neighborhood ecologies together as a single "suburbia." Portraying older notions of a suburban country as quaint and outmoded, it also served up a nostalgia that was, more or less tacitly, rooted in a higher class of suburban place. Frederick

Lewis Allen's brief history of American suburbia, published in 1954 in
Harper's, offers a revealing example. Allen's "story of Suburbia" located
its most sympathetic flowering among the "romantic" commuters of the
1920s, well-to-do arrivals such as himself. Only with the advent of "mass
produced" suburbs in the postwar years did the less well off, with their
factory-imprinted homes, make their way onto his "Suburbia" stage. Their
entrance, combined with their "segregation" by income as well as age (they
were all young) and "the discovery of the suburbs by business," made for a
postwar decline, the "metropolitanizing of Suburbia." Reportage on Levittown and other "mass-produced" places shored up Allen's and others'
sense of suburbia's "portentous" transformation. The conclusion seemed
"inescapable": the suburban countryside was nearly gone. "The days are
passing (if indeed they are not already past) when one could think of a
suburban town outside one of our great cities as a village in the country."[49]

Such a history failed to take into account how, as more rural neighborhood ecologies were vanishing in many corners of New York City's and
other urban edges, they were being actively preserved in some places and
reproduced farther out. A specialized group of geographers and economists now studied this "urban" or "metropolitan fringe" where suburban
housing had not yet overwhelmed more rural land uses.[50] But whether in
tones of regret or fascination, writers for the mass magazines such as Allen,
Whyte, and Harry Henderson characterized "suburbia," both now and in
retrospect, as distinct and separate from the countryside. So closely associated did the term "suburbs" become with its "new" or "mass" variants
by the mid-1950s that observers felt compelled to invent new terms for
places where urban commuters actively sought out neighboring farms and
"country" ways of living. The neologisms proliferated: "semi-suburbia,"
or "outer suburbs," or "ex-urbia," a first approximation of what later
emerged as the standard geographic designation. This last coinage, by
journalist August Spectorsky, started as a reference to *The Exurbanites*
(1955), upper-income professionals who, still enticed by the old vision of
a "suburban country," moved to places like Long Island's North Shore
because of its rural look and feel. Spectorsky meant to skewer the sham
of working in the city by day, but over the night and weekend thinking of
oneself as a "countryman." Hatched in social satire, exurbia would, like
suburbia, come to be seen as having a corresponding, cartographic reality.[51]

Despite the appeal of "suburbia's" expositors to the realism of census
figures, community studies, and photography, many admitted motivations
that were more autobiographical and quietly rooted in the more privileged

suburbs with which most identified. Writers like Allen and Whyte each singled out one particular suburban past that they compared most favorably to the "mass" suburbia of the postwar: their own. Allen, for instance, introduced his story of "crisis in the suburbs" by recounting his own experience in the mid-1920s of moving to a house in Westchester County. There one "could feel one was living in the country." Revisiting the area some thirty years later, he found the fields and woods were gone and "the largest remaining bit of woodland had just been selected as the site for a new high school."[52] Like Henry Bunner's lament half a century earlier, Allen's history of suburbia gained coherence and emotional force not through any studied representativeness, but out of his own personal sense of suburban loss, itself very much class-specific.

As this critical take on "mass suburbia" crystallized among elite writers like Allen and Whyte, those witnessing this "metropolitanizing" from the inside had quite different stories to tell. Whereas Allen and Whyte saw places like Levittown or Ronek Park as the city jutting outward, those moving into these places saw their own trajectories in opposing terms. The experiences of three couples who sought new homes on postwar Long Island suggest that the "suburban country" vision still found traction among new suburban home buyers, holding out the prospect for a recognizable nature nearby. It could do so even in the most "mass" and lower-end housing markets, as well as at the higher-end.

Seeing Countryside in the Home Purchase

In the early 1950s Julian and Muriel Kane and Eugene and Bernice Burnett bought homes on Long Island. Julian was soon to become prominent in a new, local and regional environmental activism, and Eugene was a future leader of the island's civil rights movement. Like so many other new arrivals in New York's mass suburbs, both couples were recently married. Seeking their first home purchase out from the city's boroughs, each couple ran up against the peculiar constraints of lower-end New York–area housing markets. For the Kanes, the tightrope walk was between location, amenities, and affordability; the Burnetts shouldered, as well, the additional burdens weighing on African American home buyers. Both couples bought into the kind of tract subdivisions that served up fodder for critics of suburbia's "metropolitanizing": the Kanes into Levittown, the Burnetts into Ronek Park. Yet both couples understood themselves to be leaving the city for places that, if by no means rural, stirred memories and expectations of the countryside.

The Kanes, the children of Russian Jewish immigrants, had grown up mostly in Brooklyn and Queens, and bought their Levitt house in 1952. They had been married five years earlier. Julian had then undertaken graduate studies in geology; Muriel, after graduating from college, had worked in Manhattan for a while, until she had become pregnant.[53] Their interest in nature and rural settings had been spurred especially by Julian, who had enjoyed childhood summers in the Catskill Mountains and who ventured out to explore mines and rock formations. Muriel, too, nourished a growing fascination with the natural world: "I found it simply broadened my horizons . . . from the standpoint of nature and being in nature." This "standpoint of . . . being in nature" helped steer their choice of an apartment in Forest Hills, Queens, "the only building within one or two square miles" with "rabbits in the field" next door. "This is wonderful," "we like the great outdoors," Julian remarked as they signed the lease, but "is it going to remain this way?" Despite the landlord's promise, it did not; a new building soon wiped away the meadow. A couple of years later, when Muriel became pregnant and Julian left school for a Manhattan job, they decided to try again, and this time to buy a home. Like many of their neighbors, they did not recall shopping around; "Levittown was the place to go." "There wasn't a lot of choice" in the early 1950s; Levitt houses still seemed nearly the only ones within the range of young families like the Kanes. The affordability of Levitt houses was also conditioned by an unyielding economic fact: farther in toward the city, there was simply no comparable space and provision available for as low a price. The Kanes remembered paying $103 a month to rent their one-bedroom Queens apartment. But the mortgage for the Levittown house, with two bedrooms, would cost them only $60 a month.

Like many early Levitt customers, the Kanes had alternating memories of what they saw in this house—between the gushing of Levitt realtors and a tempered language of sufficiency. Muriel spoke of their Levitt home as "paradise"; in her next breath she recalled a "small" yet "nice yard," where "the trees were growing" and there was "adequate, comfortable living space." "It was fine, it was fine." Like other wives involved in the decision to buy, Muriel was pleased with the neighbors, also that "we didn't have to buy appliances." Her "horrified" father perceived them to be moving to "the other end of the world," far from the city proper. But for Julian, in particular, the nearby fields and farms made the Levitt house more attractive, part of a "real suburb." As he summarized it, "We had our countryfied area."

They and others who acquired Levitt houses, whose own skin color went unremarked through the process, had a hard time seeing how their whiteness had empowered them to buy. Those kept out of Levittown *because* of their skin color, such as the Burnetts, were far more likely to recognize the profound impact that race was having on the geography of a home purchase.

In 1950 newlyweds Eugene and Bernice Burnett, who had been raised in West Indian families in Harlem, decided to buy their first house. They ruled out a return to Harlem, Eugene explained, "because at the time . . . heroin had . . . posed its ugly head. . . . We said . . . we want to raise our children somewhere else. . . . So I started looking."[54] Bernice had finished college and found an office job in Manhattan, but Eugene, a veteran without a degree, faced occupational barriers posed by his lesser education and his skin color. While working at the post office and as a chauffeur, he began looking for a house outside of New York City.[55] Scanning newspaper ads in early 1950, Eugene soon came across notices for Levittown. He telephoned an old army buddy who lived in Corona, Queens, about fifteen miles east of Levittown, and who had a car. They and Bernice then drove out to visit the Levitt model homes. On their arrival, they realized they were the only black people in sight and "that everyone was staring at us." The real estate salesman promptly turned them away, saying "It's not me . . . but the owners, the builders of this development have not as yet decided to sell this to . . . Negroes." The Burnetts came away fuming. "I don't know why I didn't start World War III," Eugene declared.

The dream dangled before them at Levittown had nevertheless distilled their ideas about what they wanted. "I was a ghetto boy who always lived in apartments and to see a plot of land and the outside of a house and this is mine and I can buy this . . . that's what I mean by beautiful. That's a whole new experience. I knew no one that owned their own home and so forth. That was a big step in the life of a young black man." For Eugene, the "plot of land," as well as the house itself, seemed an uplifting contrast to the stoops and stairs to which he was accustomed, outside apartments. Seeing house and land from "the outside," imagining himself as their owner, he read maturation and manhood in the prospect.

Bernice recalled being "on the same page" as Eugene about the importance of ownership, as well as that fateful visit to the Levittown model home. But her feminine eye was more impressed by the "modern devices" inside—"We were washing clothes by hand, and now you got a washing machine!" Used to the "closed-in" apartments of the Bronx, she was also impressed by the "airiness" of the place. All that unbuilt space around the Levitt houses held out great hopes—"You could really dream."[56] "Airiness" echoed the many official declarations of "overcrowding" in urban places like Harlem. But Bernice's words directly reflected her own more remote memories of the rural outskirts of St. Thomas's Charlotte Amalie, where she had lived until age nine. Home ownership for the Burnetts boded contacts that had been familiar to celebrants of the suburban countryside—with land (for Eugene) and air (for Bernice).

"Wide open," "fresh," "clean," "semi-rural," "it really was country"— these same impressions resounded in the recollections of the 1950s by new migrants to Levittown, as well as to other Long Island suburbs. That they gave so little initial thought to growing their own food on this land, however, went without saying. Already, the abandonment of this piece of the earlier notion of a "suburban country" was, at least in this suburbanizing region, nearly complete.

Though turned away from Levittown, the Burnetts, like many other young African American couples, persisted in their goal of buying a suburban house. They found one in "non-racial" Ronek Park.[57] The price of the Burnetts' Ronek Park house was slightly less than what the Kanes had paid at Levittown, for a variety of reasons: Ronek Park was a few miles farther from Manhattan, its lots were smaller, its houses were less provisioned, and its yards were less elaborately landscaped. In addition, its "commons" area was much less formal or developed. Ronek Park had no village green or community pool; and playgrounds and ball fields, as well as centers for shopping and community gatherings, had been left unbuilt.[58] Buying into Ronek Park meant investing in a place that remained less urbanized *or* suburbanized than the "countrified" Levittown. Thus, by dint of their skin color, the Burnetts were forced to live in a more countrified area than they would have preferred.

By contrast, racial as well as class privilege enabled those at the higher end of the housing market to be far less ambivalent about seeking out a more rural look and feel. In many of their neighborhoods, a countryside ambiance was rigorously protected. Such was the discovery of Robert Murphy and his wife Grace Barstow Murphy, who over the 1950s would become leaders of Long Island's movement for "nature" preservation. In 1952 they gave up their longtime summerhouse in Crystal Brook, along the North Shore of Suffolk County, to move into the incorporated village of

Old Field. Unlike the relocation of the Kanes and the Burnetts, this move actually brought them closer to New York City—but to a place more deliberately committed to the old "suburban country" ideal.

Robert Cushman Murphy, who for many years served as chief curator of ornithology at the American Museum of Natural History in New York City, had grown up on Long Island.[59] By the time of their move, he had been married to Connecticut native Grace Barstow, a housewife and author, for nearly four decades. The Crystal Brook residence, on the North Shore harbor of Mount Sinai, had been their vacation house for nearly as long, until Robert's impending retirement led them to give up their workaday home in Bronxville.

Most summers, they had repaired to the house in Crystal Brook, "set in trees upon a bluff above salt water." It lay several miles to the east of Old Field, in a twenty-house subdivision of one- or two-acre lots.[60] By the early 1950s, Grace Murphy still considered "our view" of the harbor to be "as fresh and beautiful . . . as it was when we first saw it"; it was "a simple view, yet so are the lines that came from Leonardo's pen." Over the same period, professional naturalist Robert Murphy kept a journal that offered a less rhapsodic and more troubled portrait. Murphy worried especially about private dredging operations, allowed by the village of Port Jefferson, that produced sand and gravel for Long Island's rapidly expanding roads, highways, and subdivisions. He had long joined in antidredging campaigns, but in 1950, opponents of dredging had faced their biggest challenge yet. A new company proposed to dig out nearly a quarter of the eastward end of the Mount Sinai harbor, across from Crystal Brook. This "very territory . . . has the greatest and most lasting residential and recreational value," Murphy bemoaned, blessed as it was with "the beauty and cleanness of the countryside." "What do you want then," he asked fellow citizens in a letter to the local paper, "a black hole, or a place where there is still room for souls to expand?"[61] Privately, Murphy also fretted about Crystal Brook itself, which had been invaded by a highway, new homes and residents, industrial activity, and vandalism, all of which the governing authorities had failed to curb. These pressures were bound to intensify "as the population increases." Moreover, at Crystal Brook field mice and squirrels nested in inconvenient places in the house, and the soil was excessively coarse and sandy.[62]

In January 1952, with the ornithologist's retirement becoming full time, the Murphys began looking for a new home. Aided by a local realtor, they began scouting out the incorporated village of Old Field, with its two-acre zoning and strict land-use provisions. Two months later, their friend Ward Melville offered the property next door to his own in Old Field. Murphy found it "a great deal." He had little to say in his journal about the house, other than that it was "substantial and attractive." But he went on at length about the property. It consisted of six acres, four times the size of their Crystal Brook lot. With "good trees" and a "spring pond," it was "a good place to feed and tame waterfowl." Moreover, the house was located along a dead-end road, "completely hidden from the highway"; the "only man-made structures visible [were the] backs of [the] Melville stables." Its siting—he did not mention Old Field zoning and land-use laws—meant that the place was "likely to keep for many years to come the spacious residential seclusion it now enjoys." And "maybe the soil will be better and the mice fewer." All told, the property seemed "a proper abode for a lady and gentleman and might be the practical solution of our problem between ages of 65 and 100."

Melville and his wife, long worried about protecting the "rural character" of Old Field,[63] passed ownership to the Murphys in a way that suggests how much less free upper-end housing markets could be than those for Levitt homes. This house next door to the Melvilles was never advertised; it changed hands without the intervention of a realtor. For the Melvilles and the Murphys, what made this purchase possible was friendship—and minimal marketing. No doubt the exclusivity of Old Field property was also sustained in more open realty markets by high prices. But in this case, exclusion operated through cronyism: land was withheld from the market until a buyer came along whom the seller knew and trusted.

From Abraham Levitt's imagery of an "isle of nightingales" through the many quests for countrified surroundings, notions of a suburban country had survived a postwar real estate boom, even as they were excised from media and social scientific talk about "suburbia." Upper-end buyers like the Murphys could afford to speak explicitly about the "nature" on their property. The sheer size of their lots made room for things this word was already known to name: conspicuous woods, even ponds. But both the Kanes and the Burnetts found, in their lower-end home shopping, some of those very sorts of land and nature contacts that promoters of the suburban countryside had hailed. The places to which they moved, without farms and with so many houses and residents, were in other ways a far cry from any countryside. If these places were no longer country but not city either, then just what kind of nature did *they* have?

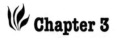

Chapter 3

Ecological Mixing and Nature Fixing

As Julian and Muriel Kane drove home from a camping trip in up-state New York sometime in the late 1940s, they spied two baby skunks darting along the highway. They, as well as another motorist, stopped. Guessing the mother had been hit by a car, the other driver persuaded them to give her one of the tiny creatures and take the other one home themselves. As babies, they would die in the woods without maternal care, she had argued; besides, with the scent gland out, "they make wonderful pets." The Kanes carried the tiny skunk back to their Queens apartment. They subsequently had a veterinarian remove the odorous organ but preserved it in a formaldehyde jar. When they moved into their new house in Levittown, the skunk and jar went along. Maturing, the small animal settled easily into its new role as house pet. Staying mostly indoors, nuzzling into their laps like a cat, it was content with a diet of table scraps. It became "a hit," especially with neighborhood children. The skunk tweaked the imaginations of Levittown's youngsters because it was so different from the other pets they knew. Julian and Muriel knew better. Yet even for them, the skunk's wildness occasionally protruded, to be captured in family stories.[1]

This creature was only one of many that the new arrivals to Nassau and Suffolk brought with them, that living multitude with which Long Island suburbanites, like other migrating human groups, surrounded themselves. Many of these, from the Kanes' pet skunk to cats, dogs, and goldfish, to lawn grasses and other ornamental plants, arrived through human intention and effort. Ideas and aspirations, like the Kanes' to bring home this living reminder of the woods, were fundamental to the ensuing transformation. Other species that proliferated had long lived there, or crept, swam, or soared in. The result, out beyond the New York City limits, was a city that was more than just the sum of its buildings and human inhabitants;

*The Kanes' skunk, one of the more unusual pets to be imported into the emblematic suburb of Levittown. (*Levittown Tribune, *March 11, 1958, courtesy of Anton Community Newspapers)*

PET SKUNK (DEODORIZED) is neighborhood attraction for youngsters at home of Julian Kane, 4 Sky Lane. Kane, who is new president of Levittown Property Owners Association, caught the skunk several years ago while on a camping trip.

it was a city astir with the greenery and commotion of nonhuman life. In this rapidly and radically altered landscape, the ability of any plant or other creature to flourish hinged, as Charles Darwin would have it, on its adaptability to its new environment, its knack for finding food and mates. From the most to the least wild, so-called generalist species like the Kanes' skunk, more flexible in diet and less demanding of their surroundings, had the easiest time. Along the postwar urban edge, adaptability could mean avoiding hazards like speeding cars and marauding children, or attracting human notice, sympathy, and care. As with domesticated plants and animals on farms, the survival of many suburban species rested on people's ideas and actions, whether more or less deliberate. During the same period, as a consequence of living amid this vast importation, the thinking of many Long Islanders about nearby nature underwent a sea change.

As the most rapidly suburbanizing slice of the nation's largest city during the post–World War II period, Long Island offers a special window into the ecological transformation associated with urban-edge sprawl, and the nature-related perceptions and politics it could in turn spark. Like the island's sudden acquisition of so many new houses, the biological changes that sprawl introduced were, for the time, unusually intensive and widespread. For this reason, their traces were more legible, harder to miss, than along the edges of other U.S. cities, where parallel developments were more isolated, fragmented, or on a smaller scale. Differences of climate, soil, and preexisting ecology meant that its waxing species most closely matched those surrounding cities in the northeastern and north central United States. But in its broadest features—a shift toward new styles of plant and animal domestication, the selective impact on wild and semidomesticated species—Long Island's ecological transformation exemplified that unfolding across the nation and the world whenever and wherever this new suburbia formed.

For the Kanes' skunk, as for increasing numbers of suburban imports (plants as well as animals), reproduction occurred at a considerable distance from what became their home. Seeds and saplings, kittens and puppies, converged on the lots and houses of suburban families through a stepped-up national commerce in ornamental plants and pets. For wilder creatures and plants, those that humans did not consciously cultivate, proliferation did still depend on local success at sustaining one's own kind, at feeding and reproducing in between the houses, roads, and malls. Except for the most mobile creatures, such as birds or butterflies, the number and diversity of less domesticated and wilder species generally rose along what urban ecologists call the "urban-rural gradient." The term refers to what America's twentieth-century urbanizing has made ever more unmistakeable: a gradual and continuous transition from those lands most densely packed with buildings and people to those where humans and their edifices were sparser.[2] On Long Island, this gradient ran roughly along an axis eastward from New York City, through those suburbs more densely covered with streets and buildings like the Kanes' Levittown, to places where structures, as well as people, were more dispersed, from the Burnetts' North Amityville to the Murphys' Old Field and beyond. Long Island's mixture of towns, factories, subdivisions, and farms had long since made it an ecological melting pot. The sprawl of the post–World War II period, by abruptly shifting the location of each of these land uses, stirred a new level of species turnover and mixing.

This mixing helped nourish a variety of movements that by the early sixties would feed into Long Island's version of environmentalism. To understand why, we need first to recognize a fundamental fact, little noted at the time. The novelty of what planners would dub the island's "spread city" lay not just in building patterns but in how, compared to an earlier and denser metropolis, it devoted far more space and solicitude to nonhuman life.[3] Abraham Levitt's vision of an "isle of nightingales" was thereby, in broad and important senses, fulfilled, but with great unevenness. Whether flora and fauna converged on or fled from a given spot depended on individual tastes, but more fundamentally on contrasts in the neighborhood ecologies available across Long Island, to people with higher versus lower incomes and with black versus white skin. Most properties acquired lawns and pets, but neighborhoods of smaller lots—the Levittowns or Ronek Parks—faced ecological challenges that wealthier ones did not. Yet when a new narrative that Long Island's nature was vanishing began to coalesce, it referred only to the least built and wildest corners of the island. And it first stirred among owners of the more spacious and leafy properties like those in Old Field, and among early buyers of shorefront or second homes.

Seen in this light, the founding of a Long Island chapter of the Nature Conservancy, with Robert Murphy as its first head, represented the application of Murphy's own "ecological" vision, but also much more. Indirectly, it expressed class and ethnic prejudices. The founders' resentment against the destructiveness of builders like the Levitts also implicated those who had made such landscapes their own. Nevertheless, the concern that surrounding urban-edge nature needed preserving gathered steam on Long Island into the early 1960s. It did so precisely because of how its advocates were able to shake off too exclusive an association with a North Shore elite. Changes in tactics were important; so was the incipient eagerness of Levittowners and others of Long Island's less well-off to lend a hand.

Haven of Horticulture

For centuries, the plant trade most crucial to Long Island landowners had consisted of seed for farmers. A few large nurseries like that of the Hicks family, in Nassau County's Westbury, had, since the late nineteenth century, also counted the island's country estates as customers. Importing and growing from seed a huge array of ornamental plants, they specialized in mature specimen trees. Into the late 1940s, however, Hicks marketing and sales still revolved around their continuing role as cultivators of nursery stock. Visiting customers shopped by strolling through the Hickses' own fields. A salesman-guide tagged their choices, and after the root-balls had been bagged or potted, shoppers returned a week later to pick up what they had purchased.[4] Combining the growing and selling of plants in this way ensured a "fresh plant" and minimized shoveling and toting "until you knew you had an order." By the early 1950s, however, the tremendous growth in horticultural sales on Long Island suddenly made these practices seem antiquated.

The woods razed during Long Island's suburbanizing had their rival in the stream of live horticultural material being implanted in home lots. Assuming that the foliage per house in Levittown lay near the average, single-family home builders in Nassau County must have furnished a veritable forest of new trees: some 1.25 million between 1945 and 1965. That total amounted to half the 1954 sum of trees across all five New York City boroughs.[5] As homeowner purchases overtook those of builders and developers, and as small-lot homeowners replaced North Shore estate owners as nurseries' prime customers, the implanted new shrubs and perennials likely ranged several times higher. Plant nurseries themselves quadrupled in Nassau and Suffolk Counties between 1939 and 1964; their sales multiplied nearly sevenfold, to reach over $8.5 billion (in 2007 dollars). Led by the rising demand around New York and other metropolitan areas, over the 1950s purchases from nurseries doubled nationwide.[6]

A number of "modernizing" measures aided the nursery business in stepping up its volume of plant sales. First, a 1930 federal Plant Protection Act had allowed for the patenting of hybrids that were propagated asexually through cuttings. With commercial hybridizers gaining such strong legal protections for their work, the variety of plants commercially available for landscaping shot up. Those species for which demand soared, such as evergreens, drew special attention from the hybridizers. Only two or three varieties of Japanese holly had been available in the 1930s, but by 1961 American growers offered nearly forty different types. Not just private nurseries but New York–area agricultural schools, not least Long Island's Farmingdale, also delved into suburban horticulture. Adding to the species hawked by Long Island nurserymen, they also sought new methods of caring for lawn and garden plants.[7] The expansion of government-sponsored pest control over the postwar period, to take on floral and arboreal threats, further shored up confidence and sales in the ornamental plant trade.

The rapid step-up in horticultural commerce on Long Island after World War II helped to make its nurseries national innovators in high-volume plant selling. Hicks, for instance, shifted toward "all-season planting," extending its greenhouses and turning to container cultivation. With older field-planting methods, trees, shrubs, and perennials had been set out only in spring or fall, usually during a "tried and true semi-dormant period," which varied widely from plant to plant. By contrast, the "modern method" of growing plants in separate containers extended the planting season for many species to as long as the weather remained frost-free. Planting in tin cans or wooden tubs, by confining root growth to a compact ball, cut down on the stress of replanting. Moreover, container plants could be grown either indoors or outside. With little ado, they could then be conveyed to a display area, where shoppers could more easily browse among available plants. Especially with the advent of cheap plastic pots, nurseries like Hicks enlarged their front buildings to provide marketing space for potted plants. Just like in self-service grocery stores, customers could pick out the plants they desired with little assistance from a sales clerk and immediately bring them home.[8]

Nurseries such as Hicks also lifted their sights beyond plant sales to become distributors for the many new lawn and garden products being marketed nationwide. Over the 1940s and 1950s, established corporations like O. M. Scott & Sons thereby consolidated their fortunes and new competitors arose—all of them reliant on local suburban distributors. On Long Island, a new business model was born: the "lawn and garden center." The City of Glass in Farmingdale epitomized the idea: it advertised itself as "America's Largest Retail Garden Center," with "thousands of hardy evergreens, shrubs, trees, . . . hardy house plants, garden tools, fertilizers, insecticides, garden accessories, lawn seeds." As smaller nurseries like Hicks added more and more gardening accoutrements, even department stores like Sears and supermarkets stepped into the business of selling container plants.[9]

By the mid-1950s, as Hicks and other nurseries sold off their own fields to concentrate on distribution and sales, a dwindling portion of these plants had first poked up through Nassau County soil, and more of them on terrain to the east. Especially in Suffolk County, more farmers abandoned potatoes for the task of supplying suburban yards with shrubbery or flowers. Suburban horticulture was more intensive than potato farming; in other words, profits could be rung from comparatively small plots of land. Besides, annuals and perennials grown so near the point of sale enjoyed some advantages over those shipped in from other parts of the country. Transport required less money and time, and Long Island–grown products were not just fresher, they could claim better adaptation to the local soil and climate. In Queens and Nassau, suburban horticulture dominated those few farms that remained; to the east in Suffolk, landscaping plants emerged after World War II as the third most valuable crop. With Suffolk in the lead, New York State growers by 1958 sold more nursery stock by volume than any other state save California.[10]

The surge in demand also led Long Island nurseries to seek more distant but potentially cheaper sources of supply. From the start of the postwar housing boom, the largest building firms like Levitt and Sons had imported plants from other states when buying in bulk; most of the Levitts' mountain laurel had come from a North Carolina dealer. By the late 1950s, as homeowner plant purchases outstretched those of builders on Long Island by a ratio of almost five to one, "more and more nursery stock [was] being imported from other states."[11] No floral material made Long Island yards more reliant on distant stockers than did grass seed.

The earliest lawn species arriving on Long Island had been those that flourished on Britain's country estates: a bluegrass (later known as "Kentucky") and red fescue. In their original climate these species had required little watering or fertilizing, but this was not so in the drier and sandier conditions of Long Island, as in other parts of the Northeast. Before, but especially after, the war, scientific breeders at agricultural research stations had set about producing new hybrids of lawn grass that could be more easily grown around a place such as New York. At the same time, national companies like O. M. Scott & Sons and Armour and Armour were moving into the business of buying grass seed in bulk. The production of grass seed for lawns was thereby transformed "from a minor to a major farm enterprise." To make it pay, farmers had to devise new techniques for producing pure strains of seed in bulk. For instance, they had to plant seeds more carefully and isolate their fields more thoroughly, to protect a crop not just from weeds and insects but from invading grass species. These and other requirements made specialized "grass seed farming" land-intensive, ideally undertaken on large acreage, at a time when land on Long Island and around other cities was becoming much more costly. Consequently, by the late 1950s, after the turf grass industry had become "larger than any other single agricultural enterprise" in the nation, grass seed for lawns was grown almost entirely outside the Northeast.[12]

On Long Island, certain innovations nevertheless ensured the competitiveness of local contributions to the grass that was sold. On the mixing and merchandising fronts, for example, a Farmingdale blend, concocted at the island's own agricultural field station, was sold as specially adapted to local conditions. Farmers, too, found an advantage in the nearby demand for suburban lawns by selling ready-made living turf. Sod farming emerged as among the fastest-growing and most profitable of island farmers' horticultural specialities, given the impatience of developers and homeowners to establish a thick velvety lawn. Promising "that matured landscape appearance overnight," businesses like the family-owned DeLea Sod Farms delivered "instant lawn" in two-foot by one-foot rectangles at a cost of thirty-six cents a slice. The high cost of live sod confined its use mostly to upper- and middle-bracket homeowners and landscapers. But by the early sixties there was sufficient demand to sustain DeLea's six hundred acres of intensive lawn grass crop on fields across northern Suffolk. To avoid contamination by weeds or other grasses, DeLea soaked its monoculture meadows in the herbicide cyanamid. To minimize soil loss, it made sure to take only one-half inch or less of dirt. Retaining little water, extracted lawn turf was highly perishable. Since the turf needed to be replanted right away, Long Island turf farmers enjoyed a tremendous edge over the off-island competition.[13]

As the exertions of the sod farmers made clear, lawns required more than just the seed. For grass to take hold in Long Island's peculiar mixture of soil and climate, it needed extra water as well as continuous work. The labor was especially demanding if the lawn was to stay a monoculture, for lawn grass did not compete well against the fast-growing generalist plants that comprised the island's weeds. Inherited from Old World agriculture, many of these weeds were the same ones that had long pestered island farms: crabgrass, long-leaf plantain, and—especially a problem on Long Island—chickweed. Then there were the insect pests. Japanese beetles (*Popillia japonica*), first arriving in North America in 1916, had, by the early forties, infested some twenty-one thousand square miles up the eastern seaboard. They were only one of a vast array of insect pests as well as plant diseases poised to proliferate amid Long Island's rapidly spreading lawns and other suburban flora.[14] Even the new hybrid varieties of fescue and bluegrass, touted as more resistant to weeds or disease, could not circumvent the continuing need of lawns for an active human hand.[15]

But just whose hand or hands should be employed? As in other agricultural as well as urban contexts that environmental historians have explored, pests and weeds confounded the logic of private property that largely governed this suburbanized landscape.[16] Their mobility, the ease with which they traversed the boundaries of property and neighborhood, undermined the degree of control that any individual owner enjoyed over his or her own lot. In places such as Old Field, the buffering of large lots diminished the sharpness of this dilemma. It was far more difficult to miss, on the other hand, in neighborhoods made up of smaller lots in places like Levittown and Ronek Park. There, not just dandelions or beetles, but dogs and children traipsed from yard to yard with visible aplomb, dispensing damage to hard-won greenery.[17] Neighbors' anger readily stirred, but also realization of the shared boon that could result from collaboration.

Abraham Levitt, among others, remained keenly aware of the additional work and expense suburban horticulture demanded, as well as the collective benefits that could follow if all Levittowners took the time and trouble to cooperate. However well-chosen and planted, all their grass, shrubs, and trees would die, and the chickweed prevail, if new owners' commitments and skills were not also fortified. Through a gardening column in the Levittown newspaper, Abraham opened up a weekly line of communication to bring home to Levittowners how "lawns, like all living things, require care." He "used to come around in a chauffeur driven car" to check on his homeowners' floral upkeep. If lawns went unmowed or unweeded, he sent his own landscapers to do the job and followed up with a bill in the mail.[18] Most developers at the lower end, like the Romano brothers, were far less solicitous, especially once their homes had been sold.

As lawn cultivation was taken up by new as well as longtime homeowners, its collective benefits, reinforced by the pressure of neighbors' peeled eyes, helped make it the most ubiquitous of horticultural practices on Long Island. Whether these residents were white or black, however, their memories downplayed the landscaping contributions of builders and developers. Early Levittowners recalled a "sea of dirt" or mud that surged with rain, an uneven respreading of the topsoil, and scrawny, "inexpensive" shrubbery and trees. Residents later remarked little about any lawn damage from roaming children or dogs, or the neglect of lawn care by a neighbor next door. Instead, whether they were Levittowners or lived in African American Ronek Park, their recollections revolved around a joint if rival pursuit of horticultural handiwork. "Everyone" took up the mowing and watering and often the fertilizing and weed killing. As with Levittowners, Eugene Burnett remembered "a kind of competition goin' with that" that made Ronek Park yards into "some of the most beautiful lawns I've ever seen anywhere." Caught up in the lawn-making enthusiasm, even Robert Murphy tried to plant one outside his Crystal Brook home. Yet for large lot owners, the dynamic was less intensely communal—the Murphys' lawn was not even visible from the road. For denizens of Old Field, but also for smaller lots of horticultural hobbyists, lawns drew less investment of emotion or energy than other vegetation they cared about.[19]

Not just in such places but also on smaller lots, Long Island's suburban horticulturalists ventured to plant an abundance of nongrass species. Broad-leaf evergreen ornamentals, including mountain laurel, rhododendrons, and hollies, vied with flower seeds and bulbs in the headlines of local nursery advertising. Exchanges with neighbors, as well, furnished both the Kanes and the Burnetts with many of their plants. Botanical connoisseur Robert Murphy imported "exotic" specimens for his home collection from travels around the country and the world, as well as from Long Island's wilder corners. Among his transplants were "holly berries" from Fire Island beach.[20] Vegetable growing, on the other hand, retained the stigma of less prosperous times for some, though by no means for all. "Many folks out here in Levittown," noted one resident, "think a vegetable garden is going to spoil the look of their property." But Abraham Levitt, for all his censure of goats and chickens, encouraged vegetable gardens, and some residents, among them the Kanes, were "very excited" to start one. Julian and Muriel planted peppers, tomatoes, and corn—at least until "we began to get corn borer." A similar enthusiasm reigned in Ronek Park, where, Eugene Burnett remembered, "all" his neighbors grew vegetables. The Murphys did so, too, in both Crystal Brook and Old Field.[21]

Planting and cultivating required at least some horticultural knowledge. While the Murphys had past experiences on which to draw, from Robert's childhood on a more rural Long Island to Grace's upbringing on an estate outside Providence, Rhode Island, newer arrivals to Long Island often had to turn to outsiders for advice. Levittowners remembered drawing less from Abraham Levitt's columns than from local nurserymen and women. At the Dengler nursery, run by "one of the old-time original farmers . . . you'd walk in there with a burned piece of grass and say, 'What do I have?' and she'd tell you you've got grubs or you have a fungus and buy this, put that." Local agricultural institutes such as the one at Farmingdale also furnished expertise. Its new research center, established in 1948 for the study of "florist and nursery crops," sponsored "turfgrass research plots." In Salisbury Park, along the western edge of Levittown, they demonstrated the latest methods for planting and maintaining lawn grass hybrids. Not just Levittowners and Ronek Parkers but people like Robert Murphy consulted county agricultural extension agents—in his case, about his failing Crystal Brook lawn.[22]

In the "lawn and garden" and allied stores, new factory-made products such as lawn mowers, pesticides, and fertilizers increasingly dwarfed commercial plants in profitability. As many petrochemical firms shifted their sights to the new homeowner market, their products such as DDT quickly garnered the approval of local horticultural experts. Not only advertisers but also authors of gardening columns, Abraham Levitt among them, espoused the new array of pesticides coming on the market just after World War II with uncritical unanimity. But so heady and overblown were the pest-preventing promises offered for many lawn troubles that prominent experts soon began counseling caution about advertisers' claims. *Consumer Reports* warned in 1955 that "ordinary weed killers are only partly effective as controls" against crabgrass. "The best solution . . . is to discover and deal with whatever opened the turf to crab grass in the first place"—usually some combination of "poor soil conditions, disease or insect injury, and poor maintenance practices."[23]

Lawn care could inspire wrath next door if lax, but it could also knit neighborhoods together. Especially in places like Levittown and Ronek Park, not just the spread of pests or weeds but the street-front vistas of yard upon contiguous yard confirmed that care for one's own small plot only went so far. Aesthetically, as well as ecologically, an informal commons was also at stake. It was comprised of like properties whose titleholders were, for the most part, similar: young and with children, closer to poor than to rich, and new to suburban home owning. The Kanes' first experiences of organizing around this local commons of small property owners came shortly after moving in. With their "wonderful neighbors," "none" of whom "had any money," they joined together with other residents to form small "cooperatives." Julian and his male neighbors pooled their funds to purchase and share a gas-powered lawn mower. If someone in the lawn mower cooperative moved, they left the machine behind with those who stayed. Similarly, for Eugene Burnett in Ronek Park, the neighborly sharing of shrubbery and horticultural knowledge helped build friendships, even lifelong bonds.

When pests struck, as Japanese beetles did at Levittown in the spring of 1951, still more formal and intensive organizing of some neighborhoods occurred. By July, the beetles' invasion had "replaced the weather as the chief topic of casual conversation in Levittown." A Mrs. Sophia Adler then launched an initiative to persuade all residents in her area to "grub-proof" their lawns. The solution they espoused was one of two newly available insect killers: either DDT or chlordane. This strictly voluntary effort to universalize the spraying of pesticides reportedly won "close to 100 per cent cooperation" among town residents. It drew hearty praise from Abraham Levitt as a "rough, tough, relentless fight," a shining exemplar of how "in union there is strength." Out of it came an enduring organization of community interest: the East Meadow Property Owners Association.[24]

At the same time, rampant usage of these many new products stirred an early skepticism among some would-be suburban consumers. The Murphys, gardening afficionados long before DDT or other sprays came on the market, had never before used pesticides on their vegetables or fruit. Into the 1950s, they saw no compelling reason to change. Robert's caution derived, perhaps, from his professional knowledge as a trained ecologist, but not so his wife's, nor the Kanes'.[25] Julian (who had trained in geology and become a high school teacher of earth science) and Muriel Kane lived in a subdivision where pesticide usage became nearly universal, at least for a time. Yet a decade or more before Rachel Carson began *Silent Spring*, the Kanes had been troubled when an indoor insecticide bomb had forced them out of their home for an entire day. When corn borers invaded their backyard crop, they decided to stop growing corn rather than risk the recommended sprays. Even as their Levittown neighbors doused grass and gardens with chlordane or DDT, a studied wariness led the Kanes to use pesticides sparingly. The new fertilizers also aroused significant aversion. Even DDT proponent Abraham Levitt favored "organic" fertilizers, especially "well-rotted stable manure," over "chemical" ones: despite its slower action, an excess did not kill plants. The Kanes preferred chicken manure; the Murphys, other detritus of animals or plants—stable manure, cotton seed meal, or even salt-hay mulch from local marshes.[26]

These inclinations created a receptive audience on Long Island for so-called organic gardening. For suburban migrants who imagined themselves headed into a traditional countryside, even back to nature, all the new chemical and other technology touted as advancing postwar horticulture could appear deeply at odds with what they sought. Plumbing this contradiction, fledgling publisher J. I. Rodale in 1942 launched a new magazine, *Organic Gardening*. By 1957 it had gained 140,000 subscribers and two years later, some 240,000 nationwide. At first ignored by agricultural officials and nursery operators, then targeted as "faddist," Rodale's publication extolled growing practices that deliberately forswore the thriving new markets for "chemical" pesticides and fertilizers. Oddly, perhaps reflecting the success with which earlier forms of American agriculture had been cast as retrograde and unscientific, Rodale traced the roots of organics not so much to U.S. predecessors as to those in exotic lands. As precedents, he pointed to the practical experiments in India by British investigator Albert Howard and to "biodynamic" gardening pursued by American adherents of Rudolf Steiner's "spiritual philosophy" of "anthroposophy." Rodale and various other authors decried the destructive effects of industry-made fertilizers and pesticides on the living components of the soil and on beneficial insects. At the same time, contributors to Rodale's magazine promoted the promise of a return to methods of cultivation that would "bring . . . nature again into connection with the cosmic creative shaping forces."[27]

Additionally, the literature on organic gardening reprised questions about how land and its care connected with human physical health. In ways that most agricultural as well as medical scientists of this period did not dare, Rodale and other writers for his publications charged that the ever-greater chemical dependence of American agriculture was endangering people. By the late forties, they argued that agricultural poisons were contributing to a rise in cancer and other ailments. Later, when the environmental impacts of pesticides on a place like Long Island were coming to be more fully understood, such an argument would make the protection of nature seem far less distinguishable from that of public health. Early on, however, these criticisms shaded easily into others—for instance, that innovations in the distribution of commodities were ruining the consumer's experience with food. "Rarely," mused Rodale, "have we heard anyone comment that the fresh, frozen or canned foods they buy at the local supermarkets have the same quality of appearance, taste, tenderness and resistance to spoilage as foods obtained years ago." Organic and biodynamic gardening gained followers on Long Island from the later 1940s onward: from the Murphys, who began calling their vegetable patch "organic," to members of the Levittown Garden Club, who invited in speakers on the subject.[28]

Whether or not they went organic, the many Long Islanders taking up backyard cultivation had to decide just who among them would get their hands dirty. The better-off might hire a gardener. A formidable fleet of local landscapers and landscaping firms arose over the postwar decades to meet this growing demand for paid yard work. But others, including the middle- or working-class residents of Levittown and Ronek Park, could not afford this service. Meanwhile, people like the Murphys received pleasure and gratification from the work itself. For all those groups who took on the upkeep of their own yards, this work became part of a larger gender and familial division of labor. For many married couples, lawn work was the husband's task; for others, the wife took it on, extending her work realm from the house into the yard.[29] However couples divvied up this labor, it resembled the domestic labor long performed by women inside the home: an uncompensated "chore" rather than an income-producing job. It might subsequently affect the property's value, but that payoff was usually far from homeowners' minds. They saw it either as self-gratifying or as social—destined for the eyes of other family members and the neighbors, whether to show off, to keep up, or merely to deflect scorn.

All the while, larger cultural changes were under way in just how suburban residents interpreted the plants that surrounded them. That so many suburban residents foisted such meanings onto their flora, that the associated work could be so routine, helped to alter how residents saw and categorized the greenery that grew around them. Biologically speaking, holly bushes and lawn grass were living organisms. The natural vitality stirring in their stalks and cells was *not* human; in important respects, it was as stubbornly autonomous as that of a towering redwood. Yet so commercial were their usual origins, so chemically and mechanically reliant was their maintenance, and so dependent were they on steady tending by human hands that their status as nature became ever more obscured. Here was the appeal of organic practices: they promised, at least, a way out, a kind of gardening that was *more* natural. The rhetoric of organic practices dismissed the nature in chemically kept gardens, cast it as compromised by industrial artifice. Nevertheless, for organicists, as well as for their more conventional counterparts, the goal was ultimately domestication, a tailoring of suburban flora toward human ends. However achieved, whether by organic or more "artificial" means, a lawn's or a garden's very status as nature might well recede from consciousness. Especially if well maintained, it was more likely to be seen as the result of the owner's hand. Or, if the aesthetic goals of neighbors were similar enough, suburban greenery might hardly be seen at all. Instead, it might simply melt into a backdrop of the generically tame. In these ways, suburban yard work subtly fed back on those who performed it, shifting their ideas about where nature could be found. Its influences ran parallel to those of another suburban domesticating practice: pet keeping.

Grass Menagerie

Along with the many new plants that Long Islanders cultivated around their houses and yards, they surrounded themselves with legions of animals. Among the many pets welcomed into Nassau and Suffolk County homes, the Kanes' skunk was exceptional; more numerous by far were dogs and cats. The total number of licensed dogs, while declining in New York City over the postwar decades, leaped upward in Nassau, doubling between 1947 and 1957 to about one dog for every eleven humans. That figure missed all the pets remaining unlicensed: as many as 20 percent more dogs (projecting from New York City estimates), all cats (perhaps half again as many as dogs, based on similar projections), and others like the Kanes' skunk. While dogs were banned in many apartments and in public housing in New York City, suburbanizing Long Island offered a well-documented if more concentrated version of what was happening in other parts of the nation. By 1960, *Consumer Reports* reckoned there were 26 million dogs in the United States, almost four times more than in 1930, compared to a 40 percent rise in the human population. By some rather enthusiastic estimates, there were as many as 2.5 pets per person.[30]

That rise brought to a head a long-building transition in the nonhuman creatures with which most Americans chose to live. No longer were domesticated animals so important for their utility; unlike in decades or centuries past, a dwindling share provided food or transportation to their human owners. The new, overwhelming preference was for animals, fish, or birds that served strictly as pets. The passage reflected many other changes that suburbanizing places shared with other corners of postwar America: greater prosperity and rising paychecks, skidding food prices, and a greater availability of grocery stores outside cities and towns. Unlike suburban landscaping, the increasing preference for pets rarely surfaced in discussions of real estate and took longer to register on the radar screen of national consumer watchdogs. *Consumer Reports* covered lawn and garden products from the 1940s onward, but only in the closing years of the 1950s did that publication begin to investigate pet-related industries. The reports were revelatory: pet keeping had spawned its own immense, highly profitable markets. By then, dogs alone outnumbered power mowers. They inspired a half-billion dollars in expenditures nationwide each year, two-thirds of the expenditures for nursery stock. These figures did not include the money spent on all the other pets people kept: cats, likely more popular than dogs, as well as rabbits, fish, canaries, and the occasional raccoon or skunk. In few places was the postwar explosion of pet culture felt as suddenly or intensively as on Long Island.[31]

As Long Islanders welcomed so many more of these creatures under their roofs, they were forgetting how much this boom in America's pet population owed to diminishing concerns about its implications for public health. Dogs in particular had long been known as carriers of rabies, a deadly virus that attacked the central nervous system of many mammals. Though a therapy had been discovered in the late nineteenth century, the last major epidemic of rabies on Long Island had struck in 1944, when rabid dogs were discovered in approximately twenty-seven Nassau County villages and towns. Nassau's health department then took effective actions. Vaccinating all dogs for free and enforcing stringent leash and licensing laws, they eradicated human cases of rabies for several decades.[32] Birds, as well, lost a disease-threatening stigma when psittacosis or "parrot fever" was largely vanquished.[33]

Of course, burgeoning pet populations and expenditures reflected more than just disease control. Incentives for pet-keeping could be reinforced by law or by contracts, such as the restrictive covenants of Levittown. But having a pet brought its own rewards.

Without any ostensible economic or other function, pets nourished human desires for a companionship stretching beyond the bounds of their own species. Much has been made of the revived emphasis on the nuclear family in the postwar media; certainly the suburban migrations of people like the Kanes and the Burnetts put new distance between themselves and their extended families of parents and grandparents. The Kanes' acquisition of their skunk, prior to the birth of their first child, suggests how the pets roaming in suburban houses and yards added a new, underrecognized extension to nuclear households. In families whose human members were not as readily at hand, pets became repositories for emotional ties. Yet they were more than just substitutes for children or grandparents. The Kanes' skunk remained a fond and familiar member of the household long after the birth of their three children. So intense was the emotional investment of its adult owners that on its death at age eleven, both Julian and Muriel "cried and cried." Similarly, the Murphys' dog sustained a special bond with Grace Murphy. Nearly deaf since childhood, she relied on him as a "hearing-ear dog," "not let[ting] anyone come near me without telling me." Her bond also went beyond the dog's utility, to companionship. Though in part standing in for a husband who traveled often, the relationship had no precise human counterpart: "My dog is my comfort. . . . The marvelous relationship between a dog and its owner can be comprehended only by actual experience."[34]

One reason that pet keeping had a low profile in the national coverage of suburbia, and made only a slight imprint on the memories of many other suburban migrants, is that demands for a new kitten or puppy often came from the children of the family. Columnists addressing how to choose a dog or a cat in *Consumer Reports* or the *New York Times* assumed that a new pet would be a "household" or "family" possession, but mostly "for the kids," as a "source of companionship and an outlet for affection." The dual statement of purpose suggested the ambiguous role pets were presumed to have for children. No doubt they provided camaraderie, but through an alliance that was not quite as real as any human-to-human relationship. Instead, as mere "emotional" outlets, pets ranked closer to those less serious, inanimate fixtures of childhood: toys.[35] If many children did treat their dog or a cat as a mere toy, however, the intensity of the love they often developed for their pets could call into question adult dismissals of their feelings.

Children's special fascination with animals had a long tradition, perpetuated by stories featuring talking animals and by their ubiquity among stuffed toys. Shifting portrayals of pets in America's popular culture fed this fascination. Whereas cinematic stories of dogs from the twenties and thirties had featured male dogs such as Rin-Tin-Tin and Baldo acting heroically in frontier settings, over the forties and fifties canine heroism came to be domesticated. Narratives like the original *Lassie*, an English novel made into a 1940 movie, affirmed the staying power of the pet-extended family. Sold off with great reluctance by her impoverished Depression-era family, the female Lassie overcame great obstacles to find her way home again. Her 1954 debut on American television adjusted the story slightly: now she roamed with a human family member, a young boy, across a countryside that was never too far from home. *Lassie* became the most watched children's show of the late 1950s.[36] Perhaps it was a coincidence that broadcast stories about Lassie were set on a small modern farm just outside "Calverton," the real-life name of a Suffolk County town. Regardless, Lassie inspired the games, stories, and names through which Long Island children interacted with their own dogs. Nassau's ten thousandth antirabies injectee was a West Hempstead Lassie. When a five-year-old Lassie belonging to the Duff family in Bethpage, Long Island, mysteriously turned up in a Los Angeles dog pound and was subsequently restored to its Long Island home, even the sober editors at the *New York Times* could not resist the story.[37]

Of those many dogs and other domesticated creatures who arrived in Nassau or Suffolk County during the postwar decades, only a small, specialized fraction entered through the commercial channels that supplied so many ornamental plants for people's yards. While kennels and pet stores multiplied, most suppliers remained small and often local, like a "tropical fish fancier" in Hempstead Village. To nearby pet shops he sold the offspring of the nearly two thousand fish he kept in fifty large tanks in his home. Breeders of pure-bred dogs usually operated on a similar scale, though increasingly, larger operations flourished. By the early 1960s, elite breeders associated with the American Kennel Club were cautioning against "puppy factories, dog farms and backyard breeders who victimize the public."[38] But the great majority of Long Island's dogs and cats likely entered households through a less formal or less lucrative exchange of cash—or no money at all. Many, like the Murphys' dog, were obtained from friends or neighbors, or through classified ads in local newspapers. Most were mixed breeds. In parallel with Long Island's human baby boom of the postwar decades, pets took reproduction into their own hands, proliferating regardless of their owners' intentions.

Even as local governments took over the job of collecting and culling stray pets, pet care blossomed into a billion-dollar private industry by 1960, with the demand in places like Long Island leading the way. By far the greatest expense—totaling $500 million in 1960—was for dog food. The Consumers Union counted more than one hundred different brands of dog food on supermarket and pet store shelves, from canned to dry mixes of meal, pellets, and biscuits. By then, total expenditures for dog health care, including medications and veterinary fees, ranged over $100 million. *Consumer Reports* found the variety of other products for dogs alone "astonishing even to most dog owners." It ranged from pajamas, raincoats, and mink coats to shampoos, deodorants, electrically heated kneeling pads, and "portable comfort stations."[39]

Ecologically speaking, the influx of so many pets in Nassau and western Suffolk Counties was not so much an advent of domesticated animals as a changeover. Those kept for agriculture were replaced by the fauna of suburban residents. As late as 1935, historically the peak year for cows and chickens on Long Island, there were likely two of them for every three residents. By 1960, the number of cows had tailed off and even the chicken populations were plummeting, as the ranks of dogs and cats approached those of humans.[40] Simultaneously, east of Long Island's subdivisions, land not so entirely converted to shopping and housing facilities retained the profit-driven production of fowl and crops. The more rural side of the urban-rural fringe persisted, and with it, not just farms but less developed land. The ecological transformations of these places, as well, helped sculpt what nature there was for postwar Long Islanders to see.

Edges Rural and Wild

Only in more cityward suburbs like Levittown did pets and ornamental plantings almost entirely supplant Long Island's agricultural or more un-worked landscapes. As the island's urban-rural ecological gradient shifted eastward, subdivisions leapfrogged not just proximate to Levittown and Ronek Park but still farther east, deep into farmland and second-growth forests. The microenvironment of the suburban subdivision brought change not only on the ground where it arose, but also through interchange with these lands more or less nearby. Farms and woods were not merely erased; some, hanging on between or beyond the tract homes, underwent their own substantive alterations. Moreover, living in residential suburbs did not necessarily mean that one lost touch with wilder or less built places and the more readily noticeable nature they harbored. Depending on what kind of neighborhood ecology people inhabited, they might still be able to find it next door, or not so far away. Local discovery of rural or wild nature also hinged on another important consideration: just what you took the "rural" or the "wild" to be.

As home building protruded farther into Suffolk, as tax assessments spiked and commodity prices fell, Long Island farmers who adapted rather than leaving still made Suffolk in 1960 the most lucrative agricultural county in New York State. Though horticultural crops and greenhouses registered the largest gains, farther east duck and potato growers still prospered through the specialized niches they had secured in the national market.[41] Early on, farms hung on even around Levittown, if more so along the North Shore, where zoning laws helped small fruit and vegetable growers and even some dairy farmers handle the pressures of sprawl. Around less densely built areas, farm stands enabled local farmers to sell their own goods at retail rather than wholesale prices. They thereby kept open a local supply stream of produce, eggs, and milk, even as grocery stores and supermarkets were coming to dominate suburban food sales. In wealthier as well as more rural areas, beyond the denser, small-lot subdivisions, sub-urban residents still cultivated not only crops, but also their own fowl and farm animals. They did so with a seriousness that was well-nigh agricul-turalist, mostly for reasons other than the sales: to have organic produce, for instance, or because, as one chicken keeper recalled, "I just liked it. . . . We got fresh eggs."[42]

In some places, though, too close a contact with farm creatures brought not just sanitary risks but, far more so than half a century earlier, a certain stigma. During the mid-1950s, for example, "a new colony" of thirty housing units was built on Hollis Warner's duck farm near Riverhead, mainly for farmworkers and others who could not afford better accommodations. In 1957 *Newsday* reported that it was "the worst [slum] between here and Buffalo." "Hometown for several hundred Negro men, women and children," it had "no paved roads, sidewalks or street lighting" and only outhouses for bathrooms. Most appallingly, though, some of its rentals were right above Warner's duck-breeding sheds. There, residents were continuously bothered not only by roaches and bedbugs but also by "the smell of those ducks in the basement. It seems to seep up here through the walls." Even as Abraham Levitt had successfully forestalled any "Goatville" around Levittown, *Newsday* took this new "Duckville" on the east end as a moniker for slums across the island: Long Island's "ugly ducklings."[43]

Interspersed among urban-edge farms as well as more suburban cultivation, wilder flora and fauna underwent adjustments of habitat, responding to the rapid extension of built land. Like the island's farmland, its suburban forests continued to shrink, receding to those corners of the island where developers were stymied or restricted. It also fractured. Chopped up by roads and highways, these woods lost many passages through which wildlife as well as human pedestrians could freely roam.[44] By the early 1960s, the fragmentation and diminishment of forests and other older habitats reached a critical point in Nassau and western Suffolk. There, the largest slices came to be almost entirely confined to public lands, along with zoning-shielded private holdings. The most unique communities of native plants—notably the Hempstead Plains, where Levittown had arisen—seemed on the road to extinction. At the same time, to the north and east, the abandonment of farmland through idling, along with the desire of well-off suburban residents for wilder surroundings, meant that long-razed forest patches were being allowed to grow back. Parts of the island's forests were thus undergoing a long-term revival, a reforestation shared by many other rural reaches of this, the nation's most urbanized region.[45]

Partly as a consequence, suburbanization ushered in new successes for some wild animal species, native generalists that, according to today's ecologists, thrive in sprawl's fragmented forests. Best documented of these were white-tailed deer. For a while considered nearly extinct on the island, by the late 1940s they found new footholds in the patchwork of forests and farms in eastern Suffolk. By 1955, the Fish and Wildlife officer taking over a new refuge noted that deer were "rapidly populating" the area. They became sufficiently numerous and intrusive for Suffolk farmers to push for an end to a thirty-year ban on a Long Island deer hunt in 1958. The proposal made it all the way through the state house, only to be defeated by worries about the safety of residential dwellers. Estimates of deer herds peaked at six thousand sometime in the late fifties, until the continuing slippage of farm acreage, along with the hazards of cars and "running dogs," started to bring their numbers down once again.[46]

Long-term trends in nonmigratory bird populations suggest that, at least in northern Nassau County, gains in new generalist varieties actually outpaced species losses. In June 1960, Robert Murphy led a team of Audubon Society birders on a bird count in Oyster Bay that followed in the footsteps of another bird-watching group led by Theodore Roosevelt some fifty years before. They found forty-six species—three more than the Roosevelt team. Among the fifteen species located in 1910 but missing in 1960, the meadowlark and the grasshopper sparrow were grassland birds, whose favored fields and meadows had been reduced by the eastward shift of agriculture. Surprisingly, Murphy's group beheld twenty species not seen by their Rooseveltian predecessors. Among them were well-known exotics often considered pests: the English sparrow and the starling. Other of the new Long Island arrivals had been more actively engineered: the mute swan, long cultivated by estate owners, and the pheasant, regularly stocked by state game officials. For others newly present, such as the northern cardinal, Murphy had no explanation for their arrival. Judging from recent studies, they may well have been pushed there by reductions of bird habitats in neighboring parts of the island.[47]

Abraham Levitt's prediction of a bird-friendly "isle of nightingales" had come partially true, but less so for places like Levittown than for others. As trees and other foliage matured in this mass suburb, it may well have invited greater avian numbers, but likely a more limited range of feathered species. Today's science indicates that a diversity of bird species is less sustained by densely built and planted places like Levittown than by landscapes along the North Shore, where forest patches and a few remaining farms coexist with suburban foliage. On the postwar landscape of Long Island, the ecological ornamentation of birds and other wildlife accrued to those microenvironments that already enjoyed social, economic, and political advantages.

Early on, residents of places like Old Field had enabled protections that made for the persistence and even regrowth of forest patches. Over the first two decades of the postwar period, Old Field and other incorporated

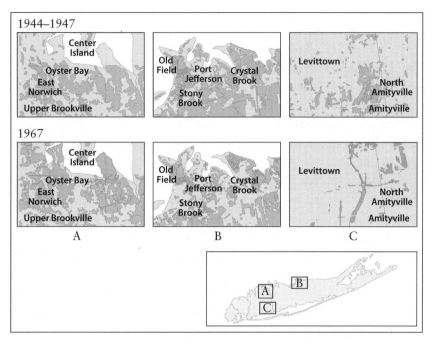

Forest cover in selected parts of Long Island, 1944–1947 versus 1967. Whereas the wealthy, often incorporated North Shore locales from Oyster Bay (Map A) to Old Field (Map B) retained their trees, much of the rest of Long Island, including the Levittown area and the North Amityville area (Map C) did not, except along parkways and in public parks. (Based on U.S. Geological Survey Maps)

villages, as well as the northerly reaches of Oyster Bay, had zoned lots for a minimum of two acres. They not only kept their existing trees; their overall forest cover expanded. By contrast, those clumps of trees and forest patches that had dotted the Levittown and Amityville areas at war's end, prior to suburbanizing, were wiped out. In these parts of Long Island, the only substantial woods hanging on were those placed in public reserves. Especially when it came to having a wilder ecology nearby, the suburban rich were getting richer, while the suburban middle and working class became poorer.

Increasingly, as the decimation of surrounding greenery joined with their own domestications, suburban dwellers sought and found a visible nature only in what seemed less tame, more wild—creatures as well as places. On Long Island as elsewhere, those enveloped by this new kind of city became more likely to recognize their surroundings as "nature" when these were less evidently worked by human hands. What people understood as "wild" hinged on what they considered to be tame or domesticated, hence, on what they were used to, as well as on their knowledge and ability to recognize human influences on the landscape. While scientists drew and debated objective distinctions between wild and tame creatures, popular notions of the wild were considerably more various and subjective. They turned at least as much on what was unfamiliar or alien as on what was known. Amid the biological tumult and admixture that sprawl unleashed across postwar Long Island, distinctions between the wild and the tame heightened in significance partly because of how much actual boundaries between the two realms blurred. In the line-drawing that ensued, just who found a wilder nature and where depended on a person's age and experience, and also on which neighborhood ecology he or she called home.

Given the prominence of young people involved in the suburban environmentalism that would erupt around the first Earth Day, children's experience of the wild in such places deserves special attention. Youngsters, it seems, could find and appreciate the wilder sides even of the most carefully tended suburban landscapes. This ability, so evident in the memories of those who grew up in as cultivated a place as Levittown, depended partly on a lack of awareness of human imprints. The children who flocked to stare in fascination at the Kanes' skunk did not realize just how tame it was. As Yi-Fu Tuan might note, their enthrallment was rooted in the minimal dominance they felt over this creature, having had little or no hand in the exercise of power by which it was tamed.[48] Children were also less troubled by the consequences that followed when adults' domesticating exertions were frustrated. While Levittown's adults sprayed Japanese beetles with pesticides, the children went about collecting them in jars, fascinated by the insects' energetic buzzing. Those who grew up in early Levittown were more likely than many adults to remember the more mundane wildlife in the vicinity.

By the same token, those remaining patches of farm or undeveloped land that Levittown's adults mainly recalled as "on the way out" seemed more remarkable to Levittown's children, and magnets for play. Many attest to being drawn to overgrown and "vacant" lots because these seemed less "sculpted" than the rest of Levittown. Places where adults had left far less signs of their own domesticating dominance, their offspring found rife with a wildness that begged discovery and exploration. They did so, in part, through playful acts of taming. They stamped down weeds to "throw a football around, play baseball, Kick the Can." Or they "ran wild" through "great big potato fields." In such places, Levittown's youngsters, as other children of these suburbs, playacted a domestication as well as a freedom for which nature itself seemed the stage. Their imaginations stirred, the undeveloped corners of their town came to be remembered—more so than other local places—as "something like nature," however susceptible to builders' bulldozers.[49]

For adults, accustomed as they were to taming their grass, shrubs, and pets, their consequent dominance helped render most next-door nature increasingly commonplace and invisible. More unusual and wilder species, on the other hand, became ever more treasured and singled out, provided they were not seen as pests. In Levittown, the Kanes' skunk no longer seemed wild at all—except during mating season, when it clawed up their front door "in search of a mate." Yet this "problem" itself proved amusing to them, at least in retrospect; it made for a quirky story, to be told and retold. Wild species could fascinate, amuse, and occasionally frighten precisely because of how exceptional the local wild had become. Even fifty years later, delight crept into the voice of Eugene Burnett's friend Eugene Reed as he remembered the "wild canaries" around North Amityville. Those "pretty little birds" would fly into his yard and "sit on the tree out there. I've never seen them anyplace else."[50] What Reed and others like him appreciated as "wild" in this bird had little to do with any biological knowledge of it or with any factual dearth of human domination over it. What mattered, instead, was how unfamiliar and out-of-place it seemed. The popular wild, in this as in other such corners of the 1950s United States, turned not just on a remembered imagery from books and films, but on mystery, on how little onlookers knew about what they saw.

Of course, actual flora and fauna only partly determined where this popular wild might be seen; much depended, as well, on the vision and values of the onlooker. Clearly, however, the neighborhood ecology of upper-end suburbs like Old Field offered Grace and Robert Murphy much basis for discovering a wilder nature nearby, ready as they were to seek and celebrate it. Surrounded by several acres of woods in Old Field, the Murphys had a greater abundance of wild life, both flora and fauna, at their doorstep, as well as a professional naturalist in the household. Shielded from the kind of development that was engulfing Levittown and Ronek Park over the 1950s, they both stayed open and welcoming to discoveries of the wild within and around their home. However, a looser and more free-floating recognition of the wild actually came easier to Grace than to her ecologist husband. The Murphys named their dog "Quis," after the Latin for blackbird, highlighting the wilder side of this most domesticated species. Moreover, Grace seems to have been the spearhead in their happy embrace of native flowers and other weeds that invaded their garden. "Far from being proper gardeners," she reported, "we let milkweed and daisies grow anywhere they want. . . . We never have disturbed the wild things by replacing them with garden growths. We treasure and protect each native flower and plant." Like the organicists' disdain for "chemicals," Grace's wilder and native-friendly gardening constituted a rebuke of "proper" ways of gardening. She defined it more or less directly in opposition to that suburban cultivation to which so many Levittowners and Ronek Parkers were aspiring.[51]

For the Kanes with their skunk in Levittown, as well as the Murphys in Crystal Brook and later Old Field, a wilder nature on their own property served as a badge of distinction within their respective communities. The Kanes became known as that couple with the pet skunk, the Murphys as that naturalist and his wife. But the degree to which one's home lot could itself repudiate the grooming of suburban lawns and shrubbery now increasingly depended on differences of class. Compared to the Kanes' Levittown lot, the Murphys' six protected acres around their Old Field house made it far easier to experiment with wilder and more organic ways.

The Kanes and others whose lots were unable to sustain much wilder flora and fauna could nevertheless travel out to find them. As they did, they helped sow the seeds for a new suburban preservationism. Leaving Long Island regularly, the Kanes continued their exploration of the national park system; the Burnetts, as well, trekked up to New Hampshire's White Mountains. Closer to home, Eugene Burnett remembered enjoyable forays with a fellow worker and "country boy" who took him clamming along the Great South Bay. Others pursued fishing or hunting and kept alive talk of "country" within these more rural corners of Long Island.[52] Out of these same impulses, demands mounted for property along its remoter islands and shores. Those who sought these purchases were not merely hoteliers, but builders of rentals and second homes.[53] At once the private demand for the visible nature of the waterfront was being fulfilled and whetted. Some 13 percent of Long Island's remaining wetlands were lost between 1954 and 1959, much of it for housing and recreational purposes. They fell victim to builders who increasingly sought newer and wilder versions of those same informal rural commons that had drawn the island's earlier postwar home buyers. Starting in the early fifties, such projects confronted second—or vacation—home residents already living there who were ready and willing to fend them off.[54]

At the same time, rural patches around places like Levittown and Ronek Park were becoming fewer and farther between. But the Kanes' and the Burnetts' communities did not undertake early collective action to stave off this destruction. It was out of the Murphys' type of neighborhood ecology, where an extensive informal commons enjoyed more formal protections, that the alliances for a new islandwide program for conserving natural lands first emerged. To understand why, we need to look at the more translocal politics that were evolving in each of these communities during the 1950s, and the ways each did, or did not, take "nature" into account.

Fixing Suburban Nature:
The Rise of Ecological Preservationism

The value of the suburban lots of many postwar homeowners in places like Long Island hinged on ample greenery and an openness that extended from theirs and neighbors' houses to the land beyond. Once they moved in, the owners of smaller lots like those in Levittown and Ronek Park faced numerous challenges in sustaining the landscape on their own and nearby lots. These difficulties consumed much of their efforts, individually and collectively, throughout the fifties. While devoted to landscapes in which lawns and other flora were omnipresent, residents found it ever more untenable to speak of any nature at stake, whether in Levittowners' politics of residential defense or in Ronek Parkers' politics of racial accessibility. Rather, it was alliances between homeowners in more privileged communities that first established the more regional pursuit of nature preservation, through the founding of a Long Island chapter of the Nature Conservancy. But for this movement for urban-edge nature parks to accomplish a conversion to environmentalism, it had first to become less elite and more public-minded. Furthermore, its leaders had to adjust their own notions of nature itself. These had to be made less narrow, less confined to ecological authenticity or purity. Ideas about what needed protecting had to be stretched cityward, beyond the Conservancy's simple goal of set-aside properties. Here, the less elite of Long Island's nature enthusiasts offered considerable insights and opportunities, albeit ones that early suburban conservationists had to be dragged into realizing.

The activities of Julian Kane and Eugene Burnett exemplified some of the new regional struggles that emanated from the dilemma of smaller-lot suburban communities during the fifties. More oriented to defense of, or access to, the tame greenery of residential neighborhoods, these groups and their leaders had little to say about what was happening in Long Island's wilder corners. Starting in 1957, Kane helped spark a townwide resistance to the zoning policies of Hempstead town officials. The goal was to prevent Levittown and other nearby residential lots from being converted into stores, shops, and gas stations.[55] To sway town officials, Kane's committee of the Levittown Property Owners Association assembled petitions, letters, public testimony, and news releases, while forging alliances with nearby homeowner associations. They sought a "comprehensive zoning plan in this Township," one that would end the township's practice of spot zoning in neighborhoods with "residential" character.[56]

In North Amityville, Eugene Burnett assumed leadership of a local chapter of the National Association for the Advancement of Colored People (NAACP)—renamed the Central Long Island chapter. Burnett and his cohorts pushed for African American access to private housing markets. One of their number, Laska Strachan, the former head of the Ronek Park Civic Association, stepped in to direct the New York NAACP's statewide housing effort. Locally, Burnett's chapter helped open larger-lot developments to the north and east of North Amityville, in places like Copiague, to more prosperous black families.[57]

Though couched in terms of "residential character" and "housing," both of these efforts pivoted around a singularly suburban ecology: neighborhoods of houses on "plots of land" that were also planted with lawns, shrubbery, and trees. But their own individual and collective work on this flora, as well as the politically and legally viable ways in which they could defend it, mediated against any mention of its natural side. Put another way, in the 1950s, the suburban nature of Levittowners and Ronek Parkers had become so normalized that they could only think about it as domesticated, not nature at all.

For this as well as other reasons, postwar residents of these suburbs channeled little of their early civic energies into preservation of Long Island's wilder lands. Many of them already had access to parks of a sort. Locally, Levittown had its village greens, installed with trees, grass, and ball fields, though Ronek Parkers had to band together to develop a similar neighborhood park. A regional system of state parks, developed by Robert Moses before the war, also offered less cultivated public lands and beaches where residents of both these developments trekked, along with many others. Whereas Jones Beach had drawn 4.1 million people in 1947, by the early sixties its visitorship had doubled to over 8.0 million.

No doubt Jones Beach remained popular because, to residents of more densely built suburban housing, as well as to those of Manhattan, it offered a contrast that seemed nature-revealing. Look away from the parking lots and pavilions, and one saw miles of sandy beach and a wave-churning ocean stretching to the horizon. However, for Long Islanders used to having forests or beaches next door, or to traveling to off-island wildernesses, a park like Jones Beach inevitably clashed with the wilder nature that they sought. Aside from its ocean, beach, and seaside bluffs, Jones Beach bore too many markers of the city: seas of asphalt to accommodate cars, a sky-scraping water tower, picnic areas covered with hundreds of tables. Even the native grasses on its dunes had been planted less for their looks than their durability.[58] Over the mid-to-late 1950s, an initiative gathered steam to undertake a more ecologically authentic style of land preserve, spear-headed by those most inclined to see Jones Beach as nature's antithesis.

The nation's third chapter of the Nature Conservancy formed on Long Island in 1954, with Robert Cushman Murphy as its first leader. Murphy's willingness to run it stemmed from what he had seen of the ecological changes under way in Crystal Bay and Old Field and in travels across the rest of his native Long Island in the late forties and early fifties. Over four decades, his ornithological work for the American Museum of Natural History had taken him to some of the remotest regions in the world, as well as to places where the effect of traveling humans and their importations were much more difficult to miss. His late 1940s study of New Zealand ecology, for instance, attributed the most rapid and disequilibrating eco-logical change to the arrival of Europeans.[59] As he watched Long Island's wilder lands transform, Murphy, more attuned to understand their eco-logical trajectory than just about any other observer, saw trends that he found increasingly alarming.

Sometimes he delighted in an unexpected abundance, as when he wit-nessed three or more least terns fishing in Port Jefferson harbor, "the first time in my life that I have seen the species there." Yet he could not mistake wrenching habitat destruction like "the slaughter of the Belle Terre woods near the Mount Sinai harbor." It brought an end to 60- to 100-year-old trees that were "beginning to look almost primeval. . . . All the forest growth that has taken place during my lifetime and more is being sacrificed." Mur-phy saw a strong connection between this disturbance and an invasion by exotic species: "The Japanese honeysuckle will now burgeon into an even worse and more monotonous jungle." He agonized over the prospect of local extinctions. Finding box turtles squashed on the local parkway, he bemoaned a reptile "the next generation of Long Islanders may never have an opportunity to know. . . . It may be gone like the gray fox, heath hen, and Labrador duck." Long Island's more genuine nature, it seemed to him, was already well on the way out. His own sense of loss could fuse with a continental one, as when he wrote about a "golden age, when game in North America was more numerous than man."[60]

If Murphy's leadership of the new group was driven, in part, by this tragic sense of what had already been lost, both he and others who became involved were also motivated to keep what they had. Like the two other local chapters that had preceded it (after the Nature Conservancy was itself chartered as an offspring of the Ecologists' Union in 1951), the Long Island chapter owed its local origins not so much to ecologists as to well-to-do property owners. The latter individuals had resolved to preserve as "natural areas" those lands that were near to, or like unto, their own. The earliest effort on Long Island, serving as the Long Island chapter's early model, was the struggle to preserve the Sunken Forest on Fire Island. A large grove of holly trees and other native vegetation that had sprouted in between dunes along the southerly barrier-island beach, the Sunken Forest lay just to the east of Point O'Woods, a community of summer homes. When a real estate developer purchased a corner of this unique "forest" in 1952, a few landowners in Point O'Woods formed a group to buy it and place the property in a private, incorporated reserve. In this effort, they secured the support of the Long Island Horticultural Society (LIHS), a group of prominent nurserymen, estate gardeners, hobbyists, and well-to-do housewives who were almost exclusively from the island's wealthy North Shore. Already, LIHS meeting places had begun to range beyond the usual—the showy gardens of upper-tier estates—to include the Sunken Forest itself and other wilder terrain. After support poured in from over forty Long Island garden clubs, the Sunken Forest group incorporated and bought up much of the vulnerable land.[61] Further spurred by a visit from the Nature Conservancy's president, Richard Hough, the LIHS in October 1954 turned its conservation committee into a full-fledged chapter of the Nature Conservancy. Its purpose was "the preservation of natural areas on Long Island as living museums for the future."[62]

By today's Nature Conservancy standards, the lands chosen for preservation were tiny—mere patches of larger ecosystems. Nor were they by any means untouched or "pristine," as Robert Murphy, who surveyed and approved their inclusion as Conservancy tracts, was quick to note. What they shared, however, was that they were either former estates or farmland; that is, they were *not* "suburban," at least in the postwar sense of the word. The "mostly mixed oak, old second growth" forest that Murphy found on one preserve prospect, a farm with trees as much as one hundred years old, had been "fairly common as tree growth" a generation earlier. What now made it "a very valuable acquisition" for the Conservancy was the ecological destruction that suburbanizing had recently wrought: "The commonplace is now beginning to be rare on our bulldozed island."[63] A better match to what they were saving was that early twentieth-century notion of a suburban countryside, albeit minus the more worked look of the farm. Murphy helped the Conservancy see past the built or planted features of potential properties, to distinguish those wild plants and creatures that, through ecological succession, had often begun to predominate. Purchase or inheritance by the Conservancy then formalized this land's status as a legal if privately owned commons. The Conservancy went on to declare what it had acquired to be "nature."

The very notion of "living museums" singled out a nature no longer taken for granted, whose wildness, partial and commonplace as it was, lay on the verge of extinction. Through such ideas, nature preservation moved suburbward over the postwar period, creating models for a more natural-looking kind of park. That Long Island by the mid-1950s already had an active chapter of the Nature Conservancy did not mean that it had gained an environmental movement, however—not by the working definition of this book. Early on, Murphy and the Long Island chapter were still guided by older conservationist models, in activism as well as goals. Mistrustful of broad participation, they held out little hope for marshaling local or state governments to assist their cause. They fancied themselves a small elite whose foresight entitled them to take charge of the island's natural resources, ostensibly for the good of all. Though declaring a goal of public education, the Conservancy did not actively invite visitors to its reserves. On the contrary, its first impulse was to restrict parking, paths, and signs.

Its vision of nature preservation was not just elite and private; it was rural and land-centered. Like the older conservationists, the group worked entirely within the boundaries of purchased property, with nary a thought about humans' physical well-being. As well, it only steered minds and sympathies to the visibly most wild of Long Island's places, plants, and creatures—those largely specific to the wealthiest suburban properties. Still shackled to standards of pristineness, the Nature Conservancy may have opened a few more eyes to the complex ecology of what it preserved. But its commitment to fixing museumlike boundaries around this particular ecology, introducing a new self-erasing type of suburban domestication, taught a narrow and segregated notion of where real nature lay. By implication, nature did not thread through the subdivisions of Long Island, nor through its farms. In its most genuine and authentic form, the Conservancy intimated, nature lay elsewhere, where humans and their work were most obscured.[64]

For all its unabashed elitism, the Nature Conservancy in its earliest initiatives worked in parallel with the evolving perceptions of many other suburban residents. Outside its North Shore elite, even those in places such as Levittown were gradually becoming more receptive to calls for a wilder version of suburban reserves, thanks to taming work in their own neighborhoods, but also to the shrinkage of nearby wilder and more open spaces. By 1961, public advocacy for what were increasingly known as "nature parks" had already widened on Long Island, in a groundswell that was spurring "the most ambitious park-buying spree in [Long Island's] history." Part of the credit goes to federal agencies like the U.S. Fish and Wildlife Bureau. As Adam Rome has pointed out, the bureau had for years studied and warned of Long Island's shrinking wetlands. But a still more critical change came in the election of 1960, when New York State voters overwhelmingly approved a $75 million park bond issue.[65] It was difficult to say what kind of parks were being envisioned by the lopsided majority of Long Islanders who voted for it. But evidence suggests that popular activism for wilder parks increasingly drew not only North Shore residents but also inhabitants of less wealthy neighborhoods. When they came to blows with Robert Moses and his more palpably built style of preservation, it was through class-confounding protests, along with federal help, that they gained the upper hand.

At the forefront of this political ferment was Grace Barstow Murphy, Robert Murphy's wife. In August 1956, Grace inaugurated the Women United for Long Island, soon renamed Conservationists, United, for Long Island. The first meeting of forty women, convened by the conservation committee of her Three Village Garden Club, drew charter members from four other garden clubs, two chapters of the League of Women Voters, and the Nature Conservancy. In part, Grace Murphy was acting to counterbalance the limitations of her husband's own nature politics. "R.C.M. is a marvelous scholar and orator," she wrote, "but he has not got the time for much public work." Women such as herself, on the other hand, were "just the ones to further the Cause of Conservation," "to arouse greater public opinion to conserve the natural resources and beauty of Long Island." Ultimately, her goal was "saving trees" and "shoreline" and promoting "public ownership of more wild areas, reservations and more parks." A language of aesthetics and beauty, more than that of ecology, conveyed her appeal. The "lovely land" was being "shaved"—and for what? Here, Murphy offered an early instance of the central place that Levittown-like mass suburbia would occupy in the new environmental imagination: "little, monotonous houses on tiny plots" and a "depressing monotony of grass, grass, grass."[66]

It is difficult to imagine a more direct expression of the class prejudice animating early suburban conservationism on Long Island. Grace Murphy's initial calls, at least, were oriented far more to mobilizing her own neighbors, already accustomed to trees and shorelines, than those who lived amid such "depressing monotony." Levittowners planning their town's tenth anniversary around this time found far more virtues in that landscape at which Murphy and her peers now scoffed. Coming "out of crowded cities," families had found there "a place in the sun." They had brought "dreams of a garden of their own . . . to fruition," "re-newing the American tradition of the Homestead."[67] The rhetoric of a suburban countryside survived not only in Murphy's screed, but also in how Levittowners lauded their own accomplishments. Nevertheless, for many who lived there, including Julian Kane, their neighborhoods were now like countryside in rhetoric alone; a wilder nature, in particular, had departed. For Kane, the disappearance of Levittown's earlier "countrified" ambience helped spur his awareness of the vulnerability of recognizable nature on other parts of the island. In 1960, about two years after his fight for master planning in Hempstead, came his first public participation in a campaign for preserving natural acreage.

In tacit concession to the lost nature around his own neighborhood, he became involved on behalf of Garvies Point. It lay outside Hempstead township itself, near Glen Cove on Nassau's North Shore. Yet the nature he sought to protect was not that of visibly wild flora or fauna, the Nature Conservancy's initial focus. Instead, what he saw as in need of preserving was the hint this beach offered of a more ubiquitous vein of natural phenomenon. Garvies Point remained "the only publicly-accessible place on Long Island that exposes the 70 million-year-old geological formations that constitute the Island's underlying bedrock." As a high school geology teacher, Kane had taken his students on field trips to this rocky beach. Sometime in early 1960, he learned that its owners were laying plans to build homes along it, and that the town was considering an alternative plan to purchase the property itself. Forming a "Save the Rocks" committee within the Hempstead Town Civic Council, he went to testify at the public hearing in favor of the town's proposal. Before a standing-room-only crowd at the city hall, spokespeople for the Nature Conservancy and Long Island chapters of Garden Clubs of America and the Audubon Society were joined, even led, by an unaccustomed ally—a Levittowner. If the public acquisition for which they called lay on the North Shore, the Save the Rocks campaign also augured a shift away from a nature so easily defined and preserved through land boundaries. For Kane, at least, the value of the "rocks" lay in the visibility they brought to a part of nature undergirding Levittown and the entire "spread city" Long Island had become.[68]

This was one of dozens of similar controversies cropping up on Long Island during the early 1960s. Their changing tactics as well as broadening support made the movement for more nature-minded parks ever less susceptible to charges that it emanated from a self-serving elite. Robert Moses had long relied on this very argument to push through his more patently constructed vision for Jones Beach and other state parks. But it was quickly losing public traction in ways of which Moses himself remained largely unaware. In 1962, the tensions erupted in the so-called Battle of Fire Island.[69]

By this time, especially along its shorefronts, Fire Island had acquired so many second homes and vacation rentals that some twenty-five thousand people were estimated to live there during the summer.[70] After mounting skirmishes over this terrain, the trigger for battle came after March 6 and 7, 1962, when a hurricane slammed into Long Island's South Shore. Robert Moses seized on the opportunity to promote a project already several years in the making. The Army Corps of Engineers had planned a four-lane public parkway spanning the length of Fire Island, whose completion, Moses promised, would "stabilize the shoreline" for homeowners. As he had with other urban "stabilization" projects closer to the city, the 73-year-old master urban planner argued that "a roadway along the Fire Island dune line" would even do the local nature a favor. After all, it "can be made to look more natural than the miles of storm-torn dunes and areas that are now stripped of vegetation." His customary alliance of local and regional officials seemed poised to have its way by mid-1962, when the required public hearings on the plan opened at a Jones Beach pavilion.[71]

There, Moses' tried-and-true ways of asserting the public's interest, as well as surmising its tastes in "nature," fell under assault. Inside the hearing room, testimony before a packed audience of fifteen hundred likened his methods to Adolf Hitler's. Outside, about nine hundred others followed the proceedings on the bathhouse promenade. Few of them were actually homeowners, still fewer genuinely "local." Almost all of them had traveled from residences in other corners of the metropolitan region via buses, ferries, and cars. Among them were Grace Murphy's customary allies, the garden clubbers and fishermen and hunters. Robert Murphy, in other venues, also lent a hand. He waxed about Fire Island as a "summerland that is still frontier . . . [that] remains as if in [an] unworldly trance which began in the time that the Indians vanished." But how this hearing differed most dramatically from that for Garvies Point was in its attendance by young people, the "groupers" who could afford Fire Island summers only by renting together. Defying categorization as well-to-do, they also brought a less staid style of protest. They strummed guitars and carried placards saying "Caution. Creeping Concrete," or "Drive Safely! But Not on Fire Island." Out of such imagery and public interchange, the balance of power was tilting. Long Island's politics of park making was taking a populist and naturalist turn.[72]

Ultimately, the victory of Fire Island's antiroad activists, as with many other preservation efforts during this period, would not come through public hearings alone. Instead, it relied on reaching up past Moses' level of government for federal support. Fire Island road fighters were able to secure the endorsement of Stewart Udall, President John F. Kennedy's secretary of the interior. The political gears were now set in motion for congressional action. In 1964, the U.S. Congress declared Fire Island the nation's fifth national seashore and New York's first national park. Federal officials then moved in to buy up and take charge of this "summerland."[73]

On this front, federal activism helped to empower those who would become environmentalists. On others, federal officials provided the foil, inviting new mobilizations of Long Island's nature advocates against them. The aggressiveness of state-based conservationism itself, ostensibly on behalf of the suburban forest, forced a few Long Island conservationists to begin a final step toward environmentalism. They were compelled, as well, toward new realizations of how deeply nature itself had become embedded, and imperiled, *within* Long Island's new "spread city" landscape.

Over the midfifties, armed with the "miracle" pesticide DDT, the U.S. Department of Agriculture (USDA) joined with New York State to commence "the largest single spray operation ever conducted" in the United States to halt the spread of the gypsy moth. First imported from China to Massachusetts in 1868, the "forest-destroying" moth seemed poised, by the late 1940s, to break out of its New England confines. It threatened that broad swathe of hardwood forest extending across the Appalachians to the Mississippi (which it soon reached) via the woods that threaded through the Greater New York City area. State and federal officials roared into action in this forest's defense. They drew up plans to poison all the moth's potential breeding grounds. In their sights lay some of the greenest corners of Long Island, where its wealthiest suburbanites lived. From April through June 1957, sixty-five planes soared over much of Suffolk County as well as the northerly reaches of Nassau, dumping DDT at a rate of one pound per acre wherever trees clustered. They crossed over nearly the entire patchwork of the island's suburban landscape: its parks, woods, farms, gardens, pastures, lawns, and homes.[74]

The DDT spray campaign sliced like a knife through the conceit, perpetuated by nature parks, that Long Island's nature lay somehow apart from its burgeoning buildings and humanity. It also augured a new phase in Long Island nature politics. Faced with such an assault on behalf of the forest, by retrofitted bombers that made as many as thirteen passes over a single residence, Long Islanders who thought the action wrongheaded turned confrontational. A lawsuit against the spray campaign commenced, the first widely publicized civil suit against pesticide use in the nation. Robert Cushman Murphy joined thirteen other plaintiffs to sue the USDA. Most of these individuals came from the same well-to-do North Shore circles from which the Nature Conservancy itself had mostly sprung. A few had more modest backgrounds: a Bethpage housewife, a Huntington chiropractor and his wife. The most unusual departure from conservationism came in their line of defense. The nature whose preservation they sought was not just distant and rural. It ran through their own properties, their yards and homes, even their own bodies. In this respect, the spray campaign was like other impositions that Long Islanders were coming to know.

Chapter 4

Worrying about the Water

M r. and Mrs. Gerald Colpas had already bought their new house in Lindenhurst, Long Island, in January 1962, when Mrs. Colpas first tasted the tap water. She gagged in disgust. When she tried to fill a cooking pot with it, "clean, crisp-looking suds" roiled up. She was not alone; soon thereafter, journalists discovered dozens of such stories. Thus was born the "saga of detergents," one more way by which Long Island became known in the nation's media over the early 1960s. As the story broke, and a reporter from the *New York Times* paid the Colpas a visit, the message quickly turned "familiar": "Ready-foaming soap substitutes"—phosphate detergents—had seethed their way into Long Islanders' private wells and faucets. To the island's mass-suburbia reputation was added another, more literal taint: the contamination of its drinking water.[1]

What went less recognized at the time (and among more recent histories of the detergent problem by William McGucken and Adam Rome) was how this experience helped confirm a larger pollution pattern, more and more evident to local experts and lay residents alike.[2] What troubled Long Island's water increasingly seemed to be a historic break from those contaminants on which a modern public health had cut its teeth half a century before. Then, the wastes of chief concern had been all too human— sewage, a physiological by-product of people's own bodies. After World War II, however, the island was becoming ground zero for the advent of another style of pollution, all too human-made. This new contamination consisted of industrial or synthetic chemicals concocted in the laboratories and factories of booming petrochemical and other industries.[3] Long Islanders stood on the early front lines of fire not only from phosphate pollution, by lab-hatched additives to detergents, but also from what Rachel Carson's *Silent Spring* would cast as the era's ur-synthetic: DDT.

Still earlier, Long Islanders had been among the nation's first to recognize a synthetics problem utterly missed by the media spotlight until decades later: hazardous industrial waste. Not just the makeup but the medley of those waterborne pollutants troubling postwar Long Island were historically significant. In few other corners of the country, possibly none, did so many of these synthetics turn up so close to one another. Locally, convictions coalesced that people's surroundings had undergone a transformation that was not just frighteningly new and pervasive, but quite possibly dangerous. That human imperviousness to environmental harms long promised by health authorities, always something of a chimera, fell open to public question. Suburb dwellers began to imagine a Pandora's box of new connections between chemical novelties and a host of worrisome health impacts they might be having. Hippocratic modes of linking place to health, common in prebacteriological times, underwent a revival. One further historic role of Long Island in postwar America was thereby consummated: as an ideological seedbed for a new environmental politics.

The new pollutants themselves proliferated because of features of Long Island's "spread city" that went unremarked in Levittown-centered media coverage. Its suburban homes lay at a varying, sometimes uncomfortable distance from one another, also from the nation's latest high-tech industries. As important in understanding why postwar Long Island became an early locus for newer pollution problems was its utter reliance on its own aquifers for water. To a unique extent, at least into the 1940s, its spread city drew ever more liberally on reservoirs running through its own porous soil and rock, a hidden river system threading into and through the earth below. Long predating Levittown, Long Island's three layers of aquifer were an Ice Age legacy of glacial carving. Filled by water percolating down from the surface, each harbored its own slow-motion stream. (See Figure 1.) In its continuing dependence on these aquifers, Long Island differed from New York City and most other midcentury American metropolises. As late as 1950, groundwater dependence was still considered a rural custom: only three of the thirty-nine American cities with populations over a quarter of a million—Houston, Memphis, and San Antonio—depended on wells alone.[4] As Long Islanders increasingly tapped these aquifers in the decades after World War II to supply all their water needs, they led what would become a nationwide trend. By the mid-1970s, 75 percent of larger U.S. cities drew on groundwater for most of their supply.[5]

Most environmental histories of aquifers' role in water management have concentrated on rural locations and usages. Long Island's experience illuminates the additional questions and concerns that arose as, over

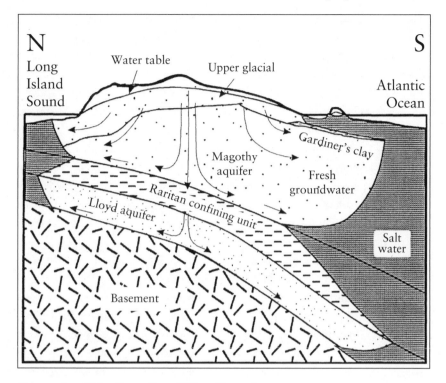

Figure 1. Long Island's aquifers. (Gilbert Hanson)

the midcentury, groundwater dependence became increasingly urbanized.[6] Long Islanders became among the first to confront the many problems involved and to explore workable solutions. Into the postwar period, the island's underground commons had remained free for the taking; small property owners could still tap at will this sea beneath their feet. But especially as prevailing practices of waste disposal turned it into a repository for many unwanted by-products of the new "spread" style of city, takings from this source became severely constricted. The aqueous free range was thus progressively, albeit partially, closed.

In the process, and partly as a consequence, Long Islanders early on took a final step toward hatching environmentalism as a popular movement. They did so by fusing the policy agendas of urban-edge conservation and public health. Yet to understand why, we need to get beyond considering each as separate issues or professional jurisdictions. In the daily lives of suburban Long Islanders, they were not separate. Medical talk about the benefits of nature contact may have largely retreated into the realm of the psychological, but in suburban practice, the pursuit of physical health and nature remained deeply entangled. Swimming in sun-warmed surf never quite lost its connotation of healthfulness. Turning on the tap still conjured up expectations that the water would remain largely as nature made it—even if also germ-free. Scrambling the boundaries between these two realms still further were the peripatetic habits of postwar Long Islanders: how those who enjoyed visits to Jones Beach or Fire Island, for instance, might well carry a thermos filled by a faucet in a tract house. What happened on Long Island was that new ways of speaking about nature and health took root that could better encompass both these sides of residents' personal experiences. From this perspective, and in light of the jurisdiction-confounding dilemmas faced by local health and water experts, we can understand the new ideology of environmentalism as emanating less from the top down than from the bottom up.

Central to its emergence was the language of chemistry and the new weight accorded to whether or not chemicals were human-made. More and more Long Islanders came to suspect industrial or artificial substances as dangerous and to favor those that were organic and natural as healthier.[7] Indirectly, the appeal of this chemically oriented naturalism reflected an insulation from infectious hazards that went less noted, as well as the rising anxiety and uncertainty about chronic diseases—now the most feared and deadly of islanders' afflictions. Casting pollution in strictly chemical terms made it easier to vilify as antiorganic and easier to pair with the ecological land preservation being pushed by urban-edge conservationists like Robert and Grace Murphy. In this fusionist effort, the Murphys themselves helped lead the way. Just as the push for a new, more authentically natural style of park ran up against a powerful officialdom with other ideas, so the newly popular politics of pollution inveighed against the prevailing public health expertise. At the same time, local health officials in particular helped confirm some of the new linkages that were being imagined. After all, phosphates seeping into local wells threatened that same newly appreciated part of Long Island's nature as did razed woods: the aquifers beneath everyone's feet.

Still more so than worries about shrinking forests or spoiled shorelines, anxieties about polluted water underwent another kind of spillage, across lines of social class. Most significantly, they filtered out from the wealthiest of Long Island's neighborhood ecologies to those of middle- and working-class whites. From the 1957 trial of DDT to a second trial in 1966, the neighborhood and class bases for litigants widened, reflecting the mobilizing potential of Long Islanders' mounting concerns about their water.

The broadened sense of crisis, achieved just as the island's environmental movement was coalescing, quietly exacted another price. Official talk of public health authorities tended to erase any references to socioeconomic differences in neighborhoods, even as they had found pollution to be the worst among the less well-off. On a personal level, the new environmentalists might have resisted this inclination, yet often they did not. Their appeals, to a nature or an ecology that was universally threatened, tended to obscure especially those dangers faced by residents who were not so middle class. Most deeply buried of these risks, not just in the ground but in the new antipollution politics of the island's environmentalists, were industrial wastes, that very type of contamination with which Long Islanders' newer worries about their water had begun.

Exploiting an Aqueous Free Range

Two realms of law had long governed the conscious and more inadvertent uses Long Islanders made of their aquifers, one for "taking" and another for "dumping." Into the late nineteenth century, groundwater in New York and other eastern states was still governed by what historian Donald Worster has described as "frontier takings doctrine." "Percolating waters" remained "the absolute property of the owner of the land under which they were found." By this principle, the owner of a plot of land could drill and extract water at will from the aquifer below, even if it depleted a neighbor's supply. A parallel, if less fully articulated, doctrine prevailed for what a property owner might do to cause contamination of the groundwater below. Into the early twentieth century, wastes could still be dumped on one's own property, seep into the aquifer below, and poison a neighbor's well without legal repercussions. This situation predominated even after the use of polluted surface waters became subject to far more stringent legal restrictions. This liberality of rights to take as well as dump made this era's law regarding aquifers under Long Island similar to that governing land in the nineteenth-century American West: an aqueous free range. By the 1940s, though some of these rights began to be circumscribed on Long Island, the freedom to take groundwater remained quite broad, and the freedom to dump into it, still more so.[8] Exercising these freedoms with gusto, the island's postwar suburbanizing laid bare a working yet underarticulated assumption. So reliably capacious were its underground reservoirs, the courts continued to imply, that taking and dumping would hardly ever interfere with one another.

Over the early twentieth century, judges in New York and other eastern states began parting ways with their western counterparts by taking civil suits over "subterranean streams" of groundwater more seriously.[9] From the moment the state stepped in to arbitrate the tapping of groundwater, issues of contamination were never far off. Among the lessons in how they could connect was the destruction of Brooklyn's aquifer in the first decades of the twentieth century. New York City's burgeoning size and demands had escalated the extraction of groundwater from Long Island. At the same time, its replenishment slowed because expanding sewers shunted waste-water into the ocean, and spreading streets and buildings kept rain from filtering back into the ground. By the 1930s, a falling water table had led to the "intrusion" or sucking in of seawater from the surrounding ocean, and Brooklyn's groundwater had become permanently contaminated with salt. Trends farther out on Long Island boded a similar fate. This prompted New York State to establish a licensing system for underground water withdrawal, overseen by the New York Water Power and Control Commission. In the early 1940s the commission's decisions greatly decreased New York City's ability to rely on Long Island groundwater, forcing it to turn west to the Delaware River for its water needs. Yet commission oversight extended only to the largest users. Property owners whose usage ran less than one hundred thousand gallons—most businesses and farms, as well as homeowners—still retained water "takings" rights underneath the land they owned. They could drill and draw without further restriction.[10]

The advent of water shortages on Long Island after World War II offers a case study in how that scarcity could be driven far less by climate or natural geography than by human development. Massive changes in water usage stemmed from the arrival of more people, homes, offices, stores, and factories, as well as from the fact that the new suburban migrants, on average, demanded more water than had earlier waves. The use of outhouses and outdoor pumps long found in poorer and more rural corners of the island, daily requiring as little as ten gallons or less per capita, markedly declined. In few other places around the nation was so little housing available without sanitary "amenities," heavily adding to per capita water consumption. In other ways, too, not only suburban living itself but also its newer demands reinforced the burden new residents imposed on Long Island's water supply.

Lawns, consolidating their reputation as emblems of the middle class, accounted for the single biggest difference between urban and suburban water usage in the postwar period.[11] The introduction of next-generation home appliances added to the demand. Automatic washing machines, such as the "Bendix Automatic DeLuxe" touted in Levitt ads, replaced manual or semiautomatic electric clothes washers. Adding soap themselves and initiating their own rinse and spin cycles, they generally consumed more water than predecessors, if only because owners did 50 percent more washer loads. Adding to the demand, electric dishwashers came with new "impellers" that directed water onto "every surface."[12] Of all the neighborhoods across Long Island's suburban landscape around 1960, fragmented as they were by race and class, the best-off residents made the largest dent in the available water supply. They had more water-dependent appliances such as dishwashers and air conditioners, more deluxe versions with extra jets and cycles, and larger lawns with more automatic sprinklers. Along the North Shore, where Long Island's richest neighborhoods were concentrated, per capita water usage rose as dramatically as any other place in the nation. In Port Washington and Manhasset-Lakeville, per capita usage surged from 50 gallons a day in 1920–25 to 95 to 110 gallons per day by 1951—at least 25 gallons more than the New York City average. By 1960, average per capita usage hit 111 gallons per day in the whole of Nassau County and 122 gallons in Suffolk County.[13]

Compounding the residential contributions to the upsurge in public groundwater withdrawals after the war were rises in industrial, commercial, and agricultural usage. Chemical and aircraft plants imbibed huge volumes of water; between 1948 and 1956, industrial water use tripled in Nassau and rose over 40 percent in Suffolk. Movie theaters and grocery and department stores that sprung up throughout Nassau and Suffolk tapped into aquifers to keep their buildings cool and comfortable. Opening just north of Levittown in 1956, Roosevelt Field, "America's largest mall," sunk wells on mall property to chill its stores. Moreover, by the midfifties Long Island's farms sucked out a significant share of groundwater—as much as 9 percent of the total. Like farms throughout the American Northeast in the postwar period, Suffolk County's irrigated more land, more often, thereby drawing more from underground pumps.[14]

Hence, the looming scarcity of water on postwar Long Island had far less to do with aridity than with suburban development, due to the extra demands it imposed and the effects it had on preexisting hydrology. As public health officials acknowledged by the midfifties, the recharge of Long Island's groundwater was threatened not just by the growth in withdrawals but by what happened to surface waters along many of the newer landscapes. Water sprinkled onto lawns and gardens tended to evaporate rather than trickling down into aquifers. The ground cover for new buildings, roads, and yards did not absorb water as readily as the agricultural land it replaced. Asphalt roads and highways and subdivision drainage systems channeled water away more quickly—another deterrent to absorption. Long Island's gradual acquisition of sewers, starting in 1949 with Nassau County's, also deprived underground reservoirs; rather than trickling back down, liquid wastes were now funneled through a treatment plant and then out to sea. For all these reasons, upper aquifers lost water that, in earlier decades, would have filtered down to replenish them. The water table was dropping, causing streams and rivers to become more and more dependent on runoff rather than springs. By the early sixties, nearly half of East Meadow Creek, which ran through Levittown, came from rainwater.[15]

Ironically, however, the long-standing opposition of many Long Islanders to sewers, and their preference for cesspools and septic tanks instead, sustained a recycling of water wastes that proved consequential. By the midsixties, 44 percent of Nassau County homes, and the vast majority of those in Suffolk, remained unconnected to sewers. Rejecting the technology that, in the view of health officials, made cities more fully sanitary, Long Islanders inadvertently helped to forestall a postwar crisis on the scale of Brooklyn's. Rather, nearly two-thirds of water withdrawals on the island wound up back in the ground. The impact of rising human usage of groundwater would have been more dire had water officials not taken some preventive measures of their own to slow the depletion. Nassau's public works engineers plotted, then dug pits throughout the county to collect and reabsorb rainwater. From around 60 planned as late as 1949, they oversaw some 405 of these recharge basins by 1958. They had a name for this strategy that will be familiar to this book's readers: "water conservation." Local water officials thereby linked their work to water-related laws and policy making at the state and federal levels, much of it centered on agricultural needs and rural locales.[16]

But on Long Island, those same strategies that addressed problems of supply with relative success exacerbated the pollution from dumping. All of the homes and factories, stores and offices that arrived anew on Long Island not only required more water. They, and those who inhabited them, also amassed an abundance of liquid and solid wastes. Sewers or not, all of their detritus had to go somewhere. In public warnings about Long Island's water woes into the 1950s, its public health and political officialdom preferred to deemphasize this rising burden of waste, and instead to sound the alarm about vanishing water resources. Not coincidentally, such a message seemed well fitted to their favored remedy: a greater centralization of the island's patchwork of private and public water companies.[17] More privately, however, health officials were forced to reckon with how problems of supply were becoming increasingly difficult to disentangle from those of contamination that resulted from property owners' continued freedom to dump.

On postwar Long Island, it became ever clearer that the mechanics of aquifers defied the logic of private property on which this freedom to dump was based. Because groundwater itself did not stay put, the boundaries of a lot, especially if small, could not contain the full range or impact of its contamination. Through underground flows, pollutants trickled into neighboring yards and wells, bathrooms and kitchens. Of special concern to surprised homeowners, whose faucet water began to foam or smell, as well as to those publicly charged to alleviate these threats, was the strangeness of the pollutants involved. While some were familiar and well understood, others were not, testing the ability of public health officials to assess their danger, much less to contain it.

New Reckonings with Seepage

Groundwater contamination like Brooklyn's, through the infiltration of the sea's salt, would periodically frustrate the efforts of health officials to protect the water supply, yet it did not prove nearly as troublesome as other intrusions.[18] Among the waterborne contaminants confronting Long Island public health officials were, in addition to the old infectious familiars, those that were much newer. Nationally, health researchers were only now establishing the means for detecting and controlling them. Compounding the conundrums posed by these pollutants were the unanticipated ways that some of them trickled not just into but through the ground below. Horizontally, they could travel hundreds of yards, even miles. As public health experts wrestled with this mobility, first revealed by the widening arc of public complaints, their understanding and practices underwent what we may, in retrospect, recognize as an ecological shift. In the process, dumping's consequences provided much of the impetus for constricting takings rights—that is, access to what had long remained, for many, an aqueous free range. Over and against the reigning narrative of public health triumphs, a counternarrative began to emerge, at least among local officials, about the new and unreckoned modernity of pollution turning up in Long Island's aquifers. These island–based experts—themselves suburbanites—thereby anticipated that very way of seeing other new pollutants that the island's environmentalists would wield against a national public health officialdom.

Dumping problems that turned up early on during Long Island's postwar suburbanizing were very much like those that had plagued America's downtowns in the nineteenth century and that the bacteriologically based public health community rose to address. Contamination of many of Nassau County's shallower wells came from human waste deposited in residential septic tanks and cesspools. Whereas in wealthier areas, the sheer acreage of large-lot subdivisions isolated inground deposits, lessening the risk of contamination from one property to the next, neighborhoods with smaller lots were far more vulnerable. Especially when each lot was only a quarter of an acre or less, neighbors' cesspools or septic tanks lay much closer to one another and thus were more likely to cause problems. Troubles were almost inevitable if the water table surged nearly to the surface, as it did in corners of Ronek Park. There, wastes could bubble up into a yard after a rainstorm and easily slough over into next-door lots. Even when the water table lay farther down, a subdivision full of leaching cesspools could so concentrate wastes below ground as to threaten not just individual but community wells. Such complaints made up much of the testimony of Ronek Parkers and others at a 1952 hearing by a congressional housing subcommittee in nearby Bay Shore. Almost everyone who spoke out about the contamination came from less-provisioned South Shore subdivisions, with their more vulnerable neighborhood ecologies. No one came to testify from the spacious, hilly enclaves on the wealthier North Shore.[19]

As such incidents occurred on postwar Long Island, the local public health officials felt well equipped to recognize and fix them. While an angry citizenry might alert them to where human sewage turned up anew, the laboratory tests for coliform bacteria, as well as standards for interpreting what levels were dangerous, had long since been established. To get ahead of the problem, they just needed to extend their monitoring. So too with the remedies. They only needed to add to the water what was, essentially, a bacteriocide—chlorine.

When tests of water in several Levittown wells, for example, showed elevated coliform levels, they gave orders to chlorinate. In one more instance of the failure of this builder to anticipate community needs, it turned out that Levittown's water company, and several others, had not yet installed chlorinators in their wells. To circumvent further shortcuts by developers, the Nassau County Board of Health in 1954 mandated that all water districts in the county had to provide chlorination facilities. Requirements for cesspools and septic tanks in new developments also became more stringent.

Yet by 1957, the inspection and approval of waste disposal systems had become so routinized that it seemed more a matter of familiar, preventive technologies than of actual disease. For this reason, Nassau's health officials turned these jobs over to the building department. Overflowing cesspools or sewage-contaminated wells certainly remained a serious concern for those whose homes were troubled by them and, in health professional circles, could still conjure up talk about typhoid. Local health officials nevertheless considered these problems old and easily solvable. Even as they and state and federal health officers continued to grapple with pollution from human sewage, suburban officials considered this problem to belong to an era of infectious disease that, especially in a place like Long Island, was passing away.[20]

The same was not true of other kinds of pollutants, newly recognized from the 1940s onward, which health officials would come to consider "modern." New sorts of substances began circulating through the wartime factories on Long Island with a solubility that easily lent itself to aqueous flushing. The aircraft industry, the island's largest manufacturer from the 1940s onward, led in the adoption of new metallochemical processes with environmental consequences. A procedure known as anodizing aimed to strengthen airplane bodies so they could withstand the stresses of air travel. To protect the aluminum surface from corrosion, it relied on chromic acid, a substance whose dangers to workers had recently become well known. Less recognized was that anodizing plants and others flushed these wastes into cesspools or lagoons, sewers, and drains, introducing novel substances into the ground.

Nassau County health officials' first contact with industrial wastes in groundwater came in 1942 near the Republic Aircraft plant in South Farmingdale. A sanitary survey by a health official revealed 0.1 parts per million (ppm) chromium contamination of a private well near a plant waste pit. By 1945, all three of Nassau's largest aircraft plants presented the same problem. Hobbled, as yet, by a dearth of analytic methods and standards for chromium-laden water, Nassau County health officials allowed the companies to treat the difficulty as one of internal plant management.[21] After the war, however, the contamination was not so easy to contain.

Part of their dilemma was that, especially compared to bacterial contamination, the consequences of these waterborne exposures had hardly been studied and were poorly understood. Only just after the war did the U.S. Public Health Service (PHS) set the first drinking water standards for hexavalent chromium, at 0.05 ppm.[22] The studies of actual human disease on which this standard was based were mainly the research on chromium exposure to workers conducted by industrial hygienists.

Essentially, the researchers dismissed any effects other than those from full-blown, clinically apparent disease. They did find that chromium caused "deep, penetrating ulcers," perhaps even cancer. But they assessed these findings via a framework of disease causality akin to those established for infectious diseases, which killed quickly. Acknowledging the body's permeability to toxins like chromium, they nevertheless maintained that people tolerated exposure, inside their bodies as well as outside, up to a measurable "threshold." At or beyond this point, the body's defenses became much more likely to break down and recognizable illnesses to develop. Already other scientists, pathologists and animal experimenters, were developing scientific challenges to this threshold assumption by detailing the longer, cumulative processes by which such ailments evolved. But far into the postwar era, threshold-based thinking governed PHS standard setting, as well as Long Island health officials' science and policy.[23]

After the war, as Long Island's chromium seepage recurred on an enlarging scale, the new federal recommendations for levels in drinking water did not help with many other puzzles posed by this new avenue of pollution.[24] Most disturbing of the several postwar episodes, in the late 1940s a groundwater plume penetrated into wells maintained by the New York City Water Department. Located near the Republic Aircraft plant, these wells' water revealed chromium levels twice those the PHS considered "safe." County health officials went on to uncover a scale of underground penetration rivaling that found three decades later at Love Canal, when industrial wastes finally attracted the attention of the national media. The "slug" of contamination had concentrations of chromium as high as 40 ppm—eighty times the official safety limit. It stretched to nearly a mile away from the plant, underneath the brushy terrain to the south. Within its circumference, some twenty-five families drew their drinking water from wells dug into their own property.

Health officials' solutions presaged their strategy for shutting down much of Long Island's aqueous free range over the postwar period. Abandoning the underlying aquifer as unusable, they pushed residents with contaminated wells to seek a more distant, cleaner water supply. Most exposed households did hook their faucets up to public water, but not everyone was convinced. Other Long Islanders would come to share this skepticism about the advice of the health experts, but for different reasons. At this early moment, doubt led some to ignore the official warnings of danger. One family refused to stop drinking the contaminated water. They "apparently fe[lt] that the additional expense for such a connection is not warranted as they have not experienced any deleterious effects to date." Three years of monitoring nevertheless showed their drinking water to contain from 5 to 25 ppm of hexavalent chromium. While the health department had no authority to force the family's compliance, it already had the power to take other actions. It closed all the public wells nearby, directed company officials to cart chromium-bearing wastes to a "sludge dump," and successfully spurred Republic and other aircraft companies to begin treating their chromium wastes. As for the slug itself, health officials did nothing, hoping that the contaminated aquifer would "continually improve" through dilution as well as "normal ground water travel."[25]

When cadmium and phenol contamination also turned up across the island by 1954, confidence in the aquifers' restorative power was shaken, and local officials who followed the plumes privately admitted a growing worry. To Nassau County's chief health engineer, "The contamination of our drinking water supply by the wastes of industry" now seemed "a most serious threat," "within five years" becoming perhaps "the number 1 public health problem." Assumptions about thresholds of bodily tolerance did not trouble him. The health-related uncertainties he saw lay beyond the bodies of the exposed; they were not so much physiological as hydrological. Factory discharges, for example, could "on occasion . . . [be] 6000 times higher in concentration than the allowable safe density." And given what was then known about the dangers of phenols, "one pound of [them] could contaminate [the entire 100 million gallons that Nassau residents drew from their aquifers daily] beyond the Public Health Service's standards." Prior to 1957, Long Island joined Southern California and Michigan, where similar industries had concentrated, as the nation's only sites where this variety and scale of industrial groundwater pollution was reported. Its uncertainties and challenges began to incline some Long Island health officials toward a worrisome narrative about pollutants, in which the new industrial contaminants figured at least as prominently as issues of supply. Enjoying a preestablished authority, however, and dreading the alarm of a lay public, Nassau's head sanitary engineer preferred to keep such ruminations between himself and his colleagues. However frightening, these problems were handled quietly, without appearing in local newspapers, through private negotiations with industrialists. "Once apprized of the facts," officials believed, "industry realizes its responsibility to the community in maintaining a healthful environment."[26] On postwar Long Island, worries about groundwater contamination only slipped out of expert circles into newspaper articles once industrialists were no longer the only culprits.

Percolating into Long Island's aquifers by the mid- to late 1950s were not just the by-products of factories, but of new commercial and home-owner usages. The companies introducing "synthetic" detergents like Dreft and Tide for automatic washers and for dish washing pitched them as having distinct advantages over their less "artificial" or "scientific" rivals. Instead of being made from animal or vegetable fats, like earlier generations of soaps, they were derived from petroleum. As with anodizing and other new industrial processes, the new detergents and many other substances seen as typifying modern "synthetics" had been born in corporate laboratories through quests for greater persistence and stability in a product. Like DDT and other pesticides steadied by the addition of a chlorine atom, among the greatest selling points of phosphate detergents was how long they kept their marketed properties, no matter where they turned up. They sudsed and cleansed not just for a few hours but for weeks, regardless of the acidity or hardness of the wash water.[27] From the mid-1950s, their unexpected endurance in Long Island's groundwater made this place the nation's canary for a new kind of pollution threat.

Remarkably, the novelty of detergent pollution necessitated that health officials initially relied on lay reportage and used methods differing little from what homeowners might do—a far cry from coliform or chromium tests. Complaints to the health department began with a Mastic family in the fall of 1954. It reported that its faucet water was "soapy" and "foaming" and had a "disagreeable odor." About two months later, homeowners in Farmingville, who like the Mastic family got their water from home wells, noted almost identical problems. The usual battery of tests for sewage pollutants, back in the health department's lab, came up negative. Laboratory officials could only confirm that the water from each of the wells had a "disagreeable" smell and "foamed when shaken."[28]

Within a few years, however, these same officials more successfully imported testing for this same hazard into their own professional turf, in the department laboratory. A quantitative test was discovered for ingredients in the detergents that were easily measurable, alkyl benzene sulfonates

(ABS). Their subsequent studies of ABS fell back on a familiar explanatory model: the large-scale industrial polluter, in this case, the local launderette or laundromat. Early on, county health officials wielded the legal tools already at their disposal to try and quell the emissions. They initiated formal public hearings, prosecuted launderette owners for a sanitary "nuisance," and stepped up requirements for launderette licenses. Yet the scope of contamination continued to mount. Press coverage heightened public awareness, and homeowner reports of foaming tap water mushroomed from tens to hundreds. Overwhelmed, Suffolk County health officials appealed to the New York Water Pollution Control Board for help. This board, created under the auspices of 1948 federal legislation and at work since the early 1950s on more traditional, organic pollutants, commenced its own broader study.[29]

Its investigators concluded that the launderettes were only the tip of an immense iceberg. Spot sampling, including in the homes of complainants far from any launderette, showed that groundwater contamination from detergents was far more widespread than county investigators had assumed. By 1960, as over 40 percent of Suffolk County residents remained dependent on home wells, half of the two thousand tested, mostly at the homeowners' request, showed measurable traces of ABS. First sought in neighborhoods near factories, then around the launderettes, the new cryptically named pollutants turned out to be far less localized and more pervasive. Postwar home building on Long Island had yielded a new mass effect, as residents of "tens of thousands of homes" poured household wastes into the same porous ground from which their drinking water came. In other corners of the nation where postwar home builders had leaned similarly on the local groundwater, an identical problem soon surfaced. Out from Minneapolis, 46.5 percent of about 63,000 wells tested were found to be contaminated with ABS.[30]

Despite later characterizations of this pollution as "suburban" and "middle class," phosphate detergents, like industrial wastes, rarely found their way into the faucets of Long Island's better-off residents. More precisely, both problems cropped up especially toward the rural side of the urban-rural fringe, in neighborhoods straddling the middle and lower classes of homeowners. Though most all victims owned houses with yards, home values around industrial plants stayed low. And those who owned the small houses and lots closest to launderettes were among the least able to afford their own washing machines. The wider contamination then charted by the pollution board affected neighborhoods that were socioeconomi-

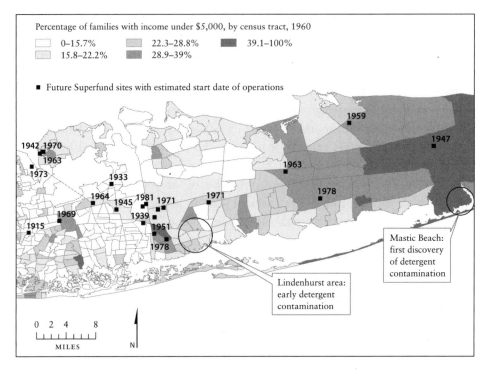

Percentage of families with income under $5,000, by census tract, 1960

☐	0–15.7%	▨	22.3–28.8%	■	39.1–100%
☐	15.8–22.2%	▨	28.9–39%		

■ Future Superfund sites with estimated start date of operations

1959

1947

1942 1970

1963

1973

1933

1963

1964   1945 1981 1971   1971

1978

1969

1939

1915

1951

1978

Mastic Beach:
first discovery
of detergent
contamination

Lindenhurst area:
early detergent
contamination

0 2 4   8

MILES   N

*Groundwater threats on Long Island by income level. Most of these Superfund sites
contain wastes dumped between 1945 and 1980. Dirty industries and waste dumps,
as well as the sites most prone to detergent pollution, lay in tracts with housing values
below the Nassau-Suffolk County average. (Based on information from National
Historical Geographic Information System and U.S. Housing Census)*

cally similar. This pollution turned out to be concentrated in the "heavily
populated southwestern portion" of Suffolk County—throughout unincorporated areas such as black North Amityville and Copiague as well as
the Colpas's white Lindenhurst. The detergents had emanated from scores
of single-family cesspools near home wells, themselves "on small plots of
4000 to 7500 square feet" (one-tenth to one-sixth of an acre). That is to
say, all of this new groundwater contamination mainly afflicted the least
wealthy and least well-provisioned Long Island homeowners.[31] Nevertheless, public health officials were ill-equipped and likely reluctant to draw
socioeconomic conclusions from their findings. They framed the detergent
issue as strictly a technical one, with considerations of class stripped away.

Their solutions amounted to a further circumscription of the freedoms
enjoyed by users of Long Island's aqueous range. Those same lower-end
homeowners who were the victims of this pollution themselves bore most

of the brunt of the ensuing changes. Early on, the health department could only advise those with a contaminated well to hook into public water supplies; officials could neither compel the switch—nor aid or otherwise fund it. Families like the Colpas in Lindenhurst were thus left to fend for themselves in finding other ways of getting water. They turned to collecting it from friends' faucets and storing it in fish tanks and camping gear. While saving the money to connect to a public water system, they wrestled with the many uncertainties about bodily risks head-on, making decisions for which health officials' blanket reassurances offered little help. The Colpas, for instance, made calculated choices to use the groundwater for cooking and coffee. At least the peculiar odor and flavor were thereby masked; and their noncontaminated supplies lasted longer.[32] If residents did choose to move, they had to absorb the decline in neighborhood housing values that contaminated water brought. People in such neighborhoods literally paid the greatest price for the new regulatory regime that health officials had begun putting in place to protect Long Island's aquifers.

Aside from urging families to connect to public water supplies, health officials sought additional fixes for groundwater contamination—all of them in the realm of takings. They set new legal restrictions on well digging, both for new building projects and for existing shafts. Standards and required certification were ratcheted upward for *all* private wells tapping into the Long Island ground, small and large.[33] Health officials encouraged water companies and well drillers to circumvent the mounting contamination of upper, glacial aquifers by digging deeper. By the early 1960s, nearly 80 percent of Nassau's groundwater came from the middle, Magothy layer, as opposed to 50 percent only three decades before. Some shafts descended to the third level, the Lloyd sands, as many as seven hundred feet below ground level.[34]

As for the upper aquifer, it was now by-passed or forbidden as a source of water. Long Island's chief water supply from the nineteenth century far onto the twentieth, it came to be increasingly abandoned, due to its polluted state, as unfit for human consumption. These very restrictions, in tandem with continuing political frustration that health officials faced over expansion of the island's sewers, helped to keep alive the freedom to dump. It was a freedom that those many homeowners still reliant on cesspools and septic tanks continued to enjoy. Proportionally speaking, it was a freedom that private enterprises of the largest scale—whether a building firm installing cesspools or a factory discharging into on-site waste ponds—most effectively exploited.

To better track and anticipate future contamination of the island's underground reservoirs, health departments greatly expanded their monitoring of well water. By the mid-1960s, Nassau County was checking 350 test wells annually for 26 chemical and physical "parameters." Identifying the newest problems as industrial and man-made, health officials had begun taking more of Long Island's underground nature into account in order to keep tabs on their magnitude and scope. They came to lean more and more on terms and tools from the nonmedical, *natural* sciences. Borrowings from the disciplines of hydrology and geology provided a more robust understanding of the dynamics of movement and equilibrium in aquifers.[35] Gravitating in these ecological directions, local health and water officials by the early 1960s had discovered heretofore unrecognized avenues by which richer and poorer neighborhood ecologies on Long Island remained connected. In other words, they had uncovered not just new pollutants, but a new natural arena through which this pollution flowed: a groundwater commons. Writing more of the island's nature into their work of oversight and regulation, public health officials in Suffolk and Nassau Counties nevertheless shunned references to "nature" or "ecology." They preferred, instead, the professional language of health and medicine or of engineering, which was largely immune to such terminology.[36]

If local health experts began providing ammunition for what would become a new environmental activism, they and a national health officialdom nevertheless served, arguably, as suburban environmentalists' most formative foil. To gain some insight into why, we need only look at how easily Nassau County health officials were able to slough off that troubling narrative about industrial wastes voiced by their own sanitary engineer. Far more significant, they insisted, was their own trajectory of accomplishment, a historic triumph over the age-old threat of germs. Nowhere was this narrative easier to substantiate than in a place like Nassau County, whose actual rates of death and disease were among the nation's lowest. A host of ongoing interventions were nevertheless necessary to sustain this achievement. In the somewhat tortured metaphor of one health official, they had to avoid "weaken[ing] and relax[ing] our grip" over the "striated cat"—i.e., tiger—of infection.

Postwar health authorities did herald a new era, still emergent, in which the chief problems were those of "the chronically [rather than the acutely] ill," those who suffered from cancer or heart disease.[37] Yet the corresponding new divisions in Nassau's and other health departments adhered almost entirely to the "prevention" of chronic disease that took place inside clinics, the detection of those already stricken with tumors or heart ailments. Local health experts, in particular, studiously refrained from connecting these diseases to exposures within the Long Island environment itself. Into the 1950s, nearly all public health interventions beyond a clinic or hospital, in the residents' food, water, and land, owed their advent to the long-standing battle against infectious ailments—precisely those to which Long Islanders no longer typically succumbed.

Outside of public health circles, other Long Islanders moved more quickly to connect these dots. They asked further questions about those new chemical and synthetic pollutants against which health officials now struggled. Might these also be having an impact on the ailments that now prevailed and that many contemporaries now found more frightening? Still more disturbing was how these pollutants resembled those very tools like chlorine with which a health officialdom battled germs. The pesticides eagerly and voluminously dispensed by mosquito control officials seemed especially suspect. After all, many witnessed the consequences of these so-called remedies firsthand—in their own yards and on their own bodies.

Mosquito Control and a New Naturalism

By the late 1950s, Long Island public health officials' widening oversight of the island's aquifers added to their other powers over other island waters, long since won. For decades, but with heightened intensity after World War II, they had watched for sewage in surface waters and for certain germ-bearing insects that bred there. This last charge had been one of the earliest for Suffolk's and Nassau's first public health appointees. What had begun as an assault on habitats and breeding grounds of *Anopheles* mosquitoes, carriers of malaria germs (a *Plasmodium*), broadened in the postwar years, becoming more ambitious even after malaria itself had long since vanished. The opposition thereby stirred counted at least one professional ecologist among its ranks—Robert Cushman Murphy. He was joined by others who, while without his professional training, drew confident surmises about the effects of the spray in their own yards. Lending further potency to this opposition were its challenges to prevailing health science, long a defender of DDT's human innocuousness. On both of these fronts, a 1957 trial against the gypsy moth spray campaign broached a host of troubling uncertainties about the pesticide's effects. The idea that this or any other single substance could, invisibly but implacably, upset the well-being of human and nonhuman creatures alike proved contagious. It formed the ideological core of what became environmentalism. Long Island's second well-publicized trial against DDT, in 1966, showed that this ideology as well as activism on nature's behalf had extended beyond the North Shore suburban elite to the less privileged South Shore.

Though the malaria-bearing *Anopheles* made up "probably only a fraction of one percent" of the island's mosquitoes, epidemics, like the 543 cases recorded in Nassau County during 1916, had spurred powerful public health initiatives. The chief targets had been those standing waters where mosquito larvae were found to breed.[38] Into the middle of the twentieth century, from New York's city limits to Long Island towns, health officials filled in many low-lying areas where water tended to accumulate. Where in-fill was impossible, on ponds and other standing bodies of water, or in cisterns or tanks, they poured a film of oil to choke off mosquito larvae's access to air. Where no one was thought to drink, the arsenical Paris Green was doused. Through large expanses of marshland stretching out onto Long Island, they dug drainage ditches to make brackish standing pools accessible to tidal flushing. Through the 1920s and 1930s, the Nassau County Mosquito Extermination Commission knocked on doors and barged into homes to seek out the typical haunt of *Anopheles* larvae, including "cesspools, rain-barrels, tin cans and other containers of water." By 1936, the ditch-digging and petroleum-pouring got started in Suffolk; five years later, Suffolk County's exterminators had nearly caught up to their Nassau counterparts.[39]

After World War II, though malaria had been vanquished on Long Island, mosquito controllers kept up the drumbeat of warnings. Thanks to "the new homes in the county with their inevitable backyard mosquito breeding places," a year's relaxation could "easily roll back our gains of all thirty-four years." Clearing existing ditches of debris, mosquito commissioners went on to shovel new ones, completing a system that stretched almost four thousand miles at its midcentury peak. They also successfully argued for a powerful chemical addition to their arsenal: the pesticide DDT. Similar to the advantages of the new synthetic detergents, DDT's toxicity was less weather-susceptible and longer-lasting than Paris Green, its predecessor. It also had a reassuring pedigree. During World War II it had proved itself as a public health "wonder drug," saving American troops from flea-transmitted typhus fever in Italy and from malaria in the Pacific theater. Also easing its adoption, mosquito control itself had by this time been delegated to its own specialized corner of county government. Outside the health department, it became still more insulated from concerns about the danger its actions might pose to human health, not to mention wildlife. Though the new pesticide was taken up slowly at first by Suffolk's Mosquito Control Commission head, Christian T. "Chris" Williamson, he eventually embraced DDT as "the most effective and economical larvicide." Single-mindedly dedicated to killing off an insect that now was only rarely an active bearer of disease germs, he and his staff gave far less thought to the effects of their environmental cure on nontargeted organisms—not least among them, the homeowners whose properties they sprayed.[40]

Clear and justifiable as this imperative for mosquito control seemed to public officials and experts, postwar Nassau and Suffolk residents had a far different relationship with malaria and other deadly infections than after the century's turn. No longer did this disease borne by mosquitoes, as well as others borne by water (typhoid) and by animals (rabies) seem such clear and present dangers. In Nassau County, by the early 1950s, tuberculosis was also in decline and the infant mortality rate was the lowest in New York State. Even the infectious poliomyelitis, though still smoldering, by mid-decade seemed headed to containment on Long Island with the Salk vaccine. Officials did find renewed urgency for mosquito control in a resurgence of equine encephalitis, or "sleeping sickness." But unlike with early twentieth-century malaria, not a single human case of equine encephalitis was confirmed on the island, and only a few virus-carrying mosquitoes were found. By 1959, Nassau and Suffolk residents were declared "virtually free of the more serious infectious diseases."[41] The growing willingness of Long Islanders to contest mosquito control practices can be understood, in part, as grounded in the diminished threat of mosquito-borne infection. Public health officials paid a price for their success. Since these historic menaces had been effectively neutralized, Long Islanders now took their protection from them for granted. The door was thereby flung open to ecological criticism of mosquito control, as well as to suspicion that the pesticides used, DDT in particular, might pose their own pathological perils.

Near the end of World War II, Robert Murphy, for several years president of the Audubon Society's board of directors, voiced to Suffolk's mosquito chief Chris Williamson a long-standing conservationist criticism of mosquito control. It had become an "engineering proposition," Murphy averred, with little regard for "the general ecological situation." It continued in "many districts" despite actual improvement in "the mosquito situation." A few years later, what the mosquito controllers did to Murphy's own pond at Briarlea magnified his outrage. "Their truck . . . barges in willy-nilly and squirts petroleum on the surface," turning it into "a hideous sticking wallow of oil." Their single-minded routine targeting of mosquito larvae also destroyed what sprayers themselves were less attuned to recognizing—but not so the professional ecologist Murphy. They had killed off the "entire fauna" of the pond, he complained. It was an accusation that did not involve any chemical tests or other special invocation of science. Murphy was an ornithologist and part of a generation of ecologists whose studies had been conducted with little or no reference to any laboratory. His strictly observational surmise was nearly indistinguishable from what any thoughtful suburban pond owner might conclude when dead fish surfaced in the days following the spray. For Williamson, the claim was sufficiently persuasive, or threatening, to make a deal with Murphy. Murphy would stock his pond with mosquito larvae–eating Gambusia fish, and it would then be spared the annual intrusions "with the petroleum hose." When Williamson switched from petroleum to DDT, Murphy's pond continued to enjoy protection—at least from the Mosquito Commission's spraying.[42]

Nevertheless, some years later DDT poured down on his property, courtesy of the 1957 gypsy moth spray campaign. Murphy was outraged. He fumed over the impact on fauna not just in his pond but all across his six acres. Other residents, soon to join him as plaintiffs in a Long Island courtroom, voiced more concern about the effect on their own and their families' person. Well before the publication of Rachel Carson's *Silent Spring*, the porousness and vulnerability of their bodies to artificial contaminants had already occurred to some inhabitants. Their thinking had begun veering from that of the island's public health officialdom, which still believed that Long Islanders were well-shielded from, and otherwise tolerant of, local environmental harms.

Mary Richards, the friend and housemate of the trial's coorganizer, Marjorie Spock, had suffered from a "digestive invalid[ism]" that drove her to bed for days at a time. Like Spock an adherent of anthroposophy, Richards went to an anthroposophy-friendly doctor for help. He diagnosed what would later be called "multiple chemical sensitivity," an extreme reaction to pesticides and other chemicals in foods bought from local grocery stores. At the doctor's recommendation, the women had planted a biodynamic garden, so extensive by the midfifties that it supplied over half the food they ate. Chiropractor Frank Reuschle and his wife Leonie thought along similar lines. Though they did not have enough room or sun for a garden of their own, they too had turned to organic food, ordered through Reuschle's sister, to avoid the chemically laden produce of grocery stores. Mary Jacobs had started growing pesticide-free fruits and vegetables for herself and her family. She thereby sought to "work with nature" in her garden on a quarter-acre lot in a Bethpage subdivision. She did so largely for health reasons after having learned about food contaminants while studying nutrition at City College of New York.[43]

By the mid-1950s, all of these individuals were not just worried about a single contaminant, or even a category of pollutants, whether pesticides or sewage or detergents. Instead, they inclined toward viewing all modern chemical artifice as suspect. Their logic resembled, even built on, that contrast between older versus more modern pollutants being crafted in public health circles, yet it also went further. Either a substance was artificial or druglike and presumed harmful. Or it was more organic or natural or drug-free and thus to be preferred. They honed a new way of distinguishing what was nature-friendly from what was not—neither by land usage, nor by a landscape's look, nor by the appearance of wildness, but by chemical nomenclature. The molecules thereby denigrated, mostly products of postwar chemical innovations, swirled invisibly to reveal a realm of nature that ranged past how older conservationists were accustomed to defining it. Unseen, waves of these molecules were washing into the bodies of Long Islanders and their loved ones. Sweeping as such visions were, their collective culmination in a thirteen-plaintiff lawsuit was very much a local occurrence. Similar anxieties over chemical artifice surfaced on the national stage, especially in congressional hearings over the regulation of food additives and the passage in 1957 of the Delaney clause outlawing carcinogenic chemicals in foods. But in these initiatives, too, a Long Islander had a curious prominence: James Delaney, the congressman responsible for both, hailed from the island-bound borough of Queens.[44]

The closer one looks at the origins of the plaintiffs' concerns about chemical artifice, as manifested in the 1957 lawsuit, the more difficult it becomes to conclude that they were driven by the science of ecology. Murphy himself seems the closest link to this formal discipline. Yet his own ecological studies had had little truck with chemistry, and only after he retired did his concern about DDT prompt him to launch a lawsuit. Biologists at Brookhaven, Long Island's national nuclear laboratory, then contributing to a new, chemically informed ecosystem ecology, had minimal interest in publicity into the late fifties, much less in this kind of civic activism.

More plausibly, these inclinations, what we might term a "chemical naturalism," were lay and experiential in origin, and themselves a cultural foundation out of which this and other formal scientific innovations would spring.[45] Their coalescing version of the human body was indeed "ecological." But it was so in a sense that Murphy as well as many younger professional ecologists of the period would have been reluctant to verify or even acknowledge. National publications such as J. I. Rodale's *Organic Gardening and Farming* and *Biodynamics*, put out by followers of Rudolf Steiner's anthroposophy, provided substantial support for the nascent worries of lay Long Islanders. So too did the publications of fringe medical groups like chiropractors and allergists, then laying the foundations for what would become "clinical ecology." After DDT had rained down on Long Islanders' gardens and heads during those spring days of 1957, Murphy's publicized call for help in suing the federal government over the spray campaign caught the eye of many of the island's nature- and organic-minded afficionados.[46] Foremost in their thoughts were the effects of DDT on themselves, their children, and favored local wildlife, not on the gypsy moths or mosquitoes that were the official justification for the spray.

On important fronts, contemporary public health authorities stood squarely in their way. In the absence of more definitive evidence of harm, the innocuousness of this and other substances from radioactive fallout to phosphate detergents were defended by a formidable scientific and official edifice. Institutionally, as well as in the published evidence they could muster, these defenders held the high ground. At first, they found it easy to fend off those who remained skeptical—the scientists as well as nonscientists worried about DDT's safety and its longer-term, less easily provable effects. But this adversity fueled the challengers' innovations. Just as political scientists have argued that the German Green Party's success in the 1970s and 1980s stemmed in part from a state that aggressively ignored it, so in late 1950s Long Island the social and ideological sinews of *Silent Spring* coalesced in confrontation with state-sanctioned expertise.[47] Public opposition to DDT honed and politicized a distinction that Rachel Carson would elaborate in a sweeping and powerful narrative, in which the ecological connections and vulnerabilities of people's bodies seemed more and more troubling. Whereas the synthetic or artificial products of modern chemical factories aroused deepening suspicion, the organic and natural furnished a reservoir of affirmative choices and values. Consolidating a lay language of nature that encompassed issues of health as well as land, anxious and angry Long Islanders united to speak for nature, to power.

To understand how pointed their battles against the public health establishment became, it helps to recall the close alliance of DDT's early opponents and the antifluoridation movement. By the early 1950s, fluoridation of public water to prevent tooth decay had gained the endorsement every major national group of health professionals. Yet when water officials agreed to turn the decision over to a local referendum, 70 percent of the votes went against fluoridation. Political scientist Morris Davis offered a discerning explanation of these results that also applied to the opponents of DDT. The antifluoridationists active on 1950s Long Island shared what Davis termed "a *drive toward naturalism* or a *naturalist syndrome.*"[48] That was the same drive that impelled the thirteen property owners who launched the first public court case against DDT in 1957; indeed, many of them opposed fluoridation as well. Economically and socially, too, the anti-DDT plaintiffs shared much with the "pure water" activists who defeated fluoridation in Manhasset. Both were, for the most part, well-to-do. Those joining the antifluoridation campaign were mostly housewives, as well as a few older men. More men than women joined the lawsuit, yet it was Marjorie Spock who did the bulk of the organization and fund-raising for the trial.

Most significantly, the two groups shared an opposition to public health officialdom, represented, first and foremost, by the U.S. Public Health Service. Fluoridation was literally a PHS offspring. The service also provided a bulwark defense of DDT, undertaking feeding studies with human prisoners that exonerated it. The health officer who designed this experiment, Dr. Wayland Hayes, asserted at the 1957 trial that these prisoners remained healthy after the tests. What he meant was that they showed no sign of pesticide-related disease that was clinically confirmable. His assumption of a threshold had steered him to neglect any more subtle or cumulative effects. PHS press releases affirmed by the PHS meanwhile called attention to the "protection of millions of people from malaria through DDT control of mosquitos." And all this spraying had yielded "no authenticated case of DDT poisoning," despite dosages "many times greater" than Long Islanders had received.[49]

At the heart of their skepticism toward these assurances, DDT's opponents drew their own surmises about links between exposure and disease. They thereby practiced a more or less speculative version of what, within the later environmental justice movement, became known as "popular epidemiology."[50] Not that the plaintiffs had no expert witnesses of their own. In addition to testimony from Robert Murphy, they introduced medical testimony: clinicians who confidently tied the pesticide to many "distressing, and sometimes fatal, manifestations" such as cancer. Laboratory analysts testified for them as well, on the DDT levels measured on crops and in soil. But lay plaintiffs who had witnessed the spraying also testified about their own experiences and the conclusions they had drawn about DDT's effects. They noted coughs that plagued them for a week afterward and, in the case of Mary Richards, a years-long worsening of her stomach ailment.[51]

Complementing this popular epidemiology was a popular ecology, extending inside as well as outside the skin. Layperson and expert alike fingered the flow of "poisons" from the environment as "cumulative," silently pooling in its victims' bodies. At the DDT trial, Murphy, speaking as a card-carrying ecologist, argued for a sweeping, general recognition of DDT's detrimental effects on a host of species beyond the targeted moth larvae. But he was less certain when it came to personal observations in his own yard, as when he stated that his Gambusia minnows had died from the spraying "so far as I know." Plaintiffs without his credentials testified with less hedging about what the spray had done on their own property. Mary Jacobs, for instance, observed a ubiquitous white residue on her garden after the spraying, along with several dead creatures that she then buried—a "jack rabbit," a squirrel, and two birds. She attributed all of their deaths to the spray.[52]

In asserting possible or actual harm from the DDT spray, many people were inclined to emphasize traditional, homey methods for eliminating pests that they were certain did not carry the same risks. From Murphy to Spock, anti-DDT plaintiffs bore witness to the effectiveness of long-standing remedies. These ranged from the natural enemies that Murphy argued had kept Long Island's gypsy moths at bay, to the pesticide-free gardening Spock recollected her father undertaking. Their talk of more natural or nature-friendly methods did tend to obscure the human history of the practices and places they defended. Gardening methods of earlier generations, for instance, likely owed much to recommendations from earlier generations of experts. Moreover, that the spray campaign so outraged these mostly well-to-do plaintiffs meant that they were little occupied with the seepage of cesspools or industrial waste pits that burdened less well-off Long Islanders. But faced with public health and other experts who brushed aside their observations as merely lay opinions, local and idiosyncratic, their naturalism offered a powerful, enabling tool. It helped them assert just how violently invasive *these* experts' interventions seemed.

Among opponents of DDT and fluoridation, it is hard to miss the gender dimension to this new naturalism that was coalescing on Long Island by the late fifties. In part, the protests represented an early stirring of a women's movement, anticipating the advent of postwar feminism. And yet the importance of male professionals to this naturalist opposition, from traveling antifluoridationists and chiropractors in Manhasset to the biologists and clinicians testifying at the first anti-DDT trial, points to how more than gender was at stake. The new, unanticipated consequences of sprawl on Long Island had opened the door to a new lay confidence in speaking for nature. They did so precisely by making plain the overconfidence, overreach, and oversights of the reigning officialdom for public health as well as parks. In corners, at least, of this spread city's mixed ecology, a new kind of civic activism was arising. Ostensibly, it was less about class or economic interests, less purely about human health, than it was about a nature that people, plants, and animals all shared.

The new chemical artifice of the postwar period, but especially the newly dichotomous terms by which people came to judge it, enabled the final steps toward the popular movement we have come to know as environmentalism. Imagining pollution less exclusively in terms of pathology, and more as a challenge to what was natural, helped empower lay activists to take up the fight against contamination. It also facilitated linkages between this and other issues long relegated to separate legal, professional, and cultural realms. In concept, pushes for parkland and against pollution seemed more on the same page. In practice, too, suburban activists moved to overcome this yawning historic divide between conservation and public health.

They were aided as well by newspaper coverage of Long Island's water woes as deeply entangled with the natural features of the island on which they lived. "Troubled Waters," a 1957 series in the islandwide paper, *Newsday*, stressed problems cropping up across it in the wake of its rapid growth, including dropping water tables and saltwater intrusion. Subsequent reports charted the rising recognition of detergent pollution, as it turned up in thousands of wells and then in the surrounding ocean.[53] By the first years of the 1960s, mounting apprehensions about contaminants, further spurred by Suffolk County's planning commission, elevated talk about threatened groundwater from the backdrop of Long Island politics to center stage. Its protection, declared Suffolk's newly elected executive Lee Dennison in 1961, was "the most desperately urgent problem in the history of the county's development."[54] The preservation of Long Island's underground drinking water supply, he and other island leaders had come to realize, hinged not just on stopping its contamination, but on keeping more land "open" and undeveloped. Unbuilt fields and woodlands were now understood to have a health-related function. They filtered as well as replenished underground reservoirs. Considering that commons whose vulnerability had become so apparent, leading politicians and planners had come to see issues of water pollution and parks as naturally linked.

These realizations stemmed not only from expert studies but also from the many local civic groups that over the late fifties made water issues their own, especially in better-off communities. Among them were garden clubs, fish and game associations, and chapters of the League of Women Voters and Conservationists, United, for Long Island, Grace Murphy's group. Murphy's own activities offer a window into how their advocacy worked. From her group's start in 1956, she sidestepped any confrontations with public health officialdom to focus on Suffolk's supply of water. This "primary resource" was not as "endless" as "we are told," she warned. It depended, among other things, on the "protection of all possible stands of spring fed fresh water and areas of deep vegetation where rain . . . may be absorbed." Into the 1960s, she still spoke of herself as a conservationist. Yet the sheer range of issues her nature talk bound together, and the emergent priority of water pollution among them all, wrought fundamental changes in what "conservation" meant for her. Also against the grain of a conservation dominated and administered mostly by male officials and experts, from afar, Grace Murphy's suburban "conservation" evolved in an expressly different direction. It entailed the protection of a nature that was nearby and intimately knowable, that included even the water flowing around and into one's residence. It was a conservation that could be pursued by garden clubs and church groups and stay-at-home housewives—as she put it in her 1961 pamphlet, "Conservation for Everyone." In these watershed years, as Rachel Carson was penning *Silent Spring*, Grace Murphy explored another, parallel way of welding concerns about the human body to those about places nearby. "Conservation is purely and simply hygiene," she announced. "We have long since accepted that word for our bodies, though few of us know very much about the biology concerned . . . it is a short step further to apply hygiene to our environment."[55]

Picking up on the talk that, decades earlier, had spurred popular initiatives and practices in fighting germs, Grace Murphy found in "hygiene" a promising model for nearby nature's care. One irony of this choice was that, on so many fronts, contemporary public health experts had sought to stymie that very anti-DDT activism pursued by her husband through their own conflicting claims about "the biology concerned." But Grace's words also pointed to a keen realization. Threats of polluted aquifers and open spaces were not separate issues that were merely linked. A bodily reconfiguration of conservation's agenda brought its core concerns closer to home,

made saving nature potentially relevant and applicable to far more suburban dwellers. Everyone needed drinking water—in the wealthiest as well
as the poorest Long Island homes. If it became contaminated, then not just
the aquifers but everyone's bodies, indeed, their very lives, might be imperiled. The conservation agenda pursued by Murphy and other North Shore
activists had initially reflected notions of nature most readily cultivated in
the neighborhood ecologies of the privileged. Now, by calling attention to
pollution in particular, she saw that she might widen the appreciation of
nature's relevance and the basis for nature-minded politics. Less privileged
suburban places and people might also be inspired to work for its defense.

Here, Grace Murphy was right, though she missed how independent
from "conservation" many new antipollution activists would consider
themselves. Prior to spurring activism, the suburban concern about contaminants spread with pollution itself, but also, through like personal experiences, a similar witnessing of connections. In many places on Long
Island, people and waterborne creatures lived side by side. There, pollutants' effects on fish or wildlife could easily be read, just as they had been
by anti-DDT plaintiffs, as clear and present dangers to the neighboring humanity. So it went among those who launched the second trial against DDT
usage on Long Island in 1966. Compared to the tiny, mostly well-to-do
group that initiated the 1957 trial, the 1966 group reflected a broadening
constituency, although the sense of biological parallelism between humans
and other local creatures was much the same.

The second lawsuit began with a young couple who, in contrast to the
Murphys, had working-class roots. Victor and Carol Yannacone resided in
Patchogue, on Long Island's South Shore. Though Victor's salary as a lawyer gave them middle-class status, he was the son of an Italian American
labor union leader, and Carol, the daughter of a mechanic. She had grown
up in an area around Yaphank Lake, whose other residents, by and large,
relied on similar blue-collar jobs. One day in 1964, she and her husband
happened upon a massive carpet of dead fish stretching across the lake.
Later they discovered that the cause of the fish kill was DDT, dumped from
a nearby facility of the Suffolk Mosquito Extermination Commission. Immediately, Carol began to worry about the children she knew to be living
around the lake. They swam in it, just as she had, and might have fallen
ill from the exposure. The Yannacones sued the commission's head, the
selfsame Chris Williamson with whom Robert Murphy had tangled.

Victor was well aware of the difficulties encountered by earlier anti-
DDT plaintiffs, as well as Rachel Carson, in proving the pesticide's ad-

verse health effects. He planned, instead, to make his case through a cross-examination of any opposing medical witness, much like he had done in workers' compensation cases. But after a group of Long Island activists known as the Brookhaven Town Natural Resources Committee (BTNRC) approached the Yannacones about joining forces, they were able to do considerably more.

The BTNRC further illustrates how a pollution-centered nature activism was overflowing the class and racioethnic fragmentation that defined Long Island's suburbanized landscape. Formed in 1965 to attack pollution from Long Island's duck farms, the committee began in the South Shore's Bellport, whose northern edges, at least, were poorer and racially diverse. The group's first members were the students of a continuing education class in high school biology taught by Art Cooley. After he assigned them to study and document this pollution, they came back to him and asked what they could do about it. Cooley then called what became the BTNRC's first meeting to discuss bringing the problem before the town board.[56] As the group gathered members and steam, a few older North Shore conservationists pitched in. Significantly, unlike the Battle of Fire Island, the BTNRC also drew in people who still made commercial use of Long Island waters, the managers of the Blue Point Oyster Company and of Fire Island Clams. What steered the group from the organic, relatively traditional pollutants of the duck farms to the synthetic threat of DDT, and a confrontation with the Mosquito Commission, was a coalition crossing lines of class identification. Ecologists George Woodwell of Brookhaven National Laboratory and Charles Wurster of the State University of New York at Stony Brook, both white-collar professionals, joined forces with the Yannacones, who despite Victor's profession were more identified with the working-class residents of Yaphank Lake.[57]

The actual case they argued against the Mosquito Commission's DDT usage, unlike the one in 1957, conceded much ground to health officialdom. Truncating mention of the bodily concerns that had motivated the Yannacones, they refused to build their case around any human suffering or pathology. Lawyer and witnesses alike dropped only the faintest hints of feared diseases such as cancer, much less the shadowy syndrome to be known as multiple chemical sensitivity. Rather than pursuing an argument centering on damage to health or private property, they framed the case as one of resource law. Legally, they thereby gained standing as representatives of the entire "class" of the county's citizens. They followed class-action precedents pioneered by rural conservationists in the 1950s and recently pursued with success in New York's suburbs via a 1965 case against a power plant for Westchester County's Storm King Mountain.[58]

Almost all of their expert testimony was about nonhuman ecology. Charles Wurster's published investigations of the effects of DDT on birds countered long-standing assertions that dead fowl were mere idiosyncratic perturbations. George Woodwell testified about lingering deposits of DDT he had measured in estuary mud. Dennis Puleston, too, who worked in the office of technical information at Brookhaven National Laboratory and was an amateur ornithologist, talked only about declining osprey populations. Together they made a case that the Mosquito Commission should stop using DDT, not because it threatened people's bodies, but because it damaged natural resources belonging to the county's citizens.

Mosquito commissioner Williamson, on the other hand, insisted that DDT's usage "be compared with certain detergents used for cleaning." Though the detergents had gotten into the groundwater and were "endangering large private and even public water supplies, . . . that is no reason why the county should be restrained from using Tide." But he could offer no counter to plaintiff witnesses' scientific documentation of ecological damages.[59] So this time, unlike eight years earlier, the pesticide's Long Island opponents won their case.

More pragmatic than principled in their commitments, this Long Island group constructed a successful argument about the impact of DDT on local nature that worked in defense of not only well-off suburbanites, but also those who were less well off. Their intermingling of science and law added up to a vision of environmental damage that was less rooted in exclusive neighborhoods or properties, one through which activists could stand in defense of county neighborhoods that were not their own. At the same time, their strategy's emphasis on nonhuman ecology, like that on aquifers by health scientists studying detergents, inclined them away from the social unevenness of human exposure and other damage. To be sure, sympathy for DDT exposure in a working-class neighborhood did spark the Yannacones' early activism, as well as steer some of the new group's later work. But its agenda did not mention many other environmental dangers that more exclusively threatened the island's less well-off residents—from older and traditional infectious hazards to those from industrial wastes.

The aftermaths of these two trials amplified Long Island's forerunning and formative contributions to the making of American environmentalism. The first became a major stimulus for Rachel Carson, just then starting on the manuscript that would become *Silent Spring*. The second would give rise to the Environmental Defense Fund. Among the first activist groups to elevate "the environment" into its own name, the Fund became one of two national groups that would emerge from the peaking movement of the 1960s and early 1970s (the other, the Natural Resources Defense Council, also arose in the suburbs of New York City). These trials owed much to the scale, timing, and composition of suburbanization on Long Island and the worries about health and nature that followed. As new knowledge, uncertainties, and anxieties stirred across this hybrid landscape, a movement on behalf of its environment was forming to channel them.

Out on the West Coast, similar changes were afoot, but across a landscape whose contrasts with Long Island could hardly have been sharper. So different was the climate and terrain of the Los Angeles basin, a sixty-mile-wide plain suspended between mile-high mountains and the warm waters of the Pacific, that until far into the twentieth-century residents and visitors alike had difficulty imagining that a city bearing the slightest resemblance to New York could arise there. By 1960, however, it had. The way New York City had extended onto Long Island bore a striking resemblance to the way the city of Los Angeles had carpeted the basin's floor and surged up its valleys and hillsides. Its arrival also provoked an environmental politics that ran in parallel.

Part II
Los Angeles

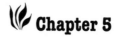

Chapter 5

Missing Nature in Los Angeles

W ho knew there was nature in Los Angeles? William Hollingsworth
Whyte, visiting the city in the late 1950s, saw hardly any. Peer-
ing out a window as he flew over the San Gabriel Valley from Los
Angeles to San Bernardino, the author of the acclaimed *The Organization Man* (1956) glimpsed only a "last remaining tract of green," on the
verge of vanishing. A "legion of bulldozers" gobbled at its eastern edge;
from San Bernardino, another "legion" was "gnawing westward." The
epic hunger of Los Angeles developers jolted Whyte's conscience, and in
the January 1958 issue of *Fortune* he first sounded a national alarm against
"urban sprawl." "Most Americans" still believed that "there will be plenty
of green space on the other side of the fence." Wrong, said Los Angeles to
Whyte and Whyte to his readers. The "progress" of Angeleno bulldozers
offered visible confirmation of how, across the nation, countryside was
being swallowed up, at the torrid pace of some three thousand acres a day.
Whyte would devote the next decade of his life to decrying and battling
this sprawl. For his, as for other jeremiads that fed a crescendoing chorus
of environmental concern over the sixties, the fate of nature in Los Angeles
supplied "an unnerving lesson in man's infinite capacity to mess up his
environment."[1]

By the middle of the twentieth century, Americans had long since become accustomed to thinking about New York as an urban place. That Los
Angeles had suffered a similar fate came as a shock, especially to easterners
like Whyte. Only a few decades before, depictions of Los Angeles filtering
back East had stressed its sunny and genial nature. John Muir, that re-
doubtable nature seeker, had rhapsodized over the very valley Whyte saw
sheared. It was, Muir found, "one of the brightest spots in all our bright
land . . . wild south sunshine in a basin rimmed about with mountains and
hills." For early-century authors lauding a suburban countryside, it epito-

mized their ideal, "where the breath of the country is sweet in the heart of the most confused metropolis." Into the mid-twentieth century, locals tended to see more of the rural in and around Los Angeles suburbs than did their New York–area counterparts. For Angelenos, the imprint of nature's hand was harder to miss. Nowhere were these inclinations more in evidence than at the opening of Los Angeles's—and the West's—first freeway, in 1940. There, California's highway commissioner modestly cast himself and his engineers as only completing what "thousands of years ago Mother Nature started." Why else would she have "carv[ed] out a beautiful canyon [the Arroyo Seco] from the mountains to the sea"? From Native American times it had served as a "natural trail for Man." Surely the Arroyo Seco Freeway, soon renamed for its Pasadena destination, fulfilled this canyon's destiny.[2]

Mother Nature as freeway builder—it is hard to imagine a starker contrast to how Whyte saw the developers' thrust that followed, as driving Mother Nature out. How could the same river-sculpted land, stretching from downtown Los Angeles up the San Gabriel Valley, inspire such different tales of the city's spread less than two decades apart? Any answer to this question must first consider the actual changes to this land during the intervening years. Those built features that throughout the midcentury said "city" covered far fewer square miles when the highway commissioner stepped up to the podium than by the time Whyte looked down from the skies. But material transformation alone cannot explain how differently Whyte and the commissioner *saw* Los Angeles's edges.

Mixtures of urban and rural that they were, urban edges amplified a capacity for ambiguity more or less shared by all human-occupied landscapes. They could serve as Rorschach blots for the beholder's ideas and favored narratives, especially those about nature.[3] William Whyte's eye was guided by another postwar narrative that he had helped craft about the spread of a natureless suburbia. Now, a pivot of focus pioneered that narrative's flip side: suburbanizing not as city building but as nature erasing. Never mind that builders or their customers might become obsessed with planting; never mind, too, that those "tracts of green" that he saw being decimated were not primeval forests but orchards. The counternarrative he and other environmentalists took to crafting posited an utter break between a spreading city and the places into which it cut, presumably far more natural. For our California freeway builder on the other hand, nature and suburbs did not seem nearly as antithetical. Like Henry Cuyler Bunner and Harlan Douglass before, this highway commissioner could still see nature's hand at work within the suburbs of the city, if not quite via a romantic "countryside." His narrative, shared by others of this period who oversaw massive human interventions in rural places, cast road building as *nature completing*.[4] In response, interpreting it as nature erasing offered a sweeping and powerful rebuke, one that has magnified this narrative's appeal among environmentalists, from Whyte up to the present day.

So why not just follow Whyte? Why seek to be more evenhanded about nature's role in suburbanizing? For one thing, recent efforts to frame cities, suburbs, and rural places as more ecologically comparable have shown this narrative, too, to have its blind spots. For another, a more evenhanded approach can better clarify the longer-term historical relationship that these narratives bore to one another. Each built on the blind spots of its predecessors, but at the expense of certain insights. Deluded as this highway builder's viewpoint may seem, it did illuminate how acts of suburban construction from roads or housing had to contend with the primary or "first nature" of the building site. This narrative of suburbanizing as nature-completing then readily gave way to city-building tales highlighting its built and social dimensions. But what both these as well as their nature-erasing antithesis tended to overlook was how suburban city building did not merely wipe away an underlying nature. It also sought to reveal or to expose it, make it *more* visible. Quests after nature even drove Los Angeles's postwar spread: most obviously, among upper-end home builders, but also in what many a middling home buyer hunted and found. An ecological narrative of suburbanizing can thereby provide greater insight into what it was like not to just soar above all this metropolitanizing, but to live in its midst. It aids our empathy for suburb dwellers, helping explain, among other things, why so many would turn into environmentalists.[5]

Ecological evenhandedness also deepens our basis for historical comparisons between metropolitanizing regions. Material contrasts of climate and topography become relevant even in and around those suburban expansions of the built that are this study's focus. More in the realm of perceptions, we gain richer terms for ascertaining differences in how, in a given period, urbanizing areas on opposing sides of the continent were *seen*. Close to New York, as around other large, long-established eastern cities, the switch from more rural to more urban interpretive strategies, from seeing land as more countrylike and nature-bearing to seeing it as citylike and built, came relatively easily. In long-rural areas like the Los Angeles basin, into the midcentury viewed as the heart of a Southern California countryside, such conversions of perspective remained hampered.

The highway engineer could cast such a nature-noting eye on the Arroyo Seco because he still understood the surrounding land and region to be essentially rural. He and others took this character for granted, even as they ushered in radical change to the terrain. Angeleno eyes and minds took a while to adjust to the major city their surroundings were becoming—even as city-building narratives became all the easier to envisage.

In the speed and scale of its rise as a metropolis, Los Angeles had few rivals in U.S. history. Over the early twentieth century, it grew from one hundred thousand to over a million residents in less than three decades, surpassing even the meteoric growth of late nineteenth-century Chicago. Between 1930 and 1960 its city limits gained 1.2 million people, more than any other American city including the much larger New York City. That suddenly, Los Angeles emerged as the nation's second largest metropolis. It provided midcentury Americans with the most dramatic example of how their cities, along with those in the rest of the industrialized world, were "exploding." A few clues as to why may be gleaned by looking at the company Los Angeles kept among American cities, those that, while smaller, grew with similar abandon. The parallel gains of Houston and Dallas, San Diego and San Antonio, reflected a larger demographic tide: over the early post–World War II decades, America's northeastern and north central regions were losing out to southwestern states, notably Texas and California. In population and share of the nation's economic pie, the Sunbelt was on the rise, with Los Angeles and to a lesser extent, Houston, as its new urban centers.

After the war, Los Angeles's metropolitan explosion concentrated especially along its edges, as in the case of New York City. Despite this broad similarity, Los Angeles's suburbanizing, like that of most other Sunbelt cities, built on only the tiniest of those dense cores that had centered the growth of New York, as well as other nineteenth-century industrial cities, including San Francisco. Not that Los Angeles had no downtown; but even as early as the 1920s, its settlements were so dispersed that some urban historians, looking back, have termed them a "suburban city." Over the postwar years, it did acquire more of a traditional, high-rise urban core.[6] Yet its burgeoning suburban development was harder to envision as a tentaclelike egress from the city itself. Less like Long Island's growth than that of other, entire Sunbelt cities of the period, the dispersed and concentrated faces of Los Angeles arrived all at once. That its suburbs themselves constituted this metropolis became harder for outsiders like Whyte, at least, to miss.[7]

Not surprisingly, then, even before serving as William Whyte's inaugural exemplar of sprawl, the Los Angeles suburbs, along with others across California, had been second only to those of New York in exemplifying the new mass suburbia. Whyte himself had helped lead the way through coverage of Los Angeles's answer to Levittown: Lakewood. It was difficult not to be impressed by the human-made dimensions of the change, as this massive subdivision joined others to constitute about 1,370 square miles of built-upon basin land by the late 1950s. In this, as in most other city-building and nature-erasing narratives, Los Angeles's significance derived from the unique scale and intensity of these processes, but also from how they *resembled* those elsewhere. Here nevertheless, as in New York City's eruption onto Long Island, the spread of urban edges had its more natural sides. Beneath and between all the building, the suburban nature arising out along Los Angeles's edges contrasted markedly with Long Island's, in ways that Whyte, and many others at the time, remained less aware.

Los Angeles's suburbs spread out, after all, in a very different climate and across the terrain of a basin rather than an island. Here, suburban builders and home buyers had to reckon, like highway engineers, with steeper topography; like farmers, with more extreme dryness; and even like park rangers, with a natural flora entirely different from that back East. And just out from many subdivisions, some of the more traditional uses of rural lands, as well as the huge federal land reserves, had few or no Long Island counterparts. As with Long Island, the neighborhood ecologies of the better-off provided a study in contrast with those of the less privileged. At the same time, the more natural currency of suburban land markets, what distinguished the ecology of richer neighborhoods from that of poorer ones around Los Angeles, was not the same as around New York City. As Los Angeles suburban dwellers over this period moved to import, to cultivate, and eventually to protect, their urban-edge biota, they, more so than their Long Island counterparts, built on a long tradition of recognizing and celebrating its regional distinctiveness.

From Nature Completing to City Building

Until World War II, any tale of Los Angeles city building invited skepticism, especially among observers from the East. The city itself, as they saw it, was only a "metropolis in the making." "Not quite gelled," without skyscrapers or identifiable circles of high culture, it was a veritable "hick town."[8] City leaders sought to turn this reputation to their advantage. They insisted on a unique alliance with "nature" in their metropolis, akin to that envisioned by our freeway engineer, as grounds for inviting factories in. Notions of a suburban countryside, as well, received more of an official impetus than around New York and lingered longer. They did so partly because more rural land uses hung on and partly because of Angelenos' regional identifications: with Southern California as a whole and with a national frontier—"the West." After the war, a new scale of building made the status of Los Angeles as a major city much easier to notice and appreciate. Suburban factories, stores, and housing developments also brought further changes. Residents became, like their New York suburban counterparts, less dependent on a visible yield from local lands; their lives coursed ever more separately from their own countryside. Nevertheless, especially at the lower end of suburban housing markets, anxieties about the rural endured more obdurately and pervasively than on Long Island. An understanding of these differences in suburban history requires a brief excursion into the natural history of the Los Angeles basin where they unfolded.

Those hills and mountains to the east, north, and west—the San Gabriel and Santa Monica ranges—had given birth to the basin itself. By the time the first humans arrived, an expanse of flat land, coated with alluvial wash and periodically shaken by earthquakes, stretched for twenty miles out to the shoreline, bordered on its other sides by mountains much higher than any within hundreds of miles of New York City. Long Island's highest point was four hundred feet above sea level. Visible from Los Angeles beaches were precipices topping the Adirondacks and Katahdin, and not much farther inland, 10,000-foot peaks, higher than anything east of the Mississippi.[9]

What this loftily rimmed basin shared with other sites that would become southwestern cities, and with no northeastern counterparts, was its exposure to the sun. The weather was consistently warm and dry. Whereas New York enjoyed forty-four inches of rain every year, Angelenos were lucky if they got sixteen. The Los Angeles climate stood out by combining infrequent, if sometimes prodigious, rainfall, with year-round temperateness. Latitude, cool ocean currents, and a unique topography made for a climate that it shared with only a few other parts of the world: South Africa, central Chile, and the lands surrounding the Mediterranean Sea.

Varying elevations within the Los Angeles basin also made for an unusual diversity of microclimates. The amount of annual rainfall could reach as high as seventeen inches close to the coastline and in the foothills, but down to twelve inches in the lower and southeasterly reaches. While

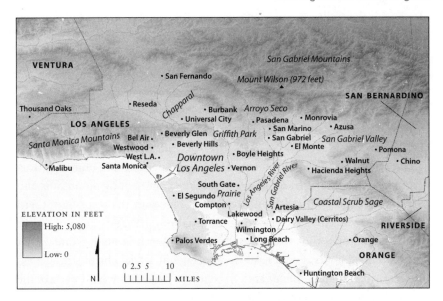

Los Angeles terrain and places (Based on information from U.S. Geological Survey, and Paula M. Schiffman, "The Los Angeles Prairie," in William Deverell and Greg Hise, eds., Land of Sunshine: An Environmental History of Metropolitan Los Angeles *[Pittsburgh: University of Pittsburgh Press, 2005], 38–51)*

most of the basin remained frost-free, belts of winter freeze traversed the foothills and ran up to mountains that stayed snowy into June and July. Long before subdividers carved up the terrain into contrasting suburban microenvironments, climatic diversity contributed to about seventeen varieties of soil, as reported by the first U.S. soil survey. The eroding soil along steep canyons stayed thin, while along the plains and riverbeds it could turn thick with alluvium and nutrients and be easy to cultivate, at least when watered.[10]

Prior to the arrival of humans, the area's plant life adapted to these variations of height, climate, and soil. Unlike in much of the East, forests made up only a small proportion of Los Angeles's floral cover. The basin flats sprouted a California version of prairie. Resembling Long Island's Hempstead Plains in general appearance, their low-growing grasses and other nonwoody plants and wildflowers nevertheless consisted of quite different species. Along the basin's elevated edges, the prairie shaded into chaparral, a diverse scrubby growth with no such eastern counterpart, dominated by species such as the needle-leaved chamise (*Adenostema fasciculatum*) and the manzanita (*Arctostaphylos*), with striking red and orange branches, along with the California lilac (*Ceanothus*), purple and fragrant in bloom. Along the coastal foothills that became known as the Santa Monica Mountains, the chaparral changed to a scruffier, thinner vegetation—the sage coastal scrub. Valleys like that around the San Gabriel River grew plant cover more familiar to eastern eyes: gallery forests, or along neighboring hills, savannas interspersed with mature oaks, sumacs, and other smaller evergreens. Farther up, yellow pines and incense cedar dotted the mountain canyons and crags.

Not only were the environments of the Los Angeles basin unusually varied, they were isolated from other parts of the continent by mountains and desert, to a degree Long Island was not. Along with the rest of Southern California, the basin gave rise to an unusual number and range of native plants and animals that were found nowhere else. It is small wonder that the less-tended lands stirred eastern reportage of a "delightful strangeness on every side." Late in the twentieth century, biologists would declare the region a continental "hot spot" of biodiversity.[11]

From successive settlements by the Tongva, Spanish, and Mexicans, through early twentieth-century city building, the promise of food cultivation remained Los Angeles's most universal drawing card. Settlers had long expected to grow most of their own food; what appealed to those who left farms in Iowa and Illinois was the promise of growing so much more besides, for market sale. Thanks to the steadiness of its sunshine, those who had honed their farming skills on midwestern fields could coax soil into produce year-round. Angeleno fields at the outset of World War II grew all manner of fruits and vegetables, also cows, hogs, chickens, ducks, and goats. By 1940, farm production on Long Island paled alongside that of Los Angeles County, *the* foremost agricultural supplier to the rest of the nation. The winter, when snow buried farms in other parts of the country, was an especially profitable time.[12]

The search for a water supply that might match the dreams not just of Los Angeles's agriculturalists but also its city builders has become perhaps the most prominent and studied theme in Los Angeles's environmental history. Early on, it led to the establishment of a federal reserve inside the county that would have significant impact on regional environmentalism: a national forest reaching into Los Angeles County, mainly to protect the basin's watershed. Unlike on Long Island, the basin's aquifers proved insufficient early on, especially as farmers and orchardists were joined by urban and suburban dwellers. Angelenos had to turn farther and farther away for their water supply—first to the Owens River Valley, then to the Colorado River.[13]

Less noted is how the irrigation needs of Angelenos' crops, as well as the sporadic distribution of oil deposits, had dispersed basin settlements nearly from the start, to wherever water or oil were most easily had. Over the early twentieth century these settlements grew into towns and the largest of them, into cities.[14] Streetcar building, threading lines through the basin during the late nineteenth and early twentieth centuries, connected settlements rendered distant by the scattered natural resources on which each relied. Road building further liberated Angelenos from living so close to where they worked or otherwise needed to go. Double-lane boulevards followed streetcar routes, while penetrating farther than the streetcars into the hills. The region's relatively high wealth per capita may have started with the basin's unusually lucrative orchards and oil, but residents also innovated new ways of selling goods to one another. Starting in the 1920s, they experimented with the self-service grocery stores and suburban shopping plazas soon to spread across the nation. Additionally, the Los Angeles area drew a remarkable array of manufacturers. It became the West Coast center for making tires, automobiles, furniture, clothing, chemicals, iron, steel, and machinery. Yet its plants were so scattered, compared to manufacturing centers in the East, that even far into the post–World War II period, locals had difficulty thinking of Los Angeles as an industrial place.[15]

Remarkably, before the war prominent Angelenos had insisted on viewing manufacturers, like farmers and oil producers, as drawing on the region's natural endowments. Los Angeles, as they put it, in a manner its freeway builders would soon echo, was "Nature's Workshop." Paralleling the suburban-country pitch for urban-edge residences, this one, to entice industrialists westward, framed even factories as profiting from a nature that was nearby. This pitch had few or no counterparts among eastern cities; no such ploy was used to sell real estate in Long Island's industrial or business centers. Los Angeles land could more easily be sold as "Nature's Workshop" because of well-known ideas about the climate of Southern California.[16] Its lack of winters and its balmy but comfortable summers obviated heavy buildings or investments in heating or cooling. According to this publicity, even the workers proved more effective, efficient, and happy—and less likely to join unions! The slice of nature referred to here was, of course, quite selective, ignoring the infrastructure of road and water systems as well as the union busting that also made the basin industry-friendly. Such sales talk built on the basin's reputation etched by John Muir, and many another pen, of a "wild south sunshine" beating down over hilly rims.[17]

With all the new wealth and jobs drawing so many more people to the Los Angeles area by wartime, real estate and home building blossomed as important industries in their own right. What enhanced the dispersive pull of home owning around the Los Angeles of this period, more so than around New York, was Angelenos' more universal embrace of backyard agriculture. Official endorsements of the "suburban homestead" flourished into the 1920s and 1930s, as when the Los Angeles Chamber of Commerce joined forces with the *Los Angeles Times* to sponsor contests highlighting "the small farm home." By 1929, the *Times* reported "thousands of little farms" around Los Angeles "on every side."[18] The Depression and New Deal gave the "small farm home" around Los Angeles a further shot in the arm. "Subsistence homestead" projects were funded by the federal government, joining some twenty-five thousand private homestead farms of a full acre and undoubtedly many more who grew for themselves on smaller plots. Backyard crops, chickens, and even goats were ubiquitous. Even developers of higher-end subdivisions accommodated the homesteading vision, as when the developer of Bel Air decided to build a "Lakewood Village" emphasizing its "semi-sustaining garden[s]."[19]

Over this same period, the city's Anglo leaders, like the state highway commissioner in 1940, found it hard to see their place in the more exclusively urban terms of William Whyte, that is, as apart from, and threatening to, the surrounding countryside. Interestingly, they talked about nature more readily and eagerly than they would later on. But for them, it served more as an aid to productivity than a place for picnics and tramping. Even as some averred a need for public parks, for those in power John Muir's mountains and hills provided plenty of "natural facilities for recreation," an informal commons that was easy to take for granted.[20] What was striking, compared to their eastern counterparts, was how they were able to frame even the most built portions of their city in such rural and frontierish terms: as homesteading, or working *with* nature—with a capital N. "Mother Nature" as the highway commissioner had put it, seemed a friend and collaborator, at least in what an Angeleno elite regarded as the region's central tasks—their own.

In postwar Los Angeles, both for the elite and others less fortunate, this sense of connection between suburban homes and factories and a surrounding nature became harder to sustain. One reason was that, between

1940 and 1970, new factories, roads, airports, and subdivisions more than doubled its urbanized area, which became almost as big as the state of Delaware. In the process, a regional military-industrial complex, taken root in wartime and in the midst of a vast Cold War–era expansion, drew in a tremendous wave of new arrivals. White and blue collar alike migrated in, engineers and draftsmen and chemists as well as industrial workers.

Yet the overall growth of the Los Angeles metropolis needs to be distinguished carefully from the expansion of its suburbs. Because of the former, a Los Angeles skyline appeared downtown, proof positive for many that a genuine city had finally arrived. But it was along the suburban outskirts of this metropolis, where buildings splayed outward into former farmland, that older perceptions and experiences of nature's nearness encountered their most serious challenges. A closer look at just what types of new buildings arose in Los Angeles's suburbs over this period suggests additional reasons why here, as on Long Island, nearby nature was becoming more difficult to see. Whether suburban nature was found or missed hinged on the perspectives of the beholders, but also on just how and how much new construction had altered the neighborhood ecologies they knew.

Among the new suburban industrial plants to open up in these years was Wham-O Manufacturing, soon to become famous as maker of the hula hoop and the frisbee. In 1955, when it was still a small, fledgling sporting goods firm, Wham-O's young executives bought land in San Gabriel, a suburb next to Pasadena. This property, the site of their first factory, did not exactly leapfrog into rural land. Rather, it filled in a suburban "light" manufacturing zone, designated by town officials a decade earlier, in what was already one of the most built-up parts of town. Just north of the railroad tracks and east of the old mission, this industrial zone lay next to the town's Mexican barrio. As yet, it consisted of mostly weed-strewn vacant lots. Not considerations of climate but of emptied, cheap, and available land, as well as labor, drew Wham-O's decision makers there. As the factory owners were likely aware, in this barrio "not only incomes [were] lower but seasonal and chronic unemployment is more common . . . than among other residents of San Gabriel." Situating its new factory in this poorer corner of greater Los Angeles, Wham-O brought jobs within walking distance of a ready-made workforce.[21]

If a visible nature was usually far from the minds of such manufacturers, it was even more so, and likely had long been, among the workers in manufacturing plants. That industrial workplaces could belong to "nature" had been a self-effacing conceit of those with the power to determine factory locations. Those whom they hired, like the employees of this San Gabriel factory, saw far less of nature there. Instead, as with the new arrivals at factories studied by Chad Montrie, new manufacturing jobs helped extend their abilities to see and appreciate nature out beyond the realm of work.[22] It might well be true that this factory's walls could be less thick, and its heating systems more minimal, than for comparable workplaces back East, as "Nature's Workshop" proponents had emphasized. But Wham-O workers were hardly in a position to appreciate such differences, much less to thank nature for them. Many of them had earlier worked in area orchards or farms; so Wham-O jobs were their first experience of working indoors (beyond whatever tasks they took on at home). They were no longer exposed to sunshine or the elements, or to crops and the soil. On the contrary, they were assembling, decorating, and packaging toys under a factory roof. For these workers, like so many others who joined the ranks of factory workers during and after the war, the assembly line, far from being "Nature's Workshop," became a place where nature was most difficult to see.[23]

A further blow to the ability to see nature not just there, but in many a suburban home and yard, came through the modernization of the materials with which goods like Wham-O toys were made. As with those processes that, on Long Island, yielded a new and modern kind of pollution, so these and other new products being channeled through store shelves and cash registers into Angeleno, and other American homes and lives, did not exactly call nature to mind. Though Wham-O began by fashioning slingshots made of wood, by the late fifties all of its toys were made from plastic. That most modern and synthetic of materials—light, highly malleable, easy to color bright red or yellow—plastics became the era's emblem for the thoroughly made. Embodying plasticity, they seemed the most transparent of receptacles for the whimsy of Wham-O's toy inventors. Thus plastic toys and other goods joined other synthetic petrochemicals to carpet Angeleno and other American homes and yards—from playthings to lawn ornaments to detergents and insecticides.[24] By the same token, contact diminished with goods made from older, more familiar textures, such as wood or ceramic or soap. These, in turn, were becoming easier to see, and embrace, as more natural. Not least of the consequences of this changeover in materials was how it furnished traction and relevance for a new chemical naturalism, soon to provide environmentalism's ideological core.

Such a subtle, gradual transformation of people's domestic environments wrought by newer manufacturing enterprises in Los Angeles could prove unsettling. It was not just because plastics were not, as later terminology would have it, "biodegradable." Disquiet stirred, as well, from how utterly obscured their earthly origins, in a primary or first nature, now seemed. The users of wooden slingshots may have thought little about where their toys' wood had come from, but at least if they did pose the question, its look and feel quickly told of the tree from which it had been cut. But how many who twirled a hula hoop or hurled a frisbee devoted even a fleeting thought to where and when its "stuff" had originated? It had begun in the ground, of course, as petroleum. Eons before, its carbon compounds had first coalesced in living plants soaking up sunlight. Prior to being cooked, reacted, molded, and painted, it had squirted up out of an oil well. By this time that oil well more likely lay in Texas, yet it could also have been closer. Southern California's inland and coastal wells remained among the nation's most prolific sources of oil into the 1960s. Having undergone transformation into a frisbee, however, this derivative of crude oil now defined nature—for contemporary Angelenos as for other Americans— only in the negative, by sheer contrast with the outdoors through which it soared.[25]

As Los Angeles factories cluttered suburban houses and backyards with so many more new emblems of the made, grocery stores penetrated the county's suburban and rural interior, obviating the need to grow one's own. Morphing into "supermarkets" as they went, their shelves grew longer and more packed, courtesy of the ease with which they could be stocked by trucks. The Los Angeles area as a whole thereby became more like Long Island, switching from local supplies of food to growers in other parts of the state and nation. From 1935 to 1956, the percentage of fresh fruits and vegetables eaten by Angelenos that were grown in the region dropped from 50 to 36 percent, as leading industry spokespeople declared "Southern California and Los Angeles in particular . . . the home of the supermarket" and of "the most efficient methods of food distribution ever known to commerce."[26] Where Greater Los Angeles more convincingly surpassed the New York area, however, was as the nation's incubator for another innovation that helped to sever suburban dwellers from a long-standing reliance on the locally grown: "fast food."

East of Los Angeles in San Bernardino, Ray Kroc in 1954 famously discovered a drive-in restaurant run by the McDonald brothers. Paring back the menu and adopting assembly-line methods in their kitchen, the McDonalds pumped out hamburgers and fries quickly, at reduced prices, to throngs of customers. Recognizing a promising business model, Kroc then turned it into a national restaurant franchise. Not only did some of the earliest McDonald's open in suburban Los Angeles, this postwar metropolis also gave birth to a host of other soon-to-be national restaurant chains: Der Wienerschnitzel, Big Boy, Baskin Robbins, International House of Pancakes, and Taco Bell.[27] With so many new options for eating that depended on more distant farms as suppliers, food prices fell, small-scale commerce between local farmers and grocers shrank, and suburban dwellers faced fewer incentives to till their own backyards.

The effects were also more subtle. Restaurants such as McDonald's lowered a still thicker curtain than did supermarkets between what suburb dwellers ate and where it originated, the land and nature out of which it had come. Not just the work of agriculture but even the handling and cooking of groceries were relegated to others, outside the home. It was no coincidence that this pioneer of fast food started with ground beef, that most malleable of animal flesh. With the woof and warp of muscle tissue churned away, it could be molded into neat discs that passed easily through the production-line kitchen and into buns. Many other reminders of the factory, more than any originating ranch or farm, attended the passage of a Big Mac from revolving grill into a customer's mouth. Uniformly cut and fried strips of potato had to be set down, and the uniform packaging of the burger peeled away. Before and after, the customer steered under another emblem of petrochemical metamorphosis, the "golden arches" of bright yellow plastic that were McDonald's trademark.

As for suburban home building itself, federal programs had opened the door, just as in the East, but it was primarily the influx of new Angelenos that ensured a scale of postwar construction rivaling New York's. As early as 1949, Los Angeles had nearly as many home builders as that eastern metropolis, the nation's leader. Housing became the most visible leading edge of Los Angeles's leapfrogging and a chief nemesis of the antisprawl campaign. As on Long Island, the most publicized contributions to sprawl's antinaturalist imagery came in the lower ranks of the housing market, in which houses before the war had often been self-built.

Largest of them all in California was Lakewood Park, just north of Long Beach, started in 1950, three years after Levittown opened. No subdivision better exemplified Angeleno builders' mammoth capacity to construct and sell houses on a scale unmatched in almost every other part of the country. Unlike the Levitts, financier Mark Taper and his collaborators Ben Weingart and Louis Boyar did have to turn eastward for financing; area lenders either could not or would not supply this kind of capital, eventually totaling $135 million. Prairie remnants as well as old bean and sugar beet farms fell under the assault of the bulldozers. They made way for seventeen thousand homes, taking three years to build and at least equaling the number in the first Levittown. Coverage of its "mass production" techniques closely paralleled that of Levittown: the countryside as blank and malleable slate, utterly reshaped by assembly-line house building.[28]

Yet the advertising of Los Angeles's prototype for mass suburbs contrasted with its New York area counterpart, especially in the minor role it reserved for planting. Abraham Levitt had sought to promote Levittown as a "garden community," a break from the strictly built. The Lakewood builders, on the other hand, promised a community that was actually an extension of Los Angeles itself, an exercise in city building. Lakewood was "completely new" and thoroughly "planned," with fully "urban conveniences," the "City as New as Tomorrow." Landscaping, so foregrounded in the advertisements for Levittown, earned only minimal attention in Lakewood ads and in the final product, considerably less care. The builders of Lakewood planted a single sapling per house, as opposed to the Levitts' seven, and seeded a lawn only in the front yard. They emphasized what was "modern," "convenient," and sanitary.[29]

That the Lakewood builders should pitch their project as city building says much about the region in which they operated. Compared to Long Island counterparts, rural settings still seemed more common. The edges of Los Angeles could still seem all too engulfed by countryside, in part because rural decrepitude was felt to pose a more pervasive threat. The Levitts' similar worries, while present, had been tucked away in measures such as restrictive covenants against farm animals. Lakewood ads addressed these same fears more directly and forthrightly. The "City as New as Tomorrow" promised the total opposite of the slumhood that troubled many semirural settlements around Los Angeles into the postwar years. The Lakewood builders anxiously broadcast the arrival of their "city" on the plain north of Long Beach by hauling in a high-rise oil derrick and festooning it with a "war surplus beacon" and strings of lightbulbs.[30]

That the builders of Lakewood sold their suburb as a novel city, however, could not disguise how unmistakably rural their new town's surroundings remained. Donald J. Waldie, in his memoir of early residence in the area, recalled the "cloudless" day the houses went on sale, the initial "interleaving of houses and fields," even a sales office that seemed "barnlike." Lakewood home shoppers noticed as well, and many were not disappointed. A builders' early survey of what new residents liked most about the development seemed to belie the builders' ad campaign. More of them stressed the value of its "country atmosphere" and "spaciousness" than its citylike conveniences.[31] To understand more of what they saw, of what drew so many Angelenos to the suburbs, aside from just the houses, requires a shift from the built to the biotic side of suburbanizing.

Selling Suburban Nature, Los Angeles Style

Los Angeles suburban home builders of the postwar period not only noticed a local nature; like the state highway commissioner, they sought to marshal it as an ally. Their noticing began with the location of their subdivisions. Like their Long Island counterparts, Lakewood and other mass builders preferred wide expanses of flat land in the basin's southeastern corner. Upper-bracket Angeleno builders, meanwhile, headed in precisely the opposite direction: to the hills. Honing publicity that departed significantly from that to richer Long Islanders, they exploited the basin's distinct topography and climate, weaving its steep slopes and semitropical balm into the suburban nature they sold. Especially when it came to planting, they and their horticultural suppliers faced difficulties their eastern counterparts did not. Among these, native chaparral or coastal scrub had little of the lushness or greenery that characterized suburban flora in the East. To achieve a similar look and feel to eastern flora, significant adjustments to the ecology of Southern California needed to be made.

Less troubled by the prospect of countryside slums, builders in upper-end Los Angeles housing markets honed a nature pitch that leveraged the basin's abundant hills and slopes. Luxury homes of twenty thousand dollars or more (by the mid-1950s, about 15 percent of Los Angeles's new houses) celebrated the view to be had from inclines and hilltops, more so than the wooded or tree-studded lots so valued around New York. With forests fewer and farther between, John Muir's "mountains and hills" enticed luxury home builders and their customers into the heights.

Among the early movers was the Bel-Air Land Company, which in 1946 erected a hundred new houses in the Santa Monica Mountains. Taking the new excavating tool of the bulldozer to peaks that had never borne a cow or an orange tree, they swept away the native chaparral, lopped off hills, and toted away about 400,000 cubic feet of earth. On the resulting plateau, some 1,300 feet above the nearby ocean, they charged $5,500 for the land alone (nearly as much as a Lakewood house) and $26,500 for the addition of a customized home. Unlike in the notices for Lakewood, sanitation and appliances went unmentioned in their advertisements. One

The view from Bel Air, enveloped by hills and vegetation, makes downtown Los Angeles seem far away. (Photograph by the author)

ad for a 1951 Bel-Air "Highlander" dwelt instead on the "panoramic view of the landscape from Mt. Wilson to Catalina," ensured by "rigid" restrictive covenants. Another summed up a promise of "country living within the city" (the area lay within Los Angeles's city limits). Nor were hillside properties confined to the most expensive housing brackets. Up the slopes from Pasadena, into the canyons of the Santa Monicas and San Gabriels, builders also constructed and sold more modestly priced homes with views.[32]

As on Long Island, landscaping was another well-touted feature of Los Angeles suburban home sales. Not just at the upper end but in any price range, lush flora could enhance a subdivision's appeal and profit. Yet the species honed to thrive in suburban yards of the East were ill-adapted to stark differences in temperature and season in Southern California. A great deal of energy and investment was poured into the search for landscaping flora that would look similar yet more easily endure Los Angeles's year-round heat and aridity.

Lawn grass posed a special problem. Species imported from the East had long carpeted golf courses and front yards in towns like Pasadena, but at great cost. Kentucky bluegrass (still recommended into the 1940s by *Los Angeles Times* horticultural writers) and other eastern "cool-season" grasses, fescue and bent, imposed heavy demands for watering. A postwar boom in the sprinkler business solved this problem, but not another. In a region where so many plants grew year-round, the dormant brown of eastern lawn species during winter frustrated expectations for unceasing greenery and invited in the still-flourishing weeds. Among the frequent invaders was common Bermuda grass, originally from tropical Africa, with thicker and coarser blades than eastern lawn species. By the mid-1950s, Angeleno landscaping experts dubbed it "devil grass," the inevitable victor in a lawn that went unmowed and unweeded. Because of such frustrations, Angeleno lawns were generally smaller than those in the East.[33]

As a solution, postwar agricultural scientists and nurserymen explored alternatives to lawn grass. Among these was dichondra. A tiny-leaved creeping herb likely originating in Central or South America, it had wild relatives that were native to Southern California's coastal scrub sage. First marketed for lawns in the 1930s, its installation was never easy. Sprouts had to be planted one by one rather than from seed. But all the effort paid off, some homeowners in Lakewood and elsewhere felt, because once installed it required little mowing and watering. Common Bermuda grass was easier to start since it was naturally invasive. But, like bluegrass, it went dormant and brown in winter and then could easily be overrun by weeds. By the early 1960s new hybrid crosses of Bermuda with African variants became available and quickly found favor among horticultural advisers in Los Angeles and other southwestern areas. The new varieties had finer textures than common Bermuda, more like eastern lawn species. They also came closer to solving the problem of seasonality, holding a green tint nearly year-round. Through such innovations, the land covered by lawns expanded considerably beyond its scope in the midfifties, when it was already estimated to occupy approximately ninety-five square miles of Los Angeles County—about four times the size of Manhattan.[34]

Just as in the East, suburban builders and dwellers outside Los Angeles cultivated an abundance of trees and shrubs. After World War II, while orange trees and other fruits and vegetables retained their foothold in suburban lots, the avocado was declared the "most popular . . . of all the evergreen fruiting trees." Originating in Mexico and Guatemala, the avocado had long been "acclimated to Southern California"; postwar suburban planting built on a history of adaptation of trees and shrubs from elsewhere to regional lands and climates. While many agricultural adaptations dated back to the early Spanish padres, after the war the Los Angeles–area nursery trade veered strongly to ornamentals.[35] Long a national as well as a local supplier, the area nursery business stepped up its production to meet the mounting demands around Los Angeles and other rapidly suburbanizing corners of America. The same new distributional tools used on Long Island served the nursery trade of suburban Los Angeles: the self-service nursery, the plastic container, and the cultivar. Monrovia, in the San Gabriel Valley near Pasadena, dubbed itself the "world's largest container nursery," with a catalog that doubled in length from the 1940s to the 1960s. By 1966, Los Angeles County was the nation's largest producer of ornamental nursery stock.[36]

In terms of local terrain, we can understand this expansion of suburban horticulture after the war as largely extending patterns of cultivation established earlier in places like the town of Pasadena. What differentiated it from the native ecology was, first of all, its soaring heights. Neither prairie nor coastal scrub nor chaparral had many trees. On the other hand, over the preceding decades, Pasadena had set up a street tree division that became a national innovator in the careful selection, nursing, and tending of trees for its neighborhoods. Postwar housing intruding into the Santa Monica foothills and elsewhere introduced similarly lofty greenery, much of it broadleaf and including some eastern species, but also geographically eclectic. Like its prewar suburban predecessors, the species had mostly originated in warm, if wetter parts of the globe: Lakewood's Jacarandas hailed from the Amazon; its pepper trees, from Peru; and the rubber trees that became a veritable fad, from India. The greatest variety of ornamental species continued to be cultivated on the wealthiest residences and estates from San Marino to Palos Verdes. But garden clubs from there to Lakewood to San Gabriel to South Gate extended a local tradition of plant importation and acclimatization running all the way back to Spanish padres. As one flower distributor bemoaned, the "salubrious" climate itself forced a reliance of commercial growers on exports rather than local sales, because "too many greens and flowers grow in backyards." One message continued to be echoed: "anything could grow" in Angeleno soil, once watered.[37]

That caveat was altogether critical. Declarations of horticultural flexibility had long been tempered by an awareness of the region's limited availability of water, especially compared to the eastern United States. After the war, this distinctiveness of Southern California's climate and soil gained new public forums, and within these, a consolidating insistence. Among them, *Sunset*, a railroad-sponsored tourism magazine, was revamped over the early forties into a Western version of *Better Homes and Gardens*. Articles provided upscale readers with ways of more deliberately attuning their landscaping to the regional climate and soil. Federal and state agricultural scientists stepped in, as well, devising new tools for the regional tailoring of horticultural advice, such as an official national map of climate zones. First widely circulated in the early sixties, it drew a clear dividing line between the "cool humid" climates of the East and Midwest and the "subtropical" areas of the Southwest. The new mapping of meteorological differences hammered home how many eastern and Eurasian plant species had trouble surviving in a place like the Los Angeles basin, where species of Mediterranean or equatorial origins were much easier to cultivate.[38]

By this time, too, a tradition of native California horticulture was gaining momentum and markets around Los Angeles, more so than native counterparts back East. Since the early twentieth century, the most lavish of the Los Angeles area's private gardens had "native" plots, by which they meant mostly drought-resistant or desert plants. A few nurseries as well as regional botanical gardens had specialized in native flora—without much specificity about which of the area's many ecological zones they belonged to. After the war, the California Horticultural Society dwelt more exclusively than its Long Island counterpart on its own region's distinctive species. Hybridizers and nursery operators tried to propagate and market some dominant plants of the area's long-standing chaparral: the ceanothus and the manzanita. If their commercial success remained limited, by the midfifties "native trees and shrubs such as California Lilac (ceanothus)" garnered regular mention by gardening columnists as needing "little irrigation."[39]

In the most suburbanized of basin places, as elsewhere, intentionally cultivated flora were joined by the straying seeds and sprouts known as "weeds." Many of these garden pests, of eastern or north Eurasian origin, were the same as those with which Levittowners contended: crabgrass and dandelions. These had an easier time in yards that were amply irrigated; in drier places, native invaders stood a better chance. Hence the menace of, among others, dodder, a relative of the morning glory, whose "yellowish-orange mats are a conspicuous feature of our native foothill vegetation." Dodder gained nourishment not from the soil but from "wartlike suckers" that engulfed a plant host, from ivies to orange trees to roses. The new possibilities for lawn grass introduced further, confounding questions about what were weeds and what were not. Dichondra, among others, could be a weed in a Bermuda grass lawn, as well as visa vera. With so many weeds and other pests looming, advisers to suburban horticulturalists around Los Angeles enthusiastically espoused the many new herbicides and insecticides that hit the market from the late forties onward.[40]

Along with all these new plants, spreading subdivisions amassed more people and a host of other creatures. Proliferating pets made up most of the nearly fivefold growth in creatures handled by the Pasadena Humane Society from the 1920s to almost fourteen thousand by 1953. The vast majority of this last sum were suburban familiars: dogs and cats. The boom in pets "far exceeded the growth ratio of the county's population." In response, across all the public shelters of the Los Angeles area, nearly two hundred thousand pets were being destroyed annually by 1970, not to mention those put down by private veterinarians. As shelter rosters made clear, within this overall growth of domesticated creatures, their balance was tilting from an agro-suburban mix more exclusively toward pets. In the 1920s cows or other large farm animals had been regular denizens of the Pasadena shelter. As backyard agriculture disappeared, the Pasadena Humane Society, by the early 1950s, handled virtually none of these except for the occasional horse. Goats, on the other hand, dwindled more slowly, and chickens still continued to turn up.[41]

That is to say, what earlier observers had called a suburban countryside had not entirely vanished from postwar Los Angeles's edges. Even into the fifties, smaller livestock continued to flourish in suburban lots and towns. As with Long Island, in some of the wealthiest areas like San Marino, alongside Pasadena, licensed hobbyists could pursue animal keeping of all sorts, provided the quarters and care were appropriate. Others like San Gabriel only allowed smaller and less troublesome beasts, though where these ordinances went unenforced, as in the Mission-area barrio, roosters still crowed. In Lakewood, unlike in Levittown, cow herds still grazed on early city lots, and no covenants banned the keeping of farm fowl. Early residents not only could but did keep chickens.[42] Those hens that clucked in early Lakewooders' backyards during the 1950s encapsulated the Los Angeles suburbs' greater friendliness to farm creatures than their Long Island counterparts. What made for the country atmosphere of Lakewood was not just the open space in and around their home lots; creatures scuttling about these spaces also called the barnyard to mind.

The countrylike setting of early Lakewood did not stop at the edge of this subdivision; the land next door, its informal commons, also figured in. And unlike with Levittown, along Lakewood's easterly flank even into the

1960s, a viable commercial agriculture flourished. Similarly, that "country living in the city" promised by Bel Air builders was not confined to the land they themselves subdivided. Here, as for many other upper-end Angeleno suburbs, the informal commons consisted of chaparral, rolling across hills and canyons that might never have been grazed or farmed. The composition of this land next door—whether dairy farms or untilled slopes—helped distinguish lower- to middle-class suburbs from those of the well-to-do. Either way, Angeleno suburbs and their denizens continued to rub up against rural lands undergoing ecological transformations of their own, with still fewer eastern counterparts.

A Roiling Rural Fringe

That "last remaining tract of greenery" observed with such alarm by William Whyte could not have been a suburban enclave like Pasadena, nor chaparral or coastal scrub sage, less greenish in hue. In all likelihood, it consisted of irrigated, chemically doused orange trees, a sort of cultivation that, in the Greater Los Angeles of the postwar years, shrank most dramatically. Whyte's nature-erasing tale about sprawl homed in on a form of agriculture that was indeed under assault. Yet it slighted other husbandry that hung on and even prospered. In particular, dairy farmers and milk cows by the early 1960s had congregated just across the San Gabriel River from Lakewood. As for wilder flora and fauna, while many were extinguished by Los Angeles's sprawl, in places just beyond the subdivisions some of them stirred and flourished anew. In broad outline, the ecological consequences resembled those on Long Island; yet differences in the pre-existing terrain, conditions, and species made for consequences that were, biological speaking, more far-reaching and dire.

Among commercial crops, the orange lost the most local ground. With an eastern market that had long cultivated the "southland's" sunny reputation, for decades it had been Los Angeles County's dominant crop. But after peaking in 1936, it fell nearly every year thereafter. In the twelve years after World War II alone, county orchards lost two-thirds of their acreage. Their vulnerability was due partly to "quick decline," a disease of citrus, and partly to national competition with Florida growers who faced fewer urbanizing pressures. With so many factory jobs opening up in places like the barrios in San Gabriel or El Monte, postwar orchardists around Los Angeles contended with shortages of seasonal workers, only partly compensated by the Mexican migrants brought in by the federal bracero program. As competition for urban-edge land sharpened, Los Angeles growers also had little say about how suburbanizing towns adjusted their property taxes to supply the services demanded by homeowners. County growers complained of tax rates as high as $40 to $90 dollars an acre by 1954, compared to the $9 or $10 assessed their Florida competitors. They also confronted pushes by suburban homeowners to suppress, by means of town ordinances, what were considered vital measures of orchard upkeep, from pesticide sprays to "smudges"—fuel burners to keep orange trees from freezing. By the late fifties, all of the San Gabriel Valley's orange packers had shut down, eliminating any possibility for profit from local orchards. Commercial orange groves continued to operate in the San Fernando Valley, but most growers gravitated to counties farther from Los Angeles and Orange, to San Bernardino and even into the Central Valley.[43]

Remarkably, however, even more so than on Long Island, some agriculturalists found advantages in remaining where they were. Nursery and cut flower growers had by the early 1960s become Los Angeles County's third most numerous type of farmer and its most lucrative.[44] Yet unlike around New York City's suburbs, cows, along with chickens and hogs, did not depart nearly as quickly. In the mid-1950s, though orange trees had been declining for two decades in Los Angeles County, its cattle population was peaking. Angeleno dairy farmers stayed put, as well as profitable, in part because of their success in industrializing the ways their cows produced milk.

The turn to factory dairying got under way around Los Angeles just after World War II. When the county health department required pasteurization, some local dairy operators went further. Streamlining the movement of milk throughout their operations, they made Los Angeles County the first place in the United States to switch to "bulk fluid milk handling." Instead of being toted from cows in cans, fresh milk was funneled directly into tank trucks "built like giant vacuum bottles placed on their sides." Taken to a pasteurizing plant, it was then quickly heated, cooled, and returned to tank trucks for delivery. Dramatic changes also came in Los Angeles dairies' land use. Pastures themselves were abandoned. Rather than sowing and tending the grassy fields on which cows traditionally grazed, dairy operators corralled their herds tightly around feeding troughs on "dry lots" bare of vegetation. The feed, meanwhile, came increasingly from outside Los Angeles County. Area dairy farmers and their cows still relied on sunshine, the ultimate fuel of ruminant biology. But even this natural contribution to their work was outsourced. The sunbeams that nourished them now fell on land far beyond Los Angeles.

Drastically reducing acreage requirements, drylot dairying alleviated tax burdens and enabled smaller property owners to accommodate larger herds. As part-time dairies were driven out of business by associated capital requirements, the number of herds in the county plummeted by half between 1940 and 1960. But as cow herds had their pastures and grass cut out from under them, those of more than 151 animals grew more than threefold.[45]

Geographically as well, dairying in postwar Los Angeles County became more concentrated. As operations enlarged and as farmers acquired more residential neighbors, objections to their presence became more aggressive. Though allowed in the most restrictive zones before World War II, dairies were increasingly shunned by postwar zoning schemes because of their "stench" and "'an unhealthy amount of flies.'" In 1956 the dairy farmers gathered in a horseshoe-shaped ring of land around Artesia, directly across the San Gabriel River from Lakewood, and resolved to fight fire with fire. Stealing a page from the playbook of industrialists and suburbanites, they incorporated themselves as a city under California law.

Right next door to Los Angeles's prototypical mass suburb, one of the nation's first serious experiments in agricultural land preservation began. The new municipality christened itself, appropriately enough, "Dairy Valley." Los Angeles County's forty-eighth city, it was arguably the county's most unusual, a place "where cows outnumber people approximately 30-1." The city council, almost totally composed of dairy farmers, promptly zoned virtually the entire city exclusively for agricultural use. They refused to levy a property tax.[46] By 1963, the county's southeastern corner in and near Dairy Valley had drawn nearly 80 percent of the county's dairy cattle. Yet its success was short-lived. Only two years later, as Sacramento passed a state-level remedy, the Williamson Act, dairy farmers' control of the city of Dairy Valley was teetering. Soon the city allowed in subdividers, instituted a property tax, and change its name to Cerritos.

The plight of urban-edge agriculturalists like Los Angeles dairy farmers caught the eye of William Whyte. Launching his antisprawl campaign, he nevertheless sought to draw a clearer line than Los Angeles dairies afforded between rural landscape and the urban sprawl that threatened it. Suburbs of bovines like Dairy Valley may well have "beat[en] the subdividers at their own game," he acknowledged. But Whyte much preferred pictures of soon-to-be-razed orange trees, along with the county-level plan for agricultural zoning devised by vegetable farmers in the Bay Area. Cow cities were not quite the kind of countryside Whyte wanted to save. Ironically,

A drylot in Dairy Valley. (Cerritos City and Public Library)

this version of the countryside was the very one to arrive on the doorstep of Lakewood, among the less privileged Angeleno suburbs.[47]

Obscured in both the dairy farmers' and Whyte's campaigns was the extent to which older possibilities, which had kept visions of a suburban countryside alive for so long around Los Angeles, were also slipping away. The agriculturalists who stayed in Los Angeles not only industrialized, they and their families also discovered the conveniences of supermarkets and fast food. In so doing, they helped seal the fate of the suburban countryside's mainstay: the small farm home. Throughout the early decades of the twentieth century, small-scale and often part-time farmers around Los Angeles had long resisted the pressure to specialize in dairy products or some intensive crop. Their produce went only occasionally to market; more often it remained with the farmers that produced it, to feed them and their families. Precisely these operations, involving tiny orchards and perhaps a single milk cow, proved most vulnerable to the pressures of urbanizing land markets. The most serious hobby farmers, as well, abandoned Los Angeles County for acreage farther out.[48] With the diminishing reliance of farmers on the produce of local land and with industrializing conversions of pastures into feedlots, the romance of the soil that had long endured in and around Los Angeles's subdivisions was on the wane. Drylot dairies, after all, hardly seemed places where contacts with nature could so readily be had. Upper-end Angeleno builders, with their hillward charges, also gravitated toward a decidedly less productive or pastoral vision for the next-door nature they promised. Even that "country living in the city" intimated, for instance, in the newer extensions of Bel Air, evoked a country devoid of agrarian imprint or desire.

Yet Los Angeles luxury builders also betrayed considerable discomfort with native versions of the wild. Looking askance at the scrubby chaparral right beside their up-scale houses, they saw a need for further domestication. A steep slope of manzanita or California lilac did not provide a lush enough "outdoor living room." Most of them replaced low-lying natives with taller, greener, and wetter flora, such as the "Highlander's . . . rare tropical shrubs."[49]

Neither builders nor conservationists of this period, nor even William Whyte, devoted much attention to how Los Angeles's sprawl was affecting wilder flora and fauna nearby. Yet the reverberations, in this, one of the most biodiverse of all North American regions, proved immense. Multiplying people, buildings, and roads, as well as new domesticated plants and animals, wrought a host of collisions with less crafted landscapes and their wilder ecology. Angelenos of this period largely overlooked the biological competition that ensued as interfaces between the suburban and the wild radiated upward and outward across the basin. Its rich array of species was withering; yet as on Long Island, many generalist species prospered. Among the changes, newcomers from the East, familiar to Long Islanders, mixed with species that were native-born.

Unlike its Long Island counterparts, hillside chaparral in the Los Angeles basin remained partly protected. The formidable steepness of its gradients kept builders away, and the remoter reaches belonged to federal reserves. But what was left of the grassland in the basin flats was almost completely erased during the postwar building boom. Only tiny remnants were left, long since dominated by naturalized species from Mediterranean Europe. Coastal sage scrub, as well, lost considerable ground—by the 1970s, it was somewhere between 10 and 15 percent of its former extent in Southern California. Not only did building projects themselves replace these wilder landscapes, imported horticulture found its way into leftover patches and neighboring canyons, especially where water was naturally to be had. Particularly prone to invade were the so-called ruderal species, the same ones that threatened many an ill-kempt Los Angeles lawn. Tolerant of trampling and even of aridity, in such places they progenerated with abandon.[50]

As for fauna, the increasing numbers of wilder species incarcerated from the 1920s to the 1950s at the Pasadena Humane Society offer a glimpse into the biotic shifts under way just beyond suburban backyards. Aggressively sneaking and poking their way into Pasadena yards and homes, some of these creatures had been driven out of wilder habitats razed by new roads and subdivisions. Birds that wound up in Humane Society cages included newcomers from the East (doves, pigeons, and starlings), generalists native both to the East and to California (crows, mockingbirds, and woodpeckers), and species more specific to the chaparral (Western scrub-jay, Anna's hummingbirds). Smaller mammals with wide-ranging appetites also found advantages along this interface, where suburban cultivation disturbed the edges of wilder lands. Like birds, animals winding up in Humane Society cages might be natives to the chaparral (raccoons, striped skunks) or eastern immigrants (fox squirrels). In postwar Pasadena, one newer arrival, the opossum, found conditions to its liking. By the 1950s Humane Society officers reported over a hundred yearly cagings of opossums, the third most frequently caught creature, after dogs and cats. This and other eastern newcomers tilted Los Angeles's suburban ecology toward a newfound resemblance with Long Island and other eastern counterparts.[51]

Hiding in the remaining patches of chaparral or woodland near Pasadena, small predators such as coyotes and foxes adapted easily to expanding suburban landscapes. Like the opossum, they left daylight to humans, feeding at night and then returning to wilder land. Coyotes, notorious opportunists, developed appetites for what suburbs offered in abundance—from human garbage to the birds and animals at the Los Angeles Zoo. The mule deer, larger and little threatened by these predators, also prospered, especially where it could retreat into upland canyons or chaparral. A herd numbering in the thousands stalked the hills "from Griffith Park in Los Angeles to Point Mugu." By the early fifties, estimated deer populations in the neighboring national forests reached historical records. State wildlife officials, declaring the era of deer restoration over, began loosening game laws. On the many deer that descended to munch on their gardens or crops, Angelenos themselves sought the right to blaze away. As late as 1959, Los Angeles County issued the second most depredation licenses of any county in California.[52]

Though neither coyotes nor mule deer lived around New York City, postwar Long Island's acquisition of white-tail herds suggests a sharing of this niche among East and West Coast urban edges. The reasons for deers' return out from Los Angeles, however, were not entirely comparable. As large a mammal as a mule deer flourished in this period partly because its main predator other than people, the cougar, now found the going rough. This fiercest of Southern California's remaining wildlife had no Long Island counterpart, at least not in the twentieth century. The wild chaparral's "keystone" predator ever since the eradication of the grizzly bear, the cougar was among the most averse to the shrinking fragments of native landscape. Over the early twentieth century, cougars had gradually retreated to the more remote, rugged mountains, assaulted by wildlife officials and bounty-seeking hunters. Nocturnal, journeying over five miles in a single night's hunt, they also ran into more and more barriers along the lower reaches of the postwar Los Angeles basin, from subdivisions to paved roads. They now confined themselves to the most mountainous retreats of the Santa Monicas and San Gabriels, even after the state abandoned its cougar bounty program in 1963.[53]

What the Los Angeles basin and the Long Island of this period most convincingly shared was the same basic process of fragmentation. Suburbanizing carved up what had been large continuous stretches of the ecosystem into increasingly smaller, more isolated islands. The most corrosive effect of fragmentation fell on floral and faunal specialists, exclusively adapted to a single landscape. And thanks to a very different natural history, Southern California had far more of this sort of species than Long Island did. Specialists of the chaparral could still find havens in the mountains. But those of the coastal sage scrub, already hemmed in by decades of agriculture, found fewer paths of retreat. As postwar builders leapfrogged across the lower elevations, they isolated the remaining patches of coastal sage more quickly. By the 1970s, it had become "the most endangered vegetative type in Southern California."

Among its natives was a tiny, gray songbird known as the "California gnatcatcher" (*Polioptila californica californica*). Capable of nesting and breeding only in the low-lying, less woody vegetation of the coastal sage scrub, the gnatcatcher rarely ventured into other terrain, even to feed. After choosing a mate, it confined itself to between one and two acres, usually for life. Probably never abundant, its range was already reported as "somewhat reduced" in 1944. By the early sixties biologists found the gnatcatcher "very rare," "driven from most of its former range along the coast of the region." By 1990, only a single "major" population of fifty pairs survived

California gnatcatcher. (Photograph by Richard Bledsoe)

in Los Angeles County, in a park on the Palos Verdes Peninsula.[54] Those species most vulnerable to sprawl were, for the most part, like the gnatcatcher, shy, unobtrusive, and unventuresome. They were also among the least likely to find their way into people's yards or their awareness.

Birders in the Los Angeles Audubon Society did have an inkling of the changes that were afoot. The 1961 Christmas Count enumerated slightly more species than half a century earlier. Along the widening interface between the suburban and the wild, a new abundance of creatures and even a burst of species diversity might erupt for a time. Yet fragmentation ensured that the larger trend was downward. As birders that same year also concluded, "The numbers have diminished considerably [since World War II] and the variety somewhat." Only later, in the wake of the 1972 Endangered Species Act and its resultant science, would the toll become clearer. Los Angeles area losses had set the pace for an exponential rise in the rate of reported extinctions in California between 1925 and 1975. By the 1990s, when the ranks of Southern California species threatened by extinction became better known, they turned out to far surpass those around Long Island or almost any other American metropolis.[55]

Why, then, was there so little fretting over this epic ecological destruction wrought by their city's spread? The question itself is in many ways anachronistic. There was as yet no formal scientific concept of *biodiversity*, and scrutiny of such places' ecology by professional investigators remained limited. Nor were there as yet laws on the books that might hold out hope for activism on behalf of any endangered species. When we look at those groups that later would take up such issues, we can also see other reasons. In appealing to what political scientists would term the postwar "political opportunity structure," local chapters of the Audubon Society and the Sierra Club sought defense only of places worlds away from any suburbs, and only of the wildest and most magnificent species.

Muir's Sierra Club, for instance, did show a new postwar willingness to engage in letter-writing campaigns against federal dam building. This "militancy" has been heralded as birthing postwar environmentalism, but that could hardly be so according to the definitions of this book. The club was not yet environmentalist, first of all, because the nature it was striving to protect still lay in the remotest of places. Most Angeleno chapter residents lived in Los Angeles's downtown or suburbs. Yet the mountain ranges in the larger region, many of them overseen by the federal government, enabled an agenda that, even while engaging federal policies, oriented Sierra's activism to a nature that seemed far away from activists' own homes and neighborhoods. Los Angeles County's long-standing federal reserves, with so few counterparts outside New York or other eastern cities, help explain why this region did not hatch a Nature Conservancy chapter at this time, despite its postwar urbanizing and suburbanizing. By the same token, the Sierra Club around 1955, after winning its celebrated campaign against Echo Park,[56] remained a small, mostly West Coast group.

Although an anti-extinction politics did stir around Los Angeles over this same period, it too stayed riveted on the most spectacular and seemingly distant wildlife. Only two creatures made it onto the agenda of Audubon and Sierra over these years, both of them charismatically human-sized and reassuringly nonsuburban in habitat. One was the tule elk, the largest of the ruminants to stalk the grasslands that predated the Spanish ranchos.[57] The other was the California condor, lumbering and awkward on land but a soaring "King of the Sky," with a six-foot wingspan. Preservation efforts were aided by the preexistence of public land here, as in other countryside of the American West. The elk resided in the dried-up Owens Valley; the condor, in the wild reaches of Ventura County's Los Padres National Park. Like the Sierra Club's more famous battles against dams, the offensive consisted mainly of letter-writing campaigns to prevent further human intrusion onto publicly owned, visibly pristine lands.[58]

Proclamations like that of the conservation chair of Sierra's Los Angeles area chapter in 1951 suggest just how far these activists had to go before they could call themselves environmentalists. As "conservationists," they aimed to "preserve" only "*natural* resources" [emphasis added]: "Our forests, parks, monuments and wild life," the "unrivaled samples of primeval America." Equally far from environmentalism was their working notions of their movement itself. As conservationists, they consisted of only a "dedicated few."[59] Only after their issues widened and their alliances broadened would they, or anyone else, feel the need to rename their cause. By then, following in the footsteps of others, they would champion those very environments that, in this early moment, they had most forsaken: those more unmistakably in the shadow of the city that Los Angeles had become.

Chapter 6

Suburban Taming
From the Personal to the Political

On the morning of Saturday, February 28, 1953, a cow suddenly appeared on an East Pasadena front lawn. Upset over "boarders" next door, nurseryman Thomas Ames had choreographed a mocking commentary on where the neighborhood seemed to be headed. Next to the heifer's feed pail he pitched a sign: "Protect Your Property from the Rooming House Menace." The cow's mooing "hasn't bothered me in the least," huffed Mrs. Arline Kraft, the widowed neighbor who was Ames's target. Others felt differently. Complaints poured in to the local police. "'You may think I'm crazy," went the refrain, "but I think I hear a cow mooing.'" Journalists got wind of the controversy and smelled a story. "Bossy," as they nicknamed the cow, "spent most of [Monday] posing for newspaper and TV cameramen" and was pronounced an "unprecedented spectacle." Within the week, Ames was declaring Bossy "worth her weight in hay." In a quid pro quo, the town forced Mrs. Kraft to expel her boarder, and Bossy's suburban sojourn ended with her return to a dairy outside of Pasadena.[1]

Sparking Pasadena's battle over Bossy, that old ideal of a "suburban homestead" no longer seemed so idyllic. Well remembered, with a vividness that on Long Island went unduplicated, its status had slipped, at least for the best-off Angelenos. Now, their suburban ideals converged with those of suburban New Yorkers: in addition to owning house and yard, their lawns had to be cowless. In the Pasadena of 1953, this suburbia rid of barnyard creatures and renters nevertheless remained, in the eyes of reporters, "posh" and "ritzy," a province of the privileged. California was indeed fast moving to the forefront of a national story about mass suburbia, featuring places far less plush such as Lakewood. Yet Los Angeles journalists were perhaps half a decade behind their New York counterparts in finding a more middling class of suburbia around their own city (see Figure 4 in the Appendix).[2] Their coverage, when it did appear in print, picked up on real changes in housing and affluence, but also, as around New York, on a longer-term constriction in what the suburban meant. The main casualty, in curious alliance with the dwindling visibility of any nature across Los Angeles's edges, was that early-century, more rustic version of the suburban as a portal to the countryside. A gap now began to yawn between how little country creatures, land uses, and appearances mattered in media depictions of suburbia, and how much they continued to matter to many suburbanites themselves, albeit in contrasting and evolving ways.

Throughout Los Angeles's urban edges, residents continued to identify with local places not just because of the buildings and human neighbors, but because of the flora, or cragginess, or open vistas. As in the case of Long Island, however, what was kept open or unbuilt varied sharply across suburban locales. As more factories as well as subdivisions arose, as basin agriculture retreated or industrialized, suburban migrants confronted very different faces of the large-scale ecological change that was afoot. Some, like Beatrice and Henry Alva in the suburban barrio of San Gabriel, witnessed urban concentration, a conversion of unbuilt lots that planners called "infill." Others, Jacqueline "Jackie" and Bud Rynerson among them, in the mass white suburb of Lakewood, strained to get a lawn to grow not far from cattle-packed drylots. Still others, such as Louise and Richard Lillard, who resided on a hillside in the Santa Monicas, gazed out on some of the basin's least developed terrain, a palpable nature next door. It too posed unexpected difficulties. Angeleno suburb dwellers faced innumerable other postwar challenges from the settings in which they lived, but these three places together illustrate the diversity of neighborhood ecologies—from yard to tract to enveloping lands—with which they contended.

Like Long Islanders, once each of these couples moved into their suburban home, switching their status from buyer to owner, their relationships with their surroundings deepened. So, with these Angeleno suburban migrants, I tell much the same story as with our suburban Long Islanders, yet differently. This time around, I focus on the many meanings our three couples discovered in nearby flora and fauna.

For each, the psychic and social ties they evolved with their settings favored the organic: the plants or pets they treasured, the less built corners of their own or neighboring terrain. What planners saw as the urban periphery, what journalists and social scientists increasingly termed "suburbia," residents imagined more intimately on what urban critic Jane Jacobs would characterize as the "human scale."[3] Practices toward flora and fauna grounded each's experience of family and community. They helped, for instance, to delineate household gender roles and, within a municipality, to demarcate differences between one's own and other groups. In each case, the neighborhood ecology underwent a significant biotic shift during the postwar period. In each case, new rounds of domesticating revised residents' claims and control over land, plants, and animals nearby, but also raised curiosity about a nature that was less domesticated. In response, each family produced its own, divergent answers. The most remarkable difference with the Long Island couples and communities was that suburban Angelenos' searches for this nature all leaned, in contrasting ways, on a regional iconography of the American West.

All three families went on to insert themselves into local politics, but only two of these individuals would actually identify themselves as environmentalists. The Rynersons' son Steve would join the Sierra Club in 1968, and Richard Lillard, through his authorship of *Eden in Jeopardy* (1966), would become the closest thing the Los Angeles region had to an environmental prophet. By setting their suburban environmentalism alongside the experience of others in these three families, I mean to suggest how this movement nevertheless reflected broader common denominators in the postwar suburban experience. Across lines not just of class, but of race or ethnicity, many others living in postwar Los Angeles suburbs also cultivated an awareness of and sensitivity to the natural sides of the city's edges. Whether they came to see their own suburban neighborhood ecologies as more or less natural, and whether their own political engagements looked more or less environmentalist, depended, in important respects, on how privileged their neighborhoods were. For some who turned environmentalist, a newfound appreciation of nature drew their eyes and allegiances closer to home. For others, it bolstered a growing sense of alienation, a heightening awareness that the land where they actually lived lay in others' hands. What these political responses shared with so many others, across neighborhoods of strikingly different class and racial composition, was a realization of the limited control they had over land and neighborhoods that were titularly their own.

Barrio In-Fill and Native Revival

Of the three suburban places highlighted in this study (San Gabriel, Lakewood, and the Santa Monicas), the barrio of San Gabriel underwent postwar changes that were the most citylike. With new factories arriving in its midst, it was one of many older and newer town cores along Los Angeles's edges that after World War II bore the brunt of industrialization. At the same time, similar not only to Pasadena and El Monte but also to East Los Angeles, San Gabriel harbored a preexisting enclave of Mexican immigrants that continued to grow. It did so in part because of how barriers of ethnicity and income kept a large number of Hispanic arrivals out of the newer postwar subdivisions. The new migrants extended a longer-term demographic tide, of those many Mexicans who had been moving from their country to the Los Angeles area since the start of the Mexican Revolution.

The Anglo-dominated leadership of their new home had, from the early twentieth century, endeavored to recover and celebrate a time to which Mexican immigrants felt less connection: the area's Spanish colonial past.[4] In San Gabriel, where related festivities concentrated, arrivals from Mexico came to rub shoulders not just with Anglo celebrants, but with residents of still longer lineage. Out of these encounters, other legacies of this colonialism came to be recollected, some of them far less rosy. In suburban San Gabriel, the Alvas' story illuminates how local ecological trajectories both aggravated the resulting tensions and helped catalyze a movement for tribal recognition highly critical of this same past.

Among the Hispanics arriving in this town on Los Angeles's periphery during the 1940s were Henry and Beatrice Alva. Married in 1938, they lived in a downtown apartment for four years, then bought their first house in San Gabriel. Their story appears a non-Anglo working-class match to the classic trajectory of a move from city to suburb—only neither had grown up downtown. They were migrating back to where they had been raised, a place that had long since been settled.

The center of San Gabriel, where they had met, was actually older than Los Angeles itself. Over the postwar period, the core of this tiny, aged town was turning denser, in ways that defied the media's tale of suburbia's rise and complicated any conclusion about when farmlike fauna were driven from America's cities. Far into the postwar decades, these creatures persisted in San Gabriel.[5] Even as these animals endured, however, they acquired new rules, meanings, and politics. The Alvas' purchase and tending of barrio property illustrates these changes, as well as the impulses propelling barrio in-fill itself. In response to this in-fill, local pushes would arise for historic preservation and park making. These only aggravated the Alvas' feelings of being ethnically as well as

The Alvas' house in San Gabriel today. The house's position allowed for only a tiny front lawn, but the yard stretched back two hundred feet from the road. Henry and Beatrice originally owned the neighboring lot, where they built another house and sold it for extra income. (Photograph by the author)

economically marginalized. These passions would inform their travel out of town, in search of wilder places. They would also impel Bea, in particular, into leadership of a new movement for Native American tribal recognition.

Site of the Los Angeles region's first Spanish mission, San Gabriel touted itself as the ancestral egg not just of California's greatest city but of its earliest crops. The barrio area, lying near the old mission, had long provided living quarters for workers in the orange orchards and their families. Site of the Alvas' childhoods, it had included not only early twentieth-century immigrants from Mexico, like Bea's and Henry's fathers, but also others. An Irish family lived next door to Bea, and her mother was descended from Native California tribes. In this place, still quite rural into the 1930s, houses had no indoor toilets or electric lights. Bea's and Henry's families, like many of their neighbors, had kept hogs and cows as well as chickens. Embarrassing as this neighborhood was to the Anglo town fathers, they leaned on it not just for agricultural labor but for the tourist trade they sought. Until the Depression hit, San Gabriel ran a "Mission Play" romanticizing its Spanish colonial period and, starting in the early 1930s, an annual Fiesta, featuring a parade and street dancing. Henry Alva had met Bea while he was a Spanish/Indian dancer in the play; Bea, too, had drawn the spotlight as the first queen of the Fiesta.[6]

After four years of marriage, family ties pulled them back to San Gabriel in 1942, at Bea's insistence. Her own parents still lived there, as did Henry's mother, who tipped them off to a house for sale across the street from her. The Alvas bought it, then watched as new industries like Wham-O moved in over the postwar years, transforming their neighborhood in ways that clashed with the media imagery of "suburbia." Although many residents of the barrio still traveled to orchards to labor, increasingly this work required a season-long trek to California's Central Valley. Other jobs were meanwhile opening up for Hispanic workers in local factories and employment allied with the boom in home building. Henry, for example, worked in the lumber industry. As new landowners, the Alvas also followed relatives and neighbors in seeking to produce income from their property.

Their two adjacent lots near San Gabriel's center, only one with a house, had the 50' x 200' "homestead" dimensions long common in county subdivisions, with plenty of room for crops and backyard animals. Bea, like the wives of other better-off Mexican Americans, mostly stayed at home. In addition to the children, she tended a family menagerie of cats and dogs and smaller barnyard creatures: geese, chickens, rabbits, a piglet, even a goat (though no cow). She tried to plant some marketable crops as well: first corn, then tomatoes; many fruit trees; a grape arbor and a blackberry vine. With competition from a door-to-door vegetable salesman and grocery stores, she made few sales; she and her family wound up eating all the tomatoes themselves. Though giving up truck gardening, she nevertheless faced growing legal obligations in other realms of property upkeep.

Historians who have recently turned to studying these new rules on yard care and animal keeping have emphasized points that apply in the case of San Gabriel: their roots in public health law, as well as their disproportionate impact on minority communities and the less well-off. Most of the studies, focused on downtowns, date these initiatives to the early twentieth century or earlier. Yet the experience in San Gabriel suggests a different timing for Los Angeles suburbs. San Gabriel's Anglo-dominated garden club had pushed through a local weed ordinance in the 1930s that forced Bea to keep her property mowed. Once she and Henry could afford it, Bea eagerly hired someone else to do the clearing.[7] Only starting in the Depression did San Gabriel follow the lead of Pasadena and other area towns in gradually clamping down on local animal ownership. Beginning with a ban on swine, during the war they also outlawed all larger or noisier creatures—cows, horses, and roosters. Only after the war did they restrict goats, rabbits, and quieter fowl to pens seventy-five or one hundred feet from the home. The new rules effectively outlawed barnyard animals for the smallest property holders, though not for better-off barrio residents like the Alvas, with their double lot. The persistent crowing of roosters, remembered by Bea and other barrio residents, suggests that these ordinances, like others issued by San Gabriel's authorities, were not strictly enforced in this corner of town.[8]

In places such as San Gabriel's barrio, this benign neglect by the police, as well as the preference shown by the Alvas and their neighbors for such creatures, kept alive Anglo stereotypes of Mexicans as primordially attached to farm animals and countryside slums. Bea Alva recalled an additional purpose for these creatures: guarding property. For the Alvas, a "feisty" pet goose squawked and their dogs bellowed when strangers approached the house. But when money got tight, even birds like the Alvas' guardian goose could wind up on the dinner table. The dual significance of animals or fowl as both pet and potential meal could make for tough decisions. When the children took a liking to a baby chick or rabbit, Henry Alva felt more conflicted about its slaughter. Their goat, christened "Clara," provided a means to fun, as well as food. She was not just milked but fitted with a straw saddle so the children could ride her around the yard. Henry himself taught her to perform in front of family and friends, to "dance on her two hind legs" while he played castanets.

Henry and his pet goat acted out an ironic commentary on the contrast between his current work life and his youthful glory days. Then, his performance in the Mission Play had led him to fancy a future as a professional actor or Spanish dancer—a prospect that soon turned illusory. As a worker of Mexican ancestry with only a grade school education, Henry had relatively few choices of job. The rise of unions in the Los Angeles area nevertheless helped bring lumberyard employees like Henry higher wages as well as health and other benefits. Labor organizing in this and other building trades, pushed by the American Federation of Labor (AFL), proved especially effective in breaking Los Angeles's "open shop" reputation.[9]

Compared to the agricultural work done by an earlier generation of barrio residents, Henry's involved fewer contacts with what he or his fellow workers might call "nature." Working with cut timber, Henry and other members of the AFL Lumber and Sawmill Workers Union had little or no contact with forests or intact trees from which this lumber had been cut. However well they got to know this wood—its types and grains, its heft and hardiness—it remained almost as difficult for lumberyard workers to see the nature in lumber as it was for those at Wham-O to see it in a frisbee, not least because of their own handiwork.

At home, domesticated plants and animals took on new roles in the barrio's neighborhood, starting with the Old Mission Church. Over the postwar period, as the Alvas joined with other families to consolidate a local sense of community, the parish membership mushroomed. Church officers added a new worship hall and joined with other community groups to restore buried or neglected parts of the old grounds, including its historic flora.[10] Chief among these, beside "La Casa Ramona Adobe," reputed home of the fictional character Ramona, grew an old grapevine. With a nine-foot thick trunk, it supposedly had been planted by the founder of the San Gabriel Mission and was thought to have initiated California viniculture. Into the fifties, restoration advocates encouraged its upkeep, as well as public acquisition of a nearby "Chiate" pueblo and its gardens, said to be the site of the region's first orange orchard.[11]

Animals, too, received new church-related roles through the revival of a "Blessing of the Animals." A Catholic ceremony that had been a major task of Mission priests during the agricultural era of the nineteenth century, it was first reprised at the downtown Los Angeles Mission. San Gabriel's restoration of the Blessing of the Animals followed suit in 1951. It commenced in the fall, during the town's Fiesta, rather than in the spring, as had been traditional. In attendance now were mostly children, their parents, and their pets; the stroll to the Mission Chapel had become a "pet and costume parade." Barnyard creatures, such as cows, roosters, and goats, still made an occasional appearance—the Alvas' Clara among them. But by the midfifties, less farmlike domesticates dominated the procession, ranging "from the traditional cat, dog and guinea pig classifications to butterflies, pigeons and even moths."[12]

Bea Alva and her family did not identify that strongly with what many saw as a companionate effort to make the San Gabriel Mission area a historic architectural zone. Leading this endeavor were the Harvard-educated lawyer Thomas Workman Temple and his wife. The Temples organized lavish "pioneer" dinners among local groups of "compadrinos" and "compadres" who claimed descent from early Spanish colonizers, excluding many of the less-connected barrio residents, like Bea Alva.[13] Joining with Anglo leaders and downtown restauranteurs, they sought to apply a kind of land-use regulation already honed in cities of the Southeast and Southwest, most ambitiously in the wealthy resort town of Santa Barbara, some hundred miles to the west.[14] Not only did all architecture have to conform to the authentic Spanish style, with tile roofs and adobe materials, the street trees and shrubbery also fell under the proposed rules. All landscaping had to use either native or Spanish-imported plants. Impeded by San Gabriel's ethnic and class fractures, also by a continued push for tax-yielding industries like Wham-O, San Gabriel's architectural zoning proved more halting and less effective than in Santa Barbara. By the mid-1960s, the zoning that was finally achieved applied almost entirely to buildings; most historic horticulture had been lost.[15]

Downtown public park making proved even less of a local priority. By the time San Gabriel adopted a full-fledged land-use plan in 1949, the town owned two tiny plots designated as parks, only one of which had been formally developed. That one, the less-than-three-acre Smith Park, lay close to the downtown barrio yet was separated by railroad tracks and an industrially zoned belt. Undertaking their own recreational version of in-fill over the postwar years, town officials converted much of it into public swimming and wading pools. While barrio residents could then walk to the pool, the rest of the town's park making was devoted to the planting and enlargement of an eight-and-a-half-acre Municipal Park along the town's far southwestern edge, next to a newer subdivision of mostly Anglo homeowners. A succession of studies by La Casa de San Gabriel, a church-sponsored community center in the barrio, meanwhile noted the small size of the more centrally located park, which "could not accommodate all the children." Its tininess, coupled with the "small yards with little grass which surround many of the houses," the studies indicated, "force children onto the sidewalks or streets to play."[16]

The Alvas' arrangement of their two lots illustrates how economic pressures pushed barrio landowners to fill in their own property, shrinking play spaces. Unable to earn extra money from their tomatoes, they decided to make another use of their "homestead"-sized landholdings. They built and sold a house on their empty lot and sought permission for a small rental right behind their own home. Zoned as R-1, the Alvas' barrio property became subject to standards that kept out factories but also outlawed additional houses. The town zoning board repeatedly rejected their request for a variance; only at the end of the fifties did it finally relent. Meanwhile, San Gabriel's Mexican American barrio was continually threatened by proposals to redevelop it as an urban renewal project or to rezone it for more factories like Wham-O.[17] This kind of pressure reinforced a disillusionment with the local elites and their politics. Bea Alva and other residents were prompted to revive a sliver of San Gabriel's past with which they could more comfortably identify.

Bea and some neighbors began to explore an identity and politics that was not Spanish but Native American. They thereby joined an ongoing effort of California tribes, ever since losing much of their land in treaties negotiated with the U.S. government in the early 1850s, to receive further restitution. Until a check for $150 arrived from the federal government—probably in 1951, from its initial settlement with Mission and California tribes—Bea recalled only vague awareness of her mother's Native American ancestry. Apparently, Bea's mother and other remaining Gabrielinos around the mission had kept that heritage secret even within their own families.[18] Bea drew lines, for instance, between her own tastes and those of "the little old Indian lady down at the corner," who was willing to cook and eat wild jackrabbits. After the government check came, she started noticing traces of an Indian past around her barrio residence, manifestations made possible by local plants. Old "Indian baskets" made of native reeds turned up in a neighbor's house. Bea recalled the few strange words that her mother would utter—among them, the name of an irrepressible weed that continued to fester in Bea's backyard. Her mother had boiled the leaves of this native invasive to rub on her children's wounds. Singling out such floral memories, Bea began to see her past quite differently from the compadrinos who pushed for historic preservation in San Gabriel. At some critical turning point, the original padres metamorphosed from being her people's predecessors to being their enslavers.[19]

By the early sixties, Bea Alva had emerged as a leader of a Gabrielino band of Native Americans. The members met regularly in each others' homes, mostly in the San Gabriel barrio, and joined with other bands of California Mission Indians to press their case for land compensation. Like Bea, band leaders as well as members tended to be blue- rather than white-collar. Like the Long Island blacks who became involved in civil rights over the same period, their embrace of an identity politics had roots not just in shared lines of descent but, at least for leaders like Bea, in their home ownership in a particular part of San Gabriel. Ownership of barrio lots, even as it brought estrangement from town fathers, also nourished expertise and confidence in confronting officialdom.[20] By 1963 Bea Alva had emerged as the spokesperson for approximately one hundred Gabrielinos, joining the leaders of other Mission bands at the federal negotiating table. The Gabrielinos flourished anew, in part, by extending their membership to others claiming local Indian ancestry across the Los Angeles area.

Enabling their meetings, as well as Bea's own participation in powwows and settlement negotiations, was the new ease of travel ushered in by Los Angeles freeways. Yet the new Gabrielino leaders lived, for the most part, in the San Gabriel barrio. Though many roots of their movement lay in the postwar transformations of this metropolitan region, they gathered in this one central hub to rectify the uprooting of their forebearers from native lands.

As some barrio residents undertook this collective quest for historic recompense, they and others periodically ventured out to wilder locales. Seeking relief from the barrio's builtness, they were drawn, as well, by the prospect of engagement with a regional as well as a familial heritage. Henry Alva, uninvolved in the compensation effort, regularly headed out from the barrio to hunt. He and his buddies took weekend trips, often to Frazier Park, in the mountainous part of Kern County to the north. Hunting, long part of Californians' lives, was by this time less a necessity—at least for an employed barrio resident like Henry—than a way of recapturing the nature contacts of an imagined frontier. He was hardly the only Los Angeles union worker to find an appeal in wildness, as when AFL locals sponsored a marching troop of "wild animals" for the 1948 Labor Day celebration.[21] Enacting a masculine belonging not just to America itself, but to an American *West*, this immigrants' son joined a growing number of blue-collar as well as middle-class men who ventured out from suburban and urban areas with gun and deer license in hand.[22]

Henry also joined Bea and their children in forays out from the San Gabriel barrio into a wilder, more or less informal commons beyond. As new buildings squeezed the space around their property, they drove west to public beaches or east to what Bea remembered as "country," the hilly boundaries of the San Gabriel Valley rearing up around La Puente and Hacienda Heights. Carrying a lunch, they would follow an old rural custom. Without bothering to inquire whether the land was publicly or privately owned, they would "find a shady tree and have a picnic." Sometimes they went still farther, across the Mexican border to Baja California, following the same route that some of their parents had traversed decades before. They always drove and never flew, given the expense of international air travel. Once there, they pitched a tent on the beach, a practice prohibited in postwar Los Angeles's official parks.

Some of the Alvas' experiences were relatively unusual, yet on the whole, their interactions with flora, fauna, and land resembled those not just of their San Gabriel neighbors but of barrio residents across the basin, from

Chihuahuita in Pasadena to the Mexican section of Boyle Heights, in East Los Angeles. The changing ecology faced by barrio residents, from the in-fill of buildings to the shifting balance of fauna and to the irrepressible weeds in their backyards, left a subtle yet indelible imprint on their personal and social identifications, as well as their politics.

Residents of the many barrios of the Los Angeles basin shared a lack of influence with local officialdom, one that limited, among other things, their aspirations for keeping nearby land undeveloped and "open." There were some exceptions, from tiny Smith Park in San Gabriel to the larger Hazard Park, a twenty-plus-acre reserve in Boyle Heights. Yet in the early 1960s, barrio residents who might have wished for more public spaces could count on little outside support. Backing from the self-styled conservationists in the Sierra Club, for instance, seemed the remotest and most inconceivable option, not only because of formidable barriers of class and ethnicity. The generally small and concrete-laden barrio parks, not to mention the ongoing in-fill around them, made it more and more difficult for the residents themselves, much less Sierrans, to recognize anything in the barrio as especially natural. It is not surprising that the opportunity seized by Bea Alva for more collective and political self-assertion had little to say about vanishing species or wilderness and far more about an aggrieved people and a land utterly lost.

Farther to the south, in Lakewood, the Rynersons also became involved in local politics. They did so on behalf of, rather than in tension with, their own town hall. Like Bea Alva and other barrio residents, Jackie Rynerson did not wind up speaking out for nature as such, yet she too, along with other Lakewooders, confronted dilemmas that were not merely built but biotic. For many growing up in such places, including her own son, encounters with this biotic side catalyzed another trajectory—also politically significant—of a wilder nature's discovery.

Tamer Turf, Wilder Wishes

Jackie and Bud Rynerson's story of moving into Lakewood matches Levittowner and other eastern tales of the "move to suburbia" much more closely than does the Alvas'. Marrying during the war, then shuffling between rentals in Los Angeles and Long Beach, they bought their first house in Lakewood in 1952. There was, however, a key difference between the Rynersons' experience and that of the Alvas and many eastern suburban migrants. Unlike many people who moved to Long Island, but like most of those moving to Los Angeles's periphery between 1940 and 1960, neither

Jackie nor Bud had been born in that American region whose suburbs they sought. Jackie's family had immigrated from Paris, France, to industrial San Pedro in the 1930s. Bud had come to the West Coast while serving in the armed forces during World War II, after growing up on a farm in Iowa. These longer trajectories, as much or more than urban apartment living, informed their confrontations with the ecology of their new suburban neighborhood. They and other Lakewooders sought to cultivate and defend the nearby flora, fauna, and open spaces of their mass suburban development. They did so in ways that, for Jackie, carried over into the political arena, through the making of a new town government. Many children, on the other hand, found these domesticating endeavors less fascinating than what escaped their clutches: the town's wilder sides. The evolving experience of the Rynersons' son Steve illuminates how this suburban wild, combined with travels and an adolescent urge to differentiate, could yield convictions about nature's sweeping banishment from Lakewood that were in close keeping with Sierra Club traditions.[23]

The Rynersons and their three children moved to Lakewood from a house they had rented in North Long Beach. Looking past Lakewood's "cookie cutters" and scant landscaping ("really just a few bushes and some lawn"), they liked its "good schools," the garbage disposal, and the stainless steel sinks. But like many others, they thought it "nice that it wasn't like a full-blown city." Its "open feeling" amplified their sense of possibility: it was, as Jackie saw it, "the first house I lived in that I could do whatever I wanted whenever I wanted to." Once in their new home, the Rynersons' gendered division of upkeep hewed to the geographic contrast in their backgrounds. Former city dweller Jackie assumed most responsibilities inside the home, while former farm boy Bud became the family "gardener."

Mowing and fertilizing what lawn there was, Bud attempted to plant the rest of their 50' x 100' lot in grass. But it was all "just hard adobe clay," stripped by the builders of its top layer. He had to break it up with a rototiller and bring in additional topsoil to get grass to take hold. Against the advice of the Lakewood Nursery, Bud also "pig-headed[ly]" sought to put in fruit trees. Though "everybody in Orange County [not far away] had orange trees in their yard," Bud soon discovered why the local nurserymen were skeptical. To carve out enough room for the root balls, he had to rent an electric auger. Even then, "You'd get down two or three feet, it's like rock." After he managed to get a peach and an avocado sapling into the ground, their maturation was cut short by the inability of this "rock" to

The Rynersons' house in Lakewood in the early 1950s. The front yard was smaller than the ones in Levittown, and the back lawn had to be installed by the owner. (Jacqueline Rynerson Papers)

absorb water. Rains, when they did arrive, came in a deluge that did not subside. Water "just [sat] there for weeks" around the trunks. The problem was made worse by the builders' negligible grading of the lot, which prevented runoff. Bud's fruit trees succumbed, drowning. Other plants struggled, as well, partly because of the soil and drainage, and because the Rynersons were just acquiring the skills of local plant care.[24]

Eventually Bud regraded the entire yard. He was then able to plant a magnolia tree in the front and to keep most of the backyard in lawn grass. But he "never really had a garden"; he grew vegetables—carrots, radishes, lettuce—in planting boxes along the driveway. Those with slightly more favorable growing conditions, such as Ted and Shirley Schnee or Charles Haynes, did get gardens and fruit trees to grow, though it was "hard." Lakewooders mostly had to give up on the higher, denser vegetative cover that grew back East. Their suburban flora remained closer to the prairie that this southeastern section of the basin had once been.

People like Bud Rynerson refused to let the developers off the hook.

Still, in the process of cultivating their land, many Lakewooders came to see their efforts as pitted against more than just the builders' neglect. They wrestled against the land's rawness, against the very nature of the soil on their small lots. Seeking its cultivation, they, like Levittowners, imagined themselves as pioneers, only with a western regional twist. Bud recalled this work as, like the first Spanish settlers, wrestling with "adobe," what these first white Californians had "made bricks out of." Bud's checkered success with planting his yard made him more skeptical about the adaptability of basin land than his wife. Jackie, meanwhile, for reasons we will soon see, continued to voice another long-standing regional conviction, that the soil was "great . . . once it gets unlocked."[25]

Optimistic as Jackie remained about the flexibility of the local soil, she and other young parents were increasingly bothered by another problem only partly addressed by the builders: where Lakewood's children would play. Advertised promises about neighborhood public parks remained unfulfilled through the early 1950s. In stark contrast to Levittown developers, Lakewood's builders had held off from putting houses on three "designated" parks, but had neither donated nor developed the land. Only a single preexisting public park joined the informal commons that threaded through and around the thousands of private home lots where, early on, Lakewood children roamed. The Rynersons' and their neighbors' children were more likely to frequent land not formally developed as a park, such as that surrounding an old well, dubbed "the green grass." Another along the San Gabriel River bed was known as the "bamboo village" for its exotic invasives. Drainage ditches and basins, sprouting weeds from the water they pooled, also attracted children. But parents raised questions about the safety of these impromtu play spaces, especially after one child died when a ditch caved in.[26] A parental concern about play space was what spurred Jackie Rynerson's involvement in Lakewood's incorporation campaign.

The development's 1954 vote to incorporate under the "Lakewood Plan" marked a critical turning point in the history of Los Angeles's suburbanizing. Afterward, as outlying towns adopted the Lakewood model, contracting with the county government for many municipal services while gaining local control over land use, this western city's suburbs became as likely to incorporate themselves as those around cities in the East.[27] The plan forged a basis for those in this mass subdivision to join forces with some residents in nearby Lakewood Village, an older, wealthier neighborhood with large lots, lakes, a golf course, and lush and leafy greenery.[28] What led the village's Lakewood Taxpayers Association to welcome newer

Lakewooders like Jackie Rynerson on board the incorporation campaign was the steady postwar encroachment by urban and industrial neighbors and land users.

From 1951, the neighboring city of Long Beach turned territorial aggressors on the entire Lakewood area. Forecasting a demand for city services in the new Lakewood that only an established municipality could supply, Long Beach officials planned to annex Lakewood Village as well the more massive subdivision one chunk at a time, trusting they could play off older against newer inhabitants.[29] After the first neighborhood vote, in Lakewood Village in 1952, went in favor of annexation, Long Beach officials did themselves no favors by foisting unsavory land uses on Lakewood's periphery: a new "prison farm" and expansions of the Municipal Airport and the Douglass aircraft plant. As anger surged over these impositions on residential areas, members of the Taxpayers Association hatched their incorporation plan.[30] Pro-incorporation spokesmen warned about the oil fields on which the city of Long Beach depended for revenues. The reserves might soon be depleted, they argued, and annexation also opened doors to the encroachment of oil wells, whose unappealing look and smell were epitomized in nearby Signal Hill. As Lakewood was "a community of young," asserted one incorporation advocate, "annexation to an oil city" was simply "not desirable."[31] Similar concerns would echo basinwide by the midsixties, as a Los Angeles–area environmental movement firmly yoked together issues of industrial pollution and parks.

But in the early to midfifties, the dearth of parks in Lakewood seemed the more immediate and actionable concern; and Jackie Rynerson was hardly alone in prioritizing them. She and other incorporation advocates achieved their first victory in a vote to create an independent park district for the area.[32] These and other electoral accomplishments, including incorporation itself, came through a grassroots campaign in which volunteers like Jackie went around knocking on hundreds of neighbors' doors. And once the Lakewood Plan was approved in March 1954, Lakewood's new mayor and city council made a point of keeping the control over local green and open spaces for themselves. They did so even while contracting with the county or preexisting districts for other services, relieving the new town from having to run its own schools, fire and police protection, sanitation and flood control, even master planning and zoning. By contrast, Lakewood quickly drafted its own weed abatement ordinance to clear unkempt vacant lots and declared park making its "highest priority."[33] Though the town would take three years to acquire and develop the park sites reserved by its developers, by 1959 it had spent $2 million on recreation, parks, and parkways—twice its total annual budget and the largest annual category of expenditure.[34]

By 1961 Lakewood's new park system had come under the leadership of Jackie Rynerson herself. From before Jackie took over, park staff built swimming pools and ball fields on the town's new formal commons, and blanketed it with greenery. Contending with the same "dense soil with poor subsurface drainage" that Bud had encountered, their funds and timing brought advantages over any individual effort. Jackie's contrary recollection, of this soil's flexibility, was premised on a sprinkler system that ensured steady irrigation as well as grading and drainage ditches that whisked the excess into the San Gabriel River. It also rested on work done for her by the park board's team of professional landscapers and their underlings. They picked and planted the newer, more adaptable grass species just then becoming available and those trees that had worked in the older sections. They also plied new cultivation tools like soil conditioners and fertilizers. The results, a year-round, manicured greenery on these public lands, invited Lakewooders to relax, to forget about the difficulties of cultivating a similar look on their own lots. Too many weeds or bare spots, too much wildness, would have defeated this purpose. The place would have cried out for the task of taming. Instead, for many users it slid into a generically pastoral backdrop for the "function" of play. Imported gestures like "a graceful palm" marked an exotic contrast with counterparts back East—so, too, the names of the parks for Latin American revolutionaries like Simon Bolivar.[35] More so than in old San Gabriel, however, these signifiers of the park's western, regional identity were incidental to a larger domesticating project.

Such places did capture one side of that sensibility that would become known as "environmentalist": the provision and care of urban and suburban parkland. Yet to fully appreciate these local parks' contribution to suburban environmentalism, we need to consider the differences between adults' and children's experiences of them. For many of Lakewood's children, these cut grasses and trimmed trees set off, by contrast, those less tamed spaces that they found more intriguing. As one of these parks was being developed, Steve Rynerson and a friend preferred its less developed portion, where the lawn grass and other landscaping had not yet been installed. It was full of insects, grasshoppers and ants. The kids could "observe . . . and see what made them tick," or catch them and take them home in glass jars. And with the YMCA Indian Guides, he enjoyed visiting an abandoned lot with the foundations of an old house, but otherwise overgrown with weeds. It "wasn't as manicured and clean as a park" and was "perhaps . . . slightly hazardous," but he found it "more fun than going to the park." Lakewood's children, like those in many other suburbs, continued to be drawn to these wilder, less developed edges where a shopping mall or houses would soon go, but which in the 1950s were "not yet taken" by suburban building *or* cultivation.

After Lakewood incorporated, its domestic animals quickly came under the scrutiny of the new government, which passed a battery of ordinances already in place in other of the basin's incorporated towns. Dogs were to be licensed and vaccinated; chickens, rabbits, and other animals were limited but not banned. With the exception of "scientific or educational uses" (for example, in the case of parakeet fanciers), pets were restricted to five fowl or small animals per household. Some residents did keep chickens early on but then, "tired of" the mess and the upkeep, got rid of them.[36] The Lakewood government initially reserved a place for preexisting commercial agriculture in the new town. But it also maintained that the river should serve as a "natural barrier" to annexations by Dairy Valley, whose large, depastured herds were judged "incommensurable" with suburban residences. By the early 1960s, after all of its own farm and dairy lots were converting into houses, shops, or parks, the Lakewood council went so far as to prohibit the keeping of any creatures other than dogs, cats, and "certain birds."[37]

As for wilder birds and animals, their diminished numbers in such a densely built-over place as Lakewood did not vanquish them from residents' attentions or memories. Some, like gophers—a prairie holdover—gained notoriety for their "infestations" and for how their bites could pass along rabies. Less threatening, but also sometimes figuring as a "problem," were the occasional opossums and raccoons that wandered into backyards. Yet living in Lakewood and being committed to its cultivation by no means ruled out an appreciation of its wilder side. Jackie Rynerson kept a fond ear out for avian neighbors, its mockingbirds, which she found "wonderful singers." Her children's fascination could go still further. When Steve and the other Rynerson children discovered a bird with a broken wing in their yard, a sparrow or a mockingbird, they made a pet of the injured creature, naming it "Chirpy." As they learned, however, wild birds did not always relish being kept as pets. After being nursed back to health, "one day Chirpy flew away."[38]

As with the Alvas, the Levittowners, and so many other families in mass

Steve Rynerson and "Chirpy." (Jacqueline Rynerson Papers)

suburbs, the Rynersons' experience with nature was far from being circum-scribed by their town's boundaries. By means of Los Angeles's expanding network of freeways, they made regular trips from their homes to wilder landscapes. Often, they followed recommendations in *Sunset* magazine, to which Jackie Rynerson subscribed. For her family members, the ap-peal of agricultural lands like those in Dairy Valley ranked far lower than those where they camped, especially during two- or three-week summer vacations. They sped by Dairy Valley cows, orchards, and the pastures visited by the Alvas—what earlier might have been deemed "suburban countryside"—to more distant places that were more recognizably wild. At the same time, they stuck *more* closely than the Alvas to the formally designated public parks and beaches. Weekend trips took them mostly to sites around Los Angeles County, but for longer vacations they traveled farther. They frequented Big Sur and other California state land, as well as national forests, "Bryce Canyon or someplace like that," and the national parks that John Muir and others had made synonymous with wilderness: Yosemite and Yellowstone.

"Until we got a little more wealthy," the Rynersons were more likely to camp than to stay in a hotel. Jackie and her daughter had more reserva-tions about camping than did Bud and the boys—"It's not like crawling into your own bed at home. You don't have the privacy that you have at home." But "the beauty of the parks" held a special appeal for Jackie Rynerson. And the very openness of their tent, not just to other people but to the outdoors, added to that "different experience" that camping brought her. "Its just not the same . . . you can really appreciate your environment much better when you're that close to it. Once you go into shelter, like you know a hotel or something like that, well that's always nice, but you don't get the same feeling."

This "feeling," remembered as a closeness or intimacy with her "environment," was not just the effect of the woods or meadows in which they camped. It also came from a contrast with the Lakewood they knew so well. The enclosed bedrooms and bathrooms of their house, as well as the immense amount of labor they had invested in their yard and neighborhood park, had ensured a certain taming but also a flip of perspective. Their Lakewood home had become second nature to them. There, they could assume an insulation from other people as well as a nonhuman world that ensured their privacy and comfort but that could itself become unsettling. Now, less so than when they had first moved in, Jackie found it difficult to see or feel any nature there that seemed so pure or primary, unaltered by human influence or imprint. Yet she seldom reflected on this absence until in a place that yielded opposing impressions. Under the thinness of a tent roof, in locales where considerable human energy and effort had been expended to reduce the appearance of domestication, her relationship with the natural world back in Lakewood was revealed as alienated.

What was true for Jackie and Bud Rynerson was doubly so for their son Steve. He "lived for those vacations." As he entered his teen years and began to become acquainted with such beautiful and natural places elsewhere, he sometimes felt "depressed about the natural environment" across the Los Angeles basin. Part of what bothered him, he began to realize, was how many of the orange trees were disappearing. By the early sixties, when he and his family drove to the beach or to other parks, they passed fewer and fewer orchards. In 1966, at age fifteen, Steve took up a pastime with which his parents were unfamiliar: backpacking. His travels began with a brief trip with a family friend into the San Gabriel Mountains. Eager for more, he then took a longer journey up into the Sierra Nevada (High Sierra), sponsored by the San Pedro YMCA.

These adventures were transformative. "Completely awed by the drama" of Muir's mountains, he also felt a newfound removal from the "artificial environment" he was coming to understand that Lakewood represented. Increasingly, "What I felt in Southern California, in Lakewood was that it was an entirely human-created environment, that there was nothing in it that wasn't created by humans." In places where he had grown up, he realized, "it takes an effort to pay attention to the fact that you are on a planet that has a natural geography, weather, stars in the sky." Significantly, Steve Rynerson's growing emotional investment in these places he could only visit, so unlike Lakewood, was generational. His earlier fascination with Lakewood's wilder corners and creatures and with camping had nourished, but now seemed increasingly overwhelmed by, what he felt among the spectacular escarpments and vistas of the Sierras. His newfound, deepening thirst for its high bare slopes not coincidentally drew a bright line between his own aspirations and those of his parents. Such intergenerational dramas played out in many other of the basin's families, as many another youth "looked forward with great anticipation to any time when we could go to where the natural environment was dominant."

The experiences of both generations of Rynersons, as well as of the Alvas, point to a swelling "call of the wild" in postwar Los Angeles. Unleashed by those same cars and freeways that enabled the sprawl of housing, demands for trails and campsites surged, especially just beyond those lands most transformed by suburbanizing. By 1958, trail use near Los Angeles was the highest in the state—over five hundred times as intensive as that in California's far north. The popular wild that drew most residents of the Los Angeles area had close associations with pristine wilderness sought by Sierrans and with the increasingly comprehensive definitions then being compiled by the era's wildlife biologists via a formal science of ecology. But popular versions also could have defining features all their own. Criteria for finding this popular wild ranged from designated park boundaries to the recommendations of *Sunset* and other publications, to the visual standards set through media depictions like Disney's *Living Nature* series. Its roots were also experiential, in the contrast with more domesticated places and creatures. Memories of national parks (like those of the Rynersons) hinged not just on these magnificent landscapes themselves, but on their departure from the familiar, from that interweaving of houses and lawns, city and country, to which Lakewooders and others had become accustomed. This popular wild was ecological, nonetheless, in the looser and broader sense of the term, suddenly common around 1970. It was ecological, that is, because it asserted the import as well as the sharpness of distinctions between the artificial and the nature-made. Revealingly, son Steve was far more eager than his parents to take sides, to affirm the least tame creatures and settings as the most tantalizing.[39]

It hardly seems surprising that adults such as the Rynersons and the Alvas made so little of this wild in their own politics. Like most Americans, they traveled to these places as families or in other small groups, forging only the most tenuous social ties with other vacationers. The fast-growing Los Angeles chapters of the eastern-based Audubon Society and the West Coast–centered Sierra Club over the 1950s seemed to offer a more solid social basis for nature advocacy. But until these old-line conservation groups more actively pursued young suburb dwellers like Steve Rynerson, until they broadened their standards for land preservation beyond a purist confinement to the most remote public lands, the birth of environmentalism as a popular movement was forestalled. Growing initiatives of professional planners, from Los Angeles County's first Master Plan for Trails in 1956 to a 1960 study of California recreation, did urge that "open space" around Los Angeles "be obtained now." But in Los Angeles both the Sierra and Audubon chapters were slow to respond to these mounting calls for urban and suburban parks.[40] Only after powerful regional constituencies had coalesced for more ecological park making inside Los Angeles, thanks to a surging mobilization of its better-off suburbanites, did these avowedly conservationist groups hop on board. The postwar paths of Richard and Louise Lillard led them into the heartland of this ferment.

Nearby Nature as Privilege and Peril

The place where the Lillards lived for several decades after the war, a canyon known as Beverly Glen, lay in the foothills of the Santa Monica Mountains but also within Los Angeles's city boundary. Entirely private property until 1968, the Santa Monicas, with their steepness and rough topography, had long stymied agriculturalists and developers alike. Yet those same features made them, like the West Los Angeles over which they loomed, a new postwar frontier for the Los Angeles suburban elite. Their slopes and hilltops, as at the new extensions of Bel Air, offered spectacular views and wild chaparral right at one's doorstep. The Beverly Glen house where Richard Lillard moved in 1947, however, was tucked in a canyon, with far more chaparral than vista. For this reason, it also was within his financial means as an entry-level college instructor. The location was well suited to Lillard's passionate eye for wild nature—the result of earlier experiences.

Though born in Los Angeles, he had spent most of his boyhood on a farm outside Sacramento. He then earned a doctorate in the East and commenced a career of teaching college English, while writing books with nature-related themes such as *The Great Forest* (1947), a history of west-

The Lillards' backyard today. On Quito Lane, in Beverly Glen, the Lillards' lot still merges with hillside chaparral. (Photograph by the author)

ern woods from Indian times to the present. Immediately after its publication, he returned with his wife and child to California to take a teaching
job at the University of California, Los Angeles, and bought the Beverly
Glen house. It lay, he later reflected, in "a modern middle environment,
an old semi-tame, semi-wild hilly tract lying between primeval brush (and
groves of oaks and black walnuts) and farm-sized parking lots devoid of
green leaves (the towers of Wilshire Boulevard)."[41]

Living there, Lillard would undergo a mental journey along a reverse
course to that of Steve Rynerson. From seeking and appreciating a nature
seen as wild and remote, he would come to embrace and defend the natural in the near at hand. Enjoying the wild slopes of a canyon just beyond
his backyard, a purchased privilege, made such a journey far easier and
more likely than in places like Lakewood or San Gabriel. Among the hills
of West Los Angeles, which contained some of the city's best-off suburbs,
Lillard went on to become an early leader in the birth of a more explicitly naturalist politics of suburban homeownership. For the Residents of
Beverly Glen, a homeowner association he helped rekindle, and for the
members of the Federation of Hillside and Canyon Associations, whose
creation followed the Residents', a nearby yet wilder nature was precisely
what they saw themselves defending. Lillard's trajectory thereby paralleled
that of the Murphys on Long Island, albeit in the face of a starkly different
ecology and through the prism of a distinctly western regional identity.

Having divorced soon after purchasing the Beverly Glen house, he might
have wound up selling it had he not soon met Louise, then a French teacher
at Beverly Hills High School. At the time, Richard still tacked between the
city's edge and a historic gold standard of wilderness, Yosemite National
Park, where over summers he lived and worked as a "naturalist" tour
guide. Louise's course, on the other hand, closely corresponds to the classic trajectory of a move from the city to suburbs, more so even than those
of our other two Angeleno couples. Though her birthplace lay back East,
she had grown up in South Central Los Angeles, the downtown. By the
time she met Richard Lillard in 1948, she too was recently divorced and
once more living in rentals. They married about a year later in Yosemite's
outdoor chapel, then settled into Richard's home in Beverly Glen. More
explicitly and dichotomously than our other two couples, they agreed that
her persona was the more "urban and the social," his the more "out-of-
doors, nature-oriented," a script about gender roles that guided their division of labor within the household.

Although she worked full-time until their daughter was born about eight years later, Louise took charge of the house's interior, just as Bea Alva and Jackie Rynerson had done. The "vaguely Spanish" structure was already twenty years old and "very run down," but their salaries as public educators left few funds for repairs. Whereas Richard reveled in its physical isolation near the end of poorly paved Quito Lane, Louise found its "very rural," "country" atmosphere more of a burden. She grumbled about the dearth of stores nearby and the distance to the supermarket and mall. Where they lived also literally made her sick. Afflicted with asthma since childhood, Louise had worsening bouts, blamed on molds that flourished in the narrow little valley's dampness and on the pollens from the "native plants" of the chaparral. From Richard, she nevertheless gleaned an appreciation for such "natural" settings and the "serenity, inner security, and contentment" they could bring. "It was a completely new environment for me and I found it delightful and amazing."[42]

As Richard assumed responsibility for the yard, part of the spectacle for Louise was Richard himself. Louise marveled at his "almost . . . sensual pleasure in watching plants grow"; "I just never knew anyone cared that much." In the Sierra Nevada, with its old-growth forests, he had witnessed a nature that remained nearly unworked, but through which he could only stroll. On his own property, he came to appreciate another way of knowing nature, through hands-on cultivation of his own flora. For what residents of Lakewood might label more perfunctorily as "yard work," Richard Lillard had another name: "personal plant culture." As "farming becomes mechanized," he reflected, it was the "home garden [that] remains the one place where specialities are lovingly raised," where "personal plant culture" could thrive. The inspiration for his early horticultural hobby came from aristocratic gardens he had visited in Europe and from the Huntington estate in San Marino, "the best thing in So. California." Tacitly distinguishing his own turf from the typical suburban yard, he emulated the "discrimination and good taste" of these elite gardens, which he found "aristocratic in the strong, good sense of the word."

On terraced ground, Richard tilled a small lawn of St. Augustine grass and planted around it a host of exotic species: a tahiwhi tree from New Zealand, a Chinese crepe myrtle, a Paraguayan philodendron, Japanese camellias, and a dawn redwood, a collector's item only recently discovered in far-away China. "A circular yard inspection," he later wrote, "is for me a kind of botanical tour of the globe."[43] Like so many Angelenos, he still grew some of his own corn, beans, and tomatoes, yet these plants lay far down the list of his horticultural priorities. Sustaining certain professional disappointments and realizing that his and Louise's teacher salaries placed the richer and more spectacular lifestyles of his neighbors out of reach, he found, in the intimacy of "personal plant culture," a saving counterbalance. "I'd rather be inches away from the stamens and corollas of my fuchsias [visible from his living room window] than leagues from the mere outline of Catalina Island," as viewed from the loftier homes of Bel Air. Against the grain of the materialist society he saw around him, Lillard resolved to "live deeply" through care for a nature near at hand.[44]

For Lillard, personal plant culture was more than a hobby; it became part of a larger quest, pursued chiefly on his suburban home lot. Traditional church or theology had little hold on either him or Louise, yet their Yosemite marriage pointed to a faith in the transcendent imprimatur of the natural world. While "in the long run few things matter," Richard decided, "conservation" did. It was, in his view, nothing short of "a religion." His words, alongside what we have seen of the importance of groups like Long Island anthroposophists, would seem to confirm environmentalism's religious roots emphasized by Thomas Dunlap, at least for some environmental activists.[45] At the same time, we do well to distinguish between the different varieties of faith that could be involved. By definition of this book, it was not so much his Yosemite sojourns as his more cityward pursuit of nature's ways that made Lillard an environmentalist. In so doing, he also took up faiths of another kind, not necessarily as religious or transcendent. With the greater ecological authenticity prescribed by the Nature Conservancy for parks, with the penchant for suspicion about the dangers of chemicals like DDT, preferences for the natural over the artificial trod into more mundane realms of actual or testable fact. The faith involved was more akin to that in a sweeping scientific hypothesis: in the greater protection that nature parks afforded local wildlife and groundwater or the lesser damage that came from biological pest control. *This* kind of faith, more so than its transcendent twin, would provide the ideological underpinnings for the popularization of environmental politics.

Lillard, as a professional humanist, left a revealing record of the bridges he and others were forging between these two sorts of faith during the 1950s. Seeking to translate his sense of nature's sacredness into daily and personal routines, he turned his Los Angeles suburban lot into a site for experimenting with practices of upkeep that seemed more nature-friendly. His search echoed that of a contemporary campaign by California conservation officials to promote how "every person has a direct stake in . . .

[the state's] resources," but with a twist. Lillard's "deeply lived" conservation came less from the vantage point of the state than that of the private individual, caring for land that he owned, but on which he also lived. The inspiration came from natural cycles, among them how "every fallen leaf has its place in tomorrow's soil." Such a faith stirred inevitable questions of natural fact—for instance, What was the most natural soil for a given kind of leaf? But sometimes the answers seemed clearer, as in the case of emanations from his own body or yard, usually carted away as "waste." Then, those acts and consequences that seemed naturally obligatory could become imbued with a sacredness approaching that of Yosemite itself. Hence, "My cesspool is my catacomb, my compost heap my shrine, my humus of leaves, salad for the land, as my prayer."[46]

In seeking more natural ways of caring for his urban-edge land, Lillard often defined these vis-à-vis the latest turns in horticultural practice, honing an anticonsumerist suspicion. The many "short cuts" sanctioned by the nurseries of the time really turned out to be "long ways around." Instead of purchasing mature nursery-grown trees, which to him often looked sickly, Lillard preferred to grow his trees from saplings or even, in the case of the Pennsylvania oak, from an acorn seed. He shunned commercial fertilizers, resorting instead to humus and compost. He gave up on pesticides after trying DDT on a moth infestation and finding it did not work. Though it is difficult to say how many Angelenos shared Lillard's fervor for chemical naturalism, in the years prior to *Silent Spring* certainly the organic gardeners did. Here, Lillard enjoyed the company of many other enthusiasts across Los Angeles County. By 1955, the county had eight organic gardening clubs, more than any other county in the nation.[47]

Lillard's personalized conservation not only guided his gardening, it also spurred a waxing recognition of the wilder plants and creatures living nearby. Compared to counterparts in Lakewood or San Gabriel, yards like his, on the edge of a capacious, unplowed spread of chaparral, invited a greater diversity of birds and other wildlife. In the vicinity of houses, the chaparral was not exactly pristine but easy to know, since Lillard could watch it year-round and close up. By the midfifties, his diary entries revolved more and more around the coyotes, deer, raccoons, and many other wild animals that strayed into his yard or that he surprised while walking in the surrounding brush. He began to ruminate about creatures he never saw, but which he knew once lived there: ringtails, cougars, and condors. His fascination grew with how, as wild creatures and people adjusted to one another, some species could actually become semidomesticated, drawn into a less timid dependence on human neighbors. A pair of blue jays nesting near his house, after he and his family started to feed them, lost much of their fear of humans. To his and Louise's delight, the birds eventually learned to eat out of their hands. Richard became aware that other, errant flora were making themselves at home among his cultivated plants. Whereas in 1955 his plant list for the yard included only what he and others had planted, by 1960 he had started a separate list of weeds, including the natives as well as the imported invasives.[48] His more intimate, detailed knowledge of the wild brought new appreciation of how it could prosper not just in distant, isolated reserves, but, at least in pieces, alongside or within the civilized.

Sometimes, though, when the wild intruded upon his plans, Lillard felt a resurgence of his own "frontier bent." When deer wrought havoc in his carefully tended yard and garden, Lillard's first reported response was to take up a gun against them, as his farmer-father might have. But "a bureaucracy stood in the way of my revenge," requiring a "depredation" license. Moreover, his wife and neighbors were dead set "against any gunplay on Quito, any killing of animals. . . . Since I didn't own a gun and didn't want to buy one and have it around, I gave up on the whole idea" and put up a five-foot-high fence instead. This decision, as he saw it, entailed a self-domestication, the achievement of a higher, more mature class of manhood. For Henry Alva, hunting had meant assimilation into more of a working-class American masculinity. Richard Lillard, by "relinquish[ing] revenge . . . became a better man."[49]

Hillside chaparral threatened more than people's gardens, however; it also posed dangers to their houses. Apparently unbeknownst to Lillard, timber-wrecking tumult came naturally to the hillsides of the Santa Monicas. Every thirty years or so, roiling infernos had swept through the combustible thickets of manzanita and chamise in the dry seasons, triggered by lightening in prehistoric times, later by human ignition. Burned-off flora then enabled mammoth mud slides, especially during Southern California's intermittent deluges of rainfall.[50] Beverly Glen and other Santa Monica hillsides had been spared such cataclysms over the 1940s and into the early 1950s, as luxury home building there had moved into high gear. Terraced lots and houses were gouged out across the mountains, including up past the Lillards' property on Quito Lane. But in mid-January 1952, the hills' natural instability returned with a vengeance.

A storm blowing down from the northern Sierras pummeled Los Angeles with over seven inches of rain, causing the worst floods since 1938. Torrents rushing down the canyons sloshed free any and all loosely packed soil. A half-million cubic yards of mud and debris slid into Los Angeles city streets, closing the Pasadena and Ventura Freeways. Almost two hundred tons of it slumped down the steep side of Beverly Glen gulch into the Lillards' yard, submerging Richard's five years of planting "improvements" under a thick layer of brown muck. Though the house remained intact, the garage door was knocked in. Never had the barriers the Lillards cultivated between their home and the chaparral beyond seemed thinner or more vulnerable. Richard was "devastated" by this setback; he remembered Louise, too, as being distressed. The Lillards got off easy compared to neighbors whose homes were completely immersed in mud "that seemed to move like a living thing."[51]

The collective response brought pause to a refrain of cultural and neighborhood criticism in Lillard's diary: suddenly, neighboring turned vital and authentic. An all-day work party "brought out scores . . . with shovels and pickaxes to help dig out five or six houses caught in mud slides." It was hard to miss the weather's contribution to the disaster. But scanning the hills, Richard early on surmised that only those streets and houses overhung by new construction, like his own, had suffered landslides. Joining with nearby neighbors, Lillard sued Quito Lane's recent developer. His and other lawsuits also provided the nuclei for a revival of the area's neighborhood association, dormant since the 1930s. In this physically isolated corner of Greater Los Angeles, a disaster, part natural and part human, had tied together canyon, society, and his own life in one neatly integrated bundle: "It was an invigorating extension of home place to canyon, of self to society." Especially for Richard, diverted from repair of his own grounds to "many night meetings, much phoning," it reprised an older regional heritage, a western Americanness with which he could heartily identify. The first president of a resurrected Residents of Beverly Glen, Lillard saw himself as revivifying that frontier democracy once celebrated by Frederick Jackson Turner.[52]

Over subsequent weeks, Lillard's neighborhood association joined together with thirteen others to form the Federation of Hillside and Canyon Associations, from its beginnings a powerful force in Los Angeles politics. The political clout that San Gabriel's barrio residents had not enjoyed even at the town level and that Lakewooders had gained only through incorporating, the Federation exercised over a power center that to the other two communities had seemed utterly distant and unapproachable—Los Angeles City Hall. Its first victory, a grading ordinance that inaugurated the city's regulation of hillside development, did not come without a struggle. The real estate and building industries made the new cut-and-fill rules "the most viciously opposed piece of legislation in recent city council history." At one point they threatened "a picket of 500 bulldozers around city hall!" But in the face of disasters starting with the 1952 landslide, the Federation effectively marshaled the very nature of Los Angeles' hills on its own behalf. They did so through their own geologists and other experts alongside a highly influential assertion of self-interest. Uniting many of the wealthiest neighborhoods "from Cahuenga Pass to Bel Air," trotting out celebrity-residents like film maker Howard Hawks, the Federation won over the media as well as Los Angeles's political elite. Over the rest of the fifties, as it took on issues from subdivision regulation to minimum lot zoning to fire prevention, it only gained in size and clout.[53]

Historian Mike Davis has taken the Federation and its homeowner allies to task for the huge class and racial distortions they brought to city politics. So effective was their lobbying that it steered the city's expenditures away from downtown neighborhoods housing ever poorer minorities, where the hazards and needs remained far greater. Among the Federation's accomplishments, in the face of successive home-destroying blazes, it helped reduce insurance rates for new houses whose siting seemed to beg for another firestorm. Bolstering the "perverse" incentives of federal disaster relief programs, it successfully pushed for, among other policies, an expansion of the city's weed clearance program to flammable hillside brush. Brimming with legal and political expertise and Hollywood addresses, its board seemed to represent the most "restrictive" and "exclusive" Los Angeles neighborhoods, where the properties were large and the owners all wealthy and Anglo.[54]

The Lillards, though represented by the Federation, saw their own lower-rent Beverly Glen differently. There "country club types" met up with older "hillsiders" as well as younger people of more middling or lesser wealth associated with Los Angeles's burgeoning schools. In stark contrast to Bel Air, the square mile surrounding the Lillard's home encompassed "a healthy diversity of incomes, interests[,] vocations and ages, of national, racial, religious and education backgrounds." It even had a "full share of temporary residents," renters whom the "Residents of Beverly Glen" welcomed into its fold, unlike many other federated groups. A reporter visiting in 1965 confirmed Lillard's observations about class blurring in Beverly Glen, a "strange cool bed . . . of local Bohemia"; where "a man from a fancy ranch house" could borrow kitchen spices from "the girls in the tickytack shack on the other side" of his street, it was "difficult . . . to notice the forest for the free spirits."[55]

Privileged as its membership and advocacy were, the Federation had a less class-specific meaning for Lillard, one that illuminated its vital contribution to the making of a more encompassing environmental ideology around Los Angeles. A new "mouthpiece" had emerged not just for one neighborhood, or even, like Lakewood, a new "city," but for a place defined by "hillside" and "canyon," its enveloping natural commons. Just as it was impossible to separate Bel Air housing values from the Santa Monica heights where this real estate sat, so the Federation turned the politics of homeownership into a forceful voice in Los Angeles–area politics for this mountainous terrain. A certain denial was also involved. Though elite homeowners wanted the hills "uncrowded," they still favored the private "quality hillside development" they themselves enjoyed, even as they sought public aid in taming the landslide and fire threats to their homes. Nevertheless, a new front had opened in the politics of nature preservation around Los Angeles, paralleling Lillard's break with the ideas of John Muir by 1955.

Muir and his admirers, Richard decided, were "socially immature." He preferred the perspective of Henry David Thoreau or Andre Gide who "balance . . . things well," "the naturalist [who] know[s] something of the humane world . . . of private love and public causes," as well as "the humane man [who] know[s] something of the nature he makes his setting."[56] Like the Federation itself, this former Yosemite nature guide was on his way to becoming an advocate for the wild not just "out there" in the High Sierra, but within Los Angeles's city limits around his hillside home.

As Lillard and Federation colleagues formulated their political defense of a suburban wild, children and adults even in less privileged suburbs such as Lakewood gravitated toward appreciation of a wilder nature. Over the 1950s, Los Angeles's suburbs—inside its city limits as well as outside— were forging eager constituencies for a more comprehensive politics of nature's defense, one that could span the entire metropolitan region. Such a politics would come closer to this book's definition of environmentalism, in part because of its widening expectations about the class of suburbanite willing to support it. But to unite those from this diverse a range of neighborhoods, more genuinely public-minded organizations were required, as well as a widened purview of which parks were in need of defense. After all, the early Federation was avowedly a self-interested lobbying arm of the most elite homeowner associations. And Los Angeles–area conservationist groups like the Sierra Club, while active in the defense of federal reserves, took a while to awaken to threats to the more cityward or downtown parks. Only in the mid-1960s did the agendas of these groups substantially converge.

Preservation's Cityward Turn

For this more broad-based and broad-minded politics of parks to consolidate around Los Angeles, some supportive changes had to occur. Wealthier homeowners needed a reason to forsake the "uncrowded" private developments first pushed by the Federation and make the leap to favor public purchase. They also had to find ways of politicking for parks that were *not* those of the homeowner association, that emphasized a more regional scale of need, while sidestepping suggestions that private or neighborhood interests were at stake. As for conservation groups like the Sierra Club, they too had to confront and at least partly surmount their own biases, first of all, against a wild that was less remote. On this front, the struggle for a new public park in the Santa Monicas—at once suburban and wild—offered an important stimulus for agenda change and coalition building. While some Sierrans also began to back parks whose nature remained considerably tamer, here they faced another barrier: their own club's tradition of racial exlusion. For similar reasons, Los Angeles's suburbanizing continued to confine blacks and Hispanics to those neighborhoods where the visibly wild was hardest to find. Sierrans' emergent defense of more cityward public lands helped stimulate tentative coalitions across racial and ethnic lines—even if only a few in the predominantly Anglo movement for nature preservation participated.

The idea of a public park in the Santa Monica Mountains dated back to Frederick Olmsted Jr., but what brought it to fruition, as in the case of the Fire Island National Seashore, was a fight against a road. Ever since San Marino had headed off a local extension of the Pasadena Freeway in the 1930s, their routes had been a bone of contention for the wealthiest and best-connected Angelenos.[57] But so vague was the initial announcement of new freeways through the Santa Monicas by the three-county Metropolitan Transportation Engineering Board in 1959 that there was little outcry. Three years later, when road planners finally announced that the new West Side Freeway would run "smack through the heart of fashionable Brentwood," it spurred not just outrage, but for the first time in Los Angeles road battles, a nature-protecting alternative.[58]

Energized by the freeway plan, Marvin Braude, a 44-year-old economist living in nearby Westwood, culled together a new group—the Santa

Monica Mountain Park Association—to lobby for a public preserve. Instead of turning over the twenty thousand hilly acres west of the San Diego Freeway to private developers, the future envisioned by both the city and the Federation, Braude suggested converting it to public ownership. Five times larger than Griffith Park, then Los Angeles's largest, the proposed park would have enjoyed the distinction of being the nation's largest urban reserve of public land. Only in corners of the proposed park would the bars against construction and usage be as strict as the "roadless" standards being argued, around this same time, for New York's Fire Island. But the justification was similar: "If we do not have the foresight to act now," Braude declared, "neither we nor coming generations will have open spaces for beauty, recreation and relief from urban sprawl." The plan sparked immediate enthusiasm in the mostly well-to-do homeowner associations closest to the park, from Brentwood's to those united in the Hillside and Canyon Federation, including Beverly Glen's. Lillard eagerly followed the press coverage, clipping newspaper articles.[59]

For all its appeal to concerns about "urban sprawl" and "open space," Braude's first proposal faltered badly. Too many people suspected that the park would formalize a natural commons only for well-off Westside homeowners, with those in other corners of the city footing the bill. The residents of distant towns, whose taxes were supposed to help finance the park, accused Braude and his allies of "want[ing] to keep their backyards vacant at public expense." They called instead for "neighborhood parks," less big and less wild, but at their own "people's doorsteps."[60] Accepting this logic, the Los Angeles County Board of Supervisors unanimously rejected the Mountain Park Association's initial plan. They proposed, instead, that the funding come from the state government. The park idea was then incorporated into a statewide park bond issue already recommended to appear on the ballot in the November 1964 election.

Whereas a sizable New York State Park bond had won passage four years earlier, California's versions were hardly a sure bet. Its electorate had narrowly rejected just such a park fund in 1962. This time around, though, as mountain park advocates geared up for the statewide vote, they took care to diffuse the neighborhood and class politics on which the Mountain Park Association's plan had foundered. A new advocacy group, the Friends of Santa Monica Park, helped sidestep accusations that theirs was merely a self-interested, property-owner campaign. Downplaying support from park-side homeowner associations like the Federation, the Friends group accentuated the park's potential access to drivers from elsewhere. This "last remaining undeveloped frontier" of the Los Angeles area, it argued, "lies within approximately one-half hour's driving distance of 25% of the state's population." Seeking support from myriad statewide groups, Friends also diverted attention from elite homeowners' self-interest by highlighting the nature to be preserved. To do so, it successfully marshaled the assistance of Angeleno scientists and conservationists. The local Audubon chapter took up the task of "acquaint[ing] the public with the geography, flora and fauna." Among the conservation groups joining this new nexus was the Sierra Club's Los Angeles chapter, otherwise still only wading into Los Angeles city and county politics. Following the successful statewide vote, Sierra supported the Friends in a letter-writing campaign aimed at both the city council and the state capital to ensure that the Mountain Park proposal stayed on course.[61]

For the Sierra Club, as well, this engagement was something of a breakthrough. Sierrans' willingness to shift their eyes and political agendas cityward had only just emerged, considerably lagging behind Lillard's own mental passage. But by the late 1950s, the Los Angeles chapter's "conservation" agenda-setters had begun to scrutinize Los Angeles County decision making regarding dumps, water pollution, and parks.[62] By no coincidence the inclusiveness that dawned was not just in regard to lands needing preservation but, at least tentatively, to those who counted as conservationists, and thereby might be admitted as members.

On questions of membership, barriers of class proved more quietly surmountable than those of race. As late as 1959, the Los Angeles chapter debated and rejected the membership application of a black woman, though she was an "ardent and experienced hiker and car camper" and "interested in conservation." An appeal to the club's San Francisco headquarters did resolve the controversy in the woman's favor. But the main office also pledged not to "aggressively seek the kinds of membership that will demonstrate religious or racial diversity as diversity."

Despite Sierra's less-than-ardent pursuit of racial diversity, its agenda continued to become more emphatically open, especially in terms of the varieties of nature whose protection the club sought. By the mid-1960s, along with their backing of the Mountain Park, Sierrans were joining campaigns for parks near the city's very heart.

In 1965, while Watts still smoldered from shocking riots that had left 34 dead, the conservation committee of Sierra's Los Angeles chapter helped spur a new campaign to defend urban parks, including those around the city's downtown barrios. It turned out that only 4 percent of Los Angeles city land was devoted to public parks, the least among America's biggest metropolises.[64] Among these preexisting, imperiled places was Hazard Park, in East Los Angeles's Boyle Heights, a 25-acre city park aside a Mexican American barrio—a neighborhood resembling that in downtown San Gabriel. Menacing Hazard was a plan to redistribute park resources to the wealthy Westside, brokered by its councilwoman in 1962. The deal would bring a "major" recreational park to her district but raze much of Hazard Park. In its stead, a new Veterans' Administration hospital, originally sited for West Los Angeles, was now to be built.

In May 1965, "unexpected" protests blossomed into a picket line outside the Westside councilwoman's Bel Air home. Organizers of a "Save Hazard Park Association," mostly neighborhood residents, put the matter in terms that Los Angeles Sierrans, undergoing their own ideological ferment, could now embrace. "Our Eastside district is the lowest in home valuations, highest in number of children per family," one local park supporter bemoaned, "yet this is the district that is plundered and given a push towards 'Asphalt Jungle' conditions."[65] Joining with a Hispanic residents' association, Sierra Club members wrote letters and spoke out at public meetings. They did so in support of not only Hazard Park but also several other threatened Los Angeles city preserves. Admittedly, Sierrans' advocacy often bore the stigmatizing inflections of the outsider: for instance, that exposure to "the out-of-doors" could stymie crime and delinquency. Eastside locals, jarred into full-time activism by the condemnation effort, more readily expressed positive sentiments about Hazard Park itself: " 'You get a feeling for the place.' " Where these very different brands of activism agreed was in the need to protect the park's "rolling hills and beautiful trees," however unwild, for the pleasant human experience they afforded. Hazard Park was one place in the barrio where residents might find a "peace and delight" that was, for Sierrans as well, what nature's presence promised.[66]

This kind of park advocacy could do little for barrios such as San Gabriel's, already shorn of most open land. Nor did it have much to say about the informal commons around places like Lakewood, only bits of which became parks, as developers gobbled up the rest. What it did mean was that the Sierra Club that Steve Rynerson would soon join had a much altered agenda from ten years earlier. Far more engaged with the park and other dilemmas attending urban and suburban environments, it was finally realizing the mobilizing potential of those many grassroots initiatives springing up in such places, basinwide. The growing ranks of activists were made up of "conservationists," but as Richard Lillard noted by 1966, many more besides: "Of Utopists, of thoughtful historians, of perennial individualists, of artists in living, of appointees to relatively powerless public commissions, and idealists . . . those who would discourage change and close down motion."[67]

What should we call this shared sense of endeavor, reaching from the zoning and preservation politics of towns like San Gabriel and Lakewood to the defense of wilder enclaves such as Beverly Glen and to the protection of the region's most isolated and inviolate wildernesses? Today, the answer seems obvious: we call it "environmentalism." But in 1966, that name was just starting to occur to its adherents. What persuaded activists that a new name was in order, that around Los Angeles "conservationist" no longer sufficed, was that imperiled land became yoked to other worrisome trends, most pivotally, the basin's long-sickening air.

 **Chapter 7**

Anxious about the Air

Here in Los Angeles, we have,
in effect, lighted a gigantic bonfire.
—Smog Brief No. 12

In late July 1943, a "low hanging cloud of acrid smoke" gathered over downtown Los Angeles. It was the fourth such "gas attack" that summer, "by far the worst." "Thousands of persons coughed, cried and sneezed" throughout the morning until the cloud broke up around noon. "What is that?" wondered commuters to downtown jobs, among them, Jackie Rynerson. "Smog," Angelenos called it by the war's end, a fusion of "smoke" and "fog" initially thought to be the same as that gusting along the streets of New York and Pittsburgh. Over the next few years, however, Los Angeles's billowing flumes defied the scientific and policy tools forged on air back East. The search for explanations and solutions forced a bewildered, angry reckoning with the new kind of city this corner of "Southern California country" was becoming, suburbs and downtown alike.[1]

As the caustic clouds swept suburbward, up the valleys and heights where so many had sought removal from factory and city, smog spawned a historic rethinking of the nature of air pollution. Over the years, Los Angeles taught Angelenos, along with the rest of the nation and the world, just how insidious and far-reaching a metropolis's impact on its atmosphere could become. The responses here, from scientific discoveries to a more delocalized system of monitoring and control, amounted to a new way of folding flame as well as air into human culture. Even as Angeleno-derived knowledge and solutions began to be transported elsewhere, more locally the basin's aerial woes prompted a further transformation. As on Long Island, across Los Angeles's spread city a chemical naturalism gained early traction, hastening the amalgamation of a new, overarching ideology of nature advocacy.

The first recorded image of smog, downtown Los Angeles, 1943. (Los Angeles Times Collection, Special Collections, University of California, Los Angeles)

Similar to Long Island's aquifers, if atop rather than below the land's surface, the atmosphere of Los Angeles had been largely taken for granted by earlier generations. Hovering inconspicuously over the basin's many suburban microenvironments, it mingled their releases with little ado until the 1940s. Then, suddenly, the precipitation of smog brought Angelenos face-to-face with the long-building burden they had placed upon the air as a receptacle for their wastes. Over these same years there was groundwater seepage around Los Angeles, as well, yet with less traumatic effect than in a place like Long Island because of the basin's dependence on distant water supplies. Instead, the tainted atmosphere was what thrust questions about pollution to the front and center of the city's postwar suburban politics.

Grounding the surprise and dismay with which many basin residents greeted smog through the fifties was the lingering assumption that theirs was still, fundamentally, a rural place. Sustaining this attitude, the dispersion of basin communities from the late nineteenth century onward had enabled an isolation of Los Angeles's major industrial corridors, even as its production surpassed that of any other city in the American West. As development proceeded in the downtown area but also out from the city limits—most notably in the southeast around Long Beach—residents in suburban Bel Air and Pasadena, and farther up the San Gabriel Valley, remained almost unaware of the expanding plants and their damaging effects. Even though these northerly communities encircled the same downtown as Los Angeles's burgeoning industry, for decades their inhabitants saw little reason to worry about the coincidence. They trusted that their own higher elevations and the miles-thick swathes of intervening land shielded them from any noxious fumes. Smog's speedy foray up the channel of the San Gabriel River dashed these presumptions. It served as an alarming reminder that industrial environs like Long Beach or the downtown were far more inextricably bound to suburban enclaves than their residents had imagined. More than that, smog's ambit recast the postwar understanding of Los Angeles's position within Southern California as a region. Beyond the city's limits, as its far-flung industry was shown to be physically yoked to its most prized residential havens, all these places were revealed to be parts of a vast metropolitan area ever more set off from the countryside for which Southern California had been known. As the smog crept farther and farther out, it raised questions about how rural even this larger region remained. Swirling into neighboring counties such as Orange and Ventura by the early sixties, smog seemed poised to ruin the pastoral repute of Southern California as a whole.[2]

As it turned out, the region's distinctive qualities of climate contributed to the precociousness of Los Angeles's aerial troubles. Los Angeles may have gone first, but other Sunbelt cities, with their year-round warmth and sunshine, soon followed, significantly ahead of Long Island. Even after the U.S. Environmental Protection Agency tackled smog nationwide from the 1970s onward, ozone levels in California and other Sunbelt states continued to top the national charts, rivaled only by air closer to the largest northeastern metropolises.[3] One of the ironies of Los Angeles's environmental history is that its early confrontation with smog owed so much to the natural features John Muir had fingered as its "wildness": the "sunshine" and air-trapping "mountainous rims."

Los Angeles's unique agglomeration not so much of people as of burning practices was what made it, in the 1940s, the first of America's Sunbelt cities to succumb. What postwar Los Angeles shared with late twentieth-century Houston, its successor as the nation's leader in ozone pollution, was not only a warm climate but also a dependence on locally extracted fuel. From early on, to a historically unprecedented degree, Angeleno fires devoured neither coal nor wood, but petroleum. Though the history of Los Angeles smog has emphasized cars as the main culprit,[4] its early intensity, like that of Houston today, owed a heavy debt to its oil industry. As important, Angelenos of all sorts continued to treat their atmosphere like Long Islanders did their aquifers and early western cattlemen did the prairie—as a free and open range. Into the mid-twentieth century, they felt few compunctions about their fires, however open and roaring, however many tons of smog-making compounds were loosed.

Smog forced a reevaluation of these practices, starting with assumptions about tainted air that tacitly undergirded them. Early observers thought air pollution to be easy to see and locally confined. But the human-made precursors of smog turned out to be invisible, even if smog itself was not. They traveled with surprising ease, not just over property but municipal lines, to the basin's farthest reaches. Scientifically and legally, Angelenos were forced to recognize an aerial commons of a larger, unprecedented scale than had been assumed for eastern cities. Los Angeles's new pollution controllers then rewrote the rule book for burning, making it far less free than an earlier smoke abatement had allowed. Setting all manner of new restrictions on what could be released skyward, they effected an enclosure of Angelenos' atmospheric range that was itself a historic accomplishment. It would be emulated widely across California and then throughout America and in many other parts of the world.

Considering the smog story alongside episodes of pollution on Long Island confirms a still larger, if initially more localized significance. Anxieties about the air fired up a sweeping new "environmental" ideology and advocacy, a reimagining of what human-made environments and human health had to do with one another. Smog presented powerful new reasons for Angelenos to suspect an alarming porosity and vulnerability of their bodies to environmental toxins. Moreover, the atmospheric circulation of smog's precursors seemed as shadowy and surreptitious as their capacity to cause disease. Exacerbating these concerns was how readily public health and medical officials shrugged off smog's seriousness. Nevertheless, the battle lines did not simply pit lay citizens and alternative practitioners against the experts. Those modern verities about air pollution just then coalescing also owed much to local, credentialed knowers: prominent Los Angeles–area doctors and scientists who, suspecting that the basin's pollutants posed greater perils, set out to prove it. As on Long Island, this one bodily peril joined an entire array of possible others that the Los Angeles area imposed on its residents. Even prior to 1962's *Silent Spring*, more and more people across the metropolitan area navigated these uncertainties via a health naturalism in which exposures considered more natural were judged to be beneficial or innocuous, while those deemed man-made were suspected of being more deleterious. As the preservation of human health and natural places thereby came to be cast in more similar terms, even the most stalwart conservation groups, like the Sierra Club, joined the anti-smog crusade.

What the resulting environmentalism shared with the earliest antismog activism, as well as with the new regime of air pollution control, was a dis-inclination to ask about where, and for whom, contamination was worst. Like the new groundwater experts on Long Island, air pollution control specialists in Greater Los Angeles spurned any scrutiny of socioeconomic inequities. At the same time, after initially focusing on the more industrial districts, they settled into tracks like those of Long Island's public health officialdom, neglecting pollutants mainly borne by the poor and racial mi-norities.[5] Popular antismog advocacy offered little corrective, driven as it was largely by those from the wealthier suburbs, whose contaminants the new officialdom of pollution control did target. The groundwork was thereby laid for the local eruption, several decades later, of a movement for environmental justice. Yet, in the waxing strength of Los Angeles's antismog movement over the first postwar decades, it is possible to trace a gradual widening of its political leadership and constituencies by gender, class, and age, if less by race.

Before Smog: An Atmospheric Open Range
Around the turn of the twentieth century, Angeleno air impressed Anglo arrivals for a different reason: how easily they could see through it. As-tronomer George Ellery Hale, visiting Pasadena to check on a proposed location for a new Carnegie Institute telescope in 1904, at first gloomily bemoaned the fog and low-hanging clouds. Then, as he made his way up Mount Wilson, the sky cleared, giving way to sparkling sunshine and blue sky.[6] What Hale and his colleagues found so striking there, at the site of the future Mount Wilson Observatory, was not only the air's freedom from rain and clouds but also its exceptional clarity. Nonscientists had similar impressions, especially when remembering the time before smog. Back then, the air had been so "crystal clear" that you could "see all the

way to Catalina Island in the Pacific." Certain peculiarities of local fires confirmed their wonderment. "Chimney-smokes," reported one observer, "go straight upward, and one may carry an unshaded and unshaken flame whither he will."[7] Throughout the basin, Muir's mountainous rim stymied those aerial movements that made starlight waver and distant panoramas blur. This near-magical transparency of Los Angeles's atmosphere licensed, over the first half of the twentieth century, another belief that turned out to be still more miraculous: in its infinite capacity to absorb human effluents. When that stinging murk arrived, to reveal just how finite the basin's atmosphere was, many Angelenos were deeply shaken.

Aggravating their shock and consternation were convictions, dating to deep in the nineteenth century, about the healing powers of the basin's balm. Entire histories have been written about how early migrants to places like Los Angeles celebrated the healthful "climate" of "Southern California."[8] Little in this literature suggests such an attitude among arrivals from Mexico, meteorologically so similar. The praise seems to have turned on contrasts with the American East. Anglo migrants found few of the features thought to bred ill health back home: coolness, the moisture of "miasmas," and abrupt temperature changes. Physicians penned entire volumes, such as Walter Lindley and J. P. Widney's *California of the South* (1896), expanding on the therapeutic beneficence of the region's land and weather. An absence of temperature shifts or dampness, they asserted, had helped make "Southern California . . . practically free from any diseases which belong especially to it, or have their habitat, as the naturalists say of a plant, in it."[9]

Long before smog's arrival, these beliefs had fallen into disrepute in many local circles. For one thing, the region's infectious ailments came to be more thoroughly documented. For another, those same health officials who did so imported a newfound confidence that any and all human environments could be rendered disease-neutral, regardless of their natural features. Modern sanitation and a well-honed monitoring and suppression of infectious threats were all that was needed. These convictions, and the "new public health" practices on which they depended, had mostly urban origins. Not surprisingly, on filtering westward, they came to predominate in Los Angeles's central and other expanding urban cores, just as these acquired more citylike infrastructure and health officers. As early as the first decade of the twentieth century, even professional climatologists were starting to see the city of Los Angeles as "not particularly a health resort, but rather a distributing center for more favored places" across the basin.

Change came not just in where healthier places were thought to lie, but in how seriously many doctors and public health officials treated aerial influences on ailments. Tellingly, analyses of climate slipped out of the regional medical journals. By the 1930s, public health departments like Pasadena's or Long Beach's offered little or no scrutiny of air at all. Clinical examinations and food-related inspections dominated their work; their laboratory tests were confined entirely to fluids—milk, water, blood, and other human emanations. Only when they began inspecting industrial workplaces in the late thirties did local health officials actually test the air.[10]

These trends notwithstanding, many enterprises across the basin remained deeply invested in the region's persisting reputation for healthiness. From local sanitoria to a Pasadena "preventorium," an abundance of doctor-run enterprises still promoted the power of fresh air to heal. Regardless of how often public health officials might refrain from linking health to weather, their own words could yield contrary interpretations. When in 1931 the health department announced that disease and death rates were the lowest in the county's history, reporters still saw confirmation of an old truism: "Los Angeles climate is one of the surest guarantees of health and longevity." In addition to the mixed beliefs of its medical mainstream, the Los Angeles area was home to an unusually diverse and influential array of medical irregulars, whom we today call "alternative practitioners." More so than regular physicians, they explicitly invoked the power of nature to ward off illness or to heal, none of them more keenly than the "naturopaths." Around Los Angeles, naturopathy enjoyed forums for expression denied New York area counterparts, including a regular column in the *Los Angeles Times*. Its authors assaulted the scientific foundation of the new public health—Louis Pasteur's germ theory—for having "set us back over sixty years." Instead of avoiding germs, Angelenos should "concentrate our attention on the soil conditions of the body," seeking out "natural food" and "fresh air." Others, from realtors to hotel owners to supermarket executives, kept alive talk of Los Angeles's regional climate as "ideal" for good health.[11]

By the time smog arrived, the reputed clarity and balm of the air across the Los Angeles basin served as what economists and geographers would later term a natural "amenity." Unlike those ecosystem services or natural capital on which ecological economists have more recently tried to put a price tag, its economic value did not go unacknowledged. On the contrary, early twentieth-century marketers of the Los Angeles climate made sure that its virtues, at least as they understood them, were widely noticed.[12]

More so than in most other cities or parts of the country, the blue expanse hovering above Angeleno heads gained a cash value, driven up by million-dollar investments. Lying all around the basin's people and land, it belonged not just to property owners with hotels or hilltop views but to everyone who ventured there: renters, tourists, even squatters. It constituted an aerial commons, but an informal one, as yet minimally encompassed by local courts or laws. The early politics of smog would formalize this "commons" status. It would do so by pitting those with the largest investments in this natural commons against others whose money had gone more into what, by the 1940s, had become the basin's "gigantic bonfire."

Until the arrival of smog, both of these groups of Angelenos remained convinced of the natural absorptive powers of their atmosphere. Reinforcing that belief were complementary assumptions about the blazes they set off, beginning with the fuel they burned. While the dark, sooty emissions of coal fires had fallen prey to an early movement for smoke abatement back East, oil became Angelenos' fuel of choice. As a liquid, it ignited more easily than coal, with a lighter, wispier flame. A propensity to vaporize meant that more of its substance and by-products escaped into the air unseen. But as state and local laws were adjusted to unleash a "free" market in oil, early conversions from coal to oil were hailed as one more example of local progress, even in fighting pollution. After the local railroads switched to oil, for instance, in 1916, "no cinder got in your eyes."[13] With coal sources lying on the far side of the continent or in the Pacific Ocean, and with oil wells tapping more and more of the basin's reserves, petroleum not only fueled Los Angeles homes and factories, it became the area's most lucrative export. For a brief period prior to the opening of East Texas oil fields, the Los Angeles basin was the largest oil producer not just in the nation but in the world.[14] With oil so easily and cheaply available, ignition and venting practices veered toward the liberal. An aerial flood of hydrocarbons swelled, one that some three decades later would culminate in stinging assaults on Angeleno corneas.

Leading the ramp-up in atmospheric emissions was the area's oil industry itself. When drillers tapped a well, a gusher sprang up out of the ground, spewing a fount of crude petroleum dozens of feet into the air for days on end. In distillation and cracking towers where this crude was then processed, temperatures as high as 800 degrees Fahrenheit were maintained by burning oil. Waste by-products were shunted through vents to the outside, where flares burned them off. The most dramatic and destructive releases came from the mammoth fires and explosions that periodically engulfed oil fields and refineries. Even greater contributions to smog would come from unignited leakage. Boiling points of the lighter petroleum products were as low as 92 degrees Fahrenheit, a temperature regularly exceeded on warmer Los Angeles days. Evaporation, little noted in the presmog era, conveyed a mighty insensible streaming of petroleum by-products from fields and refineries into the atmosphere. Oil vapors easily escaped from skimming ponds, tank "farms," joints between pipes, and at the point of transfer when oil products were poured into tank trucks and ships.[15]

The local sale of petroleum derivatives, starting with the cheap, messy, often carbonaceous residue left over at the end of higher-heat refinery processes, called "fuel oil," widened the contributions to Los Angeles's midcentury aerial burden. Houses and shops, as well as most factories, turned to this heavy extract of petroleum for their heating and other energy needs. The many industrial users, from foundries to canneries to chemical plants, shared as casual an approach to outdoor venting and burning as the oil industry itself.[16] Orchardists, too, lent a hand to keep their winters frost-free. When temperatures plummeted, they ignited fuel oil in "smudge pots," set among their fruit trees, to prevent crops from freezing. On a single frosty night in 1937, they consumed as much fuel oil as had been used by all Los Angeles manufacturers over the previous month and a half.[17] Soon afterward, even the Los Angeles Department of Water and Power—the basin's chief supplier of electricity—began turning to cheap distillates of petroleum to power its turbines.[18] A final major tributary of the oil river that fed basin fires consisted of gasoline. When vaporized and ignited, it was what, by midcentury, made the wheels of nearly all of the basin's vehicles turn. The light-colored puffs of by-product issuing from inches-wide tailpipes roused less attention or ire than the belches of smokestacks, supporting an early disbelief in cars' contribution to smog. Still less perceptible, hot days brought gasoline close to the boiling point (as low as 100 degrees Fahrenheit), cooking it away even with the engine off.

Among other torrents of hydrocarbons pouring into the basin atmosphere by the midforties were those that followed from the minimal governance of the area's dispersed towns and residences. More so than the suburbs around New York and other eastern cities, those in the Los Angeles area lacked garbage services, making residents more reliant on backyard waste burning. By the early fifties, only a third of county households had a weekly pickup of their dry and easily burnable wastes. While some Angelenos paid high fees for private garbage collection, the vast majority, within as well as outside incorporated towns, regularly burned their own wastes in "backyard incinerators," or "smoke pots." In evening hours stipulated by fire officials, flames in an estimated 1.5 million backyard incinerators danced over Angelenos' personal dumps of "tree trimmings, grass clippings, old papers, milk cartons, paper boxes, frozen food packages and other bulky combustibles," wafting strange assortments of hydrocarbons into the basin's air.[19] Joining these aerial exercises in waste disposal were more ceremonial and romantic resorts to flame: for bonfires on beaches, before football games, for barbecue pits and grills.[20]

As various and liberal as Greater Los Angeles's atmospheric releases were compared to eastern counterparts, this tremendous bonfire had already invited its share of complaints and some efforts to impose legal controls. As in the East, landowners enjoyed the freedom to launch all manner of smoke or fumes into the air above their property, with three exceptions. First, following a long tradition of "nuisance" law, the burning rights of property owners were circumscribed by neighbors' rights to sue. Any demonstrable damage to property or health from straying smoke or fumes could provide grounds for a civil suit. Second, within many city limits, town inspectors enforced smoke abatement laws. By the 1920s the city of Los Angeles had its own smoke inspectorate, the region's first paid enforcer of rules against air pollution, at least within the city limits. Issuing a handful of injunctions annually, inspectors judged violations through visits to offending sites, via eyeball observations of their smoke.[21] More broadly influential prior to 1943, but sharing the assumption that air pollution would stay local and visible, was a third, spatially oriented fix: industrial zoning. This measure restricted the messier, more odiferous industries to their own corners or "zones" within a particular city or county. Most assiduously shielded from airborne odors and hazards in this way were districts zoned as exclusively "residential," mostly occupied by Anglo homeowners of the upper or middle class. "Industrial" zones, on the other hand, might harbor a variety of nonindustrial land uses, including cheap or rental housing. Not surprisingly, their residents tended to be poorer and darker-skinned.[22]

Industrial zoning advocates as well as smoke abaters might talk about a metropoliswide problem or perhaps judge a solution's effectiveness by sweeping glances along downtown streets and skylines. In practice, however, neither zoning nor smoke control officials and experts attempted to monitor or regulate the basin's atmosphere as an interconnected whole, more than the sum of its parts. Their eyes fixated only on disparate, local sources: a smoky furnace, a neighborhood where a factory sought to relocate.

With aerial contaminants seemingly containable by these means, Los Angeles's regional and freeway planning initiatives, under way in the 1930s and 1940s, dwelled hardly at all on any atmospheric constraints or consequences to what they proposed. Also taking for granted the protective powers of modern public health, they concentrated on prospective highway routes, the provision of utilities and other infrastructure, the placement of housing and industry, even the location of recreation facilities and parks. Natural topography and aridity did figure into their deliberations, but mostly as physical limitations to be overcome. Deeply immersed in a narrative of city building, they viewed themselves as fostering an ongoing transformation of basin land into a more uniformly constructed and modern place, more or less like cities elsewhere. Throughout their discussions, even into the most contentious years of the smog debate, the atmosphere of the Los Angeles basin, its winds and weather, went unseen and unmentioned.

In the face of such denial, a forerunning countywide extension of air pollution law began not in the downtown or in an industrial district, but in a more rural corner of the region. The first law for regulating air outside a town or city limit came in San Bernardino County, fifty miles east of downtown Los Angeles. The target was agricultural: orchard smudging. Starting there in 1931, a single rule mandated cleaner smudge pots countywide—compared to city smoke control, a novel geographic scope. Grower pressure helped keep the new rule modest, prohibiting only smudges that burned the dirtiest fuel oil. Los Angeles County picked up on the new rule three years later, adding enforcement powers only after a massive smudging in 1937 blew a "smoke pall over downtown Los Angeles" that lasted three weeks.[23] With the advent of wartime industries, attempts to tether what passed from the Los Angeles area's fires into the air soon turned more ambitious and expansive. City health officials, commencing outdoor air sampling in 1942, discovered a complex brew spilling into "the outlying [suburban] districts . . . to a greater extent than at any previous time."[24] As yet, they saw little cause for alarm. But a year later, Angeleno politicos, rushing to their doors, begged to differ.

The Enigma of Smog

When that cloud of stinging mist stirred up downtown in the summer of 1943, frost-fighting smudges could hardly be blamed. Pressed by city leaders for answers, health officials speculated in ways presaging future paths of explanation: "Atmospheric conditions," along with an "accumulation of gases and fumes from industrial stacks" and "vehicular traffic" might be responsible. Soon, however, their investigations fell back onto the localist track for understanding air pollution. Fingering a single butadiene war plant that had recently opened downtown, they and the city council forced the plant to clean up its operations. The acrid cloud lifted, only to return two months later.[25] The reemergence of this haze more definitively undermined the assumption that air pollution was essentially a local problem, for it descended not only on downtown Los Angeles but also on Pasadena, seven miles away.

Suddenly and surprisingly, a suburb like Pasadena seemed much closer to those more urban or industrial places that most people were inclined to blame for the smog problem. The first goal became a new vehicle for urban-regional governance. Suburban and downtown elites thereby gained means for intervening in the dispersed industrial districts held most responsible for the smog problem. Beginning with these new imperatives of law, the smog fight then faltered on a slipperiness that frustrated scientific understanding. Defying assumptions about how air pollution worked, smog sparked much debate over what it was and what caused it. The journey to greater certitude and consensus took several years. In the process, a first round of atmospheric-range closure was accomplished, and the popularity of suburban antismog activism crescendoed.

On smog's first appearance in Pasadena, hotel managers and local government officials joined a growing chorus for action among the inhabitants of the San Gabriel Valley. Their voices joined with those from downtown civic groups to get the incriminated war plant shut down until its process was made airtight. Nevertheless, the smog returned and grew worse. As it swept farther and more frequently into the San Gabriel Valley, Pasadena quickly emerged as a basinwide leader in the first self-styled "citizen's crusade" against smog.

Among the reasons why, the town had long been home to some of the basin's best-heeled citizens. Since it had less manufacturing than the city of Los Angeles and many other towns, and no oil wells, and was experiencing a rapid departure of its orchards and herds, the wealth of 1940s Pasadena lay largely in residential real estate and tourism, where its "naturally healthy" reputation weighed heavily. On the smog issue, prominent hoteliers and realtors easily found allies among Pasadena Preferred (promoters of the Arroyo Seco Parkway), the local Chamber of Commerce, civic groups like the Shriners, the mayor and the city engineer, and, not least among them, homeowner associations. Antismog advocates from towns farther up the San Gabriel Valley also pitched in. Organizationally, this first wave of suburban antismog activism was led by a local male elite. Women handled the grassroots legwork of getting civic and property owner groups on board, and provided journalists with supportive quotations.[26] Years before an effective science and control strategy, these suburban activists parlayed a legal precedent for regulating smudges into a new countywide authority for tackling smog. Introduced by Pasadena's assemblymen in Sacramento, a new state law passed in May 1947 enabling the establishment of "air pollution districts," whose authority could override that of individual towns. Soon afterward, Los Angeles County set up its Air Pollution Control District (APCD), the nation's first to operate on a more genuinely metropolitan (rather than city-limit) scale.[27]

Before long the Los Angeles APCD had acquired more staff, funding, and authority to act against air polluters than any comparable agency in the nation or world. As researchers funded by the APCD's lucrative coffers set to work, so did its regulators, whose own ideas about the smog issue were rapidly evolving. Louis McCabe, longtime director of a Pittsburgh laboratory of the Bureau of Mines, assumed leadership of the APCD. At first McCabe subscribed to a diagnosis of Angeleno air surmised by eastern experts whom he visited. According to them, smog consisted mostly of visible liquid and solid particles, "aerosols" akin to smoke itself. But measurements of dust fall (from solid particles, or particulates) in the basin turned out to be about half those in Chicago or Detroit. McCabe then switched gears to add a chemical culprit: sulfur dioxide (SO_2).[28] This most widely feared of the era's air pollutants had recently been implicated in disasters in Belgium's Meuse Valley and in Donora, Pennsylvania, where in 1948 twenty people died and half a town was hospitalized. Given off directly by smokestacks, SO_2 had acidifying and other properties whose effects matched the eye irritations caused by smog and its corrosion of painted surfaces. By the onset of the 1951 smog season, the APCD had built an unprecedented system for the continuous monitoring of this pollutant across the basin. The thirteen stations it operated were more than those for any other suspected contaminant. But its growing focus on SO_2 led to only a partial break from local, sensory cues. Like the obscured vision created by smoke, sulfur dioxide, though detectable through measurements, was also discernible by the senses, giving off a telltale "rotten egg" smell. APCD enforcement officials used its scent to help track down industrial emitters.[29]

Curtly dismissive of automobile exhaust as a contributor, McCabe targeted all the fires across the district that were prone to aerosol (including smoke) emissions, as well as sulfurous smells. The first enclosure of atmospheric releases that followed was vast and aggressive. Refineries were required to recapture "hundred of tons" of SO_2 by-products they typically burned off. The APCD banned open burning in town dumps or incinerators. It clamped down on the profuse simmering, baking, and boiling done in Angeleno factories. Most manufacturers became subject to new requirements to reburn, contain, filter, or otherwise reduce their releases into the atmosphere, especially if sulfur-laden.

The basin's industrial workhorses, more so than its better-off residential communities, bore most of the burden of this first round of aerial enclosures. The dual emphasis on SO_2 and aerosols drew early APCD inspectors away from the San Gabriel Valley and Pasadena, where organized complaints were the loudest. Instead, inspectors converged on those parts of the county where elites had been less militant or enthusiastic about smog control, but where working and minority families were more likely to live. In municipalities along the region's south central industrial belt—Long Beach, Torrance, El Segundo, Wilmington, and South Gate, into the city of Los Angeles itself—neighboring plants by 1951 faced tight limits on dust, sulfur, and other fumes they could give off, and a strict approval process for any new facilities.

Across Los Angeles's industrial districts, the early APCD instigated an unprecedented new confinement of industrial flames. The agency boasted of a dramatic two-thirds reduction in dust fall. Sulfur emissions were even more drastically curtailed; those in the petroleum industry, from 380 tons per day in 1948 to only 80 tons three years later. Sulfurous odors and the grating of dust particles on lungs diminished across the basin's industrial heartland. Yet up the San Gabriel Valley in places like Pasadena, smog kept returning and worsening.[30]

Part of the reason was that these measures offered so little corrective to Los Angeles's natural propensity to smog. On average, so-called temperature inversions occurred 262 days annually, as cool air blowing off the Pacific was trapped within the basin's mountainous rims as well as under a warmer lid of air higher up. All manner of emissions, prevented from escaping into the stratosphere, drifted along the San Gabriel and other valleys instead. Predictably, this natural combination of weather and topography became a favored theme among smog scientists funded by the oil and gas industry, a lucrative source of research money. Louis McCabe, wary of their biases, remained skeptical of their science. But such arguments gained further credence as the APCD's crackdown on dumps, refineries, and factories brought SO_2 to 1940 levels but failed to vanquish the stinging haze. The SO_2 explanation also did not easily square with the experience of some Pasadena-based researchers, who noted the absence of any rotten egg smell in that town's haze. In their minds, other culprits began to loom larger: the backyard incinerators and, especially, cars.[31]

What more definitively tipped smog control away from aerosols and SO_2 was the discovery of a heretofore unsuspected substance, not found in factory or refinery emissions, which exactly replicated smog's most distinctive and puzzling effects. Ozone, a three-atomed and reactive version of oxygen, turned out to be the missing environmental link in the smog problem. Found at unusually high levels around Los Angeles, its oxidizing powers produced an eye irritation identical to that in smog and SO_2, as well as the same peculiar damage to car tires and leafy green plants like alfalfa and lettuce. Its role in smog came to be firmly established by Pasadena biochemist Ari Haagen-Smit.[32] In his explanatory scheme, not ozone but its precursors, the nitrogen oxides, spewed directly out of "all high temperature combustion," especially the burning of fuel oil and gasoline. Ozone's other essential ingredient, hydrocarbons, came from incomplete burning, also from what evaporated from tank farms or refineries or carburetors *before* burning, those complex compounds that drifted into the air before being broken down by combustion. Defying the long-standing assumptions of pollution scientists, ozone production happened outside of any factory or refinery, within the Los Angeles atmosphere itself. It required the most distinctive and celebrated of Southern California's natural characteristics: sunshine. Demonstrating that ozone arose from the outdoor cooking of man-made pollutants by sunlight, Haagen-Smit placed a familiar feature of Los Angeles's nature at the heart of expert thinking about smog.[33]

Haagen-Smit's model for ozone's making provided the core for a new, more expansive science of Los Angeles's aerial commons over the 1950s. Based on an elegant experimental modeling of ozone production, his theory suggested that releases in one part of Los Angeles's aerial commons could culminate in stinging mists far away. Collaborating between several disciplines, other scientists sought to characterize just how atmospheric circulation could produce ozone and other pollution across an entire metropolitan region. Efforts to chart the pathway between Long Beach refineries and Pasadena corneas involved, first of all, meteorologists. By 1954, their network of fifty-five surface wind stations—"the most concentrated network of stations ever tuned in on the direction and speed of winds above ground"—busily charted the basin's "rivers of wind."[34] What was becoming clearer, too, from this new science of pollution was that smog was not nearly as discrete, local, and unusual an event as the press and earlier regulators had assumed. Rather, what made smog were constituents of the Los Angeles basin's air that presented in high concentrations during times of "attack" but that appeared in smaller amounts the rest of the time.

With this new understanding of smog's causes came a second round of atmospheric range closure over the mid-1950s, centering on oil storage and production. Among the revelations of the new science was that ozone had myriad invisible precursors, many of which actually entered the air through evaporation rather than burning. This realization spurred a host of new rules for oil and other producers: coverage of skimming pools, for instance, and new means for preventing the accumulation or leakage of vapors in storage tanks, pipes, and transfer points. That unburned hydrocarbons contributed to smog also led to the targeting of consumer-set fires: rubbish burning and, soon to receive the bulk of the blame, "automotive exhausts." By 1954, Haagen-Smit was suggesting that automobiles were responsible for as much as 50 percent of the smog problem. APCD officials, switching gears, soon concurred.[35]

Doing the APCD's credibility no favors, this official change of tune responded not just to new science, but to an actual shift in how smog's precursors were made. When "smog" had first appeared, relatively few of the contributing hydrocarbons or nitrous oxides likely came from cars; more of them were emitted from refinery-related activities. Retrospectively, scientists estimated that the hydrocarbons streaming into the air from the petroleum industry around 1940 were over six times greater than those coming from car and truck motors. Moreover, during the wartime years just prior to the first smog attack, automobile registrations and driving had been dropping. After the war, though, in part because the APCD so effectively tackled the aerial releases from Los Angeles's oil and other manufacturers, the county's burgeoning cars and trucks became the fastest growing contributors to Los Angeles's smog-spawning discharges. Licensed cars had recovered and surged 70 percent in the ensuing decade; trucks grew larger in size and doubled in number.[36] The changes in scientific understanding thus coincided with the quickly mounting impact of internal combustion engines on the basin's air.

For a variety of reasons, then, smog's resurgence over the summer and fall of 1954 catalyzed a perfect storm of popular discontent. This smog season, along with that of the following year, marked the historic peak of measured oxidant levels in the Los Angeles basin. With the failed APCD ef-

forts suddenly so palpable, a full-blown crisis erupted over the agency's le-
gitimacy, lurching smog politics into an angry new phase. Civic restiveness
also stemmed from a loss of political savvy at the agency's helm. An engineer named Gordon Larson, ham-handed in his dealings with journalists
and the public, replaced Louis McCabe. Larson's public statements magnified impressions of the APCD's irresolution and drift. Though insisting
that "today . . . we know what smog is," he had few explanations for the
ineffectiveness of his "smog police" in the San Gabriel Valley.[37] Massaging
citizen suspicions, as well, smog experts, though now concurring in much
of their analysis, remained deeply at odds over a most pressing question for
anyone who had to breathe the air—How bad was it for human health?
In the wake of the Meuse Valley, Donora, and a recent episode in London,
most health scientists now agreed that air pollution could turn deadly. But
they were divided on the bodily consequences of Los Angeles's anomalous
clouds.

On one side were the public health experts and officials, many of them
ensconced in the state health department in Sacramento, who voiced skepticism about whether smog caused *any* serious disease. Many negative findings seemed to back them up: the dearth of extra maladies turning up in
human studies of comparable exposures (mostly of factory workers); also
statistically, the lack of a rise in county disease or death rates during the
smoggiest days. Yet among the Los Angeles area's own formidable health
experts were many who had arrived at contrary conclusions. The Los
Angeles Medical Society, citing the huge number of clinical observations
conducted by its physician members on exposed Angelenos from the late
forties, regularly articulated dire warnings. In early 1954, ratcheting up its
alarmist tone, the society pronounced smog a definite "health hazard" that
"may cause fatalities." That fall, however, Gordon Larson seemed to slide
over to the skeptics' side. In the midst of another lengthy smog assault,
he publicly shrugged off questions on whether the occurrence was almost
"dangerous" enough for a traffic shutdown.[38] Days later, a massive gathering in Pasadena offered a first glimpse into the mobilizing possibilities of
the pollution issue and a preview of the "environmental" movement that
would tap into them.

On October 20, 1954, after two solid weeks of choking "acrid blue-
gray" air over the San Gabriel Valley, activism crested to a high-water
mark with the region's single biggest antipollution protest prior to Earth
Day. A "mass meeting" at the Pasadena Civic Auditorium drew somewhere between 4,500 and 6,000 people. Most were from Pasadena but

*Early antismog protesters. A forerunning use of gas masks in a demonstration at the Highland Park Optimist Club near Pasadena. This photograph was taken around the peak of the mass protests in 1954. (*Los Angeles Times *Collection, Special Collections, University of California, Los Angeles)*

reportedly also from thirty-five of the forty-five cities across the basin. In-surance salesman Francis Packard, who had called the meeting, minced no words in saying that "scientific mumbo jumbo" and "bureaucratic inertia" stymied the control of smog. Though inexpert, he and the other speakers *knew enough* about how bad smog was and what really caused it. How could this persistent eye-stinging and coughing be innocuous? And despite the rising talk about cars, weren't the most visible culprits still out there for everyone to see? A documentary put together by Hollywood businessman Charles Peters "compared shots of heavy traffic on parkways, showing no signs of vapor, to the refineries, where there were huge clouds of smoke." The radio announcer who acted as master of ceremonies then initiated a "battle cry" of calls and responses that took the audience's tempera-ture on other official assertions. "'Do you think home incinerators are a major cause of smog?' There was slight applause. . . . 'Has the public been fooled by facts and figures.' The ringing answer was 'Yes.'" The most vociferous collective bellow parried a health expert's declaration (at a conference convened by California's Governor Goodwin Jess Knight) that smog posed no immediate health threat. Was he right? asked the emcee. "Three thousand voices [all those admitted into the packed auditorium] shouted 'NO!'"[39]

In the face of this scientific and official discord, the meeting's attendees reached their own conclusions about the air they breathed: what its contaminants were, what evidence best illuminated them, how serious was the impact on human health. All of their opinions placed them starkly at odds with the APCD. Suspicious of the automobile thesis and, by extension, of the invisible catalyzing of chemicals fingered by Haagen-Smit, they were far readier to blame the visible smoke of industrial emitters. Their ideas about smog seemed to harken back to McCabe's, to reject the recent emphasis of smog science on less visible precursors. At the same time, when it came to the crucial terrain of the human body, less visible consequences seemed more plausible to this crowd than to many scientists. For those whose own bodies lay on the line, whose eyes stung and whose throats ached from living in smog's midst, the direr possibilities of pathology weighed more heavily. Experiencing such discomfort for days on end, they found these prospects impossible to dismiss, however thin the scientific confirmations.

Taking discussion of smog "out of the scientific laboratories and [putting it] into the hands of the people," the participants at this "mass meeting" heaped scorn on air pollution's reigning experts and officials. Their movement was not as antiscientific as such spokespeople made it out to be; on important fronts, they too had medical and scientific allies. Belying contemporary critiques of suburban conformity, they spoke up, especially, for the burning eyes and throats of those in the San Gabriel Valley, among the most exclusively residential of the basin's suburban microenvironments. United over the APCD's reputed lack of enforcement in Los Angeles's industrial districts miles away, Packard and other organizers crafted a broader, more participatory framework for lay antismog activism.

Since the 1940s, a tiny group appointed by the Los Angeles mayor had laid claim to being smog's official "citizens committee." After the success of their mass meeting, Packard and company set up their own more "militant" Citizens Anti-Smog Action Committee. Encouraging voluntary, self-organizing councils in each basin community, they acquired a membership that, not coincidentally, tilted smog activism suburbward, away from downtown Los Angeles elites. Soon they boasted councils in thirty-eight basin communities, with a total of thirteen thousand members.[40] Against pollution, a more grassroots organizing and activism was coalescing early in Los Angeles's suburbs, years before the movements of the 1960s.

The hazy, stinging skies over the downtown and San Gabriel Valley had stoked a new translocal politics, addressing an aerial commons shared by the basin's separate parts. The crisis had come partly because of features of the Los Angeles area as whole: its climate and topography, its liberal burning and venting, its large and vital petroleum industry, its many cars. As fundamental, though, was how inhabitants of the region's various neighborhood ecologies—from residential and industrial—had applied such different designs to the local terrain. In one section of Los Angeles's fragmented, sprawling landscape, the San Gabriel Valley, many residents had made homes in what they understood to be healthier and more natural surroundings. In another, across the south central and eastern flatlands, industrialists and their political allies had sought suburban spaces for production, insulated from the likelihood of neighbors' complaints. Neither project had reckoned on Angeleno air. It turned from transparent to translucent, from conveying views to cooking up afflictions. Ironically, even as collective anger peaked in Pasadena, the science of smog itself was becoming less moored to visible smoke and sulfurous odors, and a better fit to what stung Pasadena eyes. Construing ozone as smog's backbone, the APCD was then able to restore confidence in itself and its experts. Appeasing these most vocal of smog sufferers, it also rebalanced the benefits of pollution control, shifting its favors from the least to the most privileged suburbanites.

Fighting Fumes, Fanning Flames

The political fallout from the smog revolt of 1954 was swift and far-reaching. Among its chief consequences was a change at the helm of the APCD, from Gordon Larson to Smith Griswold. As Griswold's enforcement officer turned more aggressive, he himself showed a much greater adeptness at public relations than his predecessor. He started a newsletter for lay readers and, along with his top officers, launched a massive campaign—through radio, television, and newspaper press releases—to educate Angelenos about smog.[41] Among his innovations was a measure that formalized Los Angeles's aerial commons anew, while insinuating smog monitoring deeper into the daily experience of residential suburbanites. Loosely modeled on the warning system for air raids, the new smog alert system inaugurated the beginnings of modern air pollution control. The world's first, it prepared the way for a third round of atmospheric closings, which was the first to target consumer-set fires. At the same time, the APCD inaugurated a new battlefront in the smog war, well-attuned not only to a changing smog science but also to pressures from suburban activists. The nation's most powerful pollution control agency mutated into a new species of consumer advocate by pushing Detroit to produce cleaner cars.

Starting in 1955, air pollution alerts began blaring regularly over radio and television, from local fire stations and air raid sirens, to warn that contaminant levels had hiked dangerously high. Their sharp, perturbing blasts did not just serve purposes of public health. Sounding in Pasadena more than any other monitoring site, the alarms showed an agency at the ready even there, as well as in the industrial districts: measuring and monitoring, always prepared to undertake preventive action. Though Angelenos might still know smog by sight and sting, expert tools and laboratories now supplied official, auditory cues about when to worry most. Unlike with smoke control, the triggers came neither from eyeball observations nor from spot-check sampling, but from measuring instruments continuously at work—an automated twenty-four-hour aerial scrutiny. Its closest precedents were the so-called threshold limit values set for individual toxins in factory air; yet in spatial scope, the new approach differed as much from industrial hygiene as from smoke control. No longer were the triggers confined to the same building or neighborhood; the legal consequences in particular could reach much further. While a first warning level prompted only voluntary actions, a second required widespread halts in industrial combustion. A third "health hazard" level demanded steps as drastic as the cessation of all basin traffic. Though unnoted at the time, the system was more *ecological* than its predecessors, because it took aim at a longer, more complex chain of causation. Screaming monitors in one place compelled shutdowns in the far reaches of this metropolitan area.[42]

Through the smog alerts and allied publicity, the Griswold APCD sought to rebuild the agency's credibility precisely by announcing less visible dangers revealed by the new science. Imperceptible as the precursors of ozone were, its spikes in concentration now gained audible cues, not only for scientists but also for a lay public. At the same time that the APCD and its experts sought to warn, however, they also hoped to discourage what they saw as the public's inclination to panic. Here, decisions about precisely what levels would trigger the alarms were critical.

To make these determinations, a committee of thirteen prominent physicians and scientists was appointed. At its head was Stafford L. Warren, one of the founders of the Medical School at the University of California, Los Angeles (UCLA), and former medical director of the Manhattan Project. Chemical by chemical, the committee drew a bright line between aesthetic effects of "visibility or discomfort," which it allowed, and "those having a potential hazard to the average healthy person," which it would divulge and combat. To make such a distinction, they drew upon what studies had been published, mostly investigations of workplace exposures and laboratory experiments with animals. If their methods foreshadowed at least the possibility of preventing less proved dangers, their scientific caution tugged against any full-blown application of this strategy, later known as the "precautionary principle." Nagging at their expectations of proof and certainty was the "peculiar intermittency or irregularity" of the outdoor measurements they were assessing, as well as "insufficient data" on many bodily effects. Human studies of most sorts, and even animal experiments on long-term or low-level exposures, seemed especially spotty. Consequently, trigger levels they set strayed little from experimental results, with minimal if any safety margins. The second stage of alert for ozone, for instance, at 1 part per million (ppm), lay only a couple of tenths from levels reported to cause chronic bronchitis and tumors in animals. They were careful to add a disclaimer: The levels set should serve only as a "starting point . . . which would enable us to proceed . . . in the public's interest." But this avowed tenuousness of their scientific base clashed with the seeming precision and solidity of their chosen numbers.[43]

Long shared informally as an amenity, the aerial commons of the Los Angeles basin now came directly under the continuous eye of APCD monitors and under the explicit rule of a metropoliswide state. Like the emerging means for controlling the contamination of Long Island's groundwater, the smog alert system originated a historically unprecedented blend of oversights: in this case, not just legal, but chemical and meteorological, as well as medical. It was a surveillance whose powers would be projected nationwide over ensuing decades, as well as across many other industrialized regions of the world. For all of its efforts to ensure scientific evenhandedness, however, this new commons regime instituted by the APCD in the mid-1950s prioritized the alleviation of some people's pollution over others'.

The changing distribution of its monitoring stations told the tale of the new regime's priorities. Ozone replaced SO_2 as the pollutant of greatest concern. Continuous monitoring for ozone expanded to twenty sites in the years just after 1955, more than for any other pollutant. A majority of these sites lay around the San Gabriel Valley and other northerly locations; most of the rest sat just downwind from other well-to-do residential districts. Only nine covered the more industrialized portion of the county, from the downtown southward, and only two of these lay in the southeast: the industrial corridor near Long Beach and Lakewood. Sulfur dioxide, by contrast, was measured continuously in only four places in 1955, down from thirteen only three years earlier.[44] It was presumed to be a more or less solved problem. Less mobile than ozone, with deadly effects that were also better established, SO_2 could nevertheless turn dangerous without registering on any of these monitors—and did. In 1956, the waste plume from a power plant at Wilmington drifted south into a harborside fire station, forcing its choking firemen to flee. At the time, no monitor was located anywhere nearby, but a measuring device placed there the following year showed SO_2 levels frequently exceeding the "warning" level of 3.0 ppm. A couple of times it reached as high as 7.9 ppm, "considerably exceeding" the "health hazard" level of 5.0. By contrast, the much more numerous monitors for ozone, though triggering nearly all the alarms by the late fifties, never elicited more than a first, "warning," level of alert.[45]

As the APCD's activities and resources concentrated increasingly on the most ozone-prone corners of the basin, still greater casualties came through its shrinking engagement with what would be called "particulates." Long known more colloquially as "smoke" or "dust," particulates were omitted from the early continuous monitoring system altogether. Small but solid, still less mobile than SO_2, their distribution had been followed into the midfifties through surveys of dust fall. Even more so than SO_2, their highest levels centered especially around Los Angeles's downtown and industrial suburbs, including parts of Lakewood and Long Beach, and many of the basin's blackest and poorest census tracts. Much later, after the smallest particulates had been shown to have among the most serious long-term health effects of any air pollutants, their high levels in many of these same locales would spur local movements for environmental justice.[46] Yet from 1955, as the APCD consolidated its energies around ozone, it stopped surveying dust fall altogether.

As with Long Island health officials' oversight of their aquifers—indeed, like much other public health science of preceding decades—the Los Angeles APCD's newly crafted instruments for monitoring the basin's atmosphere were socioeconomically skewed, favoring the troubles of some neighborhood ecologies over others. Just like other upholders of technocratic traditions, APCD administrators leaned on a technical language of health and natural science that left them underequipped to recognize those

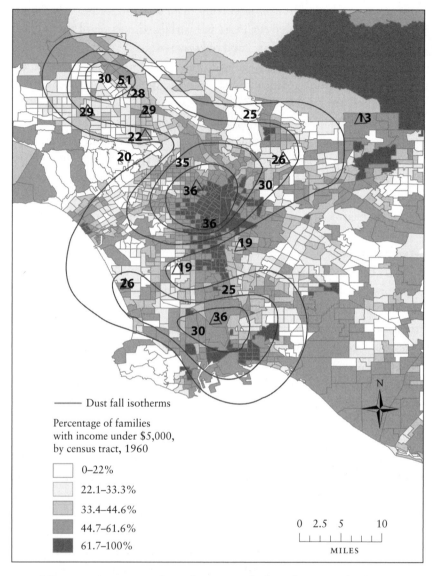

Dust fall (in tons per square mile) in the Los Angeles basin by income level.
Concentrations are from the last comprehensive study of what would become
known as "particulate" pollution in 1955. They show the vulnerability of lower-
income tracts to this kind of pollutant. But monitoring and resources were shifting
toward pollutants—notably ozone—afflicting the better-off corners of the region
more. (Based on information from National Historical Geographic Information
System, 1960 Study, and U.S. Housing Census)

issues of socioeconomic equity that were at stake. Though Griswold's APCD, chastened by a rising tide of antismog activism, did hatch more publicly minded stratagems, these harbored their own underlying bias. Revising its mission, policies, and practices, the agency aspired to become more of an official, empowered agent for what historian Lizabeth Cohen terms the "citizen consumer."[47] The consequence in this case, whether more or less intended, was that greater purchasing power trumped even-handedness. Nudged by activists and others, the agency settled on an enforcement program, as well, that most favored consumers who were wealthier.

Consider the choices the APCD made in undertaking a third round of aerial restrictions and enclosures. They started with home incinerators. In retrospect, less than 2 percent of the total burden of hydrocarbons came from incineration, mostly from large-scale municipal operations rather than backyard garbage burning. But in 1955, Smith Griswold decided to move forward on Larson's original proposal for a ban on backyard incinerators, finally implementing it with full force in 1957. The incinerator ban, in alliance with another prohibition against open burning, exacted its price primarily on the many suburban homeowners who had long burned their own trash. They now paid an extra cost for garbage collection, whether in taxes or private fees. Of all homeowners, the new rules weighed most heavily on those with lower incomes, especially if they lived in the basin's most rural reaches. Most likely to burn their own trash prior to the new rules, they could least afford the additional garbage fees. Similarly, when the APCD moved on to target cars, it first set its sights on a lower class of suburban consumers. Beginning in the early 1960s, as new requirements for emissions inspections and controls were phased in, they were first applied to older vehicles. Arguably messier, well-worn cars were also more likely to have been bought used and to belong to those priced out of the market for newer models. A flood of angry letters to pollution officials protested each measure in similar terms—how "as usual, it's the 'little fellow' getting all the blame."[48]

Perhaps in response to these protests, and to continuing pressure from antismog citizen groups, the APCD's third, late fifties round of enclosures did include some new initiatives against the basin's "big fellows." The rules for industrial enclosure were extended to mobile sources like gasoline trucks and the emerging fleet of diesel-powered cousins. With Rule 62, implemented in 1958 following strong vocal support from Packard's and other citizen groups, the agency commenced a new departure in industrial regulation. The new rule forbade the burning of low-grade petroleum distillates during the smoggy season, no matter how large or influential the user. It had especially sweeping implications for the electric power companies, whose enlarging boilers, over the peak years of smog, had doubled and tripled their consumption of fuel oil. Vigorously opposed by industry lobbyists, this seasonal fuel oil ban nevertheless pushed power plants and other Los Angeles industrial users where they were already headed: toward cleaner-burning natural gas as an energy source. More quietly, the fuel oil ban capped off a still larger transformation. By the early 1960s, the nation's second largest metropolis, born and raised on local oil, now imported the vast majority of its fossil fuels.[49]

The ban on fuel oil easily found favor among antismog activists. After all, like the steps with which smog control had begun, it mostly targeted the basin's industrial zones. Harder to swallow in Los Angeles's "citizen consumer" politics of this era, even for antismog activists, were solutions that might curtail the mobility associated with cars. Consonant with national trends noted by automobile historian Thomas McCarthy, there was a widespread reluctance to question orthodoxies of road building and suburban development, to consider measures that might have proved more far-reaching and sustainable. Even the "militant" activists at the 1954 Pasadena Assembly only went so far as a call to "electrify busses." By the 1960s, as motor vehicles were estimated to cause nearly 55 percent of smog, there were suggestions for the development of an electric car. Yet Los Angeles smog battlers of all stripes raised surprisingly few questions about freeway building. For many years, Haagen-Smit himself argued that because fast and steady-running traffic burned gasoline more efficiently, freeways were smog remedies.[50] So powerful and prevalent were the presumed rights of Angelenos to drive anywhere, to be propelled, lit, heated, and otherwise convenienced by fossil fuels, that public mass transit or other alternatives hardly seemed worth mentioning.

Once pollution controllers turned their sights to cars, they aimed not so much at Los Angeles roads or driving habits or developers as at the distant plants where automobiles were made. Probing back up the chain of production for smog's roots, local regulators and politicians established a new way of acting on behalf of citizen consumers. Rather than pitting the residential suburbs of the basin against their industrial counterparts, in an inspired switch, they opened season on a far-flung industrial foe: the "motor city" of Detroit. The APCD's confrontations with Detroit car makers had begun during the Larson era, but quietly, through exchanges of letters and visits that went little publicized. In 1958, after the nation's chief auto makers had repeatedly shrugged off Angeleno officials' insistence on cleaner-burning engines, the Los Angeles City Council went public with its frustration. It threw down the gauntlet: within three years, all automobiles sold within the city limits had to meet tough smog-reducing exhaust standards. Before its deadline had passed, a 1960 burst of antismog activism converged on Sacramento to push through the California Motor Vehicle Control Act. The battle was hard-fought and intense, but the state of California thereby wound up setting pollution-fighting terms for its vast car market. Courtesy of the new law, a Motor Vehicle Control Board began enforcing path-breaking new rules for all automobiles sold in the state, based on the amount of pollutants they produced. Incentives were thereby hatched for perfecting the catalytic converter, what many welcomed as the most promising technical fix for Los Angeles's blighted air.[51]

From its beginnings in wartime, two decades before Ralph Nader published *Unsafe at Any Speed* (1965), the smog fight had long been waged on behalf of citizen consumers, even if its early neglect of residential districts had convinced many San Gabriel Valley residents otherwise. With the APCD's reorientation under Griswold and with the state now setting pollution-fighting standards for a product manufactured half a continent away, by the early 1960s the struggle against Los Angeles smog seemed to be working in one important respect.[52] Ozone levels had stopped rising, though by no means had they tapered off. But the new regime had thereby introduced its own novel terms of inequity. The basin's atmospheric free range had been closed down, but only selectively and only for some.

Bigger producers as well as bigger consumers still enjoyed great freedom, literally, to burn. Industrialists who played by APCD rules faced few other limits on combustion. This was also true of middle- and upper-class suburban consumers, who could more easily purchase catalytic converters. More generally, they could still combust as much fossil fuel as they could afford. There was just one caveat compared to earlier: the flames had to be more thoroughly concealed or farther away. The best-off residents, in the richest suburbs like Bel Air and San Marino, had probably long since switched from fuel oil to natural gas or electricity for home heating. They were also far more likely to have larger refrigerators and more televisions, washers, and dryers—all dependent on the gas-fueled turbines of the power company. Not least among the suburban energy gobbling still allowed was that which came from driving itself or from owning more than one car. Catalytically converted emissions from a family that bought and drove two, three, or more new cars easily outstretched the lesser pollution that California's new emissions rules demanded of a single vehicle.

As for this regime's historic impact on the basin's ecology, it came not only from emissions it curtailed but also from those it did not. The green light it gave to so much more burning, its failure to consider more ambitious and far-reaching alternatives to Los Angeles's customary combustibles or modes of city building, ensured an intensified reliance on fossil fuels in the years to come. Among the consequences, pollutants—those that were measured by the APCD but especially those that were not—continued to pour into basin air. Lead and particulates, a variety of carcinogens, and other so-called air toxics, rushed skyward at an accelerating pace. Often, as would later be shown, these accumulated precisely in industrial districts where the APCD's presence had diminished and where residents' incomes were lower, their skin color was darker, and their complaints were less heard. Still less remarked over the ensuing decades, invisible gases like carbon dioxide and methane streamed skyward in ever greater volumes. Joining vast pools of chemical cousins in the upper atmosphere, they trapped more and more of the heat reflected from the earth's surface. As a consequence, the temperature of the entire planet nudged upward.

By its very success and spread, the regime of air pollution control hatched in forties and fifties Los Angeles did its share in making America the world's greatest contributor to global warming. Addressing only those pollutants detectable by sight and sting, whose bodily impact could be so direct and dire, it helped ensure that whatever else emanated from our collective bonfire lay beyond the perception of ordinary citizens. Those who would warn us about the larger consequences thus faced an immense quandary. How might we be persuaded to worry and to mobilize, given the absence of those local and widely shared experiences that earlier, in a place like postwar Los Angeles, had compelled such a broadly felt need to act?

Seedbed of Precaution and Protest

The "Los Angeles type" of pollution soon became well known among air pollution investigators across the nation and world. The city's system of aerial monitoring provided inspiration for a U.S. Public Health Service initiative, starting in 1955, to test for urban air pollution throughout the country. The World Health Organization, in its inaugural 1961 publication on air pollution, confirmed that "photochemical smog" had arrived in Los Angeles first, thanks to its unique combination of weather and topography with "smokeless fuel."[53] The scientific careers of many Los Angeles area investigators were thereby made. But the larger contributions of smog to science owed much to a far less delocalized knowledge, of a sort shared by local experts with ordinary Angelenos. Daily, firsthand experience with the basin's transformed air taught Angelenos many things beyond sheer facts about ozone and temperature inversions. To the simple act of stepping out of doors, it introduced disturbing new considerations. For the sick, especially if their ailments were lung-related, a host of new questions about the air's contributions to their maladies begged for answers. Basin physicians and health scientists lent growing credence not just to smog's but to other aerial factors' influence on disease, far more perplexing and pervasive than germ theory had allowed. Suspicions heightened by smog proved easily transferable to other environmental threats, especially if definable as chemical and artificial. In other words, like the new waterborne pollution on Long Island, the shared experience of smog helped make the Los Angeles basin a national seedbed for a new, more precautionary science of environmental health, one that treated the potential damage from toxic exposures far more searchingly and seriously.[54] The traction it was gaining into the 1960s paralleled that of antismog activism, whose social bases of support were widening.

Smog, as it intruded into the everyday lives of Angelenos, effected still another scrambling of boundaries between the natural and the human-made. Smog alerts reverberated with reminders of made-ness: spiking concentrations of a gas traceable to human emissions, signaled by piercing tocsins. After peaking at fifteen in 1955, however, the alerts then tapered off to a handful a year. Gradually, smog came to be absorbed more or less consciously into Angelenos' daily routines. The smog-related lingo and habits that many adopted were those formerly reserved for the weather. In the smoggy season, sometime between July and October, they expected what earlier might have been called "fog" to "roll in." Smog's haze might burn the eyes, but one day there was "an episode, and then the next day it didn't happen, so it could have been atmospheric conditions." Whether smog or fog stood out in Angelenos' recollections of this era depended partly on the neighborhood ecology in which they lived. Those residing in the San Gabriel Valley, such as Bea Alva, often recalled that the smog was "heavy at times." "When it was bad," and especially when smog alerts sounded, "we just dealt with it. We stayed indoors . . . just coped with it." Where smog was less likely, or less cued by alerts, as around Long Beach, the sense of crisis remained less, and ground-hugging mist was more likely deemed "foggy." Lakewooders like Jackie and Bud Rynerson encountered some smog but thought it "not that drastic." So too the Lillards, whose Beverly Glen house was in an almost smog-free section, swept by sea breezes, over much of the 1950s.[55]

Smog's palpable and immediate impact on many an Angeleno's body added to the burden of living with it. By the time of a 1956–57 survey of the Los Angeles medical community, some 91 percent of respondents had recognized a "smog disease" among their patients, including throat "irritation, [a] cough and shortness of breath."[56] The clinical ubiquity of such a diagnosis, based on patient recollections and easily recognizable physical findings, likely mirrored an abundance of similar symptoms and reasoning among lay Angelenos. Though he never saw a doctor for it, Steve Rynerson remembered smog as affecting his lungs in Lakewood, fairly close to Long Beach's industrial corridor. Not surprisingly, his assessment of local smog diverged markedly from that of his parents. "When I grew up," he recalled, "the smog was so bad on many days that after playing on the school yard taking a deep breath would make you cough." Louise Lillard's asthma worsened over the late fifties and early sixties, just when smog began sifting into Beverly Hills. In her attacks, which forced some frightening trips to hospital emergency rooms, she realized that smog may have been the culprit.[57]

A still greater concern was the longer-term health impact of smog. To appreciate why its potential affects should trouble postwar physicians and scientists around Los Angeles, we need to recall the new disease era into which they, like their Long Island counterparts, saw themselves as moving. With infectious diseases now seen as more or less conquered, the "chronic, degenerative" ailments, heart disease and cancer, now stood front and center on the agenda of health scientists in Los Angeles. Over the 1950s, their debates on the causes of a trend like the increasing rate of lung cancer were as pointed as those elsewhere, but with one difference. Angeleno experts found that the possible contribution of pollution was harder to dismiss. Over 80 percent of area physicians most closely involved with cancer, such as radiologists and oncologists, agreed that "air pollution contributes to it."[58] If such a deadly disease was exacerbated or even caused by smog, many asked, then what about the effects of other, newer environmental exposures? The question troubled many area health experts, despite long-standing notions of the modern environment's medical irrelevance. Uncertainties stirred by smog reinforced worries about a host of other contaminants, from pesticides to radioactive fallout to food additives. The floodgates opened to new scientific questions and methodologies, as well as to spiraling new anxieties. The resulting ferment, extending well beyond the science or politics of smog itself, amounted to an ecological rethinking of the human body, whose susceptibility to external influences now looked far more prominent. To assert a navigable order to this Pandora's box of toxic possibilities, many a basin expert and layperson alike leaned on familiar binaries: favoring substances seen as natural or organic, mistrusting those viewed as industrial or man-made.

Already by the late fifties, Los Angeles's role as a breeding ground for medical precautionism had been recognized by Long Islanders mobilizing for the first public trial against DDT. Two of five experts for the plaintiff who testified that the pesticide posed a danger to human health lived in the Los Angeles area. One of them, Dr. Francis Pottenger Jr., headed the Los Angeles County Medical Association's smog committee from the early 1950s onward and had himself conducted the 1956–57 survey of Los Angeles clinicians. Medical suspicions about newly recognized environmental exposures, hatched in these two rapidly suburbanizing corners of the nation, thereby nourished one another.

Pottenger's pathway toward precaution illuminates how, around Los Angeles, its roots ran back to an older vaunting of the region's natural healing powers by an earlier medicine. His father, the physician director of a respected tuberculosis (TB) sanatorium in the San Gabriel Valley, had emphasized the clinic's value in treating TB, but still attached some "importance" to fresh air and "climate." Over the 1940s, the junior Pottenger had made a scientific name for himself through experiments in another naturalist vein, demonstrating the benefits of a diet of unprocessed, "raw" meat and milk that raised questions about pasteurization. During and after his tenure as smog committee chair, Pottenger became increasingly preoccupied with health threats that were chemically defined. By the mid-1960s he was speaking out publicly about pollutants of all sorts, as the most conspicuous of those "danger factors either brought about or aggravated by increased urbanization trends in our society."[59]

Among area physicians and scientists, Pottenger was not alone. Bearing witness to the worst of smog's ravages, Angelenos made an outsized contribution to pioneering new ways of studying other chemical toxins, demonstrating their unexpected reach and toll. At Pasadena's California Institute of Technology, E. B. Lewis and Linus Pauling plumbed the dire possibilities of radioactive fallout, and Clare Patterson, the all-too-unnatural accumulations of lead around the world during the industrial era, especially the twentieth century. Working downtown at the University of Southern California but living in suburban Glendale, Paul Kotin also gained recognition for his studies of the relationship between cancer and smog and other environmental substances. Soon he would become the founding director of the National Institute of Environmental Health Sciences.[60] Angeleno scientists spearheaded what would become a national trend: the making of a new science of pollution that took noninfectious environmental exposures more seriously, that viewed humans as ecologically far more vulnerable.[61]

In the more popular realm, antismog politics continued to overflow its earlier confines. By the late 1950s there appeared a new organization of citizen activists, Stamp Out Smog (sos), the first antismog group to have a woman leader. Under Margaret Levee of Beverly Hills, it oversaw an efflorescence of antismog alliances. Identifying more forthrightly as a woman's group, sos served a bridging function similar to Grace Murphy's United Conservationists on Long Island: "Joining 422 organizations, mainly garden clubs, in calling . . . for specific legislation that will help wipe out smog." sos representatives claimed to enlist sixty thousand people "under the sos banner."[62] Among those joining the battle against smog were self-styled nature advocates, whose ideas about what and where nature was had long made smog seem like someone else's fight. Part of the reason, as when the Federation of Hillside and Canyon Associations added smog to its agenda in late 1958, was that smog continued to spread. The federation justified its new position-taking with an announcement that an "unhappy milestone" had been passed: "Smog has come to the hills, not just in little wisps now and then, as in the past, but in tearful, lung-searing clouds." About ten years later, when the Los Angeles chapter of the Sierra Club finally lent its voice and activism to the smog battle, high ozone levels were no longer confined even to the Los Angeles basin. According to state health department estimates, some 70 percent of California's population suffered from smog-induced eye irritation and 97 percent from reduced visibility attributable to smog.[63] Beyond smog's countryward spread, though, its relevance to suburban nature advocacy could also have a deeper, more personal dimension.

We may better fathom this significance by looking at the role smog played in the lives of Richard and Louise Lillard and Steve Rynerson. Whether worsening smog or mold in their damp lot at Beverly Glen was responsible, an exacerbation of Louise's asthma over the early sixties forced this couple to move. Richard was thereby forced to abandon the house and yard he had lovingly cultivated for twenty years. They settled in a neighborhood closer to the ocean, more windswept but also more urbanized, without a canyon or chaparral next door. Over the same period, Lillard was busy writing *Eden in Jeopardy: Man's Prodigal Meddling with His Environment: The Southern California Experience*, the closest thing this region acquired to an environmentalist manifesto. Although smog took up only a single chapter, the fall of the Southern California "Eden" depicted here was more than just the impersonal narrative of a region. It also expressed a personal pain, which may well have been smog-induced, over Lillard's own expulsion from an Edenic suburban enclave.

On his way to joining the Sierra Club, young Lakewooder Steve Rynerson followed an opposing trajectory, but to a similar ideological place. His trips out to the Sierra Nevada made him understand just how smog-infested his childhood haunts had been. Rynerson came to realize that a life without smog might be possible, that "not every child . . . had several days a year [of] lungs aching."[64] Smog thereby nudged him toward a felt alienation akin to Lillard's. What the stinging haze also owed to workings of the basin's mountainous rims and sunshine became steadily more difficult to remember. Instead, pollution, through the "grey pall" it cast over the entire Los Angeles metropolis, confirmed nature's utter absence there. In tandem with vanishing orange groves and other changes that Rynerson observed, smog only served to magnify the growing appreciation that he felt for "other places in the world that were more beautiful," where nature's overweaning presence filled him with awe and wonder. Even among those living in mass subdivisions such as Rynerson, smog, as it consolidated impressions of Los Angeles as a "vast wasteland of just poor planning, . . . completely man-made," was helping nourish a new species of nature advocacy.[65]

By the late sixties, smog itself, but especially the way it was interpreted, ushered Los Angles–area nature politics into a new environmental cast. As on Long Island, the groups coalescing into this region's movement adopted the pollution issue and, often at the same moment, a new name for what they sought to defend: not so much "nature" as the "environment." While not excluding traditional concerns of the conservation movement, such as park making and resource protection, the new label seemed an especially good fit for issues that conservationists had been slower to embrace, from smog to sprawl. "Environment" worked in part through its own vagueness, through the variety of issues it could yoke together. But it also stoked unexpected passions. Why? Because it tapped directly into so many personal experiences and pre-existing commitments. Because it so deftly and concretely united a panoply of concerns long seen as separate but that so many Los Angeles suburb dwellers now shared. Across the rest of the nation, as well, advocates of the environment quickly found much company.

Part III
Environmental Nation

Chapter 8

"The Environment" as a Suburban Place

T he sheer magnitude of the first Earth Day, celebrated on April 22, 1970, took many by surprise. Some twenty million people, by the organizers' count, packed its assemblies or poured into the streets. Although it surpassed the tallies of other protests that splashed across the headlines and nightly newscasts over the late sixties, Earth Day remains arguably the least understood of all these movements. Antiwar and civil rights protesters had marched on central citadels, Washington or Birmingham, but Earth Day activists assaulted a bewildering abundance of targets. In towns and cities, schools and colleges across the country, they seemed to surge from everywhere at once. Nor were the participants as easy to pigeonhole. They hailed from starkly different backgrounds and persuasions—Democrats and Republicans, elderly conservationists and students, hippies and housewives.[1] For many observers, Earth Day's outpouring seemed to either overwhelm or dilute the prevailing sense of what a movement was supposed to be.

Ubiquitous and momentous as this day's demonstration appeared, it was, far more so than most allowed, situated in, and in dialogue with, a particular kind of place. For many if not most of Earth Day's participants, those corners of the earth on which they gathered, those environments on whose behalf they rallied, were suburbs.

One hint of these hidden roots lies in how the day's most spontaneous upwelling was confined largely to the United States, the nation whose postwar cities had sprawled the most. The later rise of environmental and "green" parties in other countries has confirmed the international precedent of this vast outpouring of 1970. It signaled the arrival of the first, as yet only, mass movement for environmentalism in the Western world. Across the Atlantic, national governments did declare a year for "nature conservancy" or, in the case of Sweden, arrange an "Earth Week." The

American Earth Day also had its Washington-based initiators: Senator Gaylord Nelson (D-Wis.) joined with Representative Paul McCloskey (R-Calif.) to push the notion of a national environmental teach-in. But what stunned Earth Day's organizers, what distinguished America's 1970 version from the ones overseas, was how much the idea took off at the grass roots. Outside of the era's riots and wildcat strikes, no American protest of the late 1960s erupted more energetically from the bottom up. As Nelson put it, Earth Day "organized itself."[2]

Nowhere were Earth Day's grassroots initiatives more in evidence than in those corners of the nation most thoroughly transformed by suburbanizing. For decades, residents of Greater Los Angeles and Long Island had grappled with that array of issues, from open space to pollution, now characterized as "environmental." There, the tracing of connections between them, increasingly called "ecological," was well rehearsed. Denis Hayes, a 26-year-old Harvard Law student tapped as the event's D.C.-based coordinator, visited Southern California several times to try and craft "some central umbrella." But ultimately, a sympathetic journalist concluded, "There just wasn't time or glue to consolidate." No one could hope to "tie together hundreds of high schools," keep abreast of "what the next leaders were doing . . . assume responsibility for everything scheduled in the sprawl."[3] What amplified the Earth Day excitement there, what also aroused passions elsewhere, was how, by the end of the 1960s, such places' problems had come to be conceived as manifestations of a larger crisis.

Re-creating these local and regional struggles as national or even global ones required much doing. On the one hand, what had happened around places like Greater Los Angeles and Greater New York City had to be represented as exemplifying the fullest and most foreboding possibilities of catastrophe. Over the 1960s a host of authors, officials, and activists did just that, seizing on the sprawl and industrial pollution of these metropolises as harbingers of what might befall the rest of the nation. This environmental infamy proved a boon for Angeleno and New York–area activists, inviting a media spotlight and affirming a national-historical significance to their battles. Yet the elevation of these places' dilemmas into national news had its costs. Among them, attention was further diverted from stark differentials in just whose natural amenities were being razed and just whose neighborhoods were being polluted. The unequal distribution of each problem more locally, within metropolitan landscapes fragmented by class and race, underwent a further eclipse.

The main story line became the far-reaching, national extent of the environmental crisis, as evidenced by unmistakable similarities between metropolitan New York or Los Angeles and other parts of the country. The same problems that had reared their ugly heads so early and so perilously around the nation's largest metropolises had begun showing up elsewhere. Pollution as well as sprawl became documented around many smaller cities, especially in states with large populations and many industrial plants. Ultimately, these resemblances had their limits: many places across the nation remained as yet unscathed by sprawl and unstained by modern chemical pollutants. Ironically, these regions of the country, mostly more rural, matched the purest nature ideals of environmentalists most closely and effortlessly. Where environmental activism was slower to take hold, these parts of the nation would—in the wake of Earth Day—provide environmentalism's most powerful opponents with regional political strongholds.

Of the many issues newly identified as "environmental" by the first Earth Day, pollution, in particular, acquired an overriding significance for suburban environmentalism. Better to understand why, it is useful to compare its later 1960s construction as a national concern to that of sprawl, which culminated a few years earlier. Spearheading the antisprawl campaign were mostly well-to-do suburban residents, many of whom still enjoyed a wilder, still informal, commons near their homes. But around Long Island and Los Angeles, pollution was less exclusively an issue of the propertied; the worst of it was often concentrated in the neighborhoods of the worst-off. At the same time, DDT and smog were threats from which even the most exclusive suburban properties offered little protection. Prior to Earth Day, pollution spurred new collaborations between local residents and the campus-based: university academics, high school teachers, and students. Moreover, precisely as older conservation groups became more willing to step in and tackle the pollution problem, they experienced a great influx of new members. The rising alarm about pollution did more than any other issue to move an urban-edge politics of nature's defense beyond the conservationist goals (of preserving natural lands and resources) and the conservationist rhetoric. Not coincidentally, those suburban activists who accomplished this broadening also gravitated toward a new name for themselves: environmentalists.

Starting about 1964, this new umbrella term of the environment diffused through print and activist circles with astonishing speed. Soon, it overran the older conservationist jargon on which the Long Island Murphys and the suburban Los Angeles Lillards had relied, even as they labored to alter the latter's content and thrust. For them and their suburban colleagues, environment solved a naming problem. Finally they had a viable label for the hybrid landscapes they defended, too natural to be called "suburbia," but not "nature," either, at least not in the strictly nonhuman meaning of the term. Their concern for these places was deeply rooted in their own observations, sentiments, and surmises, yet in this era, they had also learned, such claims stood little chance against reigning experts. Hence, they too appealed to science, most frequently, "ecology," as grounding for what they asserted. But that "balance of nature" they invoked had surprisingly few roots in any formal scientific discipline. Even for the movement's many scientific professionals, who veered from the usual collegial circuits to intervene in local civics, "ecological" talk often licensed popular, rather than professional, ways of knowing.

A neighborhood as well as an urban regional advocacy were further enabled, as were other innovations intended to establish alternative, "greener" modes of consumption.[4] Forgotten, in this rush to create goods and markets that were more eco-friendly, was how suburbanizing itself had once offered an all-too-similar promise. Faced with the dense and dirty cities of the early twentieth century, more and more Americans had sought to buy their way to healthier, more natural surroundings on the urban edge. The historical ironies ran deep: many problems now being labeled as "environmental" had deep roots in this earlier consumer-oriented solution, when closeness to urban-edge nature had become a matter of private purchase. Environmentalism as a political movement required overcoming the divides that had ensued: between well-to-do suburbs, with wild lands next door, and mass suburbs, steadily joining downtowns and industrial districts in losing whatever wild patches they had had. This next round in the greening of consumer markets, just being hatched, boded a reopening of these schisms by offering still more reasons for abandoning places where nature seemed hardest to see.

At the time, however, another possibility dawned: that of an environmental altruism. Environmentalism opened the door, at least, for well-off suburban dwellers to begin confronting inequities that had been planted, as well as built, into their own fragmented metropolitan landscapes. If humans were themselves a part of ecosystems, tethered via interchanges of substance and energy, then didn't a nature exist even where human bodies were most packed and their surroundings were most industrial or human-made? And if so, then didn't environmentalism have *more* work to do there among residents of the least privileged races with the lowest incomes? Yet suburban environmentalists found powerful reasons for resisting these implications. After all, the most patently manufactured places were precisely those that, to them, seemed the most alienating. Such sites had far less appeal than the patently wild, uncultivated landscapes that they had learned to appreciate as most natural—where the human hand was far harder to notice. Environmentalists' search for salves to their own alienation, for closeness to a nature that seemed purer and more genuine to them, kept the altruistic potential of their new movement mostly unborn.

Nationalizing Sprawl

Rachel Carson's *Silent Spring* (1962), though best known for its revelations about pesticides, famously opened with her sketch of an ideal landscape: a town and countryside in balance. "Once," she wrote, "there was a town in the heart of America where all life seemed to live in harmony with its surroundings." That "heart," that "harmony" rested in the town's relationship with its informal commons of rural land. It was surrounded by "a checkerboard of prosperous farms, with fields of grain and hillsides of orchards," woods of "oak and maple and birch," and "a backdrop of pines." In these places, concord stood visible in the parallel flourishing of human and nonhuman lives, in the beauty of laurel and wildflowers along its roadsides, in the deer and fox that "silently crossed the fields," in the trout-filled streams that flowed "clear and cold out of the hills," in the "abundance and variety of bird life."[5] In Carson's telling, this avowedly fictional "fable" of equilibrium between town and country, the closest *Silent Spring* came to any mention of the urban, then fell prey to a pesticide. Yet nearly this same fabulous ideal came to be widely invoked in other literature of the period about the careening assault of sprawl.

This ascent of the sprawl critique in the early 1960s occurred as demographic change itself yielded much for its critics to work with. By 1966, for the first time in American history, suburb dwellers outnumbered residents in central cities. With a million acres being converted from nonurban to urban uses annually, metropolitan suburbs were growing seven times faster than downtowns.[6] Works framing sprawl as a national story stuck with such numbers, largely ignoring the nature seeking that propelled so much of it. Readers learned little about how many suburban migrants sought to secure countrylike land next door, or how, through the spread of subdivisions, an unprecedented proportion of open or exclusively planted land was being folded *into* America's urban fabric. Instead, what riveted sprawl's critics, from philanthropists, foundation officials, planners, architects, and other experts to a bevy of popular writers, was its destruction of the rural. Aiming at a phenomenon that had come first and was still easiest to recognize in places like Los Angeles and Long Island, popular writers strove to promote a nationwide sense of urgency by demonstrating sprawl's creeping universality. The critical coverage of sprawl followed the playbook of 1950s reportage on mass suburbia: singling out places that *were* similar with little regard for comparison or counterexample.

No individual had a greater hand in making sprawl a matter of national concern than the pundit William Whyte. Picking up the term from critics among professional planners and architects, Whyte in the late 1950s began arguing the case for a "vanishing countryside" nationwide. Starting with the San Gabriel Valley, he quickly found comparable instances around other cities, primarily in the Northeast and Midwest. Along the way, he garnered many well-endowed and powerful allies, from philanthropist Laurance S. Rockefeller to a Committee for Outdoor Recreation, appointed by President Dwight D. Eisenhower in 1958, to Stewart Udall, President John F. Kennedy's secretary of the interior. Udall's semiofficial *The Quiet Crisis* (1963) reiterated Whyte's message that American cities had been "grow[ing] too fast to grow well." They had thereby become "a focal point" for the nation's "quiet crisis in conservation."[7]

The new popular literature on sprawl, citing the nation's most urbanized regions as exemplars, went on to depict the city's spread as more and more sweeping and ominous, projecting "cancerously in all directions." Reprising the 1950s critique of "suburbia," it now had less to say about "suburbanites" and their conformity and more about their houses and enveloping landscapes. Complaints about a lower class of suburban dwellings could still echo stridently, as in Peter Blake's *God's Own Junkyard* (1964) about a subdivision's "massive, monotonous ugliness." In a new twist, though, hardly hinted at in the earlier literature, the focus now fell on the rural, "open" land being ravaged. The old overhead photographs of mass suburbia no longer dramatized heroic builders' flourish but, instead, how a countryside had been razed. Vistas swept past individual developments and communities to take in the surrounding land. Critics also ratcheted up the scale of their critiques; their jeremiads acquired a wider, regional scope. Robert Cubbedge, in his *Destroyers of America* (1964), found the entire trek from Los Angeles to San Francisco "in the short space of fifteen years . . . so scarified by man that the natural beauty of the region had been all but lost." The tone turned angrier, assailing the land's "rape" and more: "That suburban sprawl will devour the nation long before nuclear fission." The physical destruction spawned a new emblem: the bulldozer.

Barely noted in press coverage of the postwar housing boom, bulldozers by the mid-1960s were singled out in photographs and cartoons. Driverless and voracious, their images cast the making of suburbs as an utterly impersonal, mechanized, relentless process. Their gleaming blades defined the trajectory of the countryside into which they dug: it was "vanishing."[8]

As for the rural or natural-looking land that lay threatened, it acquired more personal narratives, of wilder places intimately known and tragically lost. For many people, those landscapes where they had first glimpsed a "oneness with nature," a harmony like that conjured in Carson's fable, lay in distant rural childhoods. Yet at least as frequently, others invoked what we may recognize as *suburban* places, along the edges of America's largest cities, as the locales where they had seen a nature lost. Cubbedge, who years before had moved to Long Island's Nassau County, deplored the "swallowed" land, roadside trash, and "dead" beaches witnessed around his current home. Whyte assailed the "outrages" inflicted on the suburban countryside around his childhood home outside Philadelphia. Margo Tupper, in her *No Place to Play* (1966), wrote of a neighborhood along the edge of Washington, D.C., where she had moved in 1949 to start her family. It lay near "acres of untouched woodlands which were a refuge for children—a place to play in natural surroundings." One day "the bulldozers" arrived. "These huge earth-eating machines raped the woods, filled up the creek, buried the wildflowers and frightened away the rabbits and birds. In less than a month the first of two hundred look-alike, closely set small houses rose to take the place of our beautiful forest."[9]

These were not stories about home buying or home owning, at least not directly. Rather, they were accounts of what followed after moving in, especially into those more spacious and well-provisioned neighborhoods that the authors hinted they were privileged to enjoy. Property titles, the very identity of their family as homeowners and landowners, much less as suburban dwellers, slid into an unremarkable backdrop, naturalized. Instead, the authors wrote of their awareness of a surrounding, undeclared commons—"our beautiful forest." They and their children had come to know a harmony with its trees and bushes, its birds and wildlife, its paths and playgrounds and hiding places, akin to those in Carson's fable. The meanings these places acquired seemed quite independent of the legal or the economic; they were more emotional and heartfelt. Nearby wild plants and wildlife, familiar as family, upon recollection, stirred fondness and more: well-nigh spiritual intimations of an extrahuman world.

But was this nature? Wildlife biologists or wilderness advocates would have demurred; it was too domesticated, too suburban. Indeed, by dint of "ecosystemic" approaches in postwar scientific ecology, a pristine nature was becoming increasingly undecipherable to the naked eye; it was difficult even for professionals to find. Margo Tupper acknowledged as much, designating this next-door nature as mainly for the children. All the same, her tale of its shattering resonated with many older stories about frontier loss and more ancient ones about lost gardens and lost innocence—back to the Judeo-Christian Garden of Eden. Not that it would do to mention the Bible. Tupper took care to connect her stories with John Muir's more secular gospel, even quoting his ill-fated defense of Hetch Hetchy Valley: "'No holier temple has ever been consecrated by the heart of man.'"[10] But in their more local referents, hers and these other personal narratives followed more in the tracks laid down by Henry Bunner over a half century before. They were not about some isolated corner of the Sierras; they were about a *suburban* countryside lost.

Such stories echoed a tradition building for over half a century, sharpened and spread among suburban homeowners after World War II in neighborly grumbling and, more publicly, in hearings before hundreds of zoning boards. That tales of suburban loss now surfaced as a national story reflected the growing success of only a small portion of local resistance— those who could point to a recognizably wild "nature" around the neighborhoods they defended. A 1966 article about "The Rape of the Land" in the *Saturday Evening Post*, for instance, featured a couple witnessing obliteration of "a swampy thicket . . . next to their home" on Cape Cod, where the first National Seashore had recently been created. That "builders have 'developed' 70 percent of the slopes" of Los Angeles's Santa Monica Mountains, as the *Post* also reported, echoed the cries of a five-year-old preservation movement then on the verge of celebrating the first state acquisitions of mountain land. As reporters acknowledged, land rape had become a story *because* people were fighting back, "organizing to oppose ill-planned growth and the waste of open land" "all over the nation." "The fight to preserve the spectacles of nature—the majestic rivers, the remote mountains, the wild canyons—is 100 years old," summarized the *Post*, but "the struggle to save the modest beauty of men's own backyards is new and promising."[11]

Such coverage obscured as much as it illuminated about the origins of such movements and the national "struggle" that they were now discovered to comprise. For starters, reporters reflected little, if at all, on their own geographic selectivity. Far and away the most invocations were of less developed places along the edges of the nation's biggest cities—New York, Los Angeles, Boston, Washington, D.C.—with other regions and rural places farther from cities going unmentioned. As yet there was no Atlanta or Houston counterpart to Long Island's Nature Conservancy, now almost a decade and a half old, or the Santa Monica Park Association, then celebrating an early political victory. Nevertheless, talk of a nationwide struggle for "natural beauty" worked to obscure these regional differences.

Previous chapters in this book have made clear just whose "backyards" of "modest beauty" were being defended: those of the regional elite. Homeowners in West Los Angeles or those who had second homes on Fire Island could afford the higher prices demanded for urban-edge property near a visibly wilder nature. Media depictions brushed past how activism on behalf of backyard "nature" could only occur in some corners of this era's urban edges, fragmented not just by race and class, but by differing apportionments of "natural beauty." The smaller-lot suburbs, the Levittowns and Lakewoods whose "backyards" had already become considerably less wild, were now routinely thought to be destructively antinature, their "look-alike, closely set small houses" threatening the "modest beauty" that sprawl's opponents sought to preserve.

Boosting local activism was increased support over the early to midsixties from higher levels of government. The political opportunity structure for park advocacy was changing, as states such as New York (1960) and California (1964) passed park bonds and as the federal government stepped in to finance and oversee the acquisition of urban-edge reserves.[12] Campaigns for the preservation of New York's Fire Island, Greater Boston's Cape Cod, and San Francisco's Point Reyes found success not only because of agitation by vacation homeowners and visitors, but also through the backing of Stewart Udall and others in the White House and Congress. Federal decision makers created "national seashores," starting with Cape Cod followed by Fire Island, as well as other new programs for public land purchases. Washington's funding of "open-space," first proposed by President Kennedy, was expanded by President Lyndon B. Johnson. A mammoth land and water conservation fund, set up by Congress in 1964, enabled still further acquisitions of urban-edge land. A Conference on Natural Beauty, convening over May 24 and 25, 1965, in the Johnson White House, put a federal imprimatur on the public clamor against sprawl and on behalf of "open space."

Officially organized by Laurance Rockefeller, the meeting called together about one thousand public officials, representatives from voluntary and business groups, and experts ranging from biologists to recreation and housing officials to urban planners and architects. William Whyte, tapped as a conference comanager, ensured the exclusion of "classic conservation" topics such as wilderness or forests or national parks. Instead, the agenda sought to highlight a "new conservation," centered, in Rockefeller's words, on "the environment where most people live and work—our cities and suburbs and the countryside around them." Elite policy makers, who were well represented, regarded the conference as breaking with the economism of postwar liberalism, marking a shift from "quantity to quality."[13] That "natural" features should so invariably yield beauty or quality, however, was treated far more as a matter of faith than as a point requiring demonstration or argument. The "pastoral dream" that some attendees noted running through the discussions no doubt had some downtown roots—for instance, in the City Beautiful Movement half a century before. But where this ideal had been most widely and emphatically captured over the postwar period was in upper-end suburban housing. As the downtowns of so many of the nation's largest cities had suffered from declining wealth and upkeep, as the very structure of these cities had been fundamentally altered by aspirations to live with nature nearby, this ideal had, in the America of the 1960s, become a predominantly suburban one.[14]

The floral and faunal embodiments of the wild that now, with increasing exclusivity, qualified as nature remained far more accessible in the suburbs of the most privileged. These residents enjoyed more open acreage, more trees and shrubs and wildlife, more residual or preserved wild patches, as well as stricter zoning. By contrast, suburban neighborhoods of wageworker, African American, or Hispanic families not only tended to harbor fewer such features; these places also were more vulnerable to losing what they had. Rockefeller tried to orient the conference to redress this difference. Natural beauty next door should not remain "a frill or afterthought or luxury" but should be democratized: "There can be cleanliness and touches of green no matter how pretentious or humble the home." Yet the Natural Beauty Conference had relatively little to say about the many suburbs built over the postwar period where wilder touches of green—those informal commons that had drawn residents—had already vanished. Indeed, the only session explicitly addressing suburbs was about the prospects for a "new suburbia"—a move that not-so-subtly wrote off the chances for the older one.[15]

A look at the delegations sent to this conference from our case study areas offers further insights into just whose suburban aspirations it expressed.

Among the participants were those who had led recent charges for natural land preservation around Long Island and Los Angeles: Maurice Bardash of the Citizens Committee to Save Fire Island and Marvin Braude of Santa Monica Regional Park Association. However eager they were to dissociate themselves from a mass suburbia, for their own residences, a majority of delegates from the New York and Los Angeles areas had chosen suburbs, albeit those that were the wealthiest and most naturally endowed.[16] Projecting a more Archimedean vantage point, prescribing for the many, they endeavored to embellish the "natural beauty" of entire metropolitan areas rather than a particular type of residential neighborhood. Yet theirs was an ideal that, it went unsaid, had become eminently achievable next door only for a few—a large portion of the conferees among them. The intent, certainly, was altruistic: calling for more trees and other plantings, a visible nature, for everyone. Nevertheless, the proceedings reinforced accusations that those suburbs where a vast majority of urban-edge dwellers now lived were antinatural and ugly. These suburbanites, conferees conceded—not to mention those living in urban ghettos—could find a genuine nature, and real beauty, only by driving farther and farther away from their homes.

For Angeleno and Long Island activists, the Conference on Natural Beauty seemed a heady culmination of long-standing struggles. The high-profile forum was in many ways a national projection of concerns shared, and prescriptions hatched, across the nation's most metropolitan regions, those most remade, over previous decades, by the new, more dispersed mode of urbanizing. Though nearly one-third of the delegates listed work addresses in Washington, D.C., the next biggest groups hailed from New York (155) and California (95). The California delegation contained about as many as the total attendees from all southeastern states and over twice as many as those from the entire Mountain West.[17] In the latter two regions, whose representation at the conference verged on tokenism, what conferees were calling for could seem fresher and more novel, especially where sprawl had begun to arrive. The conference served to inspire new initiatives around southeastern cities: the founding, in 1966, of Houston's Buffalo Bayou Preservation Association and, some months later, of the Georgia Conservancy, in Atlanta, described as an "idea whose time has come." But for delegates or onlookers from more rural locales, where natural beauty seemed more of an ineradicable given, the avowedly metropolitan focus of the conference rendered its proceedings largely irrelevant.[18]

If the Natural Beauty Conference had little positive to say about an older, mass suburbia, it conveyed a still more dismissive message about another place considered, if anything, *more* unmistakably human-made: the industrial factory. The reason lay partly in what the organizers decided about a related issue that soon loomed much larger in the media's spotlight: pollution. Rockefeller admitted that "perhaps no problems are more important to the quality of the environment and to our general well-being." But with "established research and action programs" devoted to air and water contamination, he concluded, "we can affirm our strong support for pollution [control] and move on."[19] For many other Americans, especially in suburbs like those around Los Angeles and Long Island, tainted air and water seemed, on the contrary, where popular knowledge and action were *most* necessary.

Nationalizing Pollution

To the old-line conservation as well as antisprawl movements, this most glaring omission from the "natural beauty" umbrella posed fundamental challenges that were less appreciated by those who viewed it as just another public issue. Open space advocates largely followed the conservationists in thinking about nature they sought to protect as "out there": that is, land, wildlife, or other natural resources that were essentially separate from the people who would destroy them. Pollution, however, left no doubt that human beings were part of ecosystems, that their very bodies belonged to nature itself. A common evolutionary heritage meant that the physiological effects of toxins on nonhuman organisms often resembled human responses—a foundation for the modern experimental science of toxicology. Furthermore, as other scientists including ecologists were demonstrating, pollutants circulated with surprising facility. Any contaminent discovered among birds or fish or wildlife might not stay "out there" for long; through the air, water, and food chain, that toxin could filter into people's neighborhoods, homes, and internal organs, to wreak havoc on human life. Hence, as pollution leaped up the list of media and popular priorities over the mid-to-late sixties, warnings echoed that human "survival" or "terracide" was at stake.

Without the possibility of a nuclear holocaust, ever looming in this Cold War era, such apocalyptic admonitions would not have gained so much ground. In retrospect, too, it is hard to miss how the "pollution" about which so many came to voice such apprehension had become freighted with meanings beyond those of chemical contamination. More indirectly, the rising clamor over pollution reflected just how many cultural boundaries, seemingly so fundamental and stable before and during World War II, now seem to have been blurred or breached. Among these were the borders between city and country, human bodies and their environments, the natural and the human-made. But social relations also turned stormy—between blacks and whites, young and old, women and men. The explosion of nationwide anxiety about pollution in the late sixties United States was no doubt overdetermined, with many earmarks of what sociologists call a "moral panic."[20] Not least among the contributors to its making was the message about pollution emanating from a swelling popular diatribe, reputedly inaugurated by Rachel Carson's 1962 masterwork.

Silent Spring never mentioned urban sprawl. But what tipped its town-and-country idyll into imbalance, a spray of "white powder," was easily more frightening. Unpacking DDT's effects, Carson wove together ideas of upset equilibria from two sorts of contemporary sciences that, to this point, had had little formal truck with one another. From a new "ecosystem ecology," increasingly grounded in chemical analysis, she took revelations of the far-reaching, often toxic effects of DDT and other pesticides on wildlife: the birds, fish, and foxes.[21] From the health sciences Carson drew on another notion of imbalance, elaborated especially through physiological, chemical, and other studies of cancer. Life-threatening tumors were now thought to begin with a cell or cells kicked into metabolic overdrive by chemical "carcinogens," DDT and other "synthetic organics" possibly among them.[22] Integrating these two versions of tipped balances, ecological and medical, *Silent Spring* suggested more harrowing conclusions than either alone would have countenanced.

As this book has gone to great lengths to argue, Rachel Carson was hardly the first to forge such a fusion. Already, scientists and regulators grappling with suburban problems like the groundwater pollution on Long Island or the smog around Los Angeles had forged interdisciplinary methodologies that were arguably more ecological, with nary a mention of any "ecosystem." And with less resort to any formal science, suburban activists had begun connecting local pollution with natural land preservation, to see these issues as of a piece. Especially in places like suburban Los Angeles and Long Island, this newly integrative political vision had leaned on a fifteen-year effort to reconsider customs—from eating and drinking to planting and cultivating—in chemical terms. Ever more searchingly and steadfastly, proponents of change had come to favor more "natural" substances, as well as practices, by distinguishing them from others that were "synthetic" or "artificial." Many were amateurs or on the margins of the mainstream, such as organic gardeners, anthroposophists, antifluoridationists, and alternative health practitioners. But in places like those showcased in this book, this same quest was finding more legitimate and influential spokespeople among "personal" or "everyman" conservationists, widely respected doctors, scientists, and other academics. Carson's great accomplishment was to meld these many scattershot, isolated, and often informal assertions of parallelism between health and nonhuman ecology into a book-length and singularly coherent vision.

By her synthesis as well, the defense of uninhabited, wild nature was no longer separate from, or at odds with, that of human health. To the contrary, both were threatened, at once, by the same thing: "a sudden rise and prodigious growth of an industry for the production of man-made or synthetic chemicals," especially those "with insecticidal properties." Nature here, in stark contrast to those meanings celebrated in the Natural Beauty Conference, was not necessarily confined to natural-looking, aesthetically appealing places. Rather, if often far less visibly, it extended everywhere, from the cells inside human bodies to the least inhabited corners of the globe. The scale of contamination revealed not only nature's pervasiveness, but also a new level of human vulnerability. A "sea of carcinogens" now lapped at humanity's heels, from Venezuela to New York, to Florida, to Wisconsin, to Germany, to Finland, to California.[23]

As global a vision as one might concoct, *Silent Spring* nevertheless had its firmest roots in suburban locales. The letter sparking Carson's commitment to write the book came from a woman in suburban Boston who had watched a DDT spraying decimate the birds in her own and her neighbors' yards. Carson also drew heavily on the 1957 anti-DDT lawsuit on Long Island. Her research began with the trial transcript, and Marjorie Spock, leader of the lawsuit, then became Carson's "chief clipping service." The web of experts Spock had brought in to testify at the trial served as Carson's own. They and others on whom Carson most relied lived and worked in suburbs, including Dr. Morton Biskind of Westport, Connecticut, and Wilhelm Hueper, at the National Institutes of Health headquarters in Bethesda, Maryland. Even Carson herself was, arguably, a suburbanite: though she loved her spot on the Maine coast, she spent most of the year in Silver Spring, Maryland, on the edge of Washington, D.C.[24]

Silent Spring reached out to suburban readers in a host of ways, both subtle and overt. Ignoring cities, limiting her invocations of the urban to "a small town in the heart of America," Carson flattered the conceit of the suburban better-off that *their* homes were not in any "suburbia," that they led essentially nonurban lives. Factories also fell into the shadowy backdrop: quick-striking maladies and death among workers appeared only briefly and in passing. Dwelling at much greater length on cancer and other chronic ailments, more likely to trouble a suburban readership, she studiously avoided mention of infectious diseases, whose absence suburb dwellers of this period, at least in metropolitan New York and Los Angeles tended to take for granted. On shifting from dangers to human health to threats to wildlife, Carson explicitly summoned the self-interest of the "suburbanite." For the "suburbanite who derives pleasure from birds in his garden," she wrote, "anything that destroys the wildlife of an area for even a single year has deprived him of a pleasure to which he has a legitimate right."[25]

The firestorm of criticism that first greeted Carson's book did delay pollution's arrival as a national preoccupation, but not for long.[26] Around the time of the Natural Beauty Conference, the first national polls were conducted of Americans' attitudes toward pollution. Respondents placed it down the list of what they would do "if it were your job to beautify America," even though over a quarter of them, and about half of those living in big cities, found it "very serious" or "somewhat serious." As pollsters continued to ask about pollution over the next five years, a veritable "miracle of public opinion" occurred. Those reporting a "very serious" concern about pollution mushroomed from only one in ten to a nationwide majority. By 1970, a whopping 82 percent of Americans named "control of air and water pollution" their top priority for governmental spending. Edging out the Vietnam War as the single most popular choice, it achieved a historic polling high for environmental issues in the United States, never equaled before or since (as of 2011). Of all the nature-related issues suddenly seen as linked, pollution, more than any other, spearheaded the making of the new "environmental" bundle.[27]

The usual explanations for this burst of concern point either to media and public fickleness (the "issue attention" cycle) or, emulating Carson, to industrial innovations themselves.[28] Surely contributing, as well, was the deluge of popular print devoted to the pollution problem (see Figure 5 in the Appendix). Though *Silent Spring* is the best-remembered, between 1962 and 1970 dozens of books followed along the path Rachel Carson had blazed, emphasizing how novel and unnatural other postwar pollutants were. Laboratory-hatched "synthetics" included not just pesticides but detergents, dyes, "germ killers," herbicides, solvents, plastics, and other petrochemicals, along with radioactive fallout. This new environmental muckraking mostly, like *Silent Spring*, evoked a nearly placeless

Organic food stores and ecology action groups by state, 1970. With a few exceptions, natural food markets and ecology action groups clustered in the same parts of the country: the Northeast, Midwest, and Pacific Coast. (Compiled from data in The Organic Directory *[Emmaus, Pa.: Rodale Press, 1971])*

ubiquity for pollution, national or global in its extent. But as the decade wore on, authors drifted away from other of Carson's premises.

The earliest publications, similar to Carson's own work, were rooted in 1950s campaigns against chemical additives and on behalf of organic gardening and more natural foods.[29] These paradigmatic preachings and practices continued to proliferate informally in the most urbanized—and suburbanized—corners of the country all the way up to the first Earth Day. Sales of Rodale publications boomed by 1970, and organic markets and cooperatives flourished. But in parallel to the assault on Carson's book, powerful groups and institutions stepped up their attacks on organic gardeners, antifluoridationists, and other alleged "faddists." To avoid accusations that they were "anti-scientific," popular antipollution authors by the midsixties were adjusting their messages accordingly. More emphasized their consultations with public health officials. In judging what substances were chemical or artificial versus organic or natural, they refrained from as sweeping or dogmatic a line drawing. They steered away especially from fights like that over fluoride, which might pit health officials against them.[30] Even so, their rhetoric on pollution heated up, thanks to what prominent health scientists were saying.

By 1964 the nation's titular public health leader, Surgeon General Luther Terry, voiced the same baleful narrative. On the opening of the National Institute for Environmental Health Science, his declarations could well have issued from Carson's pen: "Man's" "synthetic" environment, which he "himself has largely created" by expanding "urban areas" and the "wide use of chemicals," raised questions about "human survival." Both the uncertainties associated with urbanizing and industrial innovation and a widely felt lack of scientific capabilities for grappling with them led to the creation of this new institute and, more generally, to a huge increase in federal funding for pollution studies during the Kennedy and Johnson administrations.[31] Galvanizing this burst of support, cancer and other chronic diseases were still on the rise. At the same time, the development of new scientific tools and methods was nurturing the promise that the longer-term environmental causes of these maladies could be better understood.

Through lifetime animal testing, for example, toxicologists were turning up more evidence of cumulative and subtle damage in animals' bodies prior to any clinical onset. Further, new techniques in chronic disease epidemiology were yielding greater scientific understanding and consensus about slower-acting influences on disease, at least those easiest to track. From this science came that first trajectory toward imbalance picked up by Carson and her successors: that diminutive but decades-long exposures could launch the deadliest of diseases. The surgeon general's reports that smoking caused lung cancer, first asserted in 1957 and more definitively in 1964, were only the best-known conclusions to follow from this scientific efflorescence.[32] New evidence was also surfacing about the chronic consequences of a host of pollutants—among them, ozone, radiation, lead, and asbestos. That so many of these toxins came into human contact through industrial activities confirmed chemical naturalists' premises about the dangers of synthetics. Within much of the health science community into the later 1960s, the new certainties about some environmental chemicals only raised the stakes over others, far more numerous, whose effects on human health were less studied or even unknown.[33]

These findings would have been less alarming had it not been for the burgeoning new knowledge of the chemical makeup of air, water, and soil, as well as of biological tissues. The postwar technologies of chemical analysis, gas chromatography, and mass spectrometry, pioneered by petroleum engineers and nuclear scientists, had already detected substances down to the parts per million. By the mid-1960s, courtesy of the atomic absorption spectrophotometer, the sensitivity of detection shot downward from parts per million to parts per billion and, in some cases, per trillion.[34] Drawing on these innovations to expand their own analytic capabilities, public health and other investigators over the late 1950s into the 1960s crafted a message that the environmental muckrakers then took up. Pollution, instead of being confined to the most urbanized areas such as Greater Los Angeles and Greater New York City, was in fact much more widespread.

Motivating their message, as well, was a broadening surveillance of water contaminants led by the U.S. Public Health Service (PHS). In 1957 the PHS inaugurated a National Water Quality network and, starting in 1960, began comprehensive studies of the nation's twenty major river basins. The goal of these investigations was to characterize each basin's water pollution in comparable, systematic terms, and possibly to seek abatement of the worst contamination, as recently authorized by federal water pollution control laws.[35] Building on interstate surveillance pioneered in New York–area waters during the 1930s and 1940s by a Tristate Sanitary Commission, the PHS studies came to scrutinize river systems that flowed between as many as ten states. They looked for a more diverse array of pollutants than ever, from coliform bacteria to alkyl benzene sulfonates (ABS—markers for phosphates measured in Long Island wells) to a host of toxicants. By 1965, the PHS had undertaken abatement proceedings against more than one thousand communities and one thousand industrial plants in forty states. Environmental muckrakers like Donald Carr, in his *Death of the Sweet Waters* (1966), urged the service to go further. Beyond watersheds the PHS had studied, Carr stressed, another eighty-eight were "polluted to varying extents but . . . escaped government action."[36]

A similar approach evolved to study air pollution. By the mid-1960s, popularizers could point to ample scientific demonstrations that it was not just Los Angeles's or Pittsburgh's problem, but a national one. As with water pollution, the PHS had conveyed a surveillance first forged in a single corner of the country—in this case, Los Angeles—to metropolises across the country. A nationwide "air quality" monitoring network, started in 1955, included 250 stations in different cities by 1961, as state and regional health agencies expanded the arsenal for tracking air pollution. The results showed more conclusively what health officials had been arguing since the 1950s: that "Los Angeles no longer has, if it ever had, a monopoly on photochemical smog." Los Angeles still held the ozone record, but Chicago, Washington, D.C., Philadelphia, and St. Louis all had encountered from one-half to one-third as many days with comparable ozone levels. By 1966, plant damage from photochemical smog had been established in "most of the major metropolitan areas," and in twenty-seven states. The PHS reported that "no fewer than 7,300 communities are afflicted with air pollution in varying degrees." "Almost no city is safe from smog attacks," limned Thomas Aylesworth and other popular authors.[37]

Adding to these ominous disclosures of pollution's spread were indications that more than just human health was at stake; nonhuman nature was also threatened. Pollution science over the postwar period, even when pursued in city and state health departments, had borrowed from many natural sciences, from geology to meteorology. But card-carrying ecologists enjoyed special jurisdiction over public judgments of whether some balance of nature had gone awry. Even if these experts themselves disagreed about whether ecosystems had any natural equilibrium, ecologists nevertheless, especially for public audiences, navigated the uncertainties of their findings in ways similar to health scientist colleagues. That is, they drew sharp distinctions between the natural and the human-made. Whenever they detected a human hand, they suspected or declared imbalance: when DDT traces turned up in estuary mud, when it was found to damage eagle and falcon eggs, or, especially, when pollution prompted entire bodies of water to "die."

Lake "death" provided a revealing example of how ecologists interpreted trends in the natural world through metaphors at once evaluative and visceral: in this case, conjuring up the concluding event in human lives, as frightening as it was well known.[38] As a scientific concept, "eutrophication" originally named a natural process by which ponds tended to fill in. But almost invariably "eutrophication" became synonymous with "lake death" to signify a process that was not natural but "cultural," the result of human negligence. Over the midsixties, the primary demonstration of this death of waters occurred at Lake Erie. This nearly 200-mile-long freshwater lake, stretching past the suburbs and factories of Buffalo, Cleveland, and Detroit, had long borne a lion's share of postwar America's industrial discards. The furor over its pollution had been building for several years by the time a PHS investigation began in 1962. That study, and the regulatory proceedings in its wake, kicked off Lake Erie's role as a national emblem of pollution's toll on the natural world. Promptly obliging a media spotlight already turned its way, it actually caught fire in 1969. What more graphic evidence could there be of the perversion of nature's order than a lake in flames? As its surface blazed, one-third of America's lakes and ponds reportedly faced similar problems of "cultural [i.e., human-induced] eutrophication."[39]

In stressing how far pollution had insinuated itself into natural places long considered wild or pristine, the popular pollution literature followed the findings of ecologists—and the straying of pollutants themselves. As scientists by the midsixties crowded into public hearings to report pesticides in all manner of fish, birds, and other wildlife, newspapers picked up on the presence of these and other contaminants in the most natural and unexpected places. DDT was found in the remote seals and birds of the Antarctic, where "there is no record of use." That "smog in one form or another can be found just about anywhere in the U.S." was demonstrated by vignettes of its appearance in Arizona and Florida. Cars even stirred smog in Yosemite, the iconic wilderness park. As for water pollution, "even a woodland spring cannot be trusted unless it has been tested and certified." Some authors noted pollution's global scale—that air pollution troubled Paris, Tokyo, Madrid, Warsaw, Buenos Aires, and Santiago; that "empty cans, bottles and waste of all kinds litter the floors of the Atlantic Ocean, the Red Sea and the Indian Ocean." They even suggested that pollutants might be altering the entire biosphere, in ways that would melt the polar ice caps and invite "catastrophe for much of the world's inhabited land and many of its major cities."[40]

While many of the most far-reaching and insidious influences of pollution were invisible, or nearly so, an era of television and lavish photomagazines took advantage of pollution that was easy to see. Thus, although this flood of popular texts presented pollution as a worldwide problem, the largest and most industrialized metropolises—places like Los Angeles and New York—still occupied visual pride of place. In these depictions, the sunshine and oil reserves that brought smog to Los Angeles so early, the aquifers and cesspools that made Long Island so vulnerable to detergents went missing. Instead, Los Angeles provided "a portent of things to come for the motorized centers of population of the modern world." And, over the mid-1960s, the drenching of Long Island's groundwater with detergents joined many another episode in making Greater New York City the single most cited and photographed exemplar for water pollution. The visuals of antipollution tracts homed in on these and other more localized afflictions, even as texts insisted on pollution's virtual universality. Shots of smokestacks abounded, belching out their sooty tolls on full-page spreads and cover sleeves. River photographs centered on sluices or dumps, or stretches of water strewn with old tires, plastic dolls, and belly-up fish.[41]

*A fish kill image that circulated. This image from the Greater New York City
area wound up in the files of the federal agency for pollution control and then in
Thomas G. Aylesworth's* This Vital Air, This Vital Water: Man's Environmental Crisis
*(1968), one of many contemporary books on pollution aimed at a popular audience.
Images of Los Angeles's smog were also ubiquitous, winding up, for instance, on a
1967* Time *magazine cover. (National Archives)*

A January 1969 oil spill off Santa Barbara, less than a hundred miles from
downtown Los Angeles, supplied the additional spectacle of blackened
beaches and dying seal pups. As forecast in the popular antisprawl literature, these worst places augured every place's tomorrow; they were the
nation's canaries in the mine.

Like *Silent Spring*, this literature mostly reflected suburban vantage
points: factories and downtowns portrayed from a distance, from the outside. In contrast to antisprawl writers, antipollution writers hewed more
to the impersonal posture of their scientific consultants; they were less
likely either to personalize their perspective or to explicitly place it. But
occasionally, authors did refer to their own suburban residence, especially
if it lent credence to their critique. Donald Carr, who wrote early popular tracts about *The Breath of Life* (1965) as well as *The Death of Sweet*

Canaries in the mine. Despite portrayals of pollution's ubiquity, the Los Angeles and New York City areas figured heavily not just in the visuals but in the texts of pollution coverage. (Data compiled from Time *and* Newsweek *cover stories, 1967 and 1970 respectively)*

Waters (1966), offered his Los Angeles origins as a qualification.[42] Dorothy Shuttlesworth, author of *Clean Air — Sparkling Water* (1968), told of her life in East Orange, N.J., near New York City, in ways that followed the pattern in Carson's fable. A pastoral harmony, in a town where city and factory seemed comfortably distant, had fallen to urbanizing assaults from "sawmills and factories" and "many buses and cars."[43]

Such tales, marshaled amid arguments about pollution's ubiquity, revealed much but left much unmentioned. Around Long Island and Los Angeles, even for the newer pollutants found in suburbs, exposures were often the greatest in the least well-off suburban neighborhoods, around factories, or in urban cores. Only occasionally did antipollution authors acknowledge such differences. More often, they, like Carson, framed a message not for those in places long lost to pollution, but for people who had thought to escape it, among whom its presence seemed newer or just on the horizon. That is to say, they envisioned a readership of suburbanites.

Suburbanites, according to most polls, harbored the greatest concerns about the rise of pollution. City dwellers might be nearly as worried, but by the first Earth Day, suburbanites were markedly more inclined to see "worsening" pollution in the vicinity (73 percent versus 61 percent in cities, 45 percent in towns, and 34 percent in rural areas).[44] Not coincidentally, the polls showed anxiety about pollution to be much stronger in certain regions of the country: those most urbanized and industrialized, but also more inhabited by suburb dwellers. By 1970, those finding pollution "very serious" ran highest in the Northeast (51 percent for air and 53 percent for water), but almost as high for air in the Far West (41 percent, including California) and for water contamination in the Midwest (41 percent, including Illinois and Michigan). By contrast, in the Southeast pollution concerns rated "very serious" had reached only 27 percent for water and 20 percent for air).[45] Stories of antipollution activism told by the new environmental muckrakers featured groups in California and New York, as well as in the most urban, industrial—and suburbanized—states. The stage had been set not just for a string of national legislative and other victories by the new environmentalists, at this time well under way, but for the challenges to environmentalism that would later arise in the nation's more rural regions.

Pollution's "Growing Politics of Ecology"

A major message of the popular literature, from 1965 onward, was that not only professional expertise but also citizen activism was required. "Clearly," asserted Frank Graham, the "impetus must come from . . . 'the public.'" By "no coincidence," Howard Lewis observed, "the community with the most advanced pollution control technology—Los Angeles County—also has had the strongest and most vocal support of an aroused public." By the late 1960s, antipollution popularizers offered not just exemplary tales, but step-by-step guides to citizen action. The call for people to mobilize gained considerable support out of Washington, D.C., as the Johnson administration joined enterprising congressmen and senators in seeking to compel new federal standards for air and water pollution control. At the local level as late as 1965, however, federal clout still seemed glaringly absent. One commentator believed that local government was "the only organized body through which the public can control the emission of a corporation," even though local officials were the most "vulnerable . . . to pressures from industry groups."[46]

Around Long Island and Los Angeles over the mid-to-late sixties, a "growing politics of ecology" coalesced to challenge those vested interests, pollution itself, and more.[47] One difference, in particular, distinguished the new groups from earlier ones: the new community-based activists increasingly joined forces with those from college or high school campuses. Activist faculty members as well as students did not just add numbers to the ranks of citizen groups; they boosted collective claims to expertise and nourished translocal ways of thinking. Encouraged by the mushrooming media attention, by new science, and by new political opportunities, the racket of citizen antipollution activism hit a historic sweet spot. Among the consequences of the resultant barrage, paralleling a creative profusion of other "ecological" or nature-friendly thought and practice, American environmentalism acquired its modern name and cast.

The mobilizing of more people to support environmentalism was facilitated by new leverage that activists finagled within the halls of government. Agency hearing rooms opened up to their contestations; the activists also fashioned new ways of turning courtrooms and elections to their advantage. In so doing, they broached the possibility of a nature-minded politics that extended beyond the neighborhoods of a suburban middle class or their consumer interests. Citizen fights against pollution began to tackle corners of the metropolis that looked far less natural or green, places with little purchasing power or other suburban privilege. The prospect of an environmental altruism beckoned, of a serious commitment to environmental dilemmas faced in places where nature was more difficult to see. Such an altruism did stir among activists of the period. But it was rendered vulnerable by those very strategies they found so empowering.

Illustrative of the new hybrid antipollution politics was the Brookhaven Town Natural Resources Committee (BTNRC), which crystallized on Long Island during 1965–66 and quickly moved to the trial against DDT. This committee was the first group of island nature advocates to focus on pollution without also lobbying for parks; its social makeup was also new. While the earlier United Conservationists for Long Island had been led by North Shore housewives, in the BTNRC the leadership passed to men from local high school and college campuses. South Shore high school biology teacher Art Cooley started the group with night school students who wished to tackle local pollution from duck farming. Cooley proceeded to draw in professional biologists George Woodwell, then working at the Brookhaven National Laboratory, and Charles Wurster at the State University of New York (SUNY)–Stony Brook. The result was a new hybrid activism, combining the local commitments and actions of residents with the delocalized knowledge and prestige of academic scientists. Having university scientists on board, including Wurster, who had published on DDT's damages in *Science*, the group began girding itself to target local usage of what was fast becoming the most notorious of the "synthetic organic" pollutants. Their activism at this stage was irreducible to the skills and motivations of any one of the activists involved: not the scientists or teachers, or the students or housewives, or the local lawyer and his spouse who then joined them. Each, in the early days of the BTNRC, recognized how much they needed one another: theirs was a collaborative pooling of capabilities. In stark contrast to what had stirred the land preservation efforts of the local Nature Conservancy, its final synthesis was sparked by a deadly event in one of the least privileged corners of the Long Island landscape.

A fish kill at Yaphank Lake, witnessed by Carol and Victor Yannacone one day in 1964, inspired their lawsuit against the Suffolk County Mosquito Commission and, not long afterward, a partnership with the BTNRC. This very lake was where, as a child and a mechanic's daughter, Carol Yannacone had played, swam, and learned about wildlife. When, as a young adult, she saw it covered with fish carcasses and found out that DDT was the culprit, Carol was brought face-to-face with that nature's fragility and the potential human consequences that followed from its destruction. She found it all too easy to imagine similar consequences for the Lake's human neighbors, "not professional people," whose children still took dips in the same water.[48]

The quick support of the Yannacones' lawsuit by BTNRC scientists and activists consolidated a widened social basis for nature advocacy on Long Island. Over the fifties, when identifying their cause as conservation, groups of advocates had been confined mostly to the wealthy suburbs of the North Shore. Now, an activist base was building among less-privileged, if still mostly middle-class residents and communities along the South Shore. Yet the court case arose on behalf of a suburban locale where none of these activists actually lived. Even for Carol Yannacone, this neighborhood on whose behalf she acted lay on the other side of a line she herself had crossed, through an education that had brought a job at the Brookhaven Lab and her marriage to a lawyer. For her and Victor, those threatened by contamination in the lake were less middle than working class. Nourished by the political ferment of this era, their lawsuit, at least in its origins, was an act of environmental altruism. In developing the case, however, they did not dwell on the class boundaries through which their activism had broken. The BTNRC scientists, as well, focused exclusively on the natural science of DDT; they had nothing to say about the social distribution or equity of county pesticide exposures. The group as a whole was steered away from such questions in part by the very legal innovations through which they successfully pursued their cause in the courtroom.

With the 1966 anti-DDT trial and another suit against a proposed Storm

King power plant along the Hudson River, the New York area became the birthplace of a new judicial vein of citizen action against pollution: the "class action" lawsuit. To its proponents, it seemed a more direct avenue for activism than lobbying Congress or the White House. First employed in stockholder lawsuits against corporate managers and wielded to great effect by civil rights lawyers, class action suits became easier to bring against polluters when, in 1965, the American Bar Association loosened the rules for courtroom standing. As activists like those in the BTNRC won cases against public agencies as well as private companies, class action suits quickly emerged as a powerful tool with which to fight pollution.[49] This strategy essentially ruled out arguments that some residents within the fragmented metropolitan landscape of the New York area might be more exposed to contaminants than others. By the time the BTNRC joined forces with the Yannacones in 1966, a citizen lawsuit could be undertaken only on behalf of a "public" interest. Its "public" character hinged precisely on a studied indifference to the distribution of exposures; Carol Yannacone, as the named plaintiff, represented *all* Suffolk County citizens.

Antismog groups, already well ensconced in the Los Angeles area, underwent a similar evolution. What historian Scott Dewey has termed a "reawakening of local environmental anxiety by the mid-to-late 1960's" began with the smog season of 1967—the worst in eleven years. The resulting flurry of media attention brought new life to Stamp Out Smog, the decade-old group founded by wealthy Beverly Hills housewives. It also stimulated a host of university-local hybrids.[50] Exemplary of the latter was a new chapter of the Group against Smog Pollution (GASP) formed in 1968 in the San Gabriel Valley's Claremont, about fifty miles from downtown Los Angeles. John Rodman, a young Claremont College political scientist, headed the group. On its executive board were three other political science or economics professors from the college, with a local housewife and a physician added for good measure. Biologists may have dominated the university contingent on the BTNRC, but the Claremont-based GASP illustrates the important niche that social scientists also were finding in antipollution activism. Targeting a "pollution establishment," Rodman and the other social scientists in GASP argued that pollution was not just the "technical" problem that reigning experts thought it to be. They thereby meant to showcase the need for their own professional expertise—in political scientist Rodman's case, his knowledge of the inner workings of the state and its "allocation of resources." But to realize the government's "serious commitment" to pollution control, he also knew that a "growing public

Los Angeles's unvanquished smog. This photograph, taken in 1967 from the same spot as another photo some ten years earlier, at Grand Avenue between Fifth and Sixth Streets, served to demonstrate how little smog had improved. Officials did not contest this claim, but instead argued that they had kept smog from getting any thicker despite a doubling of the population of Greater Los Angeles. (© Bettmann/Corbis)

agitation" was necessary. Social and political scientists like Rodman saw much of their role in the movement as expanding participation among inexpert, ordinary citizens.[51]

GASP, as other hybrid activist groups of this era, at least opened the door to advocacy on behalf of the less well-off—those living in urban as well as suburban places where nature seemed completely erased. We have seen how these were precisely the places from which Los Angeles pollution controllers had been diverted over the 1950s and where the most dangerous of the basin's pollutants tended to concentrate. Yet the Los Angeles–area political scene provided as few entry points or incentives for remedying these inequities as Long Island courtrooms. Public hearings, long a focal point of antismog activists, encouraged them to speak for as broad a public as possible. What consumed much of their energy, and that of other antismog groups, by 1969, was the opportunity for referenda. Unique to California's constitution, the referendum enabled citizen groups, if they obtained enough signatures, to put up for a statewide vote measures that otherwise would have been the job of state legislators to enact. Referenda required statewide campaign rhetoric in which the ubiquity of smog made for a far more effective argument than differences in exposure. In 1969 antismog groups in the Los Angeles area devoted much effort, albeit unsuccessfully, to the passage of statewide referenda on a constitutional "right to clean air" and on Proposition 18 to free up gas tax funds for mass transit and pollution control.[52]

On Long Island, as around Los Angeles, pollution control became a priority especially among activists who adopted a new label for what they were defending: the environment. In 1967 key players in the BTNRC's case against DDT established the Environmental Defense Fund to bring similar lawsuits across the country. "Environment" also named new activist coalitions addressing a wider range of urban-regional issues. Prior to the creation of the national Council on Environmental Quality in mid-1969 by President Richard M. Nixon, groups coalescing across both Greater New York City and Greater Los Angeles had adopted similar names and agendas in which pollution control stood front and center. In 1967, an Action for a Better Los Angeles Environment (ABLE) catalyzed the creation of a new umbrella organization soon to gather about sixty local groups under its regional wing. Although initially the resulting group was led by a male architect and prioritized aesthetic and planning issues, the woman who cochaired it, Ellen Harris, quickly developed a reputation as Los Angeles's chief citizen warrior against water pollution.[53] On the East Coast in early 1969, the Long Island Environmental Council (LIEC) formed to coordinate and channel the efforts of about 125 environmental groups across the island. Of the matters "of interest" to the LIEC, "air pollution" and "water pollution" led the list, followed by "noise pollution, transportation, good land-use planning, power siting, open space, historical preservation, etc."[54]

Reflecting important social continuities between this newer environmental and an older conservation politics, the leaders of these self-styled "environmental" groups were often nonworking housewives living in wealthy suburbs. LIEC leader Claire Stern lived in Great Neck on the island's North Shore; Ellen Harris, in Beverly Hills. A great deal more so than their 1950s counterparts, however, they reached out to nearby universities, seeking a similar local-academic hybrid activism. They did so through consultation and correspondence with faculty, as well as conferences, among them, one on nuclear power held at SUNY–Stony Brook and another on environmental pollution in Los Angeles, both in 1969.[55] These new women leaders' personal histories also indicate that they introduced more spillage of nature advocacy out from elite circles than their own current residences might suggest. Harris had only a high school diploma. Stern had been a longtime resident of Levittown, where, she was quick to admit, her own civic acumen had been polished. And the secretary of the LIEC, who worked closely with Stern by day, still drove back each evening to a home in Levittown, the prototypical mother of all mass suburbs.

It was no coincidence that these environmental groups lent their staunch support to battles on nature's behalf in the least "natural" corners of the metropolis. Among the LIEC's oft-mentioned member groups was the Citizens for the Hempstead Plains. This 5,000-strong Levittown-area association devoted itself to saving the final remnant of a natural landscape utterly blanketed by the Levitts' development. So closely identified was the LIEC with this fight that it held its first membership picnic there. The cause of the environment could inspire activism not just in mass suburbia but in park preservation efforts downtown. Save Hazard Park Association, a largely Hispanic group seeking to preserve a grassy patch in East Los Angeles, was one of twelve charter members of ABLE's new council. The new environmentalism could inspire a defense of even the most degraded waters. Ellen Harris championed stricter water quality standards in the Dominguez Channel and Los Angeles's Inner Harbor, the basin's most industrialized waterways. Among those affected were residents of the region's poorest and least white census tracts.[56]

All the same, pollution could never have catalyzed this environmental recasting of nature advocacy had better-off citizens not felt increasingly vulnerable. Nor would its aesthetic affronts have been enough. Haunting obscured vistas and blackened beaches in this era was the looming shadow of disease and death—a question of "survival"—that many prominent experts willingly affirmed. Significant, too, was how pollution became an encompassing metaphor for much more going awry in America by the late sixties and nowhere more so than along the nation's most dynamic urban edges. Fundamental and long-trusted categories looked in danger of melting into one another, not just through pesticidal sprays or detergents, but because of the hybrid nature of these landscapes. Far more than activists of this period let on, those quests after nature that had driven suburbanizing had accomplished a blurring of city with countryside, humans with the nonhuman, the domesticated with the wild, that magnified people's discomfort.

For these reasons, as well, the rising talk about pollution in these places neatly dovetailed the mushrooming adoption of this other name for what was being defended: not so much "nature" as "the environment." Alternatively, we may understand this shift as the result of ongoing contortions in the meaning of the word "nature" itself, which made it seem self-confounding, especially in places like Long Island and Los Angeles. On the one hand, particularly in the visual realm, its associations with the nonhuman and the wild persisted and were in some respects even tightening. On the other hand, though less through visible cues than the invisible realms of chemistry, nature's realm was being stretched cityward in new ways, defining new dynamics of inhabited places and people's bodies as of a piece with the natural world. "The environment" packaged these novelties into a single term, new in itself, that also seemed less patently contradictory. Still often associated with greener and wilder locales, it more forthrightly foregrounded people's bodies and surroundings and handiwork. So rapid and far-reaching was the ascent of this new umbrella term "environment" that by the seventies its usage in the newspapers of the nation's largest metropolises would rival that of nature itself (see Figure 3 in the Appendix). And in this time, when the boundaries between the expert and the nonexpert were also being scrambled, those human bodies involved were often not passive, whether as recipients of pollutants or as scientific objects. In defense of the environment they took action, joining and mobilizing.

As national conservation groups watched the many local and regional groups singling out pollution and other suburban issues, they realized that this new environmental agenda had recruitment potential. Membership of the Sierra Club and the National Audubon Society swelled in these years, but only partly because suburb dwellers like Steve Rynerson acquired a passion for the wild settings and treks that had long been these groups' forte. Arguably more influential was how these groups adjusted their political agendas suburbward.

Their continued fixation on a nature that was reassuringly wild and remote ensured that this broadening came slowly and haltingly. The Izaak Walton League and Audubon had long fought against pollution, but mainly in rural and remote places. Leaders such as Roland Clements sought to draw the Audubon Society into the pesticide fray, but as late as 1967, his board of directors dragged its heels. Around the same time, David Brower, Sierra's executive director, encountered similar disgruntlement as he steered the club to confront nuclear power plants. Though Sierra's Los Angeles chapter waited until 1968 to join antismog campaigns, ultimately this club became the biggest of the older beneficiaries of the new environmental agenda. As late as 1960, several years after taking a more militant stand on the wilderness in its Echo Park campaign, the Sierra Club had still been largely a West Coast–based group, with only fifteen thousand members. Once Sierra took up more urban and suburban issues, its membership spread and into some unlikely quarters such as industrial Long Beach, Lakewood, and, albeit in tiny numbers, Compton, by then largely an African American enclave (see Figure 6 in the Appendix). By 1970 Sierra membership had mushroomed to 113,000, surpassing that of the Audubon Society.[57]

Driving all these new or greatly expanded groups over the mid-to-late sixties were impressions—confirmed by journalists, scientists, and politicians alike—that pollution was worsening nationwide. But what pulled together the collective action around Long Island and Los Angeles, what dominated discussion and engagement especially in such places, was that pollutants kept turning up close by. Biological and chemical expertise was vital to making local manifestations of pollution perceptible and actionable, especially where missed by a local officialdom: for instance, in demonstrating how widely DDT had spread through Long Island, or how dangerous was the pollution of Los Angeles's Inner Harbor.[58] As significant, however, were those larger categories and narratives through which experts' findings came to be interpreted for wider audiences. Among these, moving beyond Rachel Carson in important respects, suburban naturalists like Robert Murphy and Richard Lillard wove talk about pollution into new tales of land transformation that came with suburbanizing.

Though Murphy's *Fish-Shape Paumanok* (1964) was about Long Island and Lillard's *Eden in Jeopardy* (1966) was about Southern California, the trajectories they sketched from past to present were remarkably similar. Stepping into a bird's-eye view of an entire metropolitan area, they flipped the planner's narrative of city building on its head. Urbanizing dispersion was not progress but its opposite, a destruction of more natural lands and ways. Both books began with depictions of a "balance with the environment," in Native American and early colonial times for Murphy's Long Island and in the agrarian 1920s for Lillard's Los Angeles. The rest of their histories outlined the arrival of more people, of roads and cars and buildings, but also told of the decimation of forests and fields, of mountains and chaparral—the erasure of Eden. By the end of both volumes, whether the mid-twentieth-century Southern California of *Eden in Jeopardy* or the Long Island of *Fish-Shape Paumanok*, a real, unmolested nature was hardly to be found. A pervasive pollution had become "symptomatic," from the "indiscriminate spraying of chlorinated hydrocarbons (DDT)" on Long Island to the oxidizing of the Los Angeles basin's "inverted bowl . . . called the sky." The scale of contamination exemplified all that had turned "ominous and awry" in these corners of the earth.[59]

These two works also offer insights into what it meant when, in offering alternative narratives to the prevailing expertise or officialdom in this period, so many invoked "ecology" as their guide. Only Murphy had any formal claim to be an ecologist, and he was retired; Lillard's professional training lay in American literature. As their own histories make clear, both men were writing less as spokespeople for a formal scientific discipline than as testifiers about historical changes they themselves had witnessed. As statements by residents of America's most transformed urban edges, *Fish-Shape Paumanok* and *Eden in Jeopardy* followed in the tracks of Henry Bunner. They were the authors' personal narratives of suburban loss and lament, writ large. That these losses might extend to human life itself, through polluted water or air, only added to their tone of dismay. At the same time, that very impersonal holism of their reputedly ecological standpoint, their sweeping dismissal of a regional nature as utterly dead and gone, helped obscure the personal memories and experiences that motivated them. Viewing these landscapes as if from nowhere, they deftly overlooked those privileged neighborhoods, wilder and greener, where they themselves had sought and found some respite from the changes they chronicled.

A paradox thus lurked in such invocations of ecology, as well as in the celebrity status rather suddenly accorded over this same period to card-carrying ecologists like George Woodwell or Eugene Odum. This field's newfound popularity stemmed less from what professional ecologists had confirmed as scientific fact than from what so many hoped for this discipline, or claimed for it. Ecology captured people's imaginations because of how it promised a more holistic, integrative approach not just to nature itself but to humanity's relationship with it. It betokened the possibility of a science that could stay legitimately scientific, even while somehow overcoming the pitfalls of specialization or reductionism. In meeting these expectations, the actual, formal discipline of ecology at this time was greatly hobbled by the limitations of its own categories and purview. Still centered on nonhuman biota and environments, it offered only the paltriest terms and tools for more humanward and societyward insights, even if its ecosystemic concepts pointed that way. Ecologists, for instance, had had no role in the new postwar combinations of science that revealed the novel tracks of pollutants through the nature of Long Island or Greater Los Angeles, even though we may retrospectively identify these insights as ecological in character. When Murphy or Lillard did turn avowedly ecological eyes to such places, they leaned less on findings from ecology proper than on their own experiences and popular ideas. Their naturalist histories, if new in their geographic coverage, conceded much to, even reinforced, established ideas about suburbia and nature. Among these were the conservationists', of a nature "out there," but also those of city builders and planners, the very tales they sought to subvert. Narrating suburbanizing as nature's utter erasure, their ecological naturalism camouflaged not only the nature still lying in suburbs, but also environmentalism's own suburban roots.

As revealing of just what it meant to speak on ecology's behalf in this era, the younger biologists who became ecology's chief spokespeople had often not been trained in ecology proper. Barry Commoner's degree was in plant physiology, Charles Wurster's in organic chemistry. Even trained ecologists who became involved, like the BTNRC's George Woodwell, recognized that they needed other professional expertise if their own knowledge was to be translated into effective action. While some health scientists were willing to help, it is remarkable how many of those in other social, humanistic, and professional fields took up the ecological banner: social scientists like John Rodman, literati like Richard Lillard, lawyers like Victor Yannacone. As political scientists Robert Rienow and Leona Train Rienow put it, if ecology was really a "science of the relationship of all living creatures to each other and to their environment," then "what after all is the ecologist in the broadest sense but another word for . . . 'generalist'?"[60]

In this meaning, "ecology" named not so much an actual field as a stepping out from earlier versions of professionalism. Less circumscribed in subject matter, the new style was also more eagerly collaborative and more publicly engaged. In a generational shift, social and natural scientists, lawyers and doctors, mostly in their thirties and forties, discovered—in these hybrid antipollution groups of the mid-to-late sixties—new grounds for pooling professional expertise. Far more so than later, especially as these professionals applied their skills to a neglected nature not so far from their own homes, they considered what they were doing as *extra*professional. This more public-minded, civic professionalism came to serve as a generational marker—what distinguished younger lawyers, scientists, or doctors from their elders.

At the same time, these alliances were themselves yielding new realms of professional work. That greater breadth and portability many perceived in "environment" and "environmental," made these terms, rather than "ecology," the favorites of those in more exclusively professional circles. A host of specialists rebranded or newly christened themselves as environmental: engineers and scientists in aerospace; sanitary engineers, industrial hygienists, and radiation biologists; architects and urban planners; policy specialists and federal officials.[61] Allying within, as well as across disciplines, the formally trained who adopted this environmental label could gravitate away from ties to those without professional degrees. For instance, the biologists, lawyers, and other specialists who banded together to create the new Environmental Defense Fund began pouring their time and energy into lawsuits beyond Long Island. They thereby left the BTNRC, mostly lay in membership, to founder.[62] Similar to many other new environmental professionals, their own specifically suburban origins seemed incidental, even an embarrassment, to the grander, more delocalized visions of their endeavors they preferred.

Those on the other side of this era's hybrid activism, those who were neither university faculty nor local professionals, forged their own adaptations of the new "ecology" talk. The many new groups where experts and nonexperts interacted, and the explosion of popular literature about pollution, spurred a new readiness of laypeople to engage in ecospeak. "All sorts of Americans utter new words like ecosystem and eutrophication," announced a *Time* reporter in 1969, from "suburban matrons" to "busy executives and bearded hippies." On Long Island and in Greater Los Angeles, these words, increasingly accompanied by lay appropriations of scientific practices, opened eyes to just how close at hand, and serious, pollution problems were. Claire Stern declared "SUPPORT YOUR ECOSYSTEM . . . one of my favorite slogans," and ordered and distributed pollution kits to enable lay testing of local waters.[63] Around Los Angeles, Harris and many others drew their own conclusions, for instance, that because fish could not survive in the harbor, "something fishy" was afoot. Popular epidemiology went hand in hand with, and was often indistinguishable from, a popular ecology. Lay activists scouted around for contaminated streams or released balloons off the top of buildings to track wind currents. Leaning on select words and practices understood as authentically scientific, they spoke and acted with confidence. At the same time, lay activists could voice a deep skepticism about scientific professionals as well as politicians, if not the political process itself. As Ellen Harris put it, "Sometimes . . . I think professional people and political people know all the reasons why you can't change things and why you can't make better things happen. I never knew that much."[64]

Finding a special meaning in ecology were the many young people who lived on college campuses, those peculiarly detached places defined more by age than any surrounding geography. Already prone to political initiatives from the Students for a Democratic Society to the antiwar movement, by the mid-1960s those on campuses began taking up ecology and the environment as causes. High school and college students staffed and energized many of the university-local hybrid groups of these years; by the late sixties, there was a rapid proliferation of new "ecology action" groups centered on campuses themselves.[65] This shift of environmentalism onto the nation's campuses further obscured its suburban roots by enabling it to be recast as a youth movement. White and middle class as so many of these students were, *they* did not own suburban homes. Yet their activism took shape in intensive dialogue with their neighborhoods of origin and with that imagery of suburbia through which they understood these, however accurately it applied.

They might actually still be suburbanites. Such was the case with New Yorker Wendy Mollot, a twenty-year-old who continued to live in her parents' home in Levittown while cochairing a student group called SPACE (Stop Polluting the Atmosphere and Clean the Environment) at nearby Hofstra University. But more likely, as with Lakewood's Steve Rynerson, an appreciation of a wilder nature, hatched while living in the suburbs, helped steer the next steps in their lives. Selecting the seaside University of California, Santa Cruz, as his college, Rynerson commenced a years-long search for alternatives to the suburban nature his parents had chosen and cultivated.[66] For him, as for many college students of this era, turning environmentalist meant rejecting a past that matched media imagery of suburbia all too closely and seeking ways out of the thoroughgoing alienation from nature that that past now embodied for them.

Often, the starting point was confessional. "When I came here there was nothing in my middle-class background I was particularly against," admitted one new arrival to the California ecology movement. "But I began to see how a lot of things in my background could be very destructive—the love of gadgets, the concern with speed and convenience." In the searches that followed, new experiments with naturalism proliferated, far outstripping those that turned only on chemicals or parks. An "alternative" press of underground newspapers and other publications laid out a bewildering and eclectic variety of practices, as ecology for some acquired a further meaning: a new "way of life." In its name, they cultivated "people's parks," shed their automobiles and carpooled, created ecology food stores to substitute for supermarkets, showered and cleaned their clothes less, put bricks in their toilets. Within this countercultural environmentalism, there were many strands. Efforts to "purify" one's life could be communal, but could also ground new, individual patterns of consumption—a possibility realized by, among others, the *Whole Earth Catalogue* and *Mother Earth News.*[67] The search for a nature somehow less tainted, more authentic could also lead "back to the land." Perhaps it could be found by leaving the city for rural life or by camping in the High Sierras. It might also reveal itself in solitude, in a single flower, in Native American or primitive cultures, or in an eastern religion. Whatever the new direction, these many new naturalisms transported their adherents away from what, for many if not most, was a suburban past.[68]

In taking up urban and suburban issues like pollution, the politics of nature's defense had broadened and deepened. Now, it could range into the "ugliest" and most contaminated corners of the fragmented metropolitan landscape, wherever living beings, human or otherwise, lay vulnerable. Not so paradoxically, though, ideas about nature were also afoot that would draw many environmentalists' visions and energies farther away from places that were so patently polluted or human-made.

Stirring even in this time were the seeds of many new alternatives out of which, over the final three decades of the twentieth century, a "greener" style of consumption would blossom—from organic and natural foods to alternative energy technologies, to the rise of exurbia, to ecotourism.[69] At this moment, a heady idealism prevailed, that through right-minded vision and experimentation, better tools and methods might be found and spread, and the entire society transformed. In retrospect, this faith left the larger burdens of consumption, such as the burning of fossil fuels, less examined, and their accelerating trends, virtually untouched. Part of the trouble was that this prospective greening of technologies and lifestyles leaned heavily on the choices of consumers, who were neither as malleable nor as uniformly well heeled as its apostles had hoped. As well, the pitches and possibilities of green consumerism encouraged an abandonment of those less natural corners of the landscape deemed irremediable, rather than any commitment to their reconstruction. Like the long-standing suburban quest for homes with views and forest patches, the purchase of ever greener goods and gadgets could become yet another avenue by which America's wealthy could, with a clear conscience, leave the benighted rest of their society behind.

Not all of these conflicting trends were so evident at the time Gaylord Nelson and Pete McCloskey began calling for an "environmental teach-in." But those that were go a long way toward explaining the suburban response to their call. When the Nelson-named coordinators at Environmental Action sought out campus groups and leaders to coordinate this event, especially around Long Island and Los Angeles, they built on a contradictory brew of ideas and experiences that had been decades in the making.

Earth Day as Culmination

Planning for April 22, 1970, Earth Day's organizers worked hard to fashion an event that would seem totally new. In this regard, the youthful staff went further than their senatorial sponsor by changing the event's name. "Environmental teach-in" thus became "Earth Day."[70] The very idea suggested a novel allegiance transcending older geographies of citizenship, leaping upward from city, state, and nation to extend to an entire planet. It picked up on those images of earth from space that, starting in 1968, had flashed across the pages of national magazines, widely interpreted as marking a historic break, the first time Americans had seen their planet as a whole.[71] What gave Earth Day's iconography and organization such a powerful appeal, however, was that this watershed moment marked a culmination. The NASA-made image of the earth—as a singular pool of life, set off by a "desolate" moon and the black void of space—mirrored powerful, swelling historical currents. It at once built on and bolstered that naturalist line drawing that had proliferated in postwar suburban culture. Like other of these stark binaries—chemical, ecological, iconographic, and more—it affirmed that people belonged to living nature, that they themselves would suffer, even perish, from its destruction. Selecting Earth's image as the day's icon, organizers sought to transmogrify the sense of national environmental crisis into a story line still larger, one about all of humanity and its home. Among the movements of the late sixties, that culminating in Earth Day was hardly alone in the audacity of its abstractions or the perilous future toward which they pointed. But along the nation's most dynamic urban edges, no other movement's narratives had as far-reaching or stirring a resonance.

Just as suburbanizing had fragmented these places into so many different neighborhood ecologies, so the Earth Day that transpired across them was not just one but many. Among its supporters were many who had

"Joining In." Sixth graders from Beverly Hills march along Wilshire Boulevard in West Los Angeles, April 22, 1970. They adorned themselves with many familiar emblems of the first Earth Day. (Los Angeles Times Collection, Special Collections, University of California)

applauded the Natural Beauty Conference, residents of the most planted and privileged suburbs. Earth Day brought a satisfying sense of fulfillment to an older but open-minded breed of conservationists like Robert Murphy, then living in forested Old Field. When approached by a reporter, the 83-year-old Murphy declared knowingly how "it was bound to come. You can't think about this problem and see the advance of destruction and read the balance sheet without waking up." But much of Earth Day's actions happened in places that the Natural Beauty Conference had ignored: university campuses, in addition to communities across suburban Long Island and Los Angeles that were less than green and less privileged. The Levittown Public Library was among the many community centers and clubs where "teach-ins" happened outside college campuses. Among suburban high schools, activism overtook the students in well-heeled high school classes in Garden City and Pasadena, but also stirred in some less well-off districts such as Bellport and San Gabriel. Even in the more industrialized corners of the Los Angeles basin, around Long Beach, high schoolers—at least some of them black or Hispanic, as well as white—donned green armbands.[72]

Crossing the color line. More so than much of the coverage allowed, Earth Day protests spilled out beyond well-to-do white suburban communities. This photograph of African American protesters from Cathedral High School, near downtown Los Angeles, which appeared in the Los Angeles Times, *April 23, 1970, was effectively white-washed. A cropped version of this image appeared in print. Through the cropping, the figure on the left as well as many features of the African American figure on the right were cut off, along with the civil rights message of the protest sign. (*Los Angeles Times *Collection, Special Collections, University of California, Los Angeles)*

Especially in the hothouse imaginations stirring on suburban campuses and in high schools circa 1970, conservationists' nature ideals, of national parks and wilderness, went conspicuously missing. Instead, much of the point was that humans and nature had become inseparable—as much a cause for shock as for celebration. Those nature ideals expressed were precisely those that included people, from the impossibly huge—the blue dot of the Earth, humanity's home—to the small and homely—wildflowers planted along a highway or bicycles propelled by muscle power. If some did borrow ideas from the 1965 Washington conference, few made much of "natural beauty" as a goal. Humanity's, and nature's, predicaments now seemed too dire. Speeches as well as campus theatrics trafficked especially in interbred horrors, in which it was hard to tell where threats to human bodies left off and those to a nonhuman nature began. What gave so many of the event's skits and iconography their edge was how they mixed up the

Earth Day montage. Newspapers from Long Island's suburban communities, like this one from Farmingdale, just north of Levittown, enthusiastically supported the first Earth Day. They depicted Earth Day events, themes, and signage that, if more focused on water pollution, otherwise closely resembled those of counterparts in Los Angeles. (Farmingdale Observer, *April 23, 1970, courtesy of Anton Community Newspapers*)

burial or death of human bodies with imagery of destructive technologies or a nature overwhelmed. Protesters buried car engines, also "symbols of common pollutants," a globe, a human effigy made of garbage, all manner of other villains and victims. Where Earth Day protests ventured out from campus to suburbs, they carried this same tone of impending doom. Youth activists hung a skull and crossbones off a bridge over the Pasadena Freeway and trekked through the entire expanse of Los Angeles's sprawl in a "survival march."[73] Around places like Los Angeles and Long Island, this direness, these twinned warnings of humanity *and* nature on the brink, were not confined to the dramatizations of the young. Their elders—and not just the environmental activists—chimed in with similar messages. Newspaper editorialists, local experts, and public officials all spoke of a survival that was threatened, affirming the prevailing sense of dread.

Earth Day's detractors on the left were quick to note its lesser regard for the dilemmas faced by America's most aggrieved races and classes, a criticism with considerable merit. On Long Island as well as Southern California, high schools with the most reported student events often were located in towns with the highest home values and lowest densities. At events in less well-to-do suburban areas, the students who became involved were, by and large, white and college-bound. Mostly black high schools even in suburbs often had few or no reported Earth Day events.[74] In many of the suburbs where Earth Day activities were the most extensive, undertakings beyond the neighborhood itself went uncontemplated. The ubiquitous trash pickups, for instance—straight out of the playbook of suburban civics—gained a larger and more grandiose justification as caring for the Earth. But the practical effect could be exactly the same as such campaigns decades before: burnishing the tidy greenery of one's own parks, streets, and lawns.

Precisely the unevenness with which this first Earth Day was embraced forecast the fracturing of support for environmentalism over the 1970s and beyond. In regions that remained predominantly rural, even in the suburbs of a southeastern city such as Atlanta, the sense of alarm was less, the mobilizing a mere shadow of counterparts around Long Island or Los Angeles. Such places would become prime constituencies, over the 1980s and 1990s, for a new antigovernmental conservativism, with the federal laws and controls achieved around the time of the first Earth Day their foremost foil. In suburbs and downtowns where industry and its noxious legacies lay close by, where the first Earth Day's activism was nevertheless sporadic, where the residents were often working-class whites or blacks or Hispanics, the new laws and agencies of the 1970s would also fall short. From these places and oversights there would congeal other movements, socially in contrast to those of the 1950s and 1960s, avowing a need for environmental justice.

Already at the time of the first Earth Day, however, far more so than at the Natural Beauty Conference five years earlier, the new ecological and environmental frames for suburban problems transported some participants *beyond* the preoccupations of a suburban well-to-do. Tackling polluters, Earth Day's student protesters might confine themselves to the air nearby, but they also might venture forth into locations that were poorer and less green. Bellport high schoolers, for example, trouped off to photograph the polluting of a local river. Some of the day's celebrants took on urban dangers, even those to which the poor and minorities were considered far more exposed—among them, the lead paint that poisoned homes in inner cities. When they did so, an environmental altruism stirred. It did, as well, in advocacy for land preservation in places whose nature many had written off, not just downtown but in the most crowded of suburbs. On the first Earth Day, that was exactly what the LIEC and other Nassau County environmental groups achieved. The county executive announced he was formally designating forty acres of "natural meadowland" in the Mitchel Field area as a "preserve for future generations." Thanks to pressure from Levittowners and non-Levittowners alike, the last remnant of the Hempstead Plains, that prairie nearly extinguished by the most paradigmatically mass of suburbs, was finally set aside. On the fringe of Lakewood as well, civic lobbying led to the opening of the El Dorado Nature Center.[75]

In other words, the suburban invention of environmentalism constituted a movement *toward* environmental justice. It was, first and foremost, because of how, especially around places like Long Island and Los Angeles, activists broke out of the sylvan cage of elite 1950s conservationism to create a politics of nature's defense with broader appeal to a suburban middle-to-working class. It was, too, because of how the new movement enabled the spotlighting, at least, of environmental travails in more urban and industrial places. And it was because of the new environmentalism's reliance on the local claims to knowledge of a popular ecology as well as a popular epidemiology. Here, the suburban activism of the 1950s and 1960s shared much with the more suburban movements for environmental justice beginning in the late 1970s, from Buffalo's Love Canal to Houston's Northwood Manor. Whether the local knowers were laypeople or experts themselves, convictions about the dangers of pollution arose even in the face of official contentions that there was little to worry about. Their political mobilizations thereby gained a vital anchorage.

Just as any local knowledge was highly vulnerable to the power of established experts, so the mobilizing potential of any environmentalism could falter in the face of political realities. But the successes achieved by this first transformative wave of environmental politics in the United States offered an enduring precedent. Without it, any case for environmental inequities would have been far more difficult to make, and the movement that styled itself as one for environmental justice would have had much less chance of being born.

Conclusion

For anyone who recalled the giddy excitement of the original, it must have been hard not to feel disappointed by the Earth Day 2000 celebration in Glen Cove, on Long Island's North Shore. Mother Nature inscrutably scowled on the occasion, nearly raining it out. The day's only collective action, a cleanup of a nearby creek, brushed along Garvies Point Preserve, the very place Levittown's Julian Kane had defended at a packed public hearing some forty years earlier. Now strewn with spent beer bottles and decaying newspapers, its tidying mustered only a "few dozen volunteers," mostly enlistees from two local scout troops. A fair, since become standard for any self-respecting Earth Day celebration, then followed at a nearby park. Musicians strummed and sang, local politicians declaimed, booths outreached for activist groups or peddled wares for a few eco-minded entrepreneurs. The "chief attraction" of the day, in keeping with its sponsorship by the Long Island Power Authority, was a car powered by the electricity this company sold, "one of a fleet it rents out . . . to show off the power of pollutant-free automobiles." Even this self-serving marvel was not enough to pull in a larger crowd. A state senator who had spoken before the tiny audience mulled over how times had changed. Back in the 1970s, he recalled, "the drive was to stop pollution." But "Hempstead Harbor is a lot cleaner than it was 30 years ago"; so too "the air we're breathing." Now, environmentalism was different; it was more about "using natural resources in more efficient ways." And the problems it confronted—here came the obligatory refrain of global warming—were "more complex," if also "more and more out there."[1]

"More and more out there" was a resounding theme among the many charged with keeping Earth Day alive on its thirtieth anniversary. The message boomed loud and clear at the biggest and most reported event, a gathering in Washington, D.C., on the steps of the Capitol Dome that drew an estimated 150,000–300,000 people. Among all issues now qualifying as environmental, planetwide trends, especially the tumult from the earth's rising temperature, took top billing. For Denis Hayes, reprising his 1970 role as the day's main coordinator, the thirtieth anniversary edition confirmed that participation in environmentalism was "more and more out there" across the earth itself. Thanks to internet-aided organizing, he could boast of a twenty-five-fold leap in attendance compared to his first time around: some 500 million in 183 countries around the world. But Earth Day 2000's "more and more out there" seemed to mean less and less back in places like Glen Cove, in the first Earth Day's suburban heartland. Nationwide polls showed that Americans' support for many environmental causes was broad but inveterately shallow. Columnists ruminated how "many people feel that the environmental movement has become rarefied and out of touch with real people." Backing and promotion by corporations had become difficult to miss, sparking accusations that Earth Day 2000 was "corporate-sponsored." In the eyes of critics, Earth Day demonstrations now aimed mostly to entertain; they had "become little more than concerts on the mall." Older environmentalists waxed nostalgic for that "much more spontaneous and unorganized" event thirty years earlier.[2]

Yet environmentalists devoted surprisingly little reflection on how this spontaneity might have been accomplished or what its more local and popular roots might have been. The breezy ways the movement's past was being talked about bore an uncanny resemblance to the self-imagery of conservationists of the early 1950s. Tiny leadership cadres got most of the attention: that "handful of rich white males," who supposedly started the movement by selling their "esoteric enthusiasm," or iconic leaders from John Muir to Rachel Carson, whose eloquence and innovative thought had inspired the masses to follow them.[3] Even historians who sought wider explanations for environmentalism's burst of popularity in the 1960s fell back on story lines of the winning national organizations, notably the Sierra Club.[4] That there might be wider, more pervasive roots for the great participatory turn in American nature politics during the postwar period, that these might actually lie in so environmentally compromised a place as suburbs—to these possibilities most environmentalists, avowedly more oriented to the present and future, devoted little thought.

If they did think about it, scholars and practitioners in a host of environmental fields were likely more embarrassed than inspired by the original, suburban base for environmentalism's popularity. After all, they had more important things to do than ponder local or neighborhood civics. Environmentally speaking, they had work to do, full-time, paid work. Whether in government or the private sector, the sciences or the humanities, thought and action on behalf of the environment had become much more professionalized, a job for the credentialed.

Much of the impetus had come, directly or indirectly, from legislative actions of the late sixties onward. New laws at all levels of government—local, regional, and state, as well as federal—had installed new administrative terrain for environmental controversies, increasingly tilted in favor of the formally qualified. The fruits of early successes had planted seeds for later ones, but by exacting a price on the movement's grass roots. The mushrooming ranks of professional defenders, investigators, and also exploiters of "the environment" helped sunder and fragment concerns that in many suburban neighborhoods had seemed so entangled: the razing of forest patches with the contamination of air and aquifers, and the risks to human health with those to other species. In scientific, legal, and other public realms, old categories and divisions began reasserting themselves. Chief among them was the long-standing split between fields dealing with human "health" versus nonhuman "nature," whose breach had bolstered the sense that human survival itself lay on the line. On either side of this divide, new environmental professionals divvied up the most policy-relevant experiences of nature and human health, transferring both from neighborhoods of laypeople into their own white-collar places of work. As the knowledge that mattered most became far less localized, the movement's earlier participatory ideals were also sliding away.

Among the smaller groups of environmentalists who struggled to keep these ideals intact, the suburban roots of earlier activism seemed increasingly remote. From the antinuclear movement to the new alliances that surged around protests in Seattle, some environmental activists continued to experiment anew with democratic forms of decision making. Yet their actions largely centered on targets that were monumental—nuclear laboratories or power plants or global organizations like the World Trade Organization. Reliant on mobile and floating communities reminiscent of youth counterculture, these successive waves of new environmental activists dwelt less on any more permanent vision of neighborhoods or homes.

A greening of consumer markets did enable domestic possibilities that were more durable. But in so doing, it camouflaged the suburban roots of the environmental impulse still further. Whether in the realm of housing or leisure or food or clothing or cars or other energy usage, as entrepreneurship in these market niches prospered, buyer and seller alike defined them in terms of the challenge they posed to a suburban mainstream.

In the process, just as with the suburban quest for nature that had preceded it, green consumerism favored the pocketbooks and the consciences of the wealthy. On the sales side, corporate marketers discovered new profit possibilities in the ecological pitch, whose authenticity became more and more difficult to decipher. By means of green washing, tiny improvements in ecological efficiency or imprint could be loudly touted, leaving a product's larger environmental impact unremarked and unimpeded. And buyers, in a society whose infrastructure for everything from housing to transportation to food and energy supply remained resource-intensive, often found that the most thoroughgoing solutions carried hefty price tags. As with the earlier migration to a suburban countryside, when markets alone served as the primary means toward the sustainable, the society's best-off found it easiest to accomplish, often by separating themselves and their lives from everyone else's. As for *their* remaining environmental impacts—from multiple cars and houses or from the gobbling of electricity and jet fuel—these went far less scrutinized.

Also not boding well for the environmental movement by the early twentieth-first century was how its regional confines, obscured in earlier depictions of an ecological crisis that was nationwide, had, politically speaking, caught up with it. Out from New York and Los Angeles, and around the newer and faster-growing cities of the South and West, the share of Americans living in suburbs kept rising, and with it, that peculiar version of nature alienation to which modern Americans seem so prone. Yet the ongoing deracination of environmentalism from its suburban origins, fed both by green consumerism and by the mounting dependence on professionalism and federal power, helped convince many newer suburbanites that the interests of this movement were irreconcilable with their own. Around cities like Atlanta, Houston, and Phoenix, as aspiring politicians in the Republican Party massaged their mistrust, these suburbs furnished popular seats for the making of a new antienvironmental conservativism.

The predicaments in which environmentalism and environmentalists found themselves by the early twenty-first century stemmed from many circumstances beyond their control, but at least in part, from misreadings of their own history. From its beginnings in the mid-twentieth century, environmentalism had borne an uncomfortable relationship with its past. Time and again, the originators and architects of this movement had endeavored to obscure or ignore much of the history that was responsible for it. The erasures were many: from the lower class and minority neighborhoods where pollution was heaviest, to the wealthier neighborhoods from which participants in the Natural Beauty Conference hailed, to the regional concentration of early environmental problems and activism in New York, California, and similar states. Environmentalists' discomfort with their own history might seem an inevitable by-product of that sweeping alienation so many have professed, of that severance from the natural world that their society had perpetrated. But talk of nature as well as the environment has itself proved a powerful way of shoving this movement's historical complexities under the rug—among them, the class, racial, and regional skewing of many environmental dilemmas, also the movement's own evolving biases and the fraught ways it reckoned with them. Among the most dramatic of all effacements by the time of the thirtieth Earth Day was that of environmentalism's suburban roots.

Then as now, any resolve to propel an entire society toward a more sustainable future must take seriously the nature near where most people live, at least as much so as the nature where fewer reside. Better to understand what environmentalism actually is, and what its future can hold, this book has unpacked the movement's past in just such a place. The movement we call American environmentalism began, in important senses, not with the Sierra Club or with urban progressive reform, but through searches for nature along cities' elusive edges. The goal for many was to live alongside it, more so than any urban residence allowed. But the landscape they encountered there was deeply hybrid, a mixture of the city with the countryside, in large part because of suburbanites' own collective presence. After World War II, while many Americans continued to seek a nearby nature there, others felt a growing ambivalence, even trepidation, about these places. The suburban origins of the new environmental ideology in the United States, and the sense of bodily vulnerability it expressed, were hardly fortuitous. Along the rapidly suburbanizing landscapes of the postwar period, air and water pollution *were* closely and logically linked to the afflictions of wildlife and to felt needs for park making and better rules for land use. From the standpoint of suburban dwellers, the separate jurisdictions of public health and wildlife officials, freeway and land-use planners *did* overlap: in their backyards, in their very bodies. There were, of course, many other grounds for this environmental efflorescence outside suburbs and many other pathways to environmentalism: through quests for population control or energy conservation or through searches for alternative technologies or a return to the land. But around 1970, no cluster of issues contributed more to a new environmental politics than the multiple affronts to land, water, air, and human flesh in America's most transformed urban edges.

What had made the first Earth Day so galvanizing within these suburbs were shared personal experiences, a local witnessing to an array of problems that a reigning officialdom seemed unwilling or unable to quell. It had made a difference that much scientific and legal power during this period lay in the hands of those who dismissed the rising concerns. It had made a difference, as well, that so many of the concerned were not exactly untutored: high school teachers as well as students, college professors or lawyers as well as housewives. At the heart of this mass mobilization, shared by expert and nonexpert alike, was a local knowledge, born of living in a particular sort of neighborhood and in a particular type of metropolitan region. With this knowledge, especially on the edges of cities like New York and Los Angeles, came a host of uncertainties that were new and sometimes frightening; after all, the modern understanding of these problems, from causes to longer-term implications, was just being hatched. As local experts set about crafting this science and as laypeople struggled with the deficiencies of existing expertise, both had confronted these uncertainties with a new fervor for line drawing, favoring the natural over the human-made.

Some thirty years out, diminished participation of the sort seen on the first Earth Day might well have been due to changes reaching beyond environmentalists themselves, including a long-term decline in Americans' overall civic involvement. But even around 2000, environmentalism still struck a popular, community-based chord in some corners of the nation. It did so especially in places where nature itself was, at least as many environmentalists now knew it, impossible to see. By no coincidence, many of these defended places were suburbs and many of their defenders homeowners.

"The environmental justice part of the movement," often minority and working-class members, seemed to Denis Hayes and others the surest rejoinder to quips that American environmentalism was "out of touch."[5] Sure enough, the fifteen thousand people converging on Earthfaire 2000 in downtown Los Angeles did so in part because it was promoted as an event for "environmental justice." Around 1970, there had been no such movement. Its naming had come with the discovery of a type of pollution that this era's advocacy and laws had missed: hazardous industrial wastes.

The predominately minority or working-class neighborhoods where these waste sites were located had had to undertake their own local mobilizations, with little or no help from self-declared environmentalists. Coming into their own as a national movement during the 1980s, these groups had understandably coined a somewhat different name for themselves: theirs was a cause of "environmental justice." As of 2000, the Glen Cove Earth Day showed the depth of the gap between their concerns and those of the environmentalist mainstream. Whereas speakers talked about local pollution in the past tense, as a bygone, Long Island's Garvies Point still harbored two major dumps of chemical wastes. To be sure, the Environmental Protection Agency knew about them, was cleaning them up. But the prospect of seeping carcinogens still worried "many residents" who lived next door.[6]

Historians of the environmental justice movement were, by this time, eager to embrace the more local and communal roots for their movement, just as many historians of environmentalism, in a rush to celebrate singular heroes, downplayed any such origins in theirs. What both sets of chroniclers missed was how much suburban environmentalism, as it broke out of the conservationist mold of the 1950s, had looked like the movement that environmental justice historians described. Suburban environmentalism was about where activists lived and played, if not where they worked. Crossing lines of class if not race, it was grassroots and civic in impulse. Challenging conservationists' narrowed notions of "nature," it carried nature's defense into unaccustomed corners. It even brought threats to human bodies into its fold. Tapping the generalizing and legitimizing tools of academics, like its later twin it leaned on a more localized knowledge of health and place. What helped make the subsequent self-labeled environmental justice movement possible, these similarities suggest, was the failure of this earlier environmentalism to go further.

As hazardous waste dumps finally became an issue again (they were before, on postwar Long Island), those coalitions that environmental groups had established in the early seventies, across class as well as race, were coming apart.[8] While there are other reasons for these splits, much of the blame lies with middle- or upper-middle class environmentalists themselves. Idealist as they had become about preserving a nonhuman nature, many had already settled back into this as the only real meaning "nature" could have. They were losing the capacity to care about environments that were less visibly natural—and less privileged—than those *they* identified with or idealized. That is to say, they were losing the knack, so vital to the broadening of their movement in the first place, for environmental altruism.

This history of America's urban edges over the twentieth century has a message for those who would undertake or influence today's city and suburb building. When we look at such places, whether we see nature or not depends on more than just what is there. What we see also hinges on our own preferred narratives, what we have primed ourselves to look for. Clearly, both narratives of suburbanizing we have seen among our historical actors, as city building and as nature erasing, have their pitfalls.

Those looking at suburbanizing only as the extension of a city outward have largely missed the twentieth-century sea change, accelerating across the developed world, in what our cities have become. Buildings and land uses have dispersed; among them, land that is planted, space that is "open," have become far more ubiquitous and unmistakable. Over the vast majority of its land area, the American metropolis now redounds with features that our nineteenth-century forebearers would have characterized as countrylike. These more or less natural features may easily be seen as urban or "made," as parks or lawns or "suburbia"—not just by developers, industrialists, or planners, but by the many people who live there. But this natural side to our metropolises is itself a testimony to the great value recognizable nature *has* held for twentieth-century urban and suburban dwellers, and not only for those who are privileged enough to purchase homes within it. It bears remembering, as well, that cities have never been confined to what we afix to the land. Always, they have contended with elements of nature that are more mobile—water and air, not to mention the many organisms that inhabit those elements—and with that piece of nature perhaps the most difficult to see as natural: the human body.

The narrative of suburbanizing as city building has, by its very omissions, helped to catalyze its opposite: a story line revolving exclusively around the nature that city or suburb making threatens. This nature-erasing narrative brings its own share of blinders. We are likely to miss, as many environmental activists and scholars have, just how bound up nature advocacy or environmentalism has been with suburbs themselves. A central argument of this book is that the sprawling ways cities in the developed world have increasingly come to grow over the twentieth century are driven, in important ways, *by* the suburban quest for nature. This contention runs against the grain of new naturalists from Rachel Carson onward, who framed their own favored places ("a town in the heart of America") without any connection to a city. Long traditions of writing about nature as well as sub-urbia bolster these authors' assumptions: that nature is hardly to be found among tract homes in subdivisions, not to mention a denser downtown. Naturalist eyes now most often gravitate toward the largest and wildest and most open or wooded lots, with nary a glance at those that are more compactly built. Among the consequences of this viewpoint, this book has argued, is that we may wind up seeing only the nature around better-off neighborhoods as worth saving. Even pollution science, when guided solely by the objectivity of biological and other natural sciences, could favor the afflictions of the advantaged. Taking nature alone as a guide, it seems, in-clines the observer to all sorts of socioeconomic, racial, and regional biases that can warp his or her priorities and actions.

The historical record also shows just how difficult it is to keep both sides of a place simultaneously in mind: what is urban and built about it as well as what is rural or natural. Our habits of thought run dichotomously; as with a water glass that is half full or half empty, we see the one or the other. Suburbanites are famously inclined to deny the city water swirling in their glass—unless it starts to foam. Yet they are as liable as their urban critics, and many environmentalists, to regard the suburbs as among the last places to go in search of nature. This unanimity is a historical artifact. Earlier, even in the time of John Muir, most Americans did not need a "na-ture" park to find nature; they settled for a "suburban countryside." Sig-nificantly, our inclination to spatially segregate nature, to locate its bona fide versions only in those bounded plots we call "parks," is a by-product of how metropolitan our perceptions—not just of suburbs but of nature—have become.

That our lives seem so radically removed from nature has stirred the environmentalist in many of us, whether we are suburbanites or urbanites or even country dwellers. This alienation has been augmented by mate-rial changes recounted in this history: a decimation of more natural lands around America's cities, an ongoing transformation in its farms and food supply, the patently manufactured character of the objects with which we surround ourselves. But our alienation may also rely on the secret complic-ity between our dominant narratives for interpreting urbanizing change, as city-building or as nature-erasing. It may, in other words, lie inside our heads as well, a cultural legacy of the transformations this book records. Our disregard for *suburban* nature, the blooming, buzzing, bustling life lying right under most of our noses, stands out with especial poignancy. These two kinds of places, more urban and more rural, do actually meet up in our suburbs, which most twenty-first-century Americans call "home." It is by forgetting neither half of the glass, by weighing what is built and urban alongside what is more rural or natural in our suburbs, that we can better divine what our cities and our true relationship with nature have become. Only by better comprehending both, and what they have to do with one another, will we be able to undertake fuller and more effective responsibility for each.

THIS STUDY ALSO HAS MESSAGES for those who would seek a revival of the environmental movement. The advent of environmentalism as we know it is of surprisingly recent vintage, dating from the 1950s in some parts of the country and the 1960s and 1970s in others. The inventiveness that made it came from popular ranks that were, ultimately, millions strong. Heroic as Rachel Carson's contribution was, if *Silent Spring* had not come along, some other book or books would have taken its place. If there was one common denominator to the changing ideas about nature that made suburban environmentalism so popular, it was neither the spread of principles taught by ecologists nor the widening embrace of a "wilderness ideal." What united the many people who made this new movement was that they began asking nature-related questions about places where nature was *harder* to see. As a mass movement, environmentalism was borne more within the modern metropolis than without. On ground that was at once planted and built, local knowledge and concerns arose that cut across many neighborhoods and communities. The new environmentalism thereby accomplished a forgotten, but historically significant bridging of the fragmentation to which these metropolises were so prone. Empowered by new mobilizations as well as a new agenda and rhetoric, by the end of the 1960s the movement was making its historic mark.

Whether today's environmentalists can accomplish a similar feat remains to be seen. The changing distribution of wealth in our society over the last few decades has made action more difficult, if also more imperative. As the wealthiest have drawn away from the middle and lower ranks of income, environmental practice for most Americans has become increasingly confined to private purchases. Green consumerism has swelled the distribution of a few environmental commodities like hybrid cars and long-lasting light bulbs, yet at the same time has gone a long way toward tagging environmentalists with the elitism that once dogged conservationists. Expensive choices from solar heating to "green" building remain within reach, for the most part, only of the well heeled. Those who can afford them may glibly excoriate the rest of American society for environmental profligacy, but with utter complacency toward the advantages that enable their own "greenness." Meanwhile, public action that might stimulate cheaper and broader alternatives has long withered on the legislative vine.

Perhaps we need to abandon the "environmental" umbrella altogether, as did 1960s activists with conservation. Maybe we require an alternative rhetoric and agenda that can inspire and unite a broader constituency. Such was the hope that animated Michael Shellenberger and Ted Nordhaus's provocative declaration, in 2004, of the "death of environmentalism."[9]

But when it comes to global warming, that single issue in which these authors invest their main hope for a popular reawakening, historical legacies complicate the prospects. Thanks in part to the achievements of this earlier wave of environmentalism, we have become less aware of and more insensitive to the many hidden fires on which our lives depend, even as their collective emissions have elevated the pollution quagmire to a genuinely global level. That very "global" level has, despite Al Gore's *Inconvenient Truth* and a slew of other popular works, still proved a better match for a "movement" comprised more exclusively of well-paid professional scientists and activists than one in whose leadership high school teachers, housewives, and students can share.[10] The clearest avenues toward action, as yet, still lie in the hands of national and international leaders. Although many cities, states, and institutions have acted on their own, the local efficacy and significance of a community-based politics of warming is far from obvious. The earlier history of environmentalism does suggest that a single issue, especially one assigned the highest priority by the world's established scientific leadership, will, as a stimulant to popular environmental politics, only go so far.

If this history provides a model, it is that issue clusters can be as or more important than any single concern, however global and momentous. They stir collective activity not so much because of how they fit together logically from the vantage point of environmental professionals or state officials or academics, but because of shared experiences they provide "on the ground." They mobilize because they touch upon the *connective* tissue of our society, the yards and streets where ordinary people live, the air and water and food we imbibe, the meeting halls and other public spaces where we congregate. We ourselves have similar chances, starting with those new imperatives toward chemical naturalism suggested by recent science. In studies of substances such as endocrine receptors, the barriers separating health and ecological disciplines keep being challenged, breaking down.

In breast cancer and other disease-centered activism, many advocates for change have been a force in keeping alive the study of environmental factors and hypotheses. We have chances, as well, through those ideas and actual coalitions being forged over the fate of urban places. One starting point may lie in a nature-minded ethic more suited to the downtown: not just about land but about place, including its meanings for a diverse humanity. Another may lie in new urban icons of nature restoration, like an ongoing reconstruction of the Los Angeles River.[11] Whatever their beginnings, the new mobilizations should seek to engage a nature that is not just "out there" but around our collective homes, even if—especially if—we are suburbanites.

The grass roots of environmentalism, suburban and otherwise, need tending. Existing roots can be watered; better yet, in coalition with others, seeds can be planted that are altogether new. One thing the past teaches is that those who would renew this movement need to balance the global thinking that has become their forte with more small-scale civic imaginations, to bring their energies down to earth. How better might we reach into, and build on, the knowledge and the passions of neighborhoods and churches, homeowner associations and civic groups? Perhaps a dose of humility is in order and a reconciliation with our own and others' shared humanity. How else might environmentalists invent themselves anew than by a renewal of faith in the specialness of a nature that lies near at hand? And how can such a faith be, ultimately, without another fidelity, to the specialness of those human creatures who inhabit such places, whose nature we must then strain to see? Environmentalism's past is one of creativity and innovation but also empathy, and not just for the nonhuman world. That past calls on it now to shed its current self as a chrysalis, in metamorphosis toward other, unforeseeable stirrings to come.

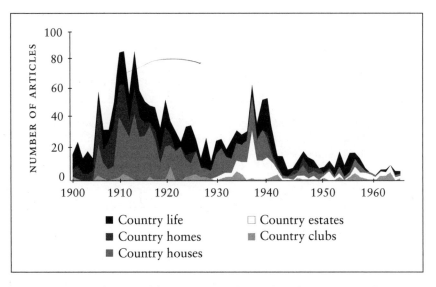

Figure 2. Decline of country life, 1900–1965. The number of magazine articles about "country" homes and customs peaked in the early twentieth century and then declined, especially after World War II. (Data compiled from A Reader's Guide to Periodical Literature*)*

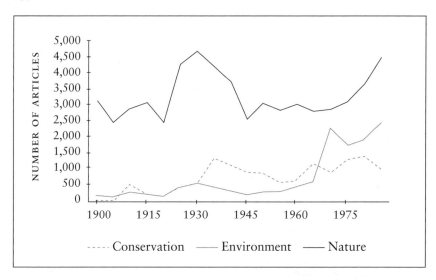

Figure 3. "Conservation," "environment," "nature": The long view, 1900–1985. Shown are the number of articles mentioning these subjects that appeared in the New York Times. *(Data compiled from ProQuest Historical Newspapers)*

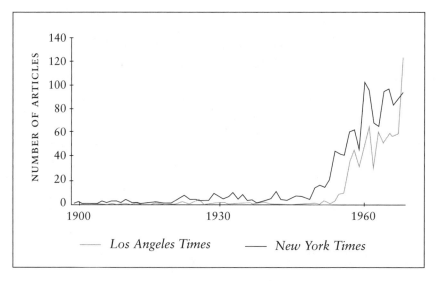

Figure 4. The rise of "suburbia" in New York and Los Angeles, 1900–1968. Shown are the number of articles mentioning this subject that appeared in the New York Times *and the* Los Angeles Times. *(Data compiled from ProQuest Historical Newspapers)*

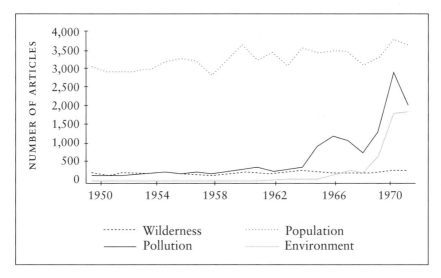

Figure 5. Pollution as a driving issue, 1950–1971. The growth of articles mentioning "pollution" precedes, yet closely parallels, that of articles mentioning the "environment"— more so than other issues mentioned. "Population" mentions are high to begin with, mostly in nonenvironmental contexts. (Data compiled from ProQuest Historical Newspapers)

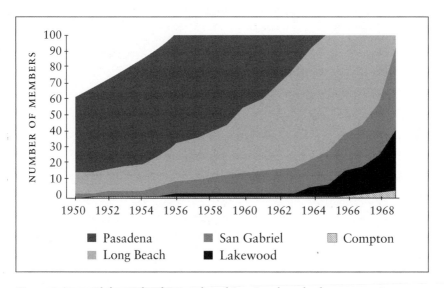

Figure 6. Sierra Club membership in selected Los Angeles suburbs, 1950–1969. Membership started out strong in Pasadena. In the 1960s, as Sierra took on more urban and industrial issues, it gained in industrial Long Beach and in San Gabriel, Lakewood (at this point mostly white- and blue-collar members), and even Compton (mostly African American). (Data compiled from Angeles Chapter of Sierra Club Papers, Special Collections, University of California, Los Angeles)

Abbreviations

APCB	Los Angeles Air Pollution Control Board Papers, Los Angeles County Board of Supervisors Archives, Los Angeles
DNR-CA	Department of Natural Resources Papers, California State Archives, Sacramento
EDF	Environmental Defense Fund Archives, Special Collections, Stony Brook University, Long Island, New York
GBM-APS	Grace Barstow Murphy Papers, American Philosophical Society, Philadelphia
JMK-SB	Julian and Muriel Kane Papers, Special Collections, Stony Brook University, Stony Brook, New York
LAT	*Los Angeles Times*
LCA	La Casa Archives, La Casa House, San Gabriel, California
LIEC	Long Island Environmental Council Papers, Special Collections, Stony Brook University, Stony Brook, New York
NAS	National Audubon Society Papers, Special Collections, New York Public Library, New York, New York
NCPH	Nassau County Department of Public Health Archives, Mineola, New York
NYT	*New York Times*
PHS	Pasadena Humane Society Archives, Pasadena Humane Society, Pasadena, California
RCM-APS	Robert Cushman Murphy Papers, American Philosophical Society, Philadelphia
RCP	Rachel Carson Papers, Beinecke Library, Yale University, New Haven, Connecticut
RLP	Richard Lillard Papers, in possession of Monique Lillard
SCP	Sierra Club Papers, Special Collections, Bancroft Library, University of California, Berkeley
SGA	San Gabriel City Archives, San Gabriel City Hall, San Gabriel, California
SGHA	San Gabriel Historical Association Archives, San Gabriel, California
UCLA	Special Collections, University of California, Los Angeles

Prologue

1. This rubric continues to hold sway in the mass media (e.g., Bruce Lambert, "Rethinking the Nation's First Suburb," *NYT*, December 25, 2005) despite historians' arguments to the contrary, such as Kenneth Jackson, *Crabgrass Frontier: The Suburbanization of the United States* (New York: Oxford University Press, 1985).

2. I thereby seek a kind of middle ground between two vast historical literatures on alienation, both of which claim roots in Karl Marx. One, revolving more or less around workplace relations, includes much labor history and geography; another, centering on the historical divorce of people from the nonhuman natural world, has evolved into environmental history. My approach builds loosely on recent efforts to bring these approaches more in dialogue with one another, among them Richard White, *The Organic Machine: The Remaking of the Columbia River* (New York: Hill and Wang, 1996); Andrew Hurley, *Environmental Inequalities: Class, Race, and Industrial Pollution in Gary, Indiana, 1945–1990* (Chapel Hill: University of North Carolina Press, 1995); Kathryn Morse, *The Nature of Gold: An Environmental History of the California Gold Rush* (Seattle: University of Washington Press, 2003); Andrew Isenberg, *Mining California: An Ecological History* (New York: Hill and Wang, 2005); Karl Jacoby, *Crimes against Nature: Squatters, Poachers, Thieves, and the Hidden History of American Conservation* (Berkeley: University of California Press, 2003); David Igler, *Industrial Cowboys: Miller & Lux and the Transformation of the Far West, 1850–1920* (Berkeley: University of California Press, 2005); and Gunther Peck, "The Nature of Labor: Fault Lines and Common Ground in Environmental and Labor History," *Environmental History* 11 (2006): 212–38.

3. Recent histories of sprawl include Robert Brueggeman, *Sprawl: A Compact History* (Chicago: University of Chicago Press, 2005), and Owen Gutfreund, *Highways and the Reshaping of the American Landscape* (London: Oxford University Press, 2004).

4. See "Homeownership Rates," http://www.census.gov/hhes/www/housing/census/historic/owner.html (March 22, 2006).

5. An international comparative view of sprawl is Peter Newman and Jeffrey Kenworthy, *Cities and Automobile Dependence: An International Sourcebook* (Aldershot, U.K.: Gower Publishing Co., 1989), expanded into Newman and Kenworthy, *An International Sourcebook of Automobile Dependence in Cities, 1960–1990* (Boulder: University of Colorado Press, 1999). On a Parisian counterexample and its fate, compare Robert Fishman, *Bourgeois Utopias: The Rise and Fall of Suburbia* (New York: Basic Books, 1989) to Brueggeman, *Sprawl*, 73–80, which also discusses many other international experiences. On shanty towns and favelas, see Robert Neuwirth, *Shadow Cities: A Billion Squatters, a New Urban World* (New York: Routledge, 2004), and Mike Davis, *Planet of Slums* (New York: Verso, 2007).

6. Christopher Sellers, *Green in Black and White: Sprawl, Race, and Environmentalism around Twentieth-Century Atlanta* (Athens: University of Georgia Press, forthcoming).

7. Adam Rome, *The Bulldozer in the Countryside: Suburban Sprawl and the Rise*

of American Environmentalism (New York: Cambridge University Press, 2001). See also Jennifer Price, *Flight Maps: Adventures with Nature in Modern America* (New York: Basic Books, 1999); Ted Steinberg, *American Green: The Obsessive Quest for the Perfect Lawn* (New York: Norton, 2006); Virginia Jenkins, *The Lawn: A History of an American Obsession* (Washington, D.C.: Smithsonian Institution Press, 1996); and Georges Teyssot, ed., *The American Lawn* (New York: Princeton Architectural Press, 1999).

8. I have drawn implicitly here on what European philosophers have termed the "Lifeworld," a realm of personal as well as intersubjective experience that remains more or less unreflected upon and, in that sense, naturalized. For an exemplary usage, see Vaclev Havel, "Anti-Political Politics," in John Keane, ed., *Civil Society and the State* (New York: Verso, 1989), 381–98.

9. Among the now voluminous literature on this movement is Robert Bullard, *Dumping in Dixie: Race, Class, and Environmental Quality*, 3rd ed. (New York: Westview Press, 2000); Robert Gottlieb, *Forcing the Spring: The Transformation of the American Environmental Movement* (Washington, D.C.: Island Press, 1993); Elizabeth Blum, *Love Canal Revisited: Race, Class, and Gender in Environmental Activism* (Lawrence: University of Kansas Press, 2008); and Eileen McGurty, *Transforming Environmentalism: Warren County, PCBs, and the Origins of Environmental Justice* (New Brunswick: Rutgers University Press, 2009). See also the bibliography of the Berkeley Workshop on Environmental Politics, "Environmental Justice and Environmental Racism," glopbetrotter.berkeley.edu/EnvirPol/Bib/B07-TurnerWu.pdf (September 2006).

10. My distinction here borrows from Linda Lorraine Nash, *Inescapable Ecologies: A History of Environment, Disease, and Knowledge* (Berkeley: University of California Press, 2006), 11–13.

11. Rachel Carson, *Silent Spring* (1962; reprint, Greenwich, Conn.: Fawcett Publications, 1970), 13–14.

12. Raymond Williams, "Ideas of Nature," in *Problems in Materialism and Culture* (London: Verso, 1980), 67–85.

13. William Greider, *The Soul of Capitalism: Opening Paths to a Moral Economy* (New York: Simon and Schuster, 2003), 316.

Chapter 1

1. Henry Cuyler Bunner, "The Story of a Path," 99–134, and "Tiemann's to Tubby Hook," 35–65, in *Jersey Street and Jersey Lane* (1896; reprint, Freeport: Books for Libraries Press, 1969), 109 ("golden hours"), 56 ("old Dame Nature"), 44 ("whacking drafts"), 43 ("my inheritance"), 39 ("comfortable farm-house"); Bunner, *The Suburban Sage; Stray Notes and Comments on His Simple Life* (1896; reprint, Freeport: Books for Libraries Press, 1969), 169 ("country life").

2. Stephen Kellert and E. O. Wilson, eds., *The Biophilia Hypothesis* (Washington, D.C.: Island Press, 1993); Samuel Hays, *Beauty, Health, and Permanence: Environmental Politics in the United States, 1955–1985* (Cambridge: Cambridge University

Press, 1985). See also Samuel Hays, *A History of Environmental Politics since 1945* (Pittsburgh: University of Pittsburgh Press, 2000), and Thomas Dunlap, *Faith in Nature; Environmentalism as a Religious Quest* (Seattle: University of Washington Press, 2004).

3. Histories of environmentalism stressing its continuities with early-century conservation include Hal Rothman, *The Greening of a Nation?: Environmentalism in the United States since 1945* (Fort Worth, Tex.: Harcourt Brace, 1998); Stephen Fox, *The American Conservation Movement: John Muir and His Legacy* (1981; reprint, Madison: University of Wisconsin Press, 1985); and Roderick Nash, *Wilderness and the American Mind*, 3rd ed. (New Haven: Yale University Press, 1982). See also Mark Harvey, *A Symbol of Wilderness: Echo Park and the American Conservation Movement* (Albuquerque: University of New Mexico Press, 1994), though Harvey notes a suburban support base (pp. 242–43). Recent histories of conservation emphasizing its more elite urban roots include Louis Warren, *The Hunter's Game: Poachers and Conservationists in Twentieth-Century America* (New Haven: Yale University Press, 1997), and Jacoby, *Crimes against Nature*, though Richard Judd, *Common Lands, Common People: The Origins of Conservation in Northern New England* (Cambridge: Harvard University Press, 1997), offers a contrasting depiction of its earlier popular roots.

4. On "risk" society, see Ulrich Beck, *Risk Society: Towards a New Modernity* (New Delhi: Sage, 1992), and Anthony Giddens, *Runaway World: How Globalization Is Reshaping Our Lives* (London: Profile, 1999). On "light-green" society, see Michael Bess, *The Light-Green Society: Ecology and Technological Modernity in France, 1960–2000* (Chicago: University of Chicago Press, 2003). As the search for "quality of life," see Hays, *Beauty, Health, and Permanence*; as consumerism, see Lizabeth Cohen, *The Consumers' Republic: The Politics of Mass Consumption in Postwar America* (New York: Vintage Books, 2003); as a "new social movement," see Claus Offe, "New Social Movements: Challenging the Boundaries of Institutional Politics," *Social Research* 52 (1985): 817–68, and Ruud Koopmans, Jan Willem Duyvendeck, and Marco G. Guigni, *New Social Movements in Western Europe: A Comparative Analysis* (Minneapolis: University of Minnesota Press, 1995).

5. Conevery Bolton Valenčius, *The Health of the Country: How American Settlers Understood Themselves and Their Land* (New York: Basic Books, 2002); Linda Lorraine Nash, *Inescapable Ecologies: A History of Environment, Disease, and Knowledge* (Berkeley: University of California Press, 2006); Gregg Mitman, *Breathing Space: How Allergies Shape Our Lives and Landscapes* (New Haven: Yale University Press, 2007); Christopher Sellers, "Thoreau's Body: Towards an Embodied Environmental History," *Environmental History* 4 (1999): 486–99.

6. From Kenneth Jackson's *Crabgrass Frontier: The Suburbanization of the United States* (New York: Oxford University Press, 1985) through a "new suburban history," most histories of suburbanization have concentrated squarely on unpacking its urban side. On how suburbs as well as suburbanites served as agents of the city's

spread, see Dolores Hayden, *Building Suburbia: Green Fields and Urban Growth* (New York: Pantheon Books, 2003), and Jackson, *Crabgrass Frontier*. Representative of much of the newer work are Kevin Kruse and Thomas Sugrue, eds., *The New Suburban History* (Chicago: University of Chicago Press, 2006), and Becky Nicolaides and Andrew Wiese, eds., *The Suburb Reader* (New York: Routledge, 2006).

7. John Stilgoe, *Borderland: Origins of the American Suburb, 1820–1939* (New Haven: Yale University Press, 1988). I have also found useful an old essay by Scott Donaldson, "City and Country: Marriage Proposals," *American Quarterly* 20 (Autumn 1968): 547–66, and Richard Harris and Robert Lewis, "Constructing a Fault(y) Zone: Misrepresentations of American Cities and Suburbs, 1900–1950," *Annals of the Association of American Geographers* 88 (1998): 622–39, as well as the classic by Peter Schmitt, *Back to Nature: The Arcadian Myth in Urban America* (New York: Oxford University Press, 1969).

8. Harlan Douglass, *The Suburban Trend* (New York: Century, 1925), 245–47. See also Graham Taylor, *Satellite Cities: A Study of Industrial Suburbs* (New York: Appleton, 1915), and many other citations in Harris and Lewis, "Constructing a Fault(y) Zone."

9. Taylor, *Satellite Cities*; Robert Lewis, "Running Rings around the City: North American Industrial Suburbs, 1850–1950," in Richard Harris and Philip Larkham, eds., *Changing Suburbs* (London: E and FN Spon, 1999), 146–67. On Brooklyn, see Jackson, *Crabgrass Frontier*, 30.

10. Marc Linder and Lawrence Zacharias, *Of Cabbages and Kings County: Agriculture and the Formation of Modern Brooklyn* (Iowa City: University of Iowa Press, 1999), 281–87; Jay Bonstell and Party, "Soil Survey of Long Island Area, New York," *Field Operations of the Bureau of Soils, 1903* (Washington, D.C.: GPO, 1903), 123–27; Louis Mesmer, "Soil Survey of the Los Angeles Area," *Field Operations of the Bureau of Soils, 1903* (Washington, D.C.: GPO, 1903), 1304–6.

11. "Why Long Island Is Popular," *Long Island Breeze*, no. 2 (1902), 8 (quotations). For similar developments elsewhere, see John Cumbler, *Reasonable Use: The People, the Environment, and the State, New England, 1790–1930* (New York: Oxford University Press, 2001); Theodore Catton, *National Park, City Playground: Mount Rainier in the Twentieth Century* (Seattle: University of Washington Press, 2006); and David Louter, *Windshield Wilderness: Cars, Roads, and Nature in Washington's National Parks* (Seattle: University of Washington Press, 2006).

12. Representative of a large literature on country homes are Michael Ebner, *Creating Chicago's North Shore: A Suburban History* (Chicago: University of Chicago Press, 1988), and Robert Mackay et al., *Long Island Country Houses and Their Architects* (New York: Society for Preservation of Long Island Antiquities and Norton, 1997). Enclaves of Garden City and Lewellyn Park in New Jersey and Frederick Law Olmsted's Riverside outside of Chicago have been discussed by many suburban historians—e.g., Hayden, *Building Suburbia*, chap. 4; Jackson, *Crabgrass Frontier*, chap. 4; and Fishman, *Bourgeois Utopias*, 126–33.

13. Hayden, *Building Suburbia*, chap. 5. On individual cities, see Sam Bass Warner Jr., *Streetcar Suburbs: The Process of Growth in Boston, 1870–1900* (Cambridge: Harvard University Press, 1962); Olivier Zunz, *The Changing Face of Inequality: Urbanization, Industrial Development, and Immigrants in Detroit, 1880–1920* (Chicago: University of Chicago Pres, 1982); Ann Durkin Keating, *Building Chicago: Suburban Developers and the Creating of a Divided Metropolis* (Columbus: Ohio State University Press, 1988); and Janet Ore, *The Seattle Bungalow: People and Houses, 1900–1940* (Seattle: University of Washington Press, 2006).

14. Henry Cuyler Bunner, "Shantytown," *Scribner's Monthly* 20 (October 1880): 855–69 (quotations, 855, 857, 865); Richard Harris, *Unplanned Suburbs: Toronto's American Tragedy, 1900 to 1950* (Baltimore: Johns Hopkins University Press, 1996); Becky Nicolaides, *My Blue Heaven: Life and Politics in the Working-Class Suburbs of Los Angeles, 1920–1965* (Chicago: University of Chicago Press, 2002); Andrew Wiese, *Places of Their Own: African American Suburbanization in the 20th Century* (Chicago: University of Chicago Press, 2004).

15. "Health—Summer as well as Winter," "Bowne Park," *NYT*, April 1, 1900; "Country vs. Town," *NYT*, April 5, 1900, 2; Hayden, *Building Suburbia*, 79–88.

16. Here again, the literature is extensive—from Brueggeman, *Sprawl*, to Fishman, *Bourgeois Utopias*, to Andrew Jackson Downing, *The Architecture of Country Houses* (New York: Appleton, 1852).

17. Frank J. Scott, *The Art of Beautifying Suburban Home Grounds of Small Extent* (New York: Appleton, 1872), 29.

18. Editor [Liberty Hyde Bailey], "What This Magazine Stands For," *Country Life* 1 (November 1901): 24–25.

19. Ibid.; "Around the Office," *Suburban Life* 9, n.s., 1 (February 1905): 1. More generally on Bailey, see Scott Peters, "'Every Farmer Should Be Awakened'; Liberty Hyde Bailey's Vision of Agricultural Extension Work," *Agricultural History* 80 (2006): 190–219, and Ben Minteer, *The Landscape of Reform: Civic Pragmatism and Environmental Thought in America* (Boston: MIT Press, 2006). See also Sarah Phillips, *This Land, This Nation: Conservation, Rural America and the New Deal* (New York: Cambridge University Press, 2004), 13–15; Steven Stoll, *The Fruits of Natural Advantage: Making the Industrial Countryside in California* (Berkeley: University of California Press, 1998), 11–16; and David Danbom, *Resisted Revolution: Urban America and the Industrialization of Agriculture* (Ames: Iowa State University Press, 1979).

20. "Mission of Country Life Magazines," *Suburban Life*, n.s., 1 (August 1905): 3; "Around the Office," *Suburban Life* 9, n.s., 1 (February 1905): 1.

21. William Dean Howells, *Suburban Sketches* (Boston: J. R. Osgood and Co., 1872); Bunner, *Suburban Sage* and *Jersey Street*.

22. Bunner, *Jersey Street*, 181, 137–38; Editor, "What This Magazine Stands For," 25.

23. Samuel Maynard, "How to Make a Country Home," *Suburban Life*, n.s., 1 (February 1905): 7 (quotations).

24. Charles Rosenberg, *The Cholera Years: The United States in 1832, 1849, and 1866* (1962; reprint, Chicago: University of Chicago Press, 1987); Sheila M. Rothman, *Living in the Shadow of Death: Tuberculosis and the Social Experience of Illness in American History* (New York: Basic Books, 1994); Mitman, *Breathing Space*.

25. Bunner, *Suburban Sage*, 192–93 ("fresh air"); Classified ads for "To Lease or for Sale in Land of Sky" ("climate unsurpassed") and for "Moosemere Park" ("pure air" and "pure and healthful water"), both in *NYT*, May 11, 1902; Classified ad for "Lots—Mohican Park" in Westchester, *NYT*, July 13, 1906 ("dry, healthy location"); Walter Lindley, "Mountain Sanatoria for Tuberculosis," *Boston Medical and Surgical Journal* 148 (1903): 468–70; "New York Sanitariums," *Polk's Medical Register and Directory of North America, 1914–1915*, http://www.bklyn-genealogy-info.com/Directory/1914.NY.Sanitariums.html (November 11, 2010). Among the secondary literature are Philip Macintosh and Richard Anderson, "The Toronto Star Fresh Air Fund: Transcendental Rescue in a Modern City, 1900–1915," *Geographic Review* 90 (2009): 539–62; Marijke Gijswijt-Hofstra, *Cultures of Neurasthenia: From Beard to the First World War* (Amsterdam and New York: Rodopi, 2001); F. J. Gosling, *Before Freud: Neurasthenia and the American Medical Community, 1870–1910* (Chicago: University of Illinois Press, 1987); and Kenneth Hawkins, "The Therapeutic Landscape: Nature, Architecture and Mind in Nineteenth Century America" (Ph.D. diss., University of Rochester, 1991).

26. Editor, "What This Magazine Stands For," 24 ("open[ed] eyes"), 25 ("growth of literature"); Bunner, *Jersey Street*, 182, 101–33.

27. Editor, "What This Magazine Stands For," 24; Bunner, *Jersey Street*, 191; Henry H. Livingtone, "What Breed of Fowl?," *Suburban Country Life*, n.s., 1 (January 1905): 26; E. I Farrington, "The Family Cow," *Suburban Life*, n.s., 1 (May 1905): 12–13; Mrs. A. Basley, "How a California Woman Makes Poultry Pay," *Suburban Life*, n.s., 1 (July 1905): 17.

28. Bunner, *Jersey Street*, 38–39, 56, 43.

29. Editor, "What This Magazine Stands For," 24.

30. Editor, "Camping Out," *Country Life*, n.s., 1 (October 1902): 229 (first three quotations); Hugo Erichsen, "How to Camp Out," *Suburban Life*, n.s., 1 (July 1905): 25–26 ("farmstead" and remaining quotations).

31. Since Garrett Hardin's "The Tragedy of the Commons", *Science* 162, no. 3859 (December 13, 1968), 1243–48, scholarship drawing on this concept has mushroomed; see the "Digital Library of the Commons," http://dlc.dlib.indiana.edu/dlc/ (January 15, 2010).

32. Samuel Maynard, "How to Make a Country Home," *Suburban Life*, n.s., 1 (February 1905): 8–10; Bunner, *Suburban Sage*.

33. Editor, "Back to the Country," *Country Life in America* 1 (1901): 25; Editors, "Mission of Country Life Magazines," *Suburban Life* 9 (August 1905): 3.

34. Bunner, *Jersey Street*, 61 ("checkered and gridironed"), 42 ("smug, mean little house[s]").

35. John M. Gries and James S. Taylor, *How to Own Your Own Home* (Wash-

ington, D.C.: GPO, 1925) (quotations from Foreword by Herbert Hoover]; Hayden, *Building Suburbia*, 121–23; Lendol Calder, *Financing the American Dream: A Cultural History of Consumer Credit* (Princeton: Princeton University Press, 1999).

36. See *A Reader's Guide to Periodical Literature* for these years. Even suburbia's early critics such as Christine Frederick and Lewis Mumford upheld a more genuine "country" experience by way of contrast; see Frederick, "Is Suburban Living a Delusion?," *Outlook* 148 (1928): 290–91, 313, and Mumford, "The Wilderness of Suburbia," *New Republic* 28 (1921): 44–45.

37. W. C. Hopper and C. W. Pierce, "Marketing and Distribution of Certain Perishable Farm Products in the Lower Hudson Valley," *Bulletin* #620 (1934): 28, 33; Jacob Arnold and Frank Montgomery, "Influence of a City upon Farming," *U.S. Department of Agriculture Farmer's Bulletin*, no. 678 (1918). A working family's food budget is from James Sullivan, *Markets for People*, in Linder and Zacharias, *Of Cabbages and Kings County*, 286. Generalizations are based on ordinances for this period in the city halls of Garden City, N.Y., Pasadena, Calif., and other suburban towns.

38. Douglass, *Suburban Trend*, 61; Linder and Zacharias, *Of Cabbages and Kings County*, 284–85 (quotation of a USDA official).

39. U.S. Bureau of the Census, *Fourteenth Census of the United States Taken in the Year 1920: Agriculture*, vol. 6 (Washington, D.C.: GPO, 1922), part 1, pp. 213, 215, part 3, p. 346.

40. Richard Harris and Robert Lewis, "The Geography of North American Cities and Suburbs, 1900–1950: A New Synthesis," *Journal of Urban History* 27 (2001): 262–93; Wiese, *Places of Their Own*; Nicolaides, *My Blue Heaven*.

41. Douglass, *Suburban Trend*, 97, 86, 242, 62, 96 ("suburban hegira").

42. Ibid., 159, 247–49.

43. Linda Lorraine Nash, *Inescapable Ecologies*; Ed Cohen, *A Body Worth Defending: Immunity, Biopolitics, and the Apotheosis of the Modern Body* (Durham, N.C.: Duke University Press, 2009); Emily Martin, *Flexible Bodies: Tracking Immunity in American Culture from the Days of Polio to the Age of AIDS* (New York: Beacon Press, 1994).

44. Hibbert Hill, *The New Public Health* (Minneapolis, Minn.: Press of the Journal-Lancet, 1913).

45. Among a vast literature, see Joel Tarr and Clay McShane, *The Horse in the City: Living Machines in the Nineteenth Century* (Baltimore: Johns Hopkins University Press, 2007); Ted Steinberg, *Down to Earth: Nature in American History* (New York: Oxford University Press, 2008), 157–74; Martin Melosi, *The Sanitary City: Urban Infrastructure in America from Colonial Times to the Present* (Baltimore: Johns Hopkins University Press, 2000); and Harold Platt, *Shock Cities: The Environmental Transformation and Reform of Manchester and Chicago* (Chicago: University of Chicago Press, 2005). Classic overviews from the perspective of public health history include John Duffy, *The Sanitarians: A History of American Public Health* (Chicago: University of Illinois Press, 1992); George Rosen, *A History of Public Health* (1958; reprint, Baltimore: Johns Hopkins University Press, 1993; and,

more recently, Dorothy Porter, *Health, Civilization and the State: A History of Public Health from Ancient to Modern Times* (New York: Routledge, 1999).

46. Hayden, *Building Suburbia*, 121–22; Melosi, *Sanitary City*. For examples of sewer controversies and incorporation, see Francis Bourget, *Manhasset: The First 300 Years* (Manhasset, N.Y.: Manhasset Chamber of Commerce, 1980), 42.

47. Daniel Rogers, *Atlantic Crossings: Social Politics in a Progressive Age* (Cambridge: Harvard University Press, 1998), 181–86; Benjamin Marsh, "The Congestion Exhibit in Brooklyn," *Charities and the Commons* 20 (1908): 209–11; New York City Board of Estimate and Approval, Committee on the City Plan, *Final Report of the Commission on Building Districts* (New York, 1916).

48. Linder and Zacharias, *Of Cabbages and Kings County*, 287–94 (288–89, quotations); Greg Hise and William Deverell, *Eden by Design: The 1930 Olmsted-Bartholomew Plan for the Los Angeles Region* (Berkeley: University of California Press, 2000).

49. Philip Bernays, "The Fiftieth Anniversary of the Los Angeles Chapter," *Southern Sierran* (November 17, 1961): 1–2; Bound Club Reports, box B-35, NAS; Raymond Torrey, Frank Place Jr., and Robert Dickinson, *New York Walk Book* (New York: American Geographic Society, 1923), 186–92.

50. Torrey, Place, and Dickinson, *New York Walk Book*, ix–x, 16; L. C. Maar, "Girl Who Hikes Tells Where and How to Go," *LAT*, June 14, 1914.

51. Torrey, Place, and Dickinson, *New York Walk Book*, ix, 13–16, 26, 138, 170; Marr, "Girl Who Hikes."

52. Gurth Whipple, *A History of Half a Century of the Management of the Natural Resources of the Empire State, 1885–1935* (Conservation Department and New York State College of Forestry, 1935), 55, 61, 127–29; Stephanie Pincetl, *Transforming California: A Political History of Land Use and Development* (Baltimore: Johns Hopkins University Press, 1999), 37–54; "Montauk Deer Overdoing Their Friendliness," *NYT*, October 21, 1956.

53. Among works that have come to constitute a large literature, see, on national parks, Richard West Sellars, *Preserving Nature in the National Parks: A History* (New Haven: Yale University Press, 1998), and Alfred Runte, *National Parks: The American Experience* (Lincoln: University of Nebraska Press, 1997); on national forests, Harold Steen, *The U.S. Forest Service: A History* (Seattle: University of Washington Press, 2004), and James Lewis, *The Forest Service and the Greatest Good: A Centennial History* (Durham, N.C.: Forest History Society, 2006).

54. Torrey, Place, and Dickinson, *New York Walk Book*, 145; Robert Caro, *The Power Broker: Robert Moses and the Fall of New York* (New York: Vintage Books, 1975), 161, but esp. 221–23; Chester Blakelock, "Know Your State Parks," *Long Island Forum* (January 1941): 13–14; Hise and Deverell, *Eden by Design*, 3, 151–56, 168–69; Paul Sabin, "Beaches versus Oil in Greater Los Angeles," in William Deverell and Greg Hise, eds., *Land of Sunshine: An Environmental History of Metropolitan Los Angeles* (Pittsburgh: University of Pittsburgh Press, 2005), 95–114.

55. Torrey, Place, and Dickinson, *New York Walk Book*. Although at this very

moment a "Wilderness Society" was being inaugurated in Washington, D.C., there seemed little prospect of backing for a wilder sort of park on a place like Long Island.

56. Fred Gendral, "The Homeless Go to Camp," *Current History* 42 (1935): 489 (quotation); Joan Crouse, *The Homeless Transient in the Great Depression: New York State, 1929–1941* (Albany: State University of New York Press, 1986); John McCarthy and Robert Littell, "Three Hundred Thousand Shacks: The Arrival of a New American Industry," *Harper's Monthly* 167 (1933): 181.

57. Ralph Borsodi, *Flight from the City: The Story of a New Way to Family Security* (New York: Harper and Brothers, 1933); Franklin D. Roosevelt, "A New Rural Planning," *National Country Life Conference* 14 (1931): 10–27. On federal subsistence homestead projects, some of them in urban fringe areas, see Phillips, *This Land*, 114–16, and Russell Lord and Paul Johnstone, eds., *A Place on Earth: A Critical Appraisal of Subsistence Homesteads* (Washington, D.C.: U.S. Department of Agriculture, 1942).

58. *Sixteenth Census of the United States, 1940: Agriculture*, vol. 1, part 1, "Statistics for Counties," 229; vol. 1, part 6, "Statistics for Counties," 697. By 1943, the proportion of hired help that was "colored" (black) averaged 70 percent in one Suffolk County study; see W. M. Curtiss, "The Labor Force on Potato and Vegetable Farms, Long Island, N.Y., 1941 and 1942," typescript, July 1943, Olin Library, Cornell University, Ithaca, N.Y. More generally on farm labor in this period, see Cynthia Hahamovitch, *The Fruits of Their Labor: Atlantic Coast Farmworkers and the Making of Migrant Poverty, 1870–1945* (Chapel Hill: University of North Carolina Press, 1997); Don Mitchell, *The Lie of the Land: Migrant Workers and the California Landscape* (Minneapolis: University of Minnesota Press, 1996); and Stoll, *Fruits of Natural Advantage*.

59. Jackson, *Crabgrass Frontier*; Hayden, *Building Suburbia*. A recent challenge to Jackson's emphasis, if not to the underlying prejudices involved, is Amy Hillier, "Redlining and the Home Owners' Loan Corporation," *Journal of Urban History* 29, no. 4 (2003): 394–420; quote from "San Gabriel Wash," "D"-Rated Areas, Los Angeles County Survey Files, Home Owners' Loan Corporation (HOLC) subsection, RG 195, Records of the Home Loan Bank Board, National Archives II, College Park, Md.

60. See Los Angeles and Queens and Westchester County Survey Files, HOLC subsection, RG 195, Records of the Federal Home Loan Bank Board, National Archives II, College Park, Md. On the Los Angeles assessments, see Becky Nicolaides, "'Where the Working Man Is Welcomed': Working-Class Suburbs in Los Angeles, 1900–1940," *Pacific Historical Review* 68 (1999); 555.

Chapter 2

1. Harry Henderson, "The Mass Produced Suburbs," *Harper's* 207 (November 1953): 25–32, (December 1953): 80–86; William Whyte, *The Organization Man* (New York: Simon and Schuster, 1956). On the methods upon which they drew, see

Sarah E. Igo, *The Averaged American: Surveys, Citizens, and the Making of a Mass Public* (Cambridge: Harvard University Press, 2007), esp. 19, and Jennifer Platt, *A History of Sociological Research Methods in America* (Cambridge: Cambridge University Press, 1996).

2. "The Lush New Suburban Market," *Fortune*, November 1953, 129 ("more open space"). For a sampling of this literature, see "Pull of Suburbs Is Stronger: Buyers, Taxpayers Move Out," *U.S. News and World Report* 26 (June 30, 1950): 11; Donald Campion and Dennis Clark, "So You're Moving to Suburbia," *America*, April 21, 1956, 80; and "Why People Move Out of Cities," *U.S. News and World Report* 40 (August 10, 1954): 69. My findings here resonate with Richard Harris and Robert Lewis, "Constructing a Fault(y) Zone: Misrepresentations of American Cities and Suburbs, 1900–1950," *Annals of the Association of American Geographers* 88 (1998): 622–39.

3. For current debates on narrative explanations of historians, see David Carr, "Narrative Explanation and Its Malcontents," *History and Theory* 47 (2008): 19–30. On the difficulty of constructing narratives of urban history, see Philip Ethington, "Los Angeles and the Problem of Urban Historical Knowledge," *American Historical Review* 105 (2000), http://www.usc.edu/dept/LAS/history/historylab/LAPUHK (February 2, 2009). For an early statement of this problem of multiple interpretations, see William Cronon, "A Place for Stories: Nature, History and Narrative," *Journal of American History* 78 (1992): 1347–76.

4. More evenhandedly ecological approaches have been fundamental to the field of environmental history. For a comprehensive introduction to this literature, see Douglas Sackman, ed., *Companion to Environmental History* (Oxford: Blackwell, 2010).

5. See, e.g., the postwar essays in Kevin Kruse and Thomas Sugrue, *The New Suburban History* (Chicago: University of Chicago Press, 2006), and Becky Nicolaides and Andrew Wiese, eds., *The Suburb Reader* (New York: Routledge, 2006).

6. Landmarks in the vast literature on Levittown include Rosalyn Baxandall and Elizabeth Ewen, *Picture Windows: How the Suburbs Happened* (New York: Basic Books, 2000), and Barbara Kelly, *Expanding the American Dream: Building and Rebuilding Levittown* (Albany: State University of New York Press, 1993).

7. A. Levitt Sr., "Welcoming Message from Founder," *Island Trees Tribune*, December 17, 1947; Abraham Levitt, "Fruit Is Fine for Little Gardens, *American Home* (January 1950): 72–73. On the advertising campaigns, see John Liell, "Levittown: A Study in Community Planning and Development" (Ph.D. diss., Yale University, 1952), 110–11; see, e.g., *NYT*, January 15, 29, 1950.

8. Abraham Levitt, "Chats on Gardening," *Levittown Tribune*, July 29, 1947.

9. "Up from Potato Fields," *Time* 56 (July 3, 1950): 67–69, 72, 68 ("grass seed").

10. "How the Land Was Formed," in "Long Island: Our Story," http://www.newsday.com/community/guide/lihistory (July 7, 2007). See also Robert Villani, *Long Island: A Natural History* (New York: Harry Abrams, 1997).

11. John Cryan, "Major Vegetation of Long Island," *Heath Hen* 1 (1981): 41;

R. M. Harper, "The Hempstead Plains: A Natural Prairie on Long Island," *Bulletin of the American Geographic Society* 43 (1911): 351–60; Jane D. Harris, "Our Vanishing Prairie," *Long Island Forum* (March 1941): 59–60.

12. For an introduction to "idling," see David Berry, "Effects of Urbanization on Agricultural Activities," *Growth and Change* 9 (1978): 2–8. More generally, see John Fraser Hart, "The Peri-metropolitan Bow Wave," *Geographical Review* 81 (1991): 35–51, and Marc Linder and Lawrence Zacharias, *Of Cabbages and Kings County: Agriculture and the Formation of Modern Brooklyn* (Iowa City: University of Iowa Press, 1999), esp. 224–33.

13. "Suffolk Protests Potato Subsidy Cut," *NYT*, November 28, 1948; "Potato Farmers Accept U.S. Offer," *NYT*, August 14, 1946; Town of Hempstead, *Building Zone Ordinance* (1930; reprint, Hempstead: Town of Hempstead, 1952), 16; Town of Babylon, *Building Zone Ordinance* (1931; reprint, Babylon: Town of Babylon, 1955), 9; Minutes of Nassau County Board of Health, December 15, 1949, p. 55, Nassau County Board of Health, Mineola, N.Y.

14. For nematode importation, see "Origin of the Infestation," from W. A. McCubbin, "The Potato Nematode Situation, Sept. 8, 1943," in folder "Potatoes (Irish and Sweet)—Insects and Diseases Affecting . . . ," box 18, Records Relating to Insects and Diseases, 1927–51, Bureau of Entomology and Plant Quarantine Papers, RG 7, National Archives II, College Park, Md.

15. Interview with Robert Rowehl, Mattituck, N.Y., March 29, 1999. See also Steven Wick, *Heaven and Earth: The Last Farmers of the North Fork* (New York: St. Martin's Press, 1996).

16. "Potato Washing Plant to Open on Saturday," *Levittown Tribune*, August 5, 1948.

17. Frank Mucha, "Employment Trends in Suburban Long Island," *Occasional Memo #33*, April 12, 1955, in folder "Long Island," box 13, Reports of Housing Market Analysts, 1937–63, RG 31, Federal Homeowners Association Archives, National Archives II, College Park, Md. More generally, see Richard Walker and Robert Lewis, "Beyond the Crabgrass Frontier: Industry and the Spread of Cities," *Journal of Historical Geography* 27 (2001): 3–19.

18. "Shopping Centers Matching Growth of Home Colonies," *NYT*, August 26, 1950; "Shopping Centers on Long Island Planned at Cost of $35,000,000," *NYT*, April 11, 1954.

19. Table 3, *Census of Housing, 1950, vol. 4: Residential Financing, part 2, Large Standard Metropolitan Areas* (Washington, D.C.: GPO, 1952), 506.

20. "Setting Your Sites," *National Real Estate and Building Journal* (May 1948): 15.

21. "Houses-Nassau-Suffolk," *NYT*, April 6, 1952.

22. "Builders Acquire Long Island Sites," *NYT*, August 18, 1948; "Extend Holdings at Lake Success," *NYT*, April 9, 1950. More generally, see "Long Island Gets New Home Groups in Luxury Bracket," *NYT*, September 21, 1947; U.S. Census of Population, 1960; *Historical Population of Long Island Communities, 1790–1980* (Hauppauge: Long Island Regional Planning Board, 1982).

23. "Distinctive *New* Country Homes [display ad]," *NYT*, August 15, 1948; "In a Community of a Lifetime! [display ad]," *NYT*, May 25, 1952.

24. "Residence Built to Fit Its Site," *NYT*, June 23, 1940; "Developers Buy Westbury Estate," *NYT*, June 7, 1936; "Open New Areas on Long Island," *NYT*, May 2, 1937.

25. "The Industry That Capitalism Forgot," *Fortune*, August 1947, 161–67; Bureau of Labor Statistics, "Structure of the Residential Building Industry in 1949," *Bulletin of the Bureau of Labor Statistics*, no. 1170 (1949): 10. On the changes in the construction industry over this period that contributed to an enlarged scale of building, see Baxandall and Ewen, *Picture Windows*; Marc A. Weiss, *The Rise of the Community Builders: The American Real Estate Industry and Urban Land Planning* (New York: Columbia University Press, 1987); Ned Eichler, *The Merchant Builders* (Cambridge: MIT Press, 1982); and Kelly, *Expanding the American Dream*, 21–25.

26. Frank LeGost, "Interim Memorandum on the Condition and Outlook for the New Home Sales Market of Western Long Island," December 10, 1948, folder "Long Island," box 13, Reports of Housing Market Analysts, 1937–63.

27. "Up from Potato Fields," *Time*; "The Industry That Capitalism Forgot," *Fortune*; Eric Larrabee, "The Six Thousand Houses That Levitt Built," *Harper's* 197 (1948): 79–88; "The Line at Levitts," *Newsweek* 33 (March 21, 1949): 66–67; William J. Levitt, "A House in Not Enough," in Sidney Furst and Milton Sherman, eds., *Business Decisions That Changed Our Lives* (New York: Random House, 1964), 66 ("breakdown").

28. The classic statement of flexible specialization is Charles Sabel and Michael Piore, *The Second Industrial Divide: Possibilities for Prosperity* (New York: Basic Books, 1982). A parallel usage in history is found in the work of Philip Scranton such as *Figured Tapestry: Production, Markets, and Power in Philadelphia Textiles, 1885–1941* (Cambridge: Cambridge University Press, 1989).

29. See n. 28 above. See also phone interview with Ralph DellaRatta, December 10, 1998.

30. Compare subdivision plans for "Ronek Park, section 1. Babylon," #1736, book 28, p. 6, Suffolk County Subdivision Plan Archive, Riverhead, N.Y., with "Island Trees, Section A," June 9, 1947, #4405, Nassau County Subdivision Plan Archives, Mineola, N.Y.

31. Abraham Levitt, "Chats on Gardening," *Levittown Tribune*, July 12, 1951.

32. Nassau County Planning Commission, *Building Activity, 1945–1965: A Twenty Year Summary* (Mineola, N.Y.: Nassau County Planning Commission, 1966), 7.

33. William Collins and Robert Margo, "Race and Home Ownership: A Century-Long View," *Explorations in Economic History* 38 (2001): 68–92; interview with Eugene Burnett, Wyandanch, N.Y., March 19, 1999; Advertising flyer for Ronek Park, in Burnett Family Papers, Wyandanch, N.Y.; "140 Dwellings Sold," *NYT*, January 31, 1950; "'Non-Racial' Colony of Houses at 7,000," *NYT*, January 27, 1950.

34. For more on Ronek Park and the experience of Eugene and Beatrice Burnett,

see text "Seeing the Countryside in the Home Purchase," below, and Christopher Sellers, "Nature and Blackness in Suburban Passage," in Diane Glave and Mark Stoll, eds., *'To Love the Wind and Rain': Essays in African American Environmental History* (Pittsburgh: University of Pittsburgh Press, 2006), 93–119.

35. "Long Island" real estate listings, *New Amsterdam Times*, April 5, 1952.

36. Real Estate listings, *Newsday*, April 5, 1952.

37. On nationwide trends in zoning on which this and the following paragraphs are based, see Stephen Sussna, "Zoning Boards: In Theory and Practice," *Land Economics* 37 (1961): 82–87, and Paul King, "Exclusionary Zoning and Open Housing: A Brief Judicial History," *Geographical Review* 68 (1978): 459–69, esp. 462.

38. "Hearing of the Village of Old Field, Oct. 1, 1948," *Minutes of the Board of Trustees of Old Field*, pp. 21, 20, Old Field Village Archives, Old Field Village Hall, Old Field, N.Y.

39. New York Regional Plan Association, *Spread City*, 40, as quoted in David Schoenbrod, "Large Lot Zoning," *Yale Law Journal* 78 (July 1969): 1418; Fred Stickel, "Trends in Court Decisions in Planning and Zoning," *American City* (December 1956): 92; "Hearing of the Village of Old Field, Oct. 1, 1948," *Minutes of the Board of Trustees of Old Field*, pp. 19, 8 (quotations).

40. Town of Babylon, *Building Zone Ordinance* (Babylon, N.Y.: Town of Babylon, 1953).

41. On the history of suburban political institutions here and elsewhere, see Jon Teaford, *Post-Suburbia* (Johns Hopkins University Press, 1997), and Paul Lewis, *Shaping Suburbia: How Political Institutions Organize Urban Development* (Pittsburgh: University of Pittsburgh Press, 1996). For an earlier period, see S. J. Makielski, *The Politics of Zoning: The New York Experience* (New York: Columbia University Press, 1966), and Richard Babcock, *The Zoning Game: Municipal Policies and Practices* (Madison: University of Wisconsin Press, 1966).

42. Abraham Levitt, "Chats on Gardening," *Levittown Tribune*, November 21, 1951.

43. "City and Country," *NYT*, June 30, 1940; "Farm Here Fades, Census Job Gone," *NYT*, April 3, 1940. On Danteville, see interview with Irwin and Cissy Botto, Hicksville, N.Y., March 29, 1999.

44. Abraham Levitt, "Chats on Gardening," November 21, 1951; Bethpage Realty, Housing Contract, March 31, 1948, p. 2, Levitt Collection, Long Island Studies Institute, Hofstra University, Hempstead, N.Y.

45. Interview with John Levitt, Felton, Ga., March 26, 2001. On changes in food markets in these years, see James Mayo, *The American Grocery Store: The Business Evolution of an Architectural Space* (Westport, Conn.: Greenwood Press, 1993), 157–91, and Harvey Levenstein, *Paradox of Plenty: A Social History of Eating in Modern America* (New York: Oxford University Press, 1993).

46. See, e.g., Tony Insolia, "The Levittown Decade," *Newsday*, September 30, 1957; Geoffrey Mohan, "Levitt's Defenses of Racist Policies," *Newsday*, September

28, 1997; D. J. Waldie, *Holy Land: A Suburban Memoir* (New York: Norton, 1996), 73.

47. On earlier settlements there, see interviews with McKinley Banks and Charles Ballenger (April 28, 1997) and Mary Leftenants (March 30, 1999), all in North Amityville, N.Y., and "'Non-Racial' Colony of Houses at $7000 Will Open Tomorrow at North Amityville," *NYT*, January 27, 1950.

48. "Town Urged to Clear Out Shanty Area," *Amityville Record*, May 21, 1953.

49. Frederick Lewis Allen, "The Big Change in Suburbia," *Harper's* 208 (June 1954): 23–28, and Allen, "Crisis in the Suburbs," *Harper's* 208 (July 1954): 47–53.

50. G. S. Wehrwein, "The Rural-Urban Fringe," *Economic Geography* 18 (1942): 217–28; *The Rural-Urban Fringe: Proceedings of the Commonwealth Conference* (Eugene: University of Oregon, 1942); W. Martin, *The Rural-Urban Fringe* (Eugene: University of Oregon Press, 1953).

51. August Spectorsky, *The Exurbanites* (Philadelphia: Lippincott, 1955); "Who Are the Suburbanites?," *Fortune*, November 1953, 231 ("semi-suburbia").

52. Allen, "Crisis in the Suburbs," 47 (quotations).

53. Interview with Julian and Muriel Kane, Great Neck, N.Y., April 2005 (these and succeeding quotations).

54. Interview with Eugene Burnett, Wyandanch, N.Y., March 19, 1999, and with Eugene and Bernice Burnett, Wyandanch, N.Y., January 7, 2004 (these and succeeding quotations).

55. For more of their story, see Sellers, "Nature and Blackness in Suburban Passage."

56. By contrast, many social scientific and media observers were critical of the Levitts' use of space; see, for example, Liell, "Levittown," 147–51.

57. On blacks' difficulties with mortgages, see "Thirty Acres Sold in Hicksville, L.I. for Housing Group," *NYT*, March 19, 1952, and phone interview with James Merrick, December 8, 1998.

58. "'Non-Racial' Colony of Houses at $7,000 Will Open Tomorrow at North Amityville," *NYT*, January 27, 1950 ("contemplated").

59. "Obituaries—Mrs. Augusta C. Murphy," *Port Jefferson Times*, May 13, 1949.

60. Grace Barstow, *There's Always Adventure: The Story of a Naturalist's Wife* (New York: Harper and Brothers, 1951), 29–30 (on Crystal Brook), 140 (on their ancestries).

61. Robert Cushman Murphy to the editor, *Port Jefferson Times*, August 23, 1946, untitled Long Island vol. See also "January 1950" and "Long Island and Elsewhere, 1950–52," RCM-APS.

62. "Aug 3–6, 1950" (mice); "Sept and Oct 1950" (lawn); "Dec. 9–10, 1950" (squirrels)—all in "Long Island and Elsewhere, 1950–52," ibid.

63. "Crystal Brook, April 5–6, 1952," "Crystal Brook and Briarlea, April 18–20, 1952," in "Long Island and Elsewhere, 1950–52," ibid.

Chapter 3

1. These and subsequent quotations of the Kanes from interview with Julian and Muriel Kane, Great Neck, N.Y., April 2005; "Pet Skunk (Deodorized)," *Levittown Tribune*, March 13, 1958.

2. On urban-rural gradients, see M. J. McConnell and S. T. A. Pickett, "Ecosystem Structure and Function along Urban-Rural Gradients: An Unexploited Opportunity for Ecology," *Ecology* 71 (1990): 1232–37, and Timothy Foresman, Stewart T. A. Pickett, and Wayne C. Zipperer, "Methods for Spatial and Temporal Land Use and Land Cover Assessment for Urban Ecosystems and Application in the Greater Baltimore-Chesapeake Region," *Urban Ecosystems* 1 (1997): 201–16.

3. New York Regional Plan Association, *Spread City: Projections of Development Trends and the Issues They Pose: The Tri-State New York Metropolitan Region, 1960–1985* (New York: Regional Plan Association, 1962).

4. Interview with Fred Hicks, Hicksville, N.Y., December 17, 1998.

5. Meyer Bergen, "About New York: Park Men, Sparing the Water, Fear They May Be Spoiling the City's 2,820,000 Trees," *NYT*, July 21, 1954.

6. U.S. Census of Agriculture, 1939, 1964; J. E. McMahon, "Home Gardeners Are Big Spenders," *NYT*, March 29, 1959.

7. Daniel Kevles and Glenn Bugos, "Plants as Intellectual Property: American Practice, Law in World Context," *Osiris*, 2nd ser., 7 (1992): 74–104; Donald Wyman, "Better Ornamental Broadleaves," *NYT*, March 26, 1961; Herbert C. Bardes, "Holly in the Landscape," *NYT*, September 28, 1958.

8. Harold Wallis Steck, "All-Season Planting to Reverse Old Rule," *NYT*, June 13, 1948; Rudy J. Favretti, "Container-Grown Material Promotes Successful Transplanting Now," *NYT*, April 30, 1961); interview with Fred Hicks.

9. On the expanding lawn care industry, see Virginia Jenkins, *The Lawn: History of an American Obsession* (Washington, D.C.: Smithsonian Press, 1994), 91–116; Ted Steinberg, *American Green: The Obsessive Quest for the Perfect Lawn* (New York: Norton, 2006); City of Glass advertisement, *Levittown Tribune*, September 27, 1951; Sears advertisement, *Levittown Tribune*, September 20, 1951.

10. Byron Porterfield, "Suffolk Extends Its Farming Role," *NYT*, May 1, 1960; J. E. McMahon, "The Demand for Beauty and Ornament Spells Big Business for Nurserymen," *NYT*, February 23, 1958).

11. Interview with Thomas Patterson, Huntington, N.Y., December 18, 1998; phone interview with Ralph DellaRatta, December 10, 1998; McMahon, "Demand for Beauty."

12. Hugh O. Graumann, "Our Sources of Seeds of Grasses and Legumes," *New York Turfgrass Association* 68 (1961): 261–63; Steinberg, *American Green*.

13. Byron Porterfield, "Sod Farms Thrive on Long Island," *NYT*, July 21, 1963.

14. "L.I. Home Owners Advised on Weeds," *NYT*, June 21, 1959). On Japanese beetles, see "Route of the Japanese Beetle," *NYT*, August 7, 1949. For an overview of plant as well as insect pests, see A. A. Hanson and F. V. Juska, eds., *Turfgrass Science* (Madison, Wis.: American Society of Agronomy, Inc., 1969).

15. Abraham Levitt, "Chats on Gardening," *Levittown Tribune*, August 9, 1951; Porterfield, "Sod Farms Thrive"; A. A. Hanson, F. V. Juska, and Glenn Burton, "Species and Varieties," in Hanson and Juska, *Turfgrass Science*, 370–409.

16. Mark Fiege, "The Weedy West: Mobile Nature, Boundaries, and Common Space in the Montana Landscape," *Western Historical Quarterly* 36 (2005): 22–47; Zachary Falck, *Weeds: An Environmental History of Metropolitan America* (Pittsburgh: University of Pittsburgh Press, 2011).

17. Abraham Levitt, "Chats on Gardening," *Levittown Tribune*, May 4, 1951; Letter to editor, "Pups and Prams," *Newsday*, February 9, 1951, from John Liell, "Levittown: A Study in Community Planning and Development" (Ph.D. diss., Yale University, 1952), 223.

18. See, e.g., Abraham Levitt, "Chats on Gardening," *Levittown Tribune*, April 15, 1948.

19. Interview with Eugene Burnett, Wyandanch, N.Y., March 19, 1999 (quotations here and elsewhere); Geoffrey Mohan, "Suburban Pioneers," *Newsday*, September 28, 1997; Harry Henderson, "Youthtown, U.S.A.," *Redbook*, February 1950, 90 ("tastes"); Robert Cushman Murphy, entry for "September–October 1950," in vol. "Long Island and Elsewhere, 1950–52"; *Journals*, RCM-APS.

20. "Better Ornamental Broadleaves," *NYT*, March 26, 1961; Robert Cushman Murphy, in vol. "Long Island and Elsewhere, 1950–52," 3–4 (Murphy plantings).

21. Frank D'Amelio, "Vegetables Can Add Color to Your Garden," *Thousand Lanes*, April 1952, 20–21; interview with Julian and Muriel Kane; Grace Murphy, "Five Hour Garden," GBM-APS.

22. Interview with Louise and Mauro Cassano, Levittown, N.Y., July 28, 1999; "L. I. Florist and Nursery Research Lab to Open Soon, at Farmingdale," *Suffolk County Farm Bureau News*, April 1948, 18; "Cornell Turfgrass Field Days," *New York Turfgrass Association Bulletin*, no. 65 (1959): 251; "Sept and Oct 1950" (lawn), in vol. "Long Island and Elsewhere, 1950–52."

23. "1956 Buying Guide Issue," *Consumer Reports* 20 (1955): 274.

24. Bureau of Entomology and Plant Quarantine, *Annual Reports of Department of Agriculture* (Washington, D.C.: GPO, 1952), 73–74; "Japanese Beetles on Rampage," *Levittown Eagle*, July 19, 1951 ("replaced the weather"); "Meadow Residents to Curb Jap Beetles," *Levittown Eagle*, September 27, 1951; "Organize Fight against Japanese Beetles," *Levittown Tribune*, September 6, 1951; "Council Hears Beetle Report," *Levittown Tribune*, September 20, 1951 (close to 100% cooperation); Abraham Levitt, "Chats on Gardening," *Levittown Tribune*, September 6, 1951.

25. Grace Murphy, "Five Hour Garden."

26. Abraham Levitt, "Chats on Gardening," *Levittown Tribune*, April 22, 1948; Robert Cushman Murphy, "Crystal Brook, August 3–6, 1950," in vol. "Long Island and Elsewhere, 1950–52."

27. See, e.g., Ehrenfried Pfeiffer, Preface to Rudolf Steiner, *Agriculture Course:*

The Birth of the Biodynamic Method, translated by George Adams (1924; reprint, London: Rudolf Steiner Press, 2004), 8 (quotation).

28. J. I. Rodale, "Open Letter to the Food Industry," *Organic Gardening* (May 1956): 37; Transcript, *Robert Cushman Murphy et al. v. Ezra Taft Benson*, Civil Action 17,610, U.S. District Court for the Eastern District of New York (1958), pp. 180–81a; "Gardeners Ready Informal Meeting," *Levittown Tribune*, February 7, 1957; Samuel Fromartz, *Organic, Inc.: Natural Foods and How They Grew* (Orlando: Harvest Books, 2007), 1–31.

29. Jenkins, *The Lawn*; Robert Cushman Murphy, "May 10–14, 1950," in vol. "Long Island and Elsewhere, 1950–52."

30. "Fewer Dogs Live in New York Now," *NYT*, April 24, 1954; "Fido Adds Up to Fancy Facts and Figures," *Consumers Union* 25 (July 1960): 340–41; "Our Expanding Pet Set," *NYT Magazine*, January 18, 1959, SM40; Alexander B. Hammer, "Affluence Is Fueling Pet Industry Growth," *NYT*, September 21, 1969 (final estimate).

31. "Fido Adds Up," *Consumers Union*; Katherine C. Grier, *Pets in America: A History* (Chapel Hill: University of North Carolina Press, 2006); Frederick Brown, "Cows in the Commons, Dogs on the Lawn: A History of Animals in Seattle" (Ph.D. diss., University of Washington–Seattle, 2010), chap. 4.

32. Bess Furman, "Health Unit Gains in Fight on Rabies," *NYT*, August 10, 1952; "Nassau Fights Rabies," *NYT*, June 11, 1946; "10,000th Dog Inoculated; Numerically Fortunate Pup Gets Round of Prizes in Nassau," *NYT*, August 20, 1946; Minutes of the Nassau County Board of Public Health, November 19, 1953, p. 2006, NCPH.

33. Arthur Gelb, "Parrots Freed of Ban by State, May Soon Get City's Pardon Too," *NYT*, June 14, 1952.

34. Grace Barstow Murphy, *Your Deafness Is Not You* (New York: Harper and Brothers, 1954), 111–12. Brown ("Cows in the Common") notes a shift from seeing pets as servants to seeing them as children.

35. "How to Buy a Dog," *Consumer Reports* 24 (1959): 578–80; Dorothy Barclay, "A Problem Puppy in the Home," *NYT*, February 10, 1952 ("source of companionship"); Nan Robertson, "Gift Ideas: Pets Please the Young," *NYT*, December 4, 1956.

36. Bernard Mergen, "Children and Nature in History," *Environmental History* 8 (2003): 643–49; Chris Magoc, "Progress, Pollution and the Pastoral Ideal in Rural-Based Television, 1954–1971," *Journal of Popular Film and Television* 19 (1991): 25–35.

37. Susan Jones, *Valuing Animals: Veterinarians and Their Patients in Modern America* (Baltimore: Johns Hopkins University Press, 2003), 116–19; Chris Magoc, "The Machine in the Wasteland," *Journal of Popular Film and Television* 19 (Spring 1991): 25–35; Tim Brooks and Earle Marsh, *Complete Directory to Prime Time Network and Cable TV Shows* (New York: Ballantine Books, 1999); "10,000th Dog Inoculated"; "Lassie Back from Jaunt," *NYT*, November 20, 1952.

38. "A.K.C. Big Business," *NYT*, June 29, 1961; "Registration Rise to 240,000 Looms," *NYT*, April 21, 1946; John Rendel, "Breeder's Advice to Buyers of Pups: Beware," *NYT*, December 7, 1961; Grier, *Pets in America*.

39. "Fido Adds Up," *Consumers Union*; "Packaged Dog Foods," *Consumer Reports* 25 (1960): 351–55; Marybeth Weston, "Now the Dog Has His Heyday," *NYT Magazine*, February 21, 1960, SM32; Alexander Hammer, "Advertising: Dog Food Drives Unleashed," *NYT*, June 14, 1959.

40. U.S. Agricultural Census, 1940, 1964.

41. On these trends for New York, see John Fraser Hart, "The Perimetropolitan Bow Wave," *Geographical Review* 81 (1991): 35–51. More generally, see Henry Lawrence, "Changes in Agricultural Production in Metropolitan Areas," *Professional Geographer* 40 (1988): 159–75.

42. Interview with Eugene Reed, Lindenhurst, N.Y., May 17, 2002 (quotation); Robert Cushman Murphy, in vol. "Long Island and Elsewhere."

43. See, e.g., letter of Herbert Hill, February 11, 1958, reel 18, and statement of Herbert Hill, September 4, 1957, reel 19, both in part 22, Legal Department Administrative Files, NAACP; Jack Ehrlich and Francis Wood, "Long Island's Ugly Ducklings," *Newsday*, September 16, 1957.

44. For an introduction to ecological fragmentation, see Elizabeth Johnson and Michael Klemens, eds., *Nature in Fragments: The Legacy of Sprawl* (New York: Columbia University Press, 2005).

45. L. C. Irland, *The Northeast's Changing Forest* (Petersham, Mass.: Harvard University Press, 1999); Alexander Pfaff and Robert Walker, "Forest Transitions & External Drivers: Looking Back and Looking Forward," (2007), http://magrann-conference.rutgers.edu/2008/_abstracts/pfaffwalkerabstract.pdf (November 22, 2010); Ellen Stroud, "Seeing the Trees: How Cities Brought Forests Back to the Northeastern United States" (forthcoming).

46. John Randolph, "The Little Deers Get Out of Hand," *NYT*, November 24, 1957; "Archery Bill Advances," *NYT*, March 28, 1957; Byron Porterfield, "Suburbs Plagued by Foraging Deer," *NYT*, December 24, 1963; John Bryant, "Narrative Report: Morton National Wildlife Refuge," May–August 1955, p. 4, in folder "EA Morton NWF," box 244, Records of Bureau of Sport Fisheries and Wildlife, U.S. Fish and Wildlife Service Archives, RG 22, National Archives II, College Park, Md. (quotation).

47. Ira Henry Freeman, "Oyster Bay Group Retraces Route President Took in Walk 50 Years Ago," *NYT*, June 11, 1960; Robert Cushman Murphy, June 10, 1960, Sagamore Hill, in folder MJR-My, box B-97, NAS. See also, more recently, Stephanie Melles, Susan Glenn, and Kathy Martin, "Urban Bird Diversity and Landscape Complexity: Species-Environment Associations along a Multi-Scale Habitat Gradient," *Conservation Ecology* 7 (2003), http://www.ecologyandsociety.org/vol7/iss1/art5 (September 7, 2011), and John Marzluff, Reed Bowman, and Roarke Donnelly, "A Historical Perspective on Urban Bird Research: Trends, Terms and

Approaches," http://www.oglethorpe/faculty/~rdonnelly/urban.pdf (September 7, 2011).

48. Yi-Fu Tuan, *Dominance and Affection: The Making of Pets* (New Haven: Yale University Press, 1984).

49. Interviews with Louise and Mauro Cassano, Levittown, N.Y., December 18, 1998; Charles Seelinger, North Babylon, N.Y., July 26, 1999; and Richard White, Tucson, Ariz., April 17, 1999 ("something like nature"). On Japanese beetles, see "Suburban Pioneers," *Newsday*, September 26, 1997; Billy Joel quotation ("great big potato fields") from Stuart Bird, *Building the American Dream: Levittown, New York*, documentary film (Hempstead, N.Y.: Hofstra University and Cablevision, 1994).

50. Interview with Eugene Reed.

51. Grace Murphy, "Five Hour Garden."

52. Interview with Eugene Reed, and with Eugene and Bernice Burnett, Wyandanch, N.Y., January 7, 2004.

53. Water Stern, "Big Rise Foreseen in Summer Homes," *NYT*, July 24, 1960.

54. "LI Wetlands Vanishing Fast," *Long Island Press*, April 21, 1961, and Robert Littell, "U.S. Unit Calls LI Wetlands Loss Alarming," *Newsday*, [1961?], clippings in folder "Zoning Wetlands," box 4, JMK-SB; interview with Eugene and Bernice Burnett.

55. For what happened along Hempstead Turnpike, see Eugene Nickerson's comments in Stan Hinden, "Dems Again Lose Bid for Master Plan," *Newsday*, July 26, 1961, clipping in folder "1954–62 Suburbia, Zoning, Tax Districts, Parks," box 1, JMK-SB.

56. Walter Michaels, "The Zoning Problem of Levittown Defined" (1958?); "Both Proposed New Gas Stations Situated on Downzoned Properties, *LPOA Newsletter* (1958) ("residential"), and "Oyster Bay's Comprehensive Zoning Plan Upheld by Courts," *LPOA Newsletter* (1958) ("in this town"), and "Latest Developments along 'Gasoline Alley,'" *LPOA Newsletter* (1958?), all in folder "1957–62 LPOA"; Herbert Goldstone, "Careful Industrial Zoning Is Boon to Long Island Communities," *Long Island Press*, March 6, 1961, in folder "1954–62 Suburbia, Zoning, Tax Districts, Parks"—all in JMK-SB.

57. Strachan to Jones, August 11, 1955, part 5, and March 4, 1957, part 5A, on reel 10, "Central Long Island" folder, Group 3, Branch Files, 1956–65, NAACP Papers, microfilm, Special Collections, Schomberg Center, New York, N.Y.; Charles Howlett, "The Long Island Civil Rights Movement in the 1960's, Part Two: Schools and Housing," *Long Island Historical Journal* 9 (1997): 25–46.

58. Grace Barstow Murphy, *Your Deafness Is Not You*; Robert Caro, *The Power Broker: Robert Moses and the Fall of New York* (New York: Vintage Books, 1974), 167–86; Michelle Kleehammer, "Robert Moses, Jones Beach, and the Legacy of Progressive-Era Conservationism," *Long Island Historical Journal* 14 (2001–2): 27–41. On the racial dimension of the planning for Jones Beach, see Caro, *Power*

Broker, 318–19, and Bernward Joerges, "Do Politics Have Artefacts?," *Social Studies of Science* 29 (1999): 411–31.

59. Robert Cushman Murphy, "The Impact of Man upon Nature in New Zealand," *Proceedings of the American Philosophical Society* 95 (1951): 569–82.

60. Robert Cushman Murphy, May 16, 1953, p. 2 (Japanese honeysuckle), in "Long Island and Elsewhere, 1953," July 17–21, 1952 (box turtles), "Long Island and Elsewhere, 1950–52"; "Crystal Brook, June 4–5, 1949" (least terns); "Crystal Brook, May 14–16, 1949"; "Crystal Brook; November 19–20, 1949" ("golden age"), "Long Island, 1946–49"—all in RCM-APS.

61. Long Island Horticultural Society (LIHS), *Newsletter*, LIHS, Planting Fields Arboreteum, Planting Fields, N.Y.; "LI Sunken Forest Drive On," *NYT*, April 28, 1953.

62. "What Is the Nature Conservancy?," *Sanctuary* 1 (1959): 5–6; "Remarks on Presentation of Certificate of Achievement to Robert Cushman Murphy by George Peters at Dinner of Long Island Horticultural Society, October 13, 1959," in "Long Island," RCM-APS; Bill Birchard, *Nature's Keepers: The Remarkable Story of How the Nature Conservancy Became the Largest Environmental Group in the World* (San Francisco: Jossey-Bass, 2005); Richard Brewer, *Conservancy: The Land Trust Movement in America* (Hanover, N.H.: Dartmouth College Press, 2003).

63. Dorothy Solow, "They're Out to Save L.I. Beauty Spots," *Long Island Press*, April 19, 1955, in "1955, Long Island and Elsewhere, 1954–55," RCM-APS, p. 2 (quotation).

64. "Natural Areas Preserved," *Nature Conservancy News* 15 (1965), table 1. This vision is also reflected in William Niering, *Nature in the Metropolis: Conservation in the Tri-State Metropolitan Area* (New York: New York Regional Planning Association, 1960).

65. Bob Greene, "Long Island's Big Push: Parks to Meet Population Growth,' *Newsday*, [1961?], clipping in box 1, folder "1954 Suburbia, Zoning, Tax Districts, Parks," JMK-SB; Adam Rome, *The Bulldozer in the Countryside: Suburban Sprawl and the Rise of American Environmentalism* (New York: Cambridge University Press, 2001).

66. Grace Barstow Murphy, "Volunteer Careers at Pembroke: Conservation," reprint from *Pembroke Alumnus*, January 1965; J. B. Murphy to "Long Islander," August 25, 1956; G. Murphy, "Talk before the Unitarian Fellowship of the Three Villages," May 19, 1963, 4a ("R.C.M."), 13a ("grass, grass, grass); and Grace Murphy, Address to Suwasset Garden Club, July 5, 1961, 5–6 ("Women . . . were just the ones")—all in GBM-APS; "Wise Use of Our Resources," October 1958, and UCLI, *Bulletin*, no. 15 (April 15, 1958), both in folder "Conservationists United for Long Island," box 8, Sharon Mauhs Papers, New York State Department of Conservation Archives, New York State Archives, Albany.

67. "'Theme' for Tenth Anniversary Celebration of Levittown, New York," folder "Levittown History 10th Anniversary Celebration," box 1, JMK-SB.

68. "Boulder Lovers Rock Glen Cove Council," *Long Island Press*, April 27, 1960, and "Nature Lovers Urge Cove Buy Rare Land," *Newsday*, April 27, 1960, both clippings in folder "1954–1962 Suburbia, Zoning, Tax Districts, Parks," JMK-SB.

69. "Fire Island Bridge Is Voted by Board," *NYT*, December 13, 1953; Richard Stengren, "Motorcade Opens Fire Island Span," *NYT*, July 5, 1959; "Citizens to Study Fire Island Park," *NYT*, February 7, 1957. See also Madeleine Johnson, *Fire Island: 1650's–1980's* (Shoreland Press, 1992 [reprint ed.]).

70. Arthur Herzog, "The Battle of Fire Island," *NYT*, July 9, 1961; Byron Porterfield, "Storm on Fire Island," *NYT*, July 17, 1962; Judy Kelmesruds, "A Summer Colony That Is an Island Unto Itself," *NYT*, July 28, 1968; Esther Newton, *Cherry Grove, Fire Island: Sixty Years in America's First Gay/Lesbian Town* (New York: Beacon Press, 1995).

71. Temporary Commission on the Protection and Preservation of the Atlantic Shore Front, *The Protection and Preservation of the Atlantic Shore Front of the State of New York*, June 25, 1962, in folder "Fire Island," box B-127, NAS; Byron Porterfield, "The Storm Has Passed, but It Has Left a Wake of Destruction That Will Remain for Some Time," *NYT*, March 12, 1962; John Devlin, "Moses Urges Dike to Save L.I. Shore," *NYT*, March 26, 1962.

72. Byron Porterfield, "Moses Quit Fire Island Hearing," *NYT*, July 11, 1962; "Young Fire Islanders Sing Out Opposition," *Newsday*, July 11, 1962; "Fire Island Holds Clambake Rally," *NYT*, August 26, 1962; Fire Island Voters Association, *Fire Island* (1962?) (photos), in folder "Fire Island," box B-127, NAS. Compare the latter with Temporary Commission, *The Protection and Preservation of the Atlantic Shore Front*. See also Robert Cushman Murphy, "Geology, Flora and Fauna of Fire Island Barrier Beach," 1 ("unworldly trance"), in "Proceedings of Symposium on the Ecology of the Fire Island Barrier Reef and Great South Bay . . . ," folder "Fire Island," box B-127, NAS.

73. Ronald Maiorana, "Udall Doubts U.S. Will Buy on L.I.," *NYT*, June 3, 1962; Warren Weaver, "Fire Island Plan Opposed by Udall," *NYT*, June 21, 1962; "Fire Island Holds Clambake Rally," *NYT*, August 26, 1962; "President Signs Measure for Fire Island Seashore," *NYT*, September 12, 1964.

74. "Clean Up Job in the North Woods," *NYT*, June 10, 1951 (the "forest-destroying" moth); "Long Island Starts War on the Gypsy Moth," *NYT*, May 8, 1955; William Blair, "U.S. Sets Sights on Gypsy Moths," *NYT*, March 20, 1957.

Chapter 4

1. Byron Porterfield, "Water Pollution Arouses Suburbs," *NYT*, April 23, 1962; Harold Smecken, "U.S. in Peril of Losing Fight on Pollution," *NYT*, February 23, 1963.

2. William McGucken, *Biodegradable: Detergents and the Environment* (College Station: Texas A&M Press, 1991); Adam Rome, *The Bulldozer in the Countryside: Suburban Sprawl and the Rise of American Environmentalism* (New York: Cambridge University Press, 2001), 104–11.

3. My approach here builds on Gabrielle Hecht's notion of a consolidating exceptionalism toward some pollutants after World War II. See Hecht, "Africa and the Nuclear World: Labor, Occupational Health, and the Transnational Production of Uranium," *Comparative Studies in Society and History* 51 (2009): 896–926.

4. Harold Thomas and Luna Leopold, "Ground Water in America," *Science* 143 (1964): 1001; John Borchert, "The Surface Water Supply of American Municipalities," *Annals of the Association of American Geographers* 44 (1954): esp. 15–16; U.S. Geological Survey, *Groundwater Atlas of the United States* (1999), http://capp.water.usgs.gov/gwa/gwa.html (October 19, 2005). On Long Island, see Lee Koppelman, "Environment vs. Development: Groundwater and Land Use Planning in Nassau and Suffolk Counties," *Long Island Historical Journal* 10 (1997): 16–24.

5. Joseph E. Upton, "Relation of Long Island Ground Water Resources to Regional Needs," *Journal of Water Works Association* 51 (1959): 287–89; R. C. Heath, B. L. Foxworthy, and Philp Cohen, "The Changing Pattern of Ground-Water Development on Long Island, New York," *Geological Survey Circular* 524 (1966): 1–12; L. B. Leopold, *Water: A Primer* (San Francisco: Freeman, 1974), as quoted in Veronica Pyle and Ruth Patrick, "Ground Water Contamination in the United States," *Science* 221 (August 19, 1983): 713.

6. The preeminent study of aquifers remains John Opie's *Oglalla: Water for a Dry Land* (Lincoln: University of Nebraska Press, 1993).

7. Linda Lorraine Nash, *Inescapable Ecologies: A History of Environment, Disease, and Knowledge* (Berkeley: University of California Press, 2006), chap. 4. For an earlier nineteenth-century counterpart, see Conevery Bolton Valenčius, *The Health of the Country: How American Settlers Understood Themselves and Their Land* (New York: Basic Books, 2002).

8. Donald Worster, *Rivers of Empire: Water, Aridity and the Growth of the American West* (New York: Pantheon, 1985), 90–95; "Point for Truck Farmers," *NYT*, April 1, 1903; *Allison Lowndes v. Huntington Water Works Company*, 148 N.Y.S. 308, 1914 N.Y. App. Div. LEXIS 6891; Frank Williams, "Memorandum of Law of Open Spaces in and around Built-up Localities, July 1925," as quoted in Regional Plan of New York, *Physical Conditions and Public Services*, vol. 8 (New York, 1929), 42.

9. Wells A. Hutchins, "The Development and Present Status of Water Rights and Water Policy in the United States," *Journal of Farm Economics* 37 (1955): esp. 868–69.

10. Russell Suter, *Engineering Report on the Water Supplies of Long Island* (New York State Department of Conservation, 1937), 41, 43–45, 56, 59; New York Water Power and Control Commission, *Annual Reports* (Albany, 1934); Fred Welsch, "Conservation of Ground Water—Practices Used on Long Island," *Water and Sewage Works* 103 (1956): 470.

11. Peveril Meigs, "Water Problems in the United States," *Geographic Review* 42 (1952): 347; Francis Wood, "Troubled Waters: Part 3, Growing Pains," *Newsday*, March 7, 1957.

12. "Automatic Washing Machines," *Consumer Reports* 25 (1960): esp. 413; Faith Corrigan, "Dishes by Machine," *NYT*, May 13, 1956; "Three Dishwasher Types Serve Most Home Needs," *NYT*, January 17, 1958.

13. Greeley and Hansen, LLC, *Report on Water Supply: Nassau County, N.Y.* (New York: Greeley and Hansen, 1962?), fig. II-2. An earlier report by Upton ("Long Island Ground Water Resources," 292–93) gives somewhat lower figures.

14. Nassau-Suffolk Regional Planning Board, *Utilities Inventory and Analysis* (Suffolk County General Services, 1969), 12–13; "Industry Is Using, Reusing Water," *NYT*, January 20, 1965); "Air-Conditioned Retail Stores," *Progressive Architecture* 39 (1958): 181; Upton, "Long Island Ground Water Resources"; Meigs, "Water Problems in the United States," 348; U.S. Census of Agriculture, 1940, 1954.

15. R. M. Sawyer, "Effect of Urbanization on Storm Discharge in Nassau County, New York" (1961), as quoted in Greeley and Hansen, *Report on Water Supply*.

16. Francis Padar, "Health Department Surveillance of Ground Water Quality" (1967?), typescript, New York State Library, Albany; Nassau-Suffolk Regional Planning Board, *Utilities Inventory*, 1; Fred W. Welsch, "Conservation of Ground Water Resources, Nassau County," *Water and Sewage Works* 102 (1949): 710, and Welsch, "Conservation of Ground Water—Practices Used on Long Island." On postwar state and federal water policies, see Karl Brooks, *Before Earth Day: The Origins of American Environmental Law, 1945–1970* (Lawrence: University of Kansas Press, 2009); Douglas Helms et al., "Water Quality in the Natural Resources Conservation Service: An Historical Overview," *Agricultural History* 76 (2002): 289–307.

17. "Long Island's Troubled Waters," *Newsday*, March 6, 1957.

18. Greeley and Hansen, *Report on Water Supply*, 26–30; Fred W. Welsch, "Water Supply Problems in Nassau County," *Water and Sewage Works* 105 (1958): 200–201. Later studies of South Shore intrusions indicated that a long-term rise in sea levels was more deleterious than overpumping; see, e.g., Koppelman, "Environment vs. Development," 20.

19. Subcommittee on Housing of the Committee on Bank and Currency, U.S. House of Representatives, "Housing Constructed under VA and FHA Programs," *Hearings on H.Res. 436, February 11, 12, 13, 1952* (Washington, D.C.: GPO, 1952)—see, e.g., 298–99, 302–5, 312–15.

20. Minutes of Nassau County Board of Health, October 21, 1954, 3032–34, NCPH; "County Board of Supervisors Gets Sewer Report Prepared by Engineer to Sanitation Commission," *Manhasset Press*, January 3, 1936; Minutes of Nassau County Board of Health, February 21, 1958, 3533, NCPH. On this new attention to stream pollution prior to the 1960s, much of it targeting rural areas, see Brooks, *Before Earth Day*.

21. Herbert Davids and Maxim Lieber, "Underground Water Contamination by Chromium Wastes," *Water and Sewage Works* 98 (1951): 528–34. More generally, see L. T. Fairhall, "Toxic Contaminants of Drinking Water," *Journal of the New England Water Works Association* 60 (1941); 404–5; more retrospectively, see Craig Colten, Peter Skinner, and Bruce Piaseki, *The Road to Love Canal: Managing Indus-*

trial Wastes before EPA (Austin: University of Texas Press, 1995), and Travis Wagner, "Hazardous Waste: Evolution of a National Environmental Problem," *Journal of Policy History* 16 (2004): 307–31.

22. Arthur Pickett, "Protection of Underground Water from Sewage and Industrial Wastes," *Sewage Works Journal* 19 (1947): 464–72. See also Patrick Gurian and Joel Tarr, "The First Federal Drinking Water Quality Standards and Their Evolution, 1914 to 1974," in Paul Fishback and Scott Farrow, eds., *Improving Regulation: Cases in Environment, Health and Safety* (Washington, D.C.: Resources for the Future, 2001), 43–69, esp. 61.

23. For more on this split, see Christopher Sellers, *Hazards of the Job: From Workplace Disease to Environmental Health Science* (Chapel Hill: University of North Carolina Press, 1997) and Sellers, "Discovering Environmental Cancer: Wilhelm Hueper, Epidemiology, and the Vanishing Clinician's Role," *American Journal of Public Health* 87 (November 1997): 1824–35.

24. Pickett, "Protection of Underground Water."

25. Davids and Lieber, "Underground Water Contamination by Chromium"; Maxim Lieber, Nathaniel Perlmutter, and Henry Frauenthal, "Cadmium and Hexavalent Chromium in Nassau County Ground Water," *Journal of the American Water Works Association* 56 (1964): 739–47; Minutes of Nassau County Board of Health, December 20, 1951, 868, NCPH; F. M. Middleton and F. Walton, "Organic Chemical Contamination of Ground Water," *Ground Water Contamination Symposium* (Washington, D.C.: GPO, 1961), 54.

26. "Mr. Terence J. McCormack—Environmental Sanitation," Minutes of Nassau Board of Health, April 15, 1954, 2058–60, NCPH (quotations); Middleton and Walton, "Organic Chemical Contamination of Ground Water"; M. Deutsch, "Incidents of Chromium Contamination in Michigan," in *Ground Water Contamination Symposium*, esp. 50–51, 98–104.

27. F. H. Brayrook, "The Development of Synthetic Detergents and Future Trends," *Chemistry and Industry* (June 26, 1948): 404–7, 409. See also McGucken, *Biodegradable*, 12–19.

28. John M. Flynn, Aldo Andreoli, and August Guerrera, "Study of Synthetic Detergents in Ground Water," *Journal of the American Water Works Association* 50 (1958): 1553–62.

29. Ibid.; C. W. Lauman and Co., "Effect of Synthetic Detergents on the Ground Waters of Long Island, New York," *New York State Department of Health Research Report*, no. 6 (1961).

30. J. M. Flynn, "Impact of Suburban Growth on Ground Water Quality in Suffolk County," *Ground Water Contamination Symposium*, 78 ("tens of thousands of homes"); L. Woodward, "Ground Water Contamination in the Minneapolis and St. Paul Suburbs," *Ground Water Contamination Symposium*, esp. 68.

31. Flynn, Andreoli, and Guerrera, "Study of Synthetic Detergents in Ground Water"; Flynn, "Impact of Suburban Growth on Ground Water Quality," 71–82, 77 ("heavily populated"), 74 ("4000 to 7500 square feet"). Five of Suffolk's public wells

also showed traces of ABS, though, unlike so many of the private homeowner wells, in amounts below "taste or foaming levels" (Flynn, "Impact of Suburban Growth on Ground Water Quality," 77).

32. Porterfield, "Water Pollution Arouses Suburbs."

33. "Suffolk Puts Ban on Well-Digging," *NYT*, August 17, 1958; Porterfield, "Water Districts Asked in Suffolk," *NYT*, January 6, 1960; *Muscillo v. Town Board of Oyster Bay*, 1961 N.Y. Misc. LEXIS 3408.

34. Nassau-Suffolk Regional Planning Board, *Utilities Inventory*, 23; Greeley and Hansen, "Report on Water Supply."

35. Padar, "Health Department Surveillance of Ground Water Quality."

36. Linda Lorraine Nash, *Inescapable Ecologies*. On the decline of "natural" talk in medicine, see John Harley Warner, *The Therapeutic Perspective: Medical Practice, Knowledge and Identity in Modern America, 1820–1885* (Princeton: Princeton University Press, 1997). On the "normal" and "pathological" language of medicine, see George Canguilhem's classic *The Normal and the Pathological* (1966; reprint, Cambridge, Mass.: Zone Books, 1991); more recently, see Peter Keating and Alberto Cambrioso, *Biomedical Platforms: Realigning the Normal and the Pathological in Late Twentieth-Century Medicine* (Cambridge: MIT Press, 2003).

37. Minutes of the Nassau County Board of Health, March 23, 1950, 662, and April 1952, 910; "Earle Browne, M.D.—Past, Present and Future," Minutes, April 1955, 3106; and "Dr. Tartakov—Shall We Relax Our Control?," 3111—all in NCPH.

38. North Shore Improvement Association, *Reports on Plans for the Extermination of Mosquitoes on the North Shore of Long Island* (New York: Press of Styles and Cash, 1902); "Malarial Fever Prevalent Here," *NYT*, August 1, 1901. For malaria in the United States during this period generally, see Margaret Humphreys, *Malaria: Poverty, Race, and Public Health in the United States* (Baltimore: Johns Hopkins University Press, 2001).

39. "Mosquito Extermination Eliminates Malaria from Nassau County," *Nassau Daily Review*, March 7, 1924, 35; Harry Davis, "Life and Times of the Mosquito," *NYT*, July 20, 1941.

40. "Nassau Opens War on Mosquito," *NYT*, April 26, 1951 ("'easily roll back our gains'"); "Generals in Jersey Mosquito War Visit Front Lines on Long Island," *NYT*, September 18, 1952; Mary Cummings, "Minnows Enlisted in Mosquito War," *NYT*, March 4, 1984, which says that 8 million feet of ditches were dug in Suffolk County, but see "Suffolk Helicopter Aids Mosquito War," *NYT*, June 26, 1958, which mentions "15 million feet of ditching" in the county. A total of 21 million feet maximum for Suffolk and Nassau adds up to just under 4,000 miles.

41. "Babies Thrive in Nassau," *NYT*, October 24, 1950; "Infant Mortality Cut," *NYT*, August 20, 1952; "Encephalitis Virus Found in L.I. Ducks," *NYT*, January 13, 1960; "Nassau Rates Drop for Births, Deaths," *NYT*, January 18, 1959 ("virtually free"). For a discussion of various diseases, see Minutes of Nassau County Board of Health, NCPH.

42. "Wildlife Experts Defend the Hawk; Mosquito Fight Scored," *NYT*, October 27, 1936; C. T. Williamson to Robert Cushman Murphy, November 16, 1944, and Murphy to Williamson, December 14, 1944; "Crystal Brook and Briarlea, May 9–10, 1952," 5; "Late June, 1954," 1 ("willy-nilly"); and Murphy to Mosquito Control Commission, February 24, 1954—all in RCM-APS.

43. Interview with Marjorie Spock, Sullivan, Maine, November 23–24, 1996; phone interview with Frank and Leonie Reuschle, June 28, 1997; Transcript, *Murphy v. Benson*, 1182, 1193 (quotations), NAS.

44. Christopher Bosso, *Pesticides and Politics: The Life Cycle of A Public Issue* (Pittsburgh: University of Pittsburgh Press, 1987); J. Weisburger, "The 36-Year History of the Delaney Clause, "*Experimental and Toxicologic Pathology* 48 (1996): 183–88; Suzanne White Junod, "The Chemogastric Revolution and the Regulation of Food Chemicals," in Seymour Mauskopf, ed. *Chemical Sciences in the Modern World* (Philadelphia: University of Pennsylvania Press, 1993), 322–55.

45. My meaning here is closer to what sociologist Pierre Bourdieu calls "habitus"; see Omar Lizardo, "The Cognitive Origins of Bourdieu's 'Habitus'" (2009), http://www.nd.edu/~olizardo/papers/jtsb-habitus.pdf (November 27, 2010). On the history of ecosystem ecology, see, e.g., Frank Golley, *A History of the Ecosystem Concept in Ecology: More Than the Sum of the Parts* (New Haven: Yale University Press, 1993), and Joel Hagen, "Teaching Ecology during the Environmental Era, 1965–1980," *Environmental History* 13 (2008): 704–23.

46. Interview with Francis Berens, Oyster Bay, N.Y., July 7, 1997, and with Marjorie Spock; Transcript, *Murphy v. Benson*, NAS.

47. John Dryzek et al., *Green States and Social Movements: Environmentalism in the United States, United Kingdom, Germany, and Norway* (New York: Oxford University Press, 2003).

48. Morris Davis, "Community Attitudes toward Fluoridation," *Public Opinion Quarterly* 23 (1959): 478. For a more detailed account, see Christopher Sellers, "The Artificial Nature of Fluoridated Water: Between Nations, Knowledges and Material Flows," *Osiris* 19 (2005): 182–202.

49. Press release, U.S. Department of Agriculture, "Federal Agencies Endorse Safety of DDT Spray Program Against Gypsy Moth," May 10, 1957, 3, in Docket of *Murphy v. Benson*, National Archives Northeast Regional Branch; testimony of Wayland Hayes, transcript of *Murphy v. Benson*, 1566–1647.

50. At the start of what has become a vast literature on popular epidemiology, see Phil Brown, "Popular Epidemiology and Toxic Waste Contamination: Lay and Professional Ways of Knowing," *Journal of Health and Social Behavior* 3 (1992): 267–81. For a critique, see Jo Melling, "Beyond a Shadow of a Doubt?: Experts, Lay Knowledge, and the Role of Radiography in the Diagnosis of Silicosis in Britain, c. 1919–1945," *Bulletin of the History of Medicine* 84 (2010): 424–66.

51. Plaintiff's Memorandum on Motion of Preliminary Injunction, 9, in Docket of *Murphy v. Benson*; interview with Marjorie Spock.

52. "Let's *Really* Protect Our Children's Teeth": "Why Fluoridation?," *Manhas-*

set Press, April 10, 1958; Transcript, *Murphy v. Benson*, 1185–89 (Jacobs), 80 (Murphy).

53. Francis Wood, "Long Island's Troubled Waters," *Newsday*, March 5, 6, 7, 8, 1957.

54. Flynn, "Impact of Suburban Growth," 76; Greeley and Hansen, *Report on Water Supply*, fig. II-2; Byron Porterfield, "Suffolk Mapping Sewage System," *NYT*, December 12, 1961 (Dennison).

55. Grace Murphy to "Long Islander," August 25, 1968, and "Conservation Simplified," 2, 4, GBM-APS.

56. Interview with Arthur Cooley, Long Island, April 7, 1997; Myra Gelband, "During the Summer of 1965," typescript, 1969, EDF.

57. Gelband, "During the Summer of 1965"; interviews with Cooley, Charles Wurster, Old Field, N.Y., November 15, 1996, and Dennis Puleston, Bellport, N.Y., September 23, 1996; Mailing list of BTNRC, EDF; Nassau-Suffolk Regional Planning Board, *U.S. Census '70; Vol.: 3, Age* (Nassau-Suffolk Regional Planning, 1972), 40–41 (table).

58. On these precedents, see Brooks, *Before Earth Day*, 149–57; Robert Lifset, "Storm King Mountain and the Emergence of Modern Environmentalism, 1962–1980" (Ph.D. diss., Columbia University, 2006).

59. Affidavits of George Woodwell, Dennis Puleston, and Charles Wurster; Affidavit of Christian Williamson, p. 6 (quotation), Docket, *Carol Yannacone et al. v. H. Lee Dennison, Suffolk County Executive, Suffolk County Mosquito Commission*, Index 139050, microfilm at County Clerk, Suffolk County, Hauppauge, N.Y. See also interviews with Puleston, Wurster, and Victor Yannacone, Patchogue, N.Y., August 21, 1996.

Chapter 5

1. William H. Whyte, "Urban Sprawl," *Fortune*, 1958, 103.

2. John Muir, *Steep Trails* (1918), chap. 11, http://www.yosemite.ca.us/john_muir_writings/steep_trails/chapter_11.html (April 23, 2011); Augustin C. Keane, "Ideal Suburbs of American Cities: California's Best Types," *Suburban Life* 10, n.s., 2 (January 1906): 10–14 ("sweet in the heart"); "Six-Million-Dollar Arroyo Seco Parkway Opened," *LAT*, December 31, 1940; "December 30, 1940," http://www.fhwa.dot.gov/byday/fhbd1230.htm (September 5, 2011).

3. That any such landscape was "second nature," the product of interaction between people and a local nature, did not preclude seeing a "first nature" there. Originating in nineteenth-century German intellectual currents, the distinction between first and second nature, revived by Donald Worster and William Cronon among others, and popularized by Michael Pollan in *Second Nature: A Gardener's Education* (New York: Atlantic Monthly, 1991), has now found wide currency across much nature-oriented scholarship.

4. This contention with an urban "first nature" has been a theme in recent environmental histories of the city such as Jared Orsi, *Hazardous Metropolis: Flooding*

and Urban Ecology in Los Angeles, 1st ed. (Berkeley: University of California Press, 2004); Mike Davis, *Ecology of Fear: Los Angeles and the Imagination of Disaster,* 1st ed. (New York: Vintage Books, 1999); Craig E. Colten, *An Unnatural Metropolis: Wresting New Orleans from Nature* (Baton Rouge: Louisiana State University Press, 2006); Ari Kelman, *A River and Its City: The Nature of Landscape in New Orleans,* 1st ed. (Berkeley: University of California Press, 2006); and Matthew Klingle, *Emerald City: An Environmental History of Seattle* (New Haven: Yale University Press, 2007).

5. The relationship between narrative and empathy in historical arguments has been a matter of debate among philosophers of history. See, e.g., Karsten Stueber, "Reasons, Generalizations, Empathy, and Narratives: The Epistemic Structure of Action Explanation," *History and Theory* 47 (2008): 31–43; F. R. Ankersmit, "The Dilemma of Contemporary Anglo-Saxon Philosophy of History," *History and Theory* 25 (1986): 1–27.

6. Robert Fishman, *Bourgeois Utopias: The Rise and Fall of Suburbia* (New York: Basic Books, 1989); Mike Davis, *City of Quartz: Excavating the Future in Los Angeles* (New York: Verso, 1990).

7. Whyte, "Urban Sprawl."

8. Duncan Aikman, "California Vibrates to 'Little Causes,'" *NYT,* September 9, 1934 ("not quite gelled"); Hedda Hopper, "Hedda Hopper's Hollywood," *LAT,* November 10, 1938 ("six suburbs," "hick town,"); Cary McWilliams, *Southern California Country: An Island on the Land* (New York: Duell, Sloane and Pearce, 1946), 375.

9. "The Los Angeles Basin—A Huge Bowl of Sand," http://www.laalmanac .com/geography/geo8e.htm (July 18. 2006); John McPhee, *The Control of Nature: Los Angeles against the Mountains* (New York: Farrar, Straus and Giroux, 1989); Raymond V. Ingersoll and Peter E. Rumelhart, "Three-Stage Evolution of the Los Angeles Basin, Southern California," *Geology* 27 (1999): 593–96.

10. Louis Mesmer, "Soil Survey of the Los Angeles Area," *Field Operations of the Bureau of Soils, 1903* (Washington, D.C.: GPO, 1903), esp. 1267. Long Island was not far behind, at 15 varieties of soil; Jay Bonstell and Party, "Soil Survey of the Long Island Area, New York," *Field Operations of the Bureau of Soils, 1903,* esp. 98.

11. Paula M. Schiffman, "The Los Angeles Prairie," in William Deverell and Greg Hise, eds., *Land of Sunshine: An Environmental History of Metropolitan Los Angeles* (Pittsburgh: University of Pittsburgh Press, 2005), 38–51; Homer Aschmann, "Evolution of a Wild Landscape and Its Persistence in Southern California," *Annals of the Association of American Geographers* 49 (September 1959): esp. 34–56; A. P. Dobson et al., "Geographic Distribution of Endangered Species in the United States," *Science* 275 (1997): 551; A. J. Wells, "The Country Life of California," *Country Life in America* 1 (1902): 80 ("delightful strangeness").

12. Liberty Hyde Bailey, "California," *Country Life in America* 1 (1902): 72; Steven Stoll, *The Fruits of Natural Advantage: Making the Industrial Countryside in California* (Berkeley: University of California Press, 1998); Douglas Sackman,

Orange Empire: California and the Fruits of Eden (Berkeley: University of California Press, 2005), esp. 84–116; Agricultural Commissioner for Los Angeles County, Livestock Commissioner, *Annual Reports.*

13. George Garrigues, "Angeles Forest Nearing 70th Anniversary Date," *LAT*, December 9, 1962; Works Progress Administration, *Los Angeles*, 52–55.

14. Robert Fogelson, *The Fragmented Metropolis: Los Angeles, 1850–1930* (Cambridge: Harvard University Press, 1967), 5–12, 34–62.

15. Ibid., 92–95, 123–34; Richard Longstreth, *The Drive-In, the Supermarket, and the Transformation of Commercial Space in Los Angeles, 1914–41* (Cambridge: MIT Press, 1999); Works Progress Administration, *Los Angeles*, 74–100; Chapin Hall, "Industrial Capital of the West," *LAT*, January 2, 1937; Ralph W. Trueblood, "Why We Grow . . . and How!," *LAT*, January 2, 1942; Christopher Boone, "Zoning and Environmental Inequity in the Industrial East Side," in Deverell and Hise, *Land of Sunshine*, 169–75.

16. Mike Davis, "Sunshine and the Open Shop: Ford and Darwin in 1920's Los Angeles," *Antipode* 29 (1997): 358–61; Greg Hise, "Nature's Workshop: Industry and Urban Expansion in Southern California, 1900–1950," *Journal of Historical Geography* 27 (2001): 74–79.

17. Los Angeles Chamber of Commerce Industrial Department, *Facts about Industrial Los Angeles: Nature's Workshop* (1924), as cited in Boone, "Zoning and Environmental Inequity," 172; Davis, "Sunshine and the Open Shop"; Hise, "Nature's Workshop"; Muir, *Steep Trails.*

18. U.S. Census of Housing, 1940; Marc A. Weiss, *The Rise of the Community Builders: The American Real Estate Industry and Urban Land Planning* (New York: Columbia University Press, 1987), esp. 79–85; Ross Gast, "The Southland Garden and Small Farm Home," *LAT*, June 23, 1929 (quotation); George Clements, "The Small Farm Home as a Factor in Industrial Life," *LAT*, September 28, 1930; "Farm and Garden," *LAT*, October 20, 1929.

19. "Many Visitors Again Inspect New Dwelling," *LAT*, March 10, 1935 ("semi-sustaining gardens"); Becky Nicolaides, *My Blue Heaven: Life and Politics in the Working-Class Suburbs of Los Angeles, 1920–1965* (Chicago: University of Chicago Press, 2002), 33–35.

20. County of Los Angeles Regional Planning District, *Master Plan of Land Use: Inventory and Classification* (Los Angeles: Regional Planning Commission, 1941), 56 ("natural facilities"). For an alternative, unimplemented plan that emphasized these recreational facilities, see Greg Hise and William Deverell, *Eden by Design: The 1930 Olmsted-Bartholomew Plan for the Los Angeles Region* (Berkeley: University of California Press, 2000).

21. "Sporting Goods Plant Started," *LAT*, February 20, 1955; Ordinances Nos. 147 and 487, Ordinance Books, SGA; Planning Program, University of Southern California, *Planning Study Research and Data: San Gabriel* (Los Angeles: University of Southern California, 1959–60), esp. A-1–9; Herbert R. Larsen and J. Walter

Cobb, "A Study of the Community of San Gabriel and the Role of La Casa de San Gabriel," typescript, July 1958, 12–13, LCA (quotation).

22. Chad Montrie, *Making a Living: Work and Environment in the United States* (Chapel Hill: University of North Carolina Press, 2009).

23. Charles Combs, "Wham-O Profits in Fun," *LAT*, May 2, 1965; "When Wham-O Was on a Roll," *LAT*, May 5, 1994—both in file "Wham-O Manufacturing," PPL Clippings Files, Pasadena Public Library, Pasadena, Calif.; interview with Richard Knerr and Richard Gillespie, Arcadia, Calif., June 2, 2003.

24. On the history of plastic manufacturing, see Jeffrey Meikle, *American Plastic: A Cultural History* (New Brunswick: Rutgers University Press, 1996). On these themes more generally, see Jennifer Price, *Flight Maps: Adventures with Nature in American Culture* (New York: Basic Books, 1999).

25. Advertisements in *LAT*: January 8, 1956, November 20, 1958, May 10, 1959; Dick Kidson, "Farmers' Market Today," *LAT*, May 18, 1958; Gene Sherman, "Cityside," *LAT*, July 4, 1958; interview with Knerr and Gillespie; Arthur Johnston, "California and the National Oil Industry," *Pacific Historical Review* 39 (1970): 155–69; Sara Elkind, "Black Gold and the Beach Offshore Oil: Beaches and Federal Power in Southern California," *Journal of the West* 44 (2005): 8–17; Paul Sabin, *Crude Politics: The California Oil Market, 1900–1940* (Berkeley: University of California Press, 2005).

26. "Analysts Told Growth of Food Chains in Southland," *LAT*, March 21, 1951 ("home of the supermarkets"); "That There May Be More for All" [advertisement for Alpha Beta], *LAT*, May 5, 1960 ("most efficient methods").

27. Agricultural Department, Los Angeles County Chamber of Commerce, *Crop Acreage Trends, 1925–1957* (Los Angeles: Los Angeles County Board of Supervisors, 1958), 10; John Jackle and Keth Sculle, *Fast Food: Roadside Restaurants in the Automobile Age* (Baltimore: Johns Hopkins University Press, 1999), 168, 193, 203, 257.

28. "Structure of the Residential Building Industry in 1949," *Bulletin of the Department of Labor*, No. 1170 (1949): 32; "Veterans Laud Home Building Industry Here," *LAT*, September 30, 1956; "Vast Homes Project to Total 17,510," *LAT*, February 19, 1950; "Record-Breaking House Production," *Architectural Forum* 92 (June 1950): 132–34, 224.

29. Among the ads exemplifying these points, see *LAT*, July 16, 30, August 6, 1950, and "Record-Breaking House Production," 134. On Lakewood, see also Donald J. Waldie, *Holy Land: A Suburban Memoir* (New York: Norton, 1996), and Allison Baker, "The Lakewood Story" (Ph.D. diss., University of Pennsylvania, 1999).

30. On semirural slums, see "Hicks' Camp Retains Touch of Old Mexico," *LAT*, December 11, 1948, and "2136 Code Violations Found at Hicks Camp," *LAT*, November 22, 1953. See also Eric Avila, *Popular Culture in the Age of White Flight: Fear and Fantasy in Suburban Los Angeles* (Berkeley: University of California Press, 2004), 145–84, and Waldie, *Holy Land*, 34 ("war surplus beacon").

31. Waldie, *Holy Land*, 3; "Lakewood Park Buyers Find Privacy Provided," *LAT*, September 24, 1950 ("country atmosphere" and "spaciousness").

32. "Extensive Leveling Made for New Tract," *LAT*, May 10, 1953; "Huge Area Purchased Here and Development Planned," *LAT*, March 17, 1946 ("rigid"); Home on Plateau Site to Be Displayed Today," *LAT*, August 12, 1951 ("country living within the city").

33. Southern California Golf Association, *Turfgrass Survey: Los Angeles County, California* (Los Angeles: Southern California Golf Association, 1954), 9–10. Cf. Pennsylvania Crop Reporting Service, *1966 Turfgrass Survey* (Harrisburg: Pennsylvania Department of Agriculture, 1966), 18. See also A. A. Hanson and F. V. Juska, eds., *Turfgrass Science* (Madison, Wis.: American Society of Agronomy, Inc., 1969), 387–88.

34. "Grass: New Hybrid Bermudas Promise to Become the Ideal Lawn," *LAT*, June 18, 1961; Dr. Robert Atkinson, "Lawns: Time to Get Yours in Order," *LAT*, September 27, 1964; "Progress Report on Grasses," *LAT*, October 14, 1956; Daniel Austin, "The Indiscriminate Vector: Human Distribution of Dichondra Micrantha (Convulvulaceae)," *Economic Botany* 52 (January–March 1998): 88–106; Hanson and Juska, *Turfgrass Science*, 388–90.

35. Jared Farmer, "Gone Native: California's Love-Hate Relationship with the Eucalyptus," *Huntington Frontiers* (Spring 2007): 18–22; Ian Tyrell, *True Gardens of the Gods* (Berkeley: University of California Press, 1999).

36. Nicolaides, *My Blue Heaven*, 34, 228; Liz McGuinness, "Top U.S. Nurseryman Still Finds Fascination in Old Seed Catalogs," *LAT*, August 11, 1965; Henry Sutherland, "Men Gardeners Are in Majority, Make Horticulture Big Business," *LAT*, June 13, 1966; Monrovia Nursery Company, "Wholesale Catalog, 1958–59," 1 ("world's largest container nursery") (compare Monrovia Nursery Company, "Monthly List on Lining Out Stock for June, 1948," to "Monthly Catalog, April 1961")—all in Library of the Los Angeles Botanical Garden, Santa Anita.

37. Monrovia Nursery Company catalogs; Armin Thurnher, "Lacy Park Development," transcript of oral history interview by Mrs. Jack Sherwood, June 27, 1965, 2–10, SMP; Charles Henry Rowan, "Ornamental Plants as a Factor in the Cultural Development of Southern California" (MA thesis, University of California, Los Angeles, 1957); "California Flower Business, Nation's Largest," *LAT*, May 12, 1963; Waldie, *Holy Land*, 55 ("salubrious," "too many greens"), 57; interview with Bud and Jackie Rynerson, Lakewood, Calif., June 9, 1999 ("anything could grow").

38. Kevin Starr, "*Sunset* Magazine and the Phenomenon of the Far West," http://sunset-magazine.stanford.edu/html/body_influences_1.html (March 11, 2011); *How to Install and Care for Your Lawn* (Menlo Park, Calif.: Lane Publishing Co., 1955); V. B. Youngner, J. H. Madison, M. H. Kimball, and W. B. Davis, "Climatic Zones for Turfgrass in California," *California Turfgrass Culture* 12 (October 1962): 25–27. See also Coleman Ward, "Climate and Adaptation," in Hanson and Juska, *Turfgrass Science*, esp. 35–38.

39. "California Native Shrubs; Are They Being Used Properly?," *Journal of the*

California Horticultural Society 21 (1960): 7–10; "California Natives," *Sunset* 97 (1946): 78–81; "Natives," *Sunset* 127 (1961): 228–40; "Home Magazine's Garden Almanac," *LAT*, October 14, 1956.

40. H. G. Baker, "Weeds—Native and Introduced," *Journal of the California Horticultural Society* 23 (1962): 97–104; Robert Atkinson, "New Foe for Crabgrass," *LAT*, August 4, 1967; Robert Wells, "The Great Dandelion Rebellion," *LAT*, May 13, 1956; Richard Durbin, "Dodder in the Garden," *LAT*, July 14, 1957; "Don't Do It to Dichondra," *LAT*, June 17, 1956; "Chemicals Winning War against Weeds," *LAT*, October 21, 1962.

41. Robert Rawitch, "Pets Outpacing Man in Population Boom," *LAT*, January 5, 1970. Compare Pasadena Humane Society, *Annual Report, 1923*, and PHS, *Annual Report, 1953*.

42. "San Marino Pet Law Permits All Fauna," *LAT*, July 5, 1953; Peyton Canary, "Uniformity in Animal Regulations Proposed," *LAT*, June 9, 1968; interview with Beatrice Alva, San Gabriel, Calif., May 20, 1999; phone interview with Esmerelda Lopez, May 21, 2001; interview with David Pinette, Arcadia, Calif., May 21, 2001; *Lakewood Municipal Code*, Section 9338, Part 3b (1958).

43. Paul Griffin and Ronald Chatham, "Population: A Challenge to California's Changing Citrus Industry," *Economic Geography* 34 (1958): 272–76; "Tracts Replacing Groves in Covina," *LAT*, July 19, 1953; "Central State Orange Crop Decline Seen," *LAT*, October 31, 1959. For Florida figures, see "Florida's Citrus Sales Gain," *LAT*, January 11, 1954, and "Former Urbanites Flourish on Farms," *LAT*, July 16, 1961. More generally, see Sackman, *Orange Empire*; Matt Garcia, *A World of Its Own: Race, Labor, and Citrus in the Making of Greater Los Angeles, 1900–1970* (Chapel Hill: University of North Carolina Press, 2001); and Stoll, *Fruits of Natural Advantage*.

44. "Turning the Soil for Farm Produce—or Building—It's a Major Money Maker," *LAT*, January 3, 1962.

45. "City Health Inspectors Guard Milk Supplies," *LAT*, June 26, 1960; *Annual Reports*, Los Angeles Livestock Department, 1940–60, and figure from "Estimated Livestock Inventory of Los Angeles County as of January 1, 1963," Los Angeles County Livestock Department, *Annual Report* (1963): 2; "2 Cows to 103,000 in County," *LAT*, June 4, 1961; Robert Sullivan, "Cows Munch Oranges, Live Assembly-Line Life in Southern California," *Wall Street Journal*, September 9, 1949; Gordon Fielding, "Dairying in the Los Angeles Milkshed: Factors Affecting Character and Location" (Ph.D. diss., University of California, Los Angeles, 1961).

46. "Protest on Dairy Flies Stirs Probe," *LAT*, May 25, 1958; "Dairies Ouster Plan to Be Heard Tuesday," *LAT*, June 8, 1958; Trudy Selleck, "Land of Dreams and Profits," esp. 72–78, and Clippings: "Cerritos Celebrates 35th Anniversary," *Cerritos News* 20 (1991): 1, "$68,000 Budget Approved by Dairy Valley City Council," June 14, 1957, and "Dairy Valley Modern 'Cowtown,'" *Long Beach Independent Press-Telegram*, April 21, 1957 ("cows outnumber people")—all in Scrapbook, Special Collections, Cerritos Public Library, Cerritos, Calif.

47. J. Herbert Snyder, "A New Program for Agricultural Land Use Stabilization: The California Land Conservation Act of 1965," *Land Economics* 42 (1966): 29–41; Whyte, "Urban Sprawl"; Whyte, "A Plan to Save Vanishing U.S. Countryside," *Life*, August 17, 1959, 88–102; and Whyte, "Open Space; Now or Never," *Landscape Architecture* 50 (1959): 8–13.

48. U.S. Agricultural Censuses for 1945, 1964; Los Angeles County Livestock Department, "Biennial Report, 1959–61," 7.

49. "New Home Project Is Visited by 10,000 in Three Days," *LAT*, September 9, 1951, and "10 New Homes Totaling $363,000 Are Announced," *LAT*, October 14, 1951.

50. Paula Schiffman, "The Los Angeles Prairie," 49; J. M. Klopatck et al., "Land-Use Conflicts with Natural Vegetation in the United States," *Environmental Conservation* 6 (1979): 191–99; J. L. Atwood, "California Gnatcatchers and Coastal Sage Scrub: The Biological Basis for Endangered Species Listing," in John E. Keeley, ed., *Interface between Ecology and Land Development in California* (Los Angeles: Southern California Academy of Sciences, 1993), esp. 154–55; Tracy Tennant, Michael Allen, and Fred Edwards, "Perspectives in Conservation Biology in Southern California: I. Current Extinction Rates and Causes" (2001), http://escholarship.org/uc/item/7ck5d6oj (September 5, 2011); A. C. Alberts et al., "Effects of Habitat Fragmentation on Native and Exotic Plants in Southern California Coastal Scrub," in Keeley, *Interface between Ecology and Land Development*, 103–10.

51. Pasadena Humnae Society, *Annual Report, 1953*; Joseph Grinnell, "The Tennessee Possum Has Arrived in California," *California Fish and Game* (1914): 114–16.

52. Emil Ott, Executive Officer, to General W. T. Hannum, February 13, 1948, "Abalone-Deer, 1935–40," folder F3735:108, and "Summary of Deer Depredation Kill," folder F3498:288, both in box 5, Director's Files, Game Management Branch, Deer, 1962–65, DNR-CA; W. M. Longhurst, A. S. Leopold, and R. F. Dasmann, "A Survey of California Deer Herds: Their Ranges and Management Problems," *California Department of Fish and Game Bulletin*, no. 6 (1952): 1–136; William Dasmann, Henry Hjerson, and Daly Gilsenan, "California's First General Either-Sex Deer Hunting Season," *California Fish and Game* 44 (1958): esp. 232; Richard Gordon Lillard, *My Urban Wilderness in the Hollywood Hills: A Year of Years on Quito Lane* (Lanham, Md.: University Press of America, 1983).

53. In the mid-1980s, two decades further into home builders' march across the mountains, the cougar struck back. See Mike Davis, *Ecology of Fear*, 228–49, and Paul Beier, "Determining Minimum Habitat Areas and Habitat Corridors for Cougars," *Conservation Biology* 7 (1993): 94–108.

54. J. L. Atwood, "California Gnat Catchers and Coastal Sage Scrub," in Keeley, *Interface between Ecology and Land Development* (quotations, 155, 158). More generally on sprawl's ecological effects, see Elizabeth Johnson and Michael Klemens, eds., *Nature in Fragments: The Legacy of Sprawl* (New York: Columbia University Press, 2005).

55. Kevin Crooks, Andrew Suarez, and Douglas Bolger, "Avian Assemblages along a Gradient of Urbanization in a Highly Fragmented Landscape," *Biological Conservation* 115 (2004): 451–62; Douglas Bolger et al., "Response of Rodents to Habitat Fragmentation in Coastal Southern California," *Ecological Applications* 7 (1997): 552–63; Hugh Kingery, "Christmas Countdown—1962," *Western Tanager* 29, no. 6 (February 1963): 47, 55 (quotation); Tennant, Allen, and Edwards, "Perspectives in Conservation Biology in Southern California."

56. On the Echo Park campaign, see especially Mark Harvey, *A Symbol of Wilderness: Echo Park and the American Conservation Movement* (Seattle: University of Washington Press, 2000); John Cosco, *Echo Park: Struggle for Preservation* (Boulder, Colo.: Johnson Books, 1995).

57. See Elna Bakker, "The Tule Elk," *Western Tanager* 27, no. 5 (1961): 29–30.

58. California condors were among the first birds entered on the federal tally of endangered species in 1967, in a mounting but futile effort to preserve their capability to reproduce themselves in the wild. See "Condor of Ice Age Battles to Survive," *LAT*, March 14, 1949; "Binoculars to Be Aimed at Condors," *LAT*, October 23, 1956; Noel Snyder and Helen Snyder, *The California Condor: A Saga of Natural History and Conservation* (Princeton: Princeton University Press, 2000).

59. Ralph Mocine, "Conservation," *Southern Sierran*, no. 10 (1951): 2.

Chapter 6

1. Jack Cressman, "Highbrow Cow Stirs Society Feud; Mama Bossie Causes Fuss on El Molino," *Pasadena Independent*, March 2, 1953; "Officials Take Dim View of Ritzy Feud, Say Canvas Not Proper Cow Home," *Pasadena Independent*, March 3, 1953; "Bossy Taken from Front Yard as 'Mission Accomplished'" [no citation provided]—all in "1953" scrapbook, PHS.

2. Coverage kicked off especially with a seven-part series in 1957 on "What Price Suburbia?" starting with Norris Leap, "What Price Suburbia?: Thousands Gladly Pay," *LAT*, December 22, 1957.

3. Jane Jacobs, *The Death and Life of Great Cities* (1961; reprint, New York: Vintage Books, 1992); Alice Alexiou, *Jane Jacobs: Urban Visionary* (New Brunswick: Rutgers University Press, 2006).

4. Some highlights of the large historiography are Douglas Monroy, *Rebirth: Mexican Los Angeles from the Great Migration to the Great Depression* (Berkeley: University of California Press, 1999); George Sánchez, *Becoming Mexican American: Ethnicity, Culture and Identity in Chicano Los Angeles, 1900–1945* (New York: Oxford University Press, 1993); and David G. Gutiérrez, *Walls and Mirrors: Mexican Americans, Mexican Immigrants and the Politics of Ethnicity* (Berkeley: University of California Press, 1995).

5. This and all subsequent quotations regarding the Alvas' experience are from my interview with Beatrice Alva in San Gabriel on May 20, 1999. On farmlike city fauna, see Ted Steinberg, *Down to Earth: Nature in American History* (New York: Oxford University Press, 2008), 157–74; Joanna Dyl, "Urban Disaster: An Environ-

mental History of San Francisco after the 1906 Earthquake" (Ph.D. diss., Princeton University, 2006), esp. 289–95; and Frederick Brown, "Cows in the Commons, Dogs on the Lawn: A History of Animals in Seattle" (Ph.D. diss., University of Washington–Seattle, 2010), 91–152. Brown's findings of the continuing presence of chickens in some poorer neighborhoods and houses (pp. 209–28) accord with my own.

6. The literature on this vein of Spanish "fantasy" heritage is vast—from Carey McWilliams (*Southern California Country: An Island on the Land* [New York: Duell, Sloane and Pearce, 1946]) to William Deverell (*Whitewashed Adobe: The Rise of Los Angeles and the Remaking of Its Mexican Past* [Berkeley: University of California Press, 2004]) to Phoebe Kropp (*California Vieja: Culture and Memory in a Modern American Place* [Berkeley: University of California Press, 2008]).

7. San Gabriel City Council Ordinances 244, 269, SGA.

8. San Gabriel City Council Ordinances 254, 398, 459, SGA.

9. For an overview, see Michael Kazin, "The Great Exception Revisited: Organized Labor and Politics in San Francisco and Los Angeles," *Pacific Historical Review* 55 (1986): 371–402, and Grace H. Stimson, *Rise of the Labor Movement in Los Angeles* (Berkeley: University of California Press, 1955).

10. Richard Mathison, "Churchmen Wondering about Religious Boom," *LAT*, March 15, 1959; "New Chapel Going Up at Mission Site," *LAT*, August 19, 1956.

11. "Civic Group to Restore La Casa Ramona Adobe," *LAT*, November 20, 1948; "18 Nations Combine to Honor Grapevine," *San Gabriel Post-Advocate*, October 18, 1957, in Scrapbook 1957–58, SGHA; "House Used by Padres in 1776 Still Occupied," *LAT*, November 26, 1956.

12. "Garlanded Animals Stand Humbly for Benediction," *LAT*, April 9, 1950; Cordell Hicks, "500 Animals Blessed in Animal Ceremony," *LAT*, April 17, 1940; "Pets Receive Blessing at San Gabriel Mission," *LAT*, April 1, 1956.

13. "Early Interest in Past Blossoms into Career of Historical Study," *LAT*, December 12, 1960; "Chamber Group Will Perpetuate Traditions," *LAT*, May 4, 1952.

14. Charles Gould, "Plaza Redevelopment Plan at Mission Gains Support," *LAT*, September 16, 1956; "City Okays Plan of Architecture," *San Gabriel Sun*, October 17, 1956; "'Spanish' Zone Okayed," *San Gabriel Sun*, April 29, 1957; "Council Acts to Control Plaza Permits," Scrapbook 1956–58, SGHA.

15. "San Gabriel Weighs Future Control, Financing of Mission Plaza Project," *LAT*, February 3, 1957; "San Gabriel City Hall Site Vote Hailed," *LAT*, December 14, 1958; Ed Ainsworth, "Crucial Decision for San Gabriel," *LAT*, April 8, 1965.

16. "Official Land Use Plan of San Gabriel," Ordinance 556, April 26, 1949, SGA; University of Southern California, *Planning Study Research and Data: San Gabriel* (University of Southern California, 1960), D-13; "$300,000 to Be Spent on San Gabriel City Park," *LAT*, August 12, 1956; Typescripts of Herbert Larsen and J. Walter Cobb, "The Role of La Casa de San Gabriel," May 1959, 9 ("small yards"), and Larsen and Cobb, "A Study of the Community of San Gabriel and the Role of La Casa de San Gabriel," July 1958, 10—both in LCA.

17. On repeated redevelopment and rezoning proposals, see Arnold Rios, "Roughly

Speaking," *El Chismoso (The Tattler)*, August 10, 1952, LCA; University of Southern California, *Planning Study*, A-5.

18. For a summary of this Native American history, see Edward Castillo, "A Short Overview of California Indian History," http://www.nahc.ca.gov/califindian .html (December 16, 2010). On the Gabrielinos, see Heather Singleton, "Surviving Urbanization: The Gabrielino, 1850–1928," *Wicazo Sa Review* 19 (2004): 49–59; William McCawley, *The First Angelinos: The Gabrielino Indians of Los Angeles* (Banning, Calif.: Maliki Mus. Pr.; Novato, Calif.: Ballena, 1996); and Claudia K. Jurmain and William Mccawley, eds., *O, My Ancestor: Recognition and Renewal for the Gabrielino-Tongva People of the Los Angeles Area* (Berkeley: Heyday Books, 2009).

19. "Indians Vote on U.S. Offer for Old Lands," *LAT*, September 8, 1963.

20. Interviews with Ernie Salas, San Gabriel, Calif., June 9, 1999, June 12, 2003, and Victoria Cordova, Duarte, Calif., June 4, 1999.

21. "Paraders Roll on Rubber Tires behind Color Guard," *LAT*, September 7, 1948.

22. On Los Angeles hunters, see, e.g., "Study of LA County 1939 Deer Kill," folder F3735:96, box 5, Natural Resources-Administration-Director, DNR-CA. On a similar impulse among Michigan auto workers, see Chad Montrie, *Making a Living: Work and Environment in the United States* (Chapel Hill: University of North Carolina Press, 2009), 91–112.

23. This and all subsequent testimony about the Rynersons' history is from interviews with Bud and Jackie Rynerson in Lakewood, Calif., on June 9, 1999, with Jackie alone in Lakewood on October 21, 2006, and from a phone interview with Steve Rynerson on February 5, 2009.

24. These problems were widely shared, according to the soil and water well analysis cited in Community Facilities Planners, "Analysis and Proposals of Recreation Facilities for the Community of Lakewood," June 1955, 45–50, in Local History Collection, Angelo M. Iacoboni Library, Lakewood, Calif.

25. Interviews with Charles Haynes, Lakewood, Calif., June 5, 1999, and Ted and Shirley Schnee, Lakewood, Calif., June 10, 1999.

26. Allison Baker, "The Lakewood Story" (Ph.D. diss., University of Pennsylvania, 1999), 178–79 ("bamboo village"). The well site may have been one of those developed by the Lakewood Parks, Recreation, and Parkway District as a Tot Lot. See also John Todd, *A History of Lakewood, 1949–1954* (Lakewood, Calif.: City of Lakewood, 1984), 5; "Citizens Seek End to Lakewood Ditch Hazards," *Lakewood Enterprise*, June 28, 1951.

27. By 1960, of the sixty plus incorporated cities in this single county, one-third had adopted some version of the Lakewood Plan. On the Lakewood Plan, see Todd, *History of Lakewood*.

28. Donald J. Waldie, *Holy Land: A Suburban Memoir* (New York: Norton, 1996); Lakewood Taxpayers Association, Inc., letter, March 8, 1954, as quoted in Harry Klissner, "How Agencies of Communications Can Convert a Gigantic Real

Estate Operation (Lakewood) into a Socially Cohesive Community" (M.A. thesis, University of California, Los Angeles, 1854), 116–17; Baker, "Lakewood Story," 75.

29. Todd, *History of Lakewood*, 9–24.

30. Ibid.; "Airport Opposition Mounts," *Lakewood Enterprise*, January 31, 1952.

31. "LTA to Study Annexation, Plazans Will Petition for It," *Lakewood Enterprise*, February 28, 1952; "LW City Prospects Told at Chamber Meeting," *Lakewood Enterprise*, January 21, 1954 ("annexation to an oil city"); "Crowd of 380 Jams School at Incorporation Debate," *Lakewood Enterprise*, February 18, 1954; "Lakewood Eying Tideland Revenue," *LAT*, July 7, 1953.

32. Todd, *History of Lakewood*, 4–6.

33. Baker, "Lakewood Story," 113, 115 ("highest priority").

34. City of Lakewood, *Annual Report, 1961–62*, 13.

35. City of Lakewood, *Annual Report, 1959*, 5, and *1961–62* ("graceful palm"), 8. On sprinklers, see Todd, *History of Lakewood*.

36. Four of the first twenty-five ordinances in the town's first five months targeted animals. See Lakewood City Ordinances, Lakewood City Hall Archives, Lakewood City Hall, Lakewood, Calif.; "Canine and Feline Population Jumps Fourfold in County," *Lakewood Enterprise*, January 10, 1954; "Lakewood Dog License Issue Starts Saturday," *Lakewood Enterprise*, July 6, 1954; "Bird Fanciers Peck at LW City Council," *Lakewood Enterprise*, September 16, 1954; interview with David Pinette, Arcadia, Calif.; May 21, 2001.

37. On the town's farmland, see "Farm Lease of Lakewood Acres Voted," *Lakewood Enterprise*, April 9, 1954; "Protest Delayed on DV Move to Hurdle San Gabriel River," *Lakewood Enterprise*, April 18, 1957.

38. There were also instances of residents keeping other wild pets. See "Lakewood Gardens Boy Facing Shots for Gopher Bite," *Lakewood Enterprise*, April 4, 1954, and "Pet Lover's Ocelot Ruled Wild Animal," *LAT*, January 28, 1965.

39. California Public Outdoor Recreation Committee, *California Public Outdoor Recreation Plan* (Sacramento, 1960), part I, 44; Gregg Mitman, *Reel Nature: America's Romance with Wildlife on Film* (Cambridge: Harvard University Press, 1999); Margaret J King, "The Audience in the Wilderness: The Disney Nature Films," *Journal of Popular Film and Television* 24, no. 4 (1996): 60–68.

40. Outdoor Recreation Committee, *California Public Outdoor Recreation Plan*, 105–7, 105 ("open space").

41. This and subsequent testimony obtained from interview with Louise Lillard in North Hollywood, Calif., on June 12, 2003; Richard Lillard's curriculum vitae, RLP; Richard Gordon Lillard, *Desert Challenge: An Interpretation of Nevada* (New York: Knopf, 1942), *The Great Forest* (New York: Knopf, 1947); and R. Lillard, *My Urban Wilderness in the Hollywood Hills: A Year of Years on Quito Lane* (Lanham, Md.: University Press of America, 1983), 10 (quotation). See also Otis Coan and Richard Lillard, *America in Fiction; An Annotated List of Novels That Interpret Aspects of Life in the United States* (Stanford, Calif.: Stanford University Press, 1941).

42. R. Lillard, *My Urban Wilderness*, 143.

43. Ibid., 44.

44. Lillard Journal, RLP.

45. Among the recent literature, see Thomas Dunlap, *Faith in Nature: Environmentalism as a Religious Quest* (Seattle: University of Washington Press, 2004), and Lynn Ross-Bryant, "Sacred Sites: Nature and Nation in the U.S. National Parks," *Religion and American Culture: A Journal of Interpretation* 15 (2005): 31–52. See also John Gatta, *Making Nature Sacred: Literature, Religion, and Environment in America from the Puritans to the Present* (New York: Oxford University Press, 2004).

46. Lillard Journal, 167, RLP; "Conservation Held Job for Individual," *LAT*, January 28, 1951.

47. "Citizens Conference Studies Conservation," *LAT*, October 17 1952; "Conservation Council" folder, SCP; "Organic Gardening Clubs of America," *Organic Gardening and Farming* 2 (October 1955): 77.

48. Lillard, *My Urban Wilderness*; Lillard Journal, RLP; Statistics, PHS.

49. Lillard, *My Urban Wilderness*, 136–37 (quotations).

50. Edward Owen, "The Inevitable Cycle: Fire, Denudation, Flood and Disaster: Report and Recommendations for Fire and Flood Control in Hollywood Hills and Santa Monica Mountains," typescript, 1936 (quotations from E. C. Eaton, Chief Engineer, L. A. County Flood Control District, p. 52), in folder 11, box 1, Weaver Collection, no. 1447, UCLA. See also Mike Davis, *Ecology of Fear: Los Angeles and the Imagination of Disaster*, 1st ed. (New York: Vintage Books, 1999), and Jared Orsi, *Hazardous Metropolis: Flooding and Urban Ecology in Los Angeles*, 1st ed. (Berkeley: University of California Press, 2004).

51. "Storm Damage in Millions, Hundreds Left Homeless," *LAT*, January 17, 1952; "Southland Storm Ends, Flood Waters Recede," *LAT*, January 19, 1952; "Mopping Up Started in Storm Areas," *LAT* January 20, 1952; interview with Louise Lillard ("devastated"); Lillard, *My Urban Wilderness*, 49–52.

52. Lillard, *My Urban Wilderness*, 55 (all quotations); Los Angeles Census Tracts, 1960.

53. George Beronius, "A Successful Fight for Safer Hillsides," *LAT*, June 16, 1957; G. E. Morris, "Hillside Planning Topic of Official City Report," *LAT*, May 25, 1958; "The Federation in Action . . . Gets Results," flyer (1963?), in Federation of Hillside and Canyon Associations Papers, UCLA.

54. Davis, *Ecology of Fear*, 105–9, 146. On the area's fire history, see Stephen Pyne, *Fire in America: A Cultural History of Wildland and Rural Fire* (Princeton: Princeton University Press, 1982), 404–15.

55. Lillard, *My Urban Wilderness*, 113; Art Seidenbaum, "Back to Nature in Beverly Glen," *LAT*, July 16, 1965 ("girls in the tickytack shack"); "Beverly Glen Artists Ready Spring Festival," *LAT*, February 10, 1963.

56. "The Federation in Action . . . Gets Results," flyer; Lillard Journal, 157, RLP ("balance . . . things well").

57. The idea was suggested several times earlier. See "Apartments in 'Wilds' Pos-

sible on Tract Here," *LAT*, March 12, 1958; "Largest City Park Seen for Valley," *LAT*, December 28, 1958; "Population Needs to Be Surveyed," *LAT*, October 18, 1959; Tom Cameron, "Residential Expansion Spreading from Valleys to Malibu Shorelines," *LAT*, August 12, 1962.

58. "4 Billions for Freeways in New Plan," *LAT*, August 8, 1959; "City Asks 6 New Valley Freeway Links," *LAT*, April 21, 1957; L. R. Gillis, District Engineer, to James Hartzell, President of Federation, November 13, 1959, in folder "Freeways," box 12, Federation of Hillside and Canyon Associations Papers, UCLA; "New Era of the Freeway," *LAT*, January 2, 1959.

59. Henry Sutherland, "Santa Monica Mountain Plan Draws Opposition," *LAT*, July 17, 1962; Ray Hebert, "Stakes High in Row over Mountain Park," *LAT*, February 2, 1964 (quotations pro-park); "Group Seeks to Form Park in Mountains," *LAT*, September 8, 1963 (Braude quotation); "Brentwood Group Chief Backs Mountain Park," *LAT*, December 6, 1962; "Urban Planning" folder, box 16, Richard Lillard Papers, UCLA.

60. Ray Hebert, "Mountain Park Vote Plan Killed," *LAT*, March 25, 1964 ("backyards vacant"); Art Seidenbaum, "The Santa Monica Mountain Hassle—Trouble on Olympus," *LAT*, September 20, 1964 ("neighborhood parks"); Ray Hebert, "Park Could Hike Taxes, Cities Told," *LAT*, January 4, 1964.

61. "Group Launches 'All-Out' Drive for Santa Monica Mountains Park," *LAT*, August 9, 1964; Ralph Stone, "People Deserve Park in Santa Monica Mountains," *LAT*, September 26, 1964; "Park Group Plans Day in Mountains," *LAT*, June 11, 1964; "Walton Chapter to Back Prop. 1," *LAT*, October 16, 1964; "Mountain Friends' Unit Plans Parties," *LAT*, August 30, 1964; "Women Voters Back Mountain Park Plan," *LAT*, October 1, 1964; Evelyn Gayman, "Santa Monica Mountain Park," *Southern Sierran* 19, no. 10 (1964): 1; Gayman, "Park Poor Los Angeles," *Southern Sierran* 20, no. 2 (1965): 1.

62. Anonymous, "Dump for Los Angeles Trash," *Southern Sierran* (October 1955): 3; Dan Thrapp, "Notes on Conservation," *Southern Sierran* 11 (December 1956): 1; Walt Wheelock, "Water Pollution," *Southern Sierran* 14 (October 16, 1959): 4.

63. Brower to Amneus, February 24, 1959; Amneus to Board of Directors, February 19, 1959; Margaret Barry Wehle to Secretary of the Sierra Club, March 18, 1959; Thomas Hunt to David Brower, March 26, 1959, in pp. 2312–19, folder "Membership Committee General, 1953–59," box 41, SCP.

64. Gayman, "Park Poor Los Angeles."

65. "Wyman Home Picketed in Land Swap Protest," *LAT*, May 23, 1965; Patricia Sanchez, "'Save Park' Group Clarifies Stand," *LAT*, May 29, 1965; Elinor Lenz, "Right on, Lillian!," *LAT*, July 11, 1971; Kenneth Rosen, "Hazard Park," *Cry California* 4 (1968–69): 30–34. See also Alexander M. Man Papers, folders 8, 9, box 2, Southern California Library for Social Studies and Research, Los Angeles.

66. Gayman, "Park Poor Los Angeles"; "Elysian Park" [another similar park fight], *Southern Sierran* 10, no. 8 (October 1965): 2; Evelyn Gayman, "Our Local

Parks," *Southern Sierran* 21, no. 4 (1966): 2 ("peace and delight"); Minutes of Conservation Committee, Sierra Club–Angeles Chapter, February 2, 1966, 3, SCP.

67. Robert Kirsch, "Consider What Man Hath Wrecked in Southern California," *LAT*, September 11, 1966 (Lillard's quotation); Richard G. Lillard, *Eden in Jeopardy: Man's Prodigal Meddling with His Environment: The Southern California Experience* (New York: Knopf, 1966).

Chapter 7

1. "City Hunting for Source of 'Gas Attack,'" *LAT*, July 27, 1943; interview with Jackie Rynerson, Lakewood, Calif., October 21, 2006 ("What is that?"); Carey McWilliams, *Southern California Country: An Island on the Land* (1946; reprint, Salt Lake City: Peregrine Smith, 2009).

2. For a contemporary version, see McWilliams, *Southern California Country*.

3. "Houston, Los Angeles Tops in Ozone—The Smoggiest Cities in the US," *Public Roads* (November 2000), http://www.findarticles.com/p/articles/mi_m3724/is_3_64/ai_70203634 (September 23, 2006); American Lung Association, "Best and Worst Cities," in *State of the Air, 2006*, http://lungaction.org/reports/sota06_cities.html#table2b (September 27, 2006).

4. An emphasis similar to mine appears in Sara Elkind, "Los Angeles' Nature: Urban Environmental Politics in the Twentieth Century," in Jeffery Diefendorf and Kurk Dorsey, eds., *City, Country, Empire: Landscapes in Environmental History* (Pittsburgh: University of Pittsburgh Press, 2005), 89–51. Among the earlier literature emphasizing automobiles, see Scott Dewey, *Don't Breathe the Air: Air Pollution and U.S. Environmental Politics, 1945–1970* (College Station: Texas A&M Press, 2000); James Krier and Edmund Ursin, *Pollution and Policy: A Case Essay on California and Federal Experience with Motor Vehicle Air Pollution, 1940–1975* (Berkeley: University of California Press, 1977); and Marvin Brienes, "The Fight against Smog in Los Angeles, 1943–1957" (Ph.D. diss., University of California, Davis, 1975).

5. Natalie Molina, *Fit to Be Citizens?: Public Health and Race in Los Angeles, 1879–1939* (Berkeley: University of California Press, 2006). On the bubonic plague in the 1920s, see William Deverell, *Whitewashed Adobe: The Rise of Los Angeles and the Remaking of Its Mexican Past* (Berkeley: University of California Press, 2005), chap. 5; also in a comparable period in San Francisco, see Naya Shah, *Contagious Divides: Epidemics and Race in San Francisco's Chinatown* (Berkeley: University of California Press, 2001).

6. Michael Simmons, "Bringing Astronomy to an Isolated Mountaintop," Mount Wilson Observatory Association, 1983, http://www.mtwilson.edu/Simmons1.php (March 11, 2011).

7. Walter Lindley and J. P. Widney, *California of the South* (New York: D. Appleton, 1896), 34, 40; Lawrence Wechsler, "L.A. Glows: Why Southern California Doesn't Look Like Any Place Else," *New Yorker*, February 28, 1998, 90–97.

8. Helen Hunt Jackson, *Glimpses of California and the Missions* (Boston: Little, Brown, 1907), 214; Lindley and Widney, *California*, 150.

9. Lindley and Widney, *California of the South*, 46–51, 62–66; Jackson, *Glimpses of California*, 214 (quotation) and ff. On nineteenth-century miasmatic theory, see Linda Lorraine Nash, *Inescapable Ecologies: A History of Disease, Environment and Knowledge* (Berkeley: University of California Press, 2007), and Conevery Bolton Valenčius, *The Health of the Country: How American Settlers Understood Themselves and Their Land* (New York: Basic Books, 2002). Examples in the *Southern California Practitioner* include P. C. Remondino, "The Climate of Southern California in Its Relation to Renal Diseases," 4 (1889): 369–87, and B. Reed, "Climate in Relation to Disorders of Metabolism and the Circulation," 3 (1906): 559–61. Among many others in *LAT*, see John Davis, "Health in California," December 30, 1889.

10. Linda Lorraine Nash, *Inescapable Ecologies*; Frank McCoy, "Health and Diet Advice: Health and Climate," *LAT*, September 16, 1927. See, e.g., City of Pasadena, *Community Health Organization and Appraisal 1932* (Pasadena, 1932).

11. "New Health Records Set By County," *LAT*, July 1, 1931; "Proves Southland Sun Is Elixir," *LAT*, July 14, 1924; "Health in California Explained," *LAT*, August 29, 1926; Harry Ellington Brook, "Care of the Body," *LAT*, June 1, 1924 (Pasteur); Philip Lovel, M.D. "Care of the Body," *LAT*, February 23, 1930.

12. Edward Ullman, "Amenities as a Factor in Regional Growth," *Geographical Review* 44 (1954): 119–32.

13. Charles Lummis, "Southern California," *Mentor*, December 15, 1916, 7.

14. Paul Sabin, *Crude Politics: The California Oil Market, 1900–1940* (Berkeley: University of California Press, 2005); Nancy Arthur Johnson, "California and the National Oil Industry," *Pacific Historical Review* 39 (1970): 155–69; James C. Williams, "Fuel at Last: Oil and Gas for California, 1860's–1940's," *California History* 55 (Summer 1996): 115–27.

15. "Refinery Blast Death List at 20," *Long Beach Press Telegram*, June 2, 1933; "Life in an Oil Refinery Flows Fast and Hot," *LAT*, October 12, 1959; Los Angeles APCD, *Technical Progress Report: Air Quality of Los Angeles County* (Los Angeles: Los Angeles APCD, 1961), 2:269, 1:84–104, APCB. On gasoline's boiling point, see Ted Sell, "Smog Declared Worst Since '55," *LAT*, November 27, 1958.

16. Los Angeles APCD, *Technical Progress Report*, 2:269, 1:9–13, APCB.

17. "Warming Up Nature," *LAT*, December 30, 1926; "Ranchers Fight Frost with 32,400,000 Gallons of Oil," *LAT*, January 9, 1937.

18. Los Angeles APCD, *Technical Progress Report*, 1:19–20, APCB.

19. "Clamor for Rubbish Disposal Leads to Survey by Times," *LAT*, October 1949; "Center for Burning Junk Worst Smog Offender," *LAT*, September 29, 1947; "L.A. Area Jumble of Rubbish Plans," *LAT*, May 16, 1956; "LA 'Smoke Pots' to Be Abolished," *APCD Report* 3, no. 11, April 1955.

20. "Goblins Will Ride to the Playground," *LAT*, October 31, 1949; "Bonfires

Well Patronized in Chilly Dawn," *LAT*, January 2, 1949; "Barbecue Pits Feature of Western Hospitality," *LAT*, April 19, 1940.

21. "Belching and Dark Anti-Smoke Tokens," *LAT*, January 1, 1908. For smoke abatement generally, see David Stradling, *Smokestacks and Progressives: Environmentalists, Engineers, and Air Quality in America, 1881–1951* (Baltimore: Johns Hopkins University Press, 1999); Harold Platt, "Invisible Gases: Smoke, Gender and the Redefinition of Environmental Policy in Chicago, 1900–1920," *Planning Perspectives* 10 (1994): 67–97; and Stephen Moseley, *The Chimney of the World: A History of Smoke Pollution in Victorian and Edwardian Manchester* (Cambridge, U.K.: White Horse Press, 2001).

22. Christopher Boone, "Zoning and Environmental Inequity in the Industrial East Side," in William Deverell and Greg Hise, eds., *Land of Sunshine: An Environmental History of Metropolitan Los Angeles* (Pittsburgh: University of Pittsburgh Press, 2005), 169–75.

23. "Smudge Change Delay Granted," *LAT*, October 21, 1931; "Orchard Smudge Smoke Engulfs Valley," *LAT*, January 9, 1937; "How the Southland Looks Fighting Cold," *LAT*, January 25, 1937; "Citrus Orchard Smudging Hangs Smoke Pall over Downtown Los Angeles," *LAT*, January 23, 1937.

24. Frank M. Stead, "Industrial Hygiene in Los Angeles County," *Industrial Medicine* 11 (November 1942): 542–46; Brienes, "The Fight against Smog, 35 ("outlying districts"), 54 n. 6. More generally on industrial hygienists who undertook such studies, see Christopher Sellers, *Hazards of the Job: From Industrial Disease to Environmental Health Science* (Chapel Hill: University of North Carolina Press, 1997).

25. "Industry Blamed for 'Gas Attack,'" *LAT*, July 29, 1943; "Butadiene Plant Confirmed as Source of Gas Fumes Here," *LAT*, July 29, 1943. For earlier precedents, see Brienes, "The Fight against Smog," 33–39.

26. "Anti-Smog Campaign Gets Backing," *Pasadena Star-News*, May 9, 1946. See also Dewey, *Don't Breathe the Air*, esp. 85–87, and Karl Brooks, *Before Earth Day: The Origins of American Environmental Law, 1945–1970* (Lawrence: University of Kansas Press, 2007), 61–73.

27. Harold Kennedy, "The History, Legal and Administrative Aspects of Air Pollution Control in the County of Los Angeles" (M.S. thesis, University of Southern California, 1954), esp. 9–14.

28. L. C. McCabe et al., "The Nature of Industrial Dusts and Fumes in the Los Angeles Area," March 28, 1949, at American Chemical Society Symposium on Air Contaminants, APCB.

29. On Donora, see Lynn Page Snyder, "The Death-Dealing Smog over Donora, Pennsylvania: Industrial Air Pollution, Public Health, and Federal Policy, 1915–1963" (Ph.D. diss., University of Pennsylvania, 1994), and McCabe et al., "Nature of Industrial Dusts and Fumes," 6.

30. Ronald Schiller, "The Los Angeles Smog," *National Municipal Review* 44 (1955): 561; Arthur Stern and Leonard Greenberg, "Air Pollution—The Status

Today," *American Journal of Public Health* 41 (1951): 27–37; Evaluation and Planning Staff, "Analysis of Shutdown Plans Submitted under Regulation VII, July 25, 1956," 2–10, APCD; California Department of Health, *Clean Air for California* (San Francisco: State Department of Health, 1955), esp. 14.

31. McCabe et al., "Nature of Industrial Dusts and Fumes," 1; Ed Ainsworth, "Refineries Held Smog Leaders," *LAT*, September 15, 1948; Stanford Research Institute, *Third Interim Report on the Smog Problem in Los Angeles County* (Los Angeles: Western Oil and Gas Association, 1950); Ed Ainsworth, "Experts Demand 7 Smog War Steps," *LAT*, December 6, 1953; Ari Haagen-Smit, interview by Shirley K. Cohen, Pasadena, Calif., March 16, 20, 2000, p. 23, Oral History Project, California Institute of Technology Archives, http://resolver.caltech.edu/CaltechOH:OH_Haagen-Smit_Z (February 15, 2008).

32. Haagen-Smit interview, 25; Arnold O. Beckman interview by Mary Terrall, Pasadena, Calif., October 16–December 4, 1978, Oral History Project, California Institute of Technology Archives, http://resolver.caltech.edu/CaltechOH:OH_Beckman_A (September 29, 2006).

33. Ari Haagen-Smit, "The Air Pollution Problem in Los Angeles," *Engineering and Science* 14 (December, 1950): 7–13; Haagen-Smit, C. E. Bradley, and Margaret Fox, "Formation of Ozone in Los Angeles Smog," *Proceedings of the Second National Air Pollution Symposium, May 5 and 6, 1952, Huntington Hotel, Pasadena, California* 2 (1952): 54–56.

34. "Nine Smog Test Stations Will Be Set Up in Area," *LAT*, July 15, 1954; "Balloons Help Trace Smog Flow," *LAT*, September 7, 1954 ("most concentrated network").

35. Kennedy, "History, Legal and Administrative Aspects of Air Pollution Control," 70–71.

36. "Text of Report and Conclusions of Smog Expert," *LAT*, January 19, 1947; Los Angeles APCD, *Technical Progress Report*, 2:268, APCB; Scott Bottles, *Los Angeles and the Automobile* (Berkeley: University of California Press, 1987).

37. On Larson, see Dewey, *Don't Breathe the Air*, 88–95. See also "District Observes Sixth Anniversary," *Newsletter of APCD* 2 (1954): 1.

38. California Department of Health, *Clean Air for California*, 7; "State Official Doubts Smog Injures Health," *LAT*, October 15, 1953; Ed Ainsworth, "Doctors Enlist in Fight to End Smog as Menace to Angelenos' Health," *LAT*, January 5, 1947, and Ainsworth, "Endless Smog War Urged at Parley," *LAT*, January 24, 1954 ("health hazard"); "Poulson Says Larson, Due as First Witness, Lied about Their Talk," *LAT*, October 22, 1954.

39. "6000 Citizens Demand Action on Smog Menace," *Pasadena Independent*, October 21, 1954; "An Emergency, Ill Mayor Says," *Pasadena Star-News*, October 21, 1954, 1, 4 (quotation).

40. "Pasadenans Will Take to Phones in Smog War," *LAT*, October 31, 1954; "Smog's Seeping into Brown Office—By Mail," *LAT*, November 27, 1954.

41. Dewey, *Don't Breathe the Air*, 96–97.

42. Stafford Warren, Report of the Special Advisory Smog Committee, February

15, 1955, APCB. For a broader context, see California Department of Public Health, *Technical Report of California Standards for Ambient Air Quality and Motor Vehicle Exhaust* (Berkeley: California Department of Public Health, 1959), 20–23.

43. Warren, "Report."

44. "The Air Monitoring Program," *APCB Report*, March 1956. See also APCD, *Technical Progress Report*, 2:86, 287–90, APCB; Air Resources Board, *Ten Year Summary of California Air Quality Data, 1963–1972* (Sacramento: Air Analysis Section, 1974), 200.

45. California Department of Public Health, *Technical Report of California Standards*, esp. 21; Testimony of Robert Chass, Director of Engineering for the Los Angeles County APCD, "Hearing on Rule 62," 20–21, APCB.

46. Manuel Pastor, "Racial/Ethnic Inequality in Environmental-Hazard Exposure in Metropolitan Los Angeles," (2001), http://www2.ucsc.edu/cjtc/docs/r_racial hazardexp_fullreport.pdf (January 17, 2011); R. A. Morello-Frosch, M. Pastor, and J. Sadd, "Environmental Justice and Southern California's 'Riskscape': The Distribution of Air Toxics Exposures and Health Risks among Diverse Communities," *Urban Affairs Review* 36 (2001): 551–78.

47. Lizabeth Cohen, *The Consumers' Republic; The Politics of Mass Consumption in Postwar America* (New York: Vintage Books, 2003).

48. "Incinerators Head List of Public Complaints," *Newsletter of APCB* 2 (April 23, 1954): 2; Dewey, *Don't Breathe the Air*, 53–54, 69–70. Over a hundred letters against the incinerator ban are filed in box APBP-1-A, folder 1, APCB. See also Krier and Ursin, *Pollution and Policy*, 158–63.

49. Los Angeles APCD, *Technical Progress Report*, 1:esp. 20, 2:269, APCB.

50. Thomas McCarthy, *Auto Mania: Cars, Consumers and the Environment* (New Haven: Yale University Press, 2007); "An Emergency, Ill Mayor Says," *Pasadena Star News*, October 21, 1954 ("electrify busses"); Ari Haagen-Smit, "The Control of Air Pollution in Los Angeles," *Engineering and Science* (December 1954): esp. 15.

51. Dewey, *Don't Breathe the Air*; interview with Lester Breslow, Los Angeles, Calif., October 19, 2006; California Department of Public Health, *Technical Report*.

52. Ralph Nader, *Unsafe at Any Speed: The Designed-In Dangers of the American Automobile* (New York: Grossman, 1965).

53. K. Barker et al., *Air Pollution* (Geneva: World Health Organization, 1961).

54. Though only formulated explicitly in the last couple of decades, the so-called precautionary principle has roots that have been investigated in studies such as Gerald Markowitz and David Rosner, "Industry Challenges to the Principles of Prevention in Public Health: The Precautionary Principle in Historical Perspective," *Public Health Reports* 117 (2002): 501–12, and Nancy Langston, "The Retreat from Precaution: Regulating Diethylstilbestrol (DES), Endocrine Disrupters, and Environmental Health," *Environmental History* 13 (2008): 41–65.

55. Los Angeles APCD, *Profile of Air Pollution Control* (Los Angeles: County of Los Angeles, 1973), 72; "Fog Wanes along Coast, Deepens in Inland Cities," *Long Beach Press Telegram*, November 28, 1954; Typescript by Beatrice Alva (June 20,

2003), in author's possession; phone interview with Richard Gillespie, June 6, 2003; interviews with Ernie Salas, San Gabriel, Calif., June 12, 2003, David Pinette, Arcadia, Calif., May 21, 2001, Jackie Rynerson, Lakewood, Calif., October 21, 2006, and Louise Lillard, North Hollywood, Calif., June 12, 2003; Richard G. Lillard, *Eden in Jeopardy: Man's Prodigal Meddling with His Environment: The Southern California Experience* (New York: Knopf, 1966).

56. Graham Berry, "Smog Can Cause Human Malignancies, Doctors Say," *LAT*, April 5, 1957. See also "Physicians Give Opinions on Smog," *APCD Report*, nos. 2, 9 (1961): 1; Maury Beam, "Told of Health Peril, Board Votes to Tighten Smog Rule," *LAT*, March 17, 1961.

57. Phone interview with Steve Rynerson, February 5, 2009; interview with Louise Lillard.

58. Berry, "Smog Can Cause Human Malignancies"; "Physicians Give Opinions on Smog."

59. Francis Pottenger Sr., "Four Fundamental Principles of the Treatment of Tuberculosis Established by Bremner," *Chest* 1 (1935): 7–8; Francis Pottenger Jr., "The Effect of Heat-Processed Foods and Metabolized Vitamin D Milk on the Dentofacial Structures of Experimental Animals," *American Journal of Orthopedic and Oral Surgery* 32 (1946): 467–85; "Nation's Top Nutrition Experts Meet in Pasadena," *LAT*, April 10, 1965.

60. See, e.g., Paul Kotin and H. L. Faulk, "Atmospheric Factors in the Pathogenesis of Lung Cancer," *Advances in Cancer Research* 57 (1963): 475–514. On the scientific debates over cancer causation, see Robert Proctor, *Cancer Wars: How Politics Shapes What We Know and Don't Know about Cancer* (New York: Basic Books, 1996), and Christopher Sellers, "Discovering Environmental Cancer: Wilhelm Hueper, Epidemiology, and the Vanishing Clinician's Role," *American Journal of Public Health* 87 (November 1997): 1824–35.

61. E. B. Lewis, "Leukemia and Ionizing Radiation," *Science*, May 17, 1957, 965–72; Linus Pauling, "How Dangerous Is Radioactive Fallout?," *Foreign Policy Bulletin*, June 15, 1957, 149; Jennifer Caron, "E. B. Lewis and Radioactive Fallout: The Impact of Caltech Biologists on the Debate over Nuclear Weapons Testing in the 1950's and 60's" (B.S. thesis, California Institute of Technology, 2003); Clare Patterson, "Contaminated and Natural Lead Environments of Man," *Archives of Environmental Health* 11 (1965): 344–60; Christian Warren, *Brush with Death: A Social History of Lead Poisoning* (Baltimore: Johns Hopkins University Press, 2001).

62. "West Siders Ask Laws to Fight Smog," *LAT*, October 4, 1959; "MTA Promises Action in Year on Rapid Transit," *LAT*, December 17, 1959; "Women Ask for Aid to Stamp Out Smog," *LAT*, May 18, 1959; "Women's Group Joins Fight on Air Pollution," *LAT*, January 8, 1959.

63. Irving Bengelsdorf, "Damaging Blanket of Smog Spreads to Much of State," *LAT*, May 26, 1963; "Heavy Smog Hits Central Valley," *APCD Report* 9 (May 1961): 1; Jim Hartzell, President, "'The Air We Breathe,'" announcement of December 2, 1958, meeting, and "Mild Hope for the Right to Breathe," *Canyon Crier*,

November 27, 1958—both in folder "Air Pollution and Smog," box 1, Weaver Collection, no. 1244, UCLA.

64. Phone interview with Steve Rynerson.

65. Ibid.

Chapter 8

1. See, e.g., Flora Lewis, "Instant Mass Movement," *LAT*, April 29, 1970. For a recent less critical account than what follows, with a review of the slim historiography, see Adam Rome, "Give Earth a Chance: The Environmental Movement and the Sixties," *Journal of American History* 90 (2003): 525–54, and Rome, "The Genius of Earth Day," *Environmental History* 15 (2010): 194–205.

2. "Nordic Nations Set Earth Week Events," *LAT*, June 9, 1970; John Dryzek, David Downes, Christian Hunold, and David Scholsberg, *Green States and Social Movements: Environmentalism in the United States, United Kingdom, Germany and Norway* (New York: Oxford University Press, 2003), esp. 28, 109; Martin Janicke and Helmut Wiedner, eds., *National Environmental Policies: A Comparative Study of Capacity-Building* (Berlin: Springer, 1997); Bill Christofferson, *The Man from Clear Lake: Earth Day Founder Senator Gaylord Nelson* (Madison: University of Wisconsin Press, 2004), esp. 305.

3. Art Seidenbaum, "The Lack of Glue," *LAT*, March 13, 1970.

4. See, e.g., Andrew Kirk, *Counterculture Green: The Whole Earth Catalogue and American Environmentalism* (Lawrence: University of Kansas Press, 2007).

5. Rachel Carson, *Silent Spring* (1962; reprint, Greenwich, Conn.: Fawcett Publications, 1970), 13–14.

6. President's Council on Natural Beauty, *From Sea to Shining Sea: A Report on the American Environment—Our Natural Heritage* (Washington D.C.: GPO, 1968), 104; Margo Tupper, *No Place to Play* (Philadelphia: Chilton Books, 1966), 15.

7. Adam Rome, "William Whyte, Open Space, and Environmental Activism," *Geographic Review* 88 (1998): 259–74; Stewart Udall, *The Quiet Crisis* (New York: Holt, Rinehart and Winston, 1963), 159–60.

8. Ben Bagdikian, "The Rape of the Land," *Saturday Evening Post* 25 ("cancerously in all directions"); Peter Blake, *God's Own Junkyard: The Planned Deterioration of America's Landscape* (New York: Holt, Rinehart and Winston, 1964), 17 ("massive, monotonous ugliness"), photos 104–7 (Lakewood-to-be); Robert Cubbedge, *The Destroyers of America* (New York: Macfadden Books, 1964), 8 ("so scarified"), 57 ("before nuclear fission").

9. Cubbedge, *Destroyers*, 124, 42 (roadside "trash"), 36 ("swallowed" land), 74 ("dead" beaches); William Whyte, *The Last Landscape* (Garden City: Doubleday, 1968), 15–18; Tupper, *No Place to Play*, 3, 19.

10. Tupper, *No Place to Play*, 12.

11. Bagdikian, "The Rape of the Land," 27 ("organizing to oppose," "all over the nation"), 26 ("modest beauty").

12. For an introduction to this concept and literature, see David Meyer and

Debra C. Minkoff, "Conceptualizing Political Opportunity," *Social Forces* 82 (2004): 1457–92.

13. *Beauty for America: Proceedings of the White House Conference on Natural Beauty, Washington, D.C., May 24–25, 1965* (Washington, D.C.: GPO, 1965), 2, 20, 19 ("the environment where most people live), 687. On the "quantity to quality" shift, see Rome, "Give Earth a Chance."

14. *Beauty for America*, 527, 514 ("pastoral dream").

15. Ibid., 19, 22 (Rockefeller quote).

16. Of seventeen Los Angeles–area delegates, all nine with home addresses found in *LAT* keyword searches lived in suburban towns, many of them exclusive and well-to-do. Among a sample of twenty-two who listed New York City work addresses, seven of twelve found in *NYT* keyword searches lived outside New York City boroughs in well-to-do communities; at least one other also listed a home in East Hampton. *Beauty for America*, 693–756.

17. *Beauty for America*, 693–756. Ninety-seven attendees had addresses in southeastern states, whereas only thirty-three were from the Mountain West.

18. Teresa Tomkins-Walsh, "'To Combine Many and Varied Forces': The Hope of Houston's Environmental Activism, 1923–1999," in Martin Melosi and Joseph Pratt, eds., *Energy Metropolis; An Environmental History of Houston and the Gulf Coast* (Pittsburgh: University of Pittsburgh Press, 2007), 20; Memo of Betty Vinson to Mackay, November 25, 1966 ("idea whose time has come"), in folder "Misc. Memos," box 7, Georgia Natural Areas Council, Georgia Archives, Atlanta.

19. *Beauty for America*, 20 ("no problems are more important"). See also Cubbedge, *Destroyers*, chaps. 6, 7, and Tupper, *No Place to Play*, chap. 4.

20. For a definition of this term and a review of the social science literature, see Arnold Hunt, "'Moral Panic' and Moral Language in the Media," *British Journal of Sociology* 48 (1997): 629–48.

21. On the history of ecosystem ecology, see Joel Hagen, "Teaching Ecology during the Environmental Age, 1965–1980," *Environmental History* 13 (2008): 704–23, and Frank Golley, *A History of the Ecosystem Concept in Ecology: More than the Sum of the Parts* (New Haven: Yale University Press, 1993).

22. Carson, *Silent Spring*; Maril Hazlett, "'Woman vs. Man vs. Bugs': Gender and Popular Ecology in Early Reactions to Silent Spring," *Environmental History*, October 2004, http://www.historycooperative.org/journals/eh/9.4/hazlett.html (March 20, 2009).

23. Carson, *Silent Spring*, 24 ("sudden rise," "insecticidal properties"), 213 ("sea of carcinogens")

24. Rachel Carson to Marjorie Spock, September 1958, RCP; Linda Lear, *Rachel Carson: Witness for Nature* (New York: Henry Holt, 1997), 318–20, 330–38.

25. Carson, *Silent Spring*, 37, 118 (on orchard workers), 84 ("legitimate right").

26. Hazlett, "'Woman vs. Man vs. Bugs'"; Lear, *Rachel Carson*.

27. Hazel Erskine, "The Polls: Pollution and Its Cost," *Public Opinion Quarterly*

36 (1972): 120–35, 120 ("miracle of public opinion"); Erskine, "The Polls: Pollution and Industry," *Public Opinion Quarterly* 36 (1972): 263–80.

28. For a summary of these explanations, see Richard Andrews, *Managing the Environment, Managing Ourselves: A History of American Environmental Policy* (New Haven: Yale University Press, 1999), 223–26, 237–39.

29. Leonard Wickenden, *Our Daily Poison: The Effects of DDT, Fluoride, Hormones, and Other Chemicals on Modern Man* (New York: Devin Adair, 1955); Lewis Herber [later Murray Bookchin], *Our Synthetic Environment* (New York: Knopf, 1962); J. I. Rodale, *Our Poisoned Earth and Sky* (Emmaus, Pa.: Rodale Press, 1964).

30. These trends started with works such as Howard Lewis, *With Every Breath You Take: The Poisons of Air Pollution and How They Are Injuring Our Health* (Crown Publishers, 1965); Alfred Lewis, *Clean the Air: Fighting Smoke, Smog and Smaze across the Country* (New York: McGraw-Hill, 1965); and Donald Carr, *The Breath of Life: The Problem of Poisoned Air* (New York: Norton, 1965).

31. Gladwin Hill, "New Agency and New Policy to Enter Fight against Water Pollution," *NYT*, December 21, 1965; Paul Milazzo, *Unlikely Environmentalists: Congress and Clean Water, 1945–1972*, 94–111, 118–20; President's Science Advisory Committee, Environmental Pollution Panel, *Restoring the Quality of Our Environment* (Washington, D.C.: The White House, 1965); "Pollution Peril Is Called Grave," *NYT*, April 2, 1964.

32. Allan Brandt, *The Cigarette Century: The Rise, Fall, and Deadly Persistence of the Product That Defined America* (New York: Basic Books, 2007), 211–39.

33. Mark Parascandola, "Cigarettes and the US Public Health Service in the 1950s," *American Journal of Public Health* 91 (2001): 196–205; William Rothstein, *Public Health and the Risk Factor: A History of an Uneven Medical Revolution* (Rochester, N.Y.: University of Rochester Press, 2003); Robert Proctor, *Cancer Wars: How Politics Shapes What We Know and Don't Know about Cancer* (New York: Basic Books, 1995); J. Samuel Walker, *Permissible Dose: A History of Radiation Protection in the Twentieth Century* (Berkeley: University of California Press, 2000).

34. J. D. Ratcliff, "Do Traces of Metals Decide Our Fate?," *Today's Health* 44 (1966): 35; J. T. Watson, "A Historical Perspective and Commentary on Pioneering Developments in Gas Chromatography/Mass Spectrometry at MIT," *Journal of Mass Spectrometry* 33 (1998): 103–8.

35. Karl Brooks, *Before Earth Day: The Origins of American Environmental Law, 1945–1970* (Lawrence: University of Kansas Press, 2009), 125–33.

36. Harold Smeck, "U.S. in Peril of Losing Fight on Water Pollution," *NYT*, February 28, 1963; Hill, "New Agency and New Policy"; Donald Carr, *The Death of the Sweet Waters* (New York: Norton, 1966), 141–44.

37. Marjorie Hunter, "U.S. Pushes Drive on Air Pollution," *NYT*, October 15, 1961; President's Science Advisory Committee, *Restoring the Quality of Our En-*

vironment, 204 ("major metropolitan areas"); Gladwin Hill, "Nation Is Facing All-Out Battle for Cleaner Air," *NYT*, September 26, 1966 ("no fewer than 7,300 communities"); Thomas Aylesworth, *This Vital Air, This Vital Water: Man's Environmental Crisis* (Chicago: Rand McNally, 1968), 82.

38. For other examples, see Greg Mitman, "In Search of Health: Landscape and Disease in American Environmental History," *Environmental History* 10 (2005): 184–210.

39. President's Science Advisory Committee, *Restoring the Quality of Our Environment*, 174–91; "Lake Erie Called a Health Danger," *NYT*, July 31, 1965; William McGucken, *Lake Erie Rehabilitated* (Akron, Ohio: University of Akron Press, 2000), 36–53; David Stradling and Richard Stradling, "Perceptions of the Burning River: Deindustrialization and Cleveland's Cuyahoga River," *Environmental History* 13 (2008): 515–35.

40. "DDT Traces Found in Antarctic Animals," *NYT*, July 11, 1965; "From Sea to Shining Sea," *Newsweek*, January 26, 1970, 38 ("just about anywhere"); Philip King Brown, "Yosemite Park Acts to Ease Over-Crowding," *NYT*, July 14, 1968; Aylesworth, *This Vital Air*, 18–22; Robert Rienow and Leona Train Rienow, *Moment in the Sun: A Report on the Deteriorating Quality of American Environment* (New York: Dial Press, 1967), 191 ("empty cans, bottles"); Barry Commoner, *Science and Survival* (New York: Viking Press, 1966), 11 ("catastrophe").

41. Carr, *Breath of Life*, 14 ("a portent"), and *Sweet Waters*, 195 ("Long Island"). Three of the fourteen photos in *Sweet Waters* between pp. 130 and 131 are reported as being from the New York area, two from Ohio, and the rest from different states. See also Frank Graham Jr., *Disaster by Default: Politics and Water Pollution* (New York: M. Evans and Co., 1966), 91, 106, and John Perry, *Our Polluted World: Can Man Survive* (New York: Franklin Watts, 1967), 125.

42. Carr, *Breath of Life*, 13.

43. Dorothy Shuttlesworth, *Clean Air — Sparkling Water* (Garden City, N.Y.: Doubleday, 1968), 9, 17.

44. Erskine, "The Polls: Pollution and Its Cost," 124.

45. Louis Harris and Associates, *The Harris Survey Yearbook of Public Opinion, 1970* (New York: Louis Harris and Associates, 1970), 49–55. See also Erskine, "The Polls: Pollution and Its Cost."

46. Graham, *Disaster by Default*, 211 ("impetus must come from"); Howard Lewis, *With Every Breath You Take* (New York: Crown Publishers, 1965), 259 ("no coincidence"); League of Women Voters, *The Big Water Fight* (Brattleboro, Vt.: Stephen Greene Press, 1966), 34–77; Federal Water Pollution Control Administration, *Focus on Clean Water: An Action Program for Community Organizations* (Washington, D.C.: GPO, 1966); Michael Chester and Albert Micale, *Let's Go to Stop Air Pollution* (New York: Putnam, 1968); John Bird, "Our Dying Waters," *Saturday Evening Post*, April 23, 1966 ("the only organized body").

47. The quotation is from Barry Weisberg, "The Politics of Ecology," widely reprinted in alternative media of the period, as well as in Robert Disch, ed., *The*

Ecological Conscience: Values for Survival (Englewood, N.J.: Prentice Hall, 1970), 154–60.

48. Interview with Carol Yannacone, Patchogue, N.Y., August 21, 1996.

49. Robert Lifset, "Storm King and the Birth of Modern Environmentalism, 1964–1980" (Ph.D. diss., Columbia University, 2005); Andrews, *Managing the Environment*, 220–21; precedents also lay in suits to fight federal dam building: Brooks, *Before Earth Day*, 149–51.

50. Mrs. Sherman Slade, "A Protest," *LAT*, April 15, 1965; Scott Dewey, *Don't Breathe the Air: Air Pollution and U.S. Environmental Politics, 1945–70* (College Station: Texas A&M Press, 2000), esp. 106–7; Andrews, *Managing the Environment*, esp. 240; James Longhurst, "'Don't Hold Your Breath, Fight for It': Women's Activism and Citizen Standing in Pittsburgh and the United States, 1965–1975" (Ph.D. diss., Carnegie-Mellon University, 2004).

51. John Rodman, "Smog Apologists Chided for Pap of Euphemism," *LAT*, September 7, 1969; Charles Elwell, "Claremont Professors Join Smog Battle," *LAT*, September 21, 1969; Dewey, *Don't Breathe the Air*, 107.

·52. Elwell, "Claremont Professors Join Smog Battle"; "Proposition to Finance Transit, Smog War Loses," *LAT*, November 5, 1970.

53. Art Seidenbaum, "Digging at the Grassroots for Help," *LAT*, November 7, 1967; Seidenbaum, "A Foe of Noise, Waste, Pollution," *LAT*, December 26, 1969.

54. Maxwell Wheat to Franklin Bear, January 22, 1969 (quotation), Claire Stern to Arnold Miller, August 27, 1969 (quotation), and Stern to Peter Pratt, December 2, 1969, all in LIEC.

55. Claire Stern to Peter Pratt, December 2, 1969, folder "LIEC Corr and Memos 1969 F1," box 1, LIEC; Seidenbaum, "Digging at the Grassroots"; Seidenbaum, "A Foe of Noise, Waste."

56. "CV–Claire Stern," "Member Groups LIEC," and "A Picnic on the Prairie," LIEC; "Tide Turns in Water Pollution," *LAT*, October 19, 1969.

57. Thomas Wellock, *Critical Masses: Opposition to Nuclear Power in California, 1958–1978* (Madison: University of Wisconsin Press, 1998), 46–49, 68–96; Michael Cohen, *The History of the Sierra Club, 1892–1970* (San Francisco: Sierra Club Books, 1988); Stephen Fox, *The American Conservation Movement: John Muir and His Legacy* (1981; reprint, Madison: University of Wisconsin Press, 1985); Frank Graham and Carl Buchheiser, *The Audubon Arc: The History of the National Audubon Society* (Austin: University of Texas Press, 1992). On Izaak Walton, see Gregory Summers, *Consuming Nature: Environmentalism in the Fox River Valley, 1850–1950* (Lawrence: University of Kansas Press, 2006). See also Figure 6 in the Appendix; figure culled from Angeles Chapter of Sierra Club Papers, UCLA.

58. Quietly, not only did Ellen Harris consult with "ecological experts," but also she found a steady ally in a fish and wildlife official on the Water Control Board. See Seidenbaum, "A Foe of Noise, Waste," and Lynn Lilliston, "Woman Leads Fight for Cleaner Water," *LAT*, March 28, 1969.

59. Robert Murphy, *Fish-Shape Paumanok: Nature and Man on Long Island* (Phil-

adelphia: American Philosophical Society, 1964), 58–60; Richard G. Lillard, *Eden in Jeopardy: Man's Prodigal Meddling with His Environment: The Southern California Experience* (New York: Knopf, 1966), 245 ("inverted bowl").

60. "Ecology: The New Jeremiads," *Time*, August 15, 1969, http://www.time.com/time/magazine/article/0,9171,901238,00.html (January 12, 2007); Robert Rienow and Leona Rienow, *A Moment in the Sun*, ix ("ecologist in the broadest sense"—they were partly quoting Stuart Chase in *Some Things Worth Knowing: A Generalist's Guide to Useful Knowledge* [New York: Harper, 1958]); Michael Egan, *Barry Commoner and the Politics of Survival* (Cambridge: MIT Press, 2007). On these questions in the context of professional ecology itself, see Paul Milazzo, *Unlikely Environmentalists: Congress and Clean Water, 1945–1972* (Lawrence: University of Kansas Press, 2006), esp. 105–7, and Stephen Bocking, *Ecologists and Environment Politics* (New Haven: Yale University Press, 1997).

61. Lynton Caldwell, "Environment: A New Focus for Policy?," *Public Administration Review* 23 (1963): 132–39. See also charts on the rise of environmental journals in Unsettlingground.com.

62. Christopher Sellers, "Body, Place, and the State: The Makings of an 'Environmentalist' Imaginary in the Post–World War II United States," *Radical History Review* 94 (1999): 31–64.

63. Stern to Editor, *Look* magazine, November 12, 1969; Outstanding Obligations as of July 5, 1970, LIEC.

64. Harris, "Water in the Harbor," *LAT*, October 20, 1967; Seidenbaum, "A Foe of Noise, Waste," 18.

65. Interview with Arthur Cooley, Long Island, N.Y., April 7, 1997; Marion Lane Rodgers, *Acorn Days: The Environmental Defense Fund and How It Grew* (New York: Environmental Defense Fund, 1990); Myra Gelband, "During the Summer of 1965," typescript, April 1969, EDF; Wellock, *Critical Masses*, 78; Ray Ripton, "Fear for Environment Reaches Grass Roots," *LAT*, February 15, 1970; Gladwin Hill, "Environment May Eclipse Vietnam as College Issue," *NYT*, November 30, 1969.

66. "Mother, Daughter Join Environmental Program," *Levittown Tribune*, April 9, 1970; phone interview with Steve Rynerson, February 5, 2009.

67. Richard Goldstein, "The Flower Children and How They Grew," *LAT*, May 28, 1967; Steven Roberts, "The Better Earth," *NYT*, March 29, 1970; Garrett de Bell, ed., *The Environmental Handbook: Prepared for the First National Environmental Teach-In* (New York: Ballantine, 1970), 243, 252. See also Kirk, *Counterculture Green*.

68. Roberts, "The Better Earth"; Gary Snyder, *Earth House Hold*, reprinted in Robert Disch, ed., *The Ecological Conscience: Values for Survival*, 203; Thomas Dunlap, *Faith in Nature: Environmentalism as a Religious Quest* (Seattle: University of Washington Press, 2004), 110–14.

69. Kirk, *Counterculture Green*. For a useful survey of French counterparts, see Michael Bess, *The Light-Green Society: Ecology and Technological Modernity in France, 1960–2000* (Chicago: University of Chicago Press, 2003).

70. Christofferson, *The Man from Clear Lake*, 306.

71. Neil Maher, "Shooting the Moon," *Environmental History*, July 2004, http://www.historycooperative.org/journals/eh/9.3/maher.html (May 23, 2007); Denis Cosgrove, "Contested Global Visions: One-World, Whole-Earth, and the Apollo Space Photographs," *Annals of the Association of American Geographers* 84 (1994): 270–94.

72. "Repentance on Long Island," *Newsday*, April 23, 1970 (Murphy); "Cousteau Leads Earth Day Rites," *Long Beach Press-Telegram*, April 23, 1970. Generalizations are based on a survey of Earth Day coverage in Long Island and suburban Los Angeles newspapers.

73. "Earth Day Observances Slated," *LAT*, April 19, 1970; Kenneth Pannuchi, "Votes Called Way to Force Cleaner Earth," *LAT*, April 22, 1970; Gordon Grant, "Earth Day: A Many-Symboled Observance," *LAT*, April 22, 1970; Charles Reilly, "San Gabriel High Crew Plays Dead," *Pasadena Star-News*, April 23, 1970.

74. Whitney Young Jr., "Pollution and Life in the Slums," *Chicago Defender*, April 25, 1970; Environmental Action, *Earth Day — The Beginning* (New York: Arno Press and the New York Times, 1970), 95–106, 169–72. See also Jack Rosenthal, "Some Troubled by Environment Drive," *NYT*, April 22, 1970.

75. "'Earth Day' Trek Leads to Debris-Filled Sites," *Long Island Advance*, April 23, 1970; "Nassau Plans Park in Mitchell Field," *Newsday*, April 23, 1970; "80-Acre Nature Center Will Open to Public in El Dorado Park," *Long Beach Independent*, May 15, 1969; George Robeson, "Small Wilderness at the City's Edge," *Long Beach Independent Press-Telegram*, April 20, 1970.

Conclusion

1. Victor Chen, "Earth Day Program Tackles Pollution," *Newsday*, April 29, 2000.

2. Peter Dykstra, "Earth Day at 30: Having a New Day or Passe?," *CNN Interactive*, April 20, 2000, http://edition.cnn.com/SPECIALS/views/y/2000/04/dykstra.earthday.apr20/ (September 12, 2011); Don Hopey, "Earth Day at 30," *Pittsburgh Post-Gazette*, April 17, 2000, http://www.Post-gazette/healthscience/20000417eday2.asp (June 29, 2007); John Judis, "Marchers and Their Imprints," *NYT*, May 14, 2000 ("concerts on the mall"); "Earth Day 2000 Organizer Denis Hayes," America Online Transcript, April 22, 1999, http://www.time.com/time/community/transcripts/1999 (June 29, 2007) ("out of touch with real people"); Donella Meadows, "Earth Day at 30," April 21, 2000 ("commercial occasion"), http://www.tidepool.org/gc/gc4.21.00.cfm (June 29, 2007); "The Battle for Planet Earth," *Newsweek*, April 24, 2000; Benjamin Soskis, "Green with Envy," *New Republic*, May 8, 2000, 13; Richard Stenger, "Planet Green, Still Troubled on 30th Earth Day Anniversary, *CNN Interactive*, April 14, 2000 ("much more spontaneous" quoted from Donella Meadows), http://articles.cnn.com/2000-04-14/nature/earth.day.then.now_1_green-movement-pollution-earth-day?_s=PM:NATURE (September 12, 2011).

3. Philip Shabecoff, "Environmentalists Need to Bulk Up," *Newsday*, April 20, 2000.

4. Samuel Hays's magisterial *Beauty, Health, and Permanence: Environmental Politics in the United States, 1955–1985* (Cambridge: Cambridge University Press, 1985) did offer a larger sweep of environmental politics in detail, but when seeking a more synthetic narrative (pp. 52–57), it affirmed the Sierra-centric tale. Many other historians of the environmental movement have as well; see, e.g., Philip Shabecoff, *A Fierce Green Fire: The American Environmental Movement* (Washington, D.C.: Island Press, 2000); Hal Rothman, *The Greening of a Nation?: Environmentalism in the United States since 1945* (Fort Worth, Tex.: Harcourt Brace, 1998); and Kirkpatrick Sale, *The Green Revolution: The American Environmental Movement, 1962–1992* (Hill and Wang, 1993).

5. "Earth Day 2000 Organizer Denis Hayes" ("out of touch").

6. John T. McQuiston, "Cancer Study Renews Old Concerns," *NYT*, April 13, 1994.

7. See, e.g., Robert Gottlieb, "Expanding Environment Horizons," *LAT*, April 16, 2000.

8. This period's and other coalitions with labor unions have been the subject of growing scholarship—among them, Robert Gordon, "Poisons in the Fields: The United Farm Workers, Pesticides, and Environmental Politics," *Pacific Historical Review* 68 (1999): 51–78, and Brian Obach, *Labor and the Environmental Movement: The Quest for Common Ground* (Cambridge: MIT Press, 2004). For one example of the less studied coalitions with African American leaders, see Andrew Hurley, *Environmental Inequalities: Class, Race, and Industrial Pollution in Gary, Indiana, 1945–1980* (Chapel Hill: University of North Carolina Press, 1995).

9. Michael Shellenberger and Ted Nordhaus, "The Death of Environmentalism: Global Warming Politics in a Post-Environmental World," http://www.thebreak through.org/images/Death_of_Environmentalism.pdf (September 28, 2007).

10. Al Gore, *An Inconvenient Truth: The Planetary Emergency of Global Warming and What We Can Do about It* (Emmaus, Pa.: Rodale, 2006). For one graphic account of its local consequences, see Elizabeth Kolbert, *Field Notes from a Catastrophe: Man, Nature and Climate Change* (New York: Bloomsbury, 2006).

11. Nancy Langston, *Toxic Bodies: Hormone Disruptors and the Legacy of DES* (New Haven: Yale University Press, 2010); Phil Brown, *Toxic Exposures: Contested Illnesses and the Environmental Health Movement* (New York: Columbia University Press, 2007); Matthew Klingle, *Emerald City: An Environmental History of Seattle* (New Haven: Yale University Press, 2007); Jennifer Price, "Remaking American Environmentalism: On the Banks of the L.A. River," *Environmental History* 13 (2008): 536–55.

Note on Sources

This book draws on an unusual variety of sources, cited as well as uncited. Of special note for future historical inquirers, many of these lead below the surface of received stories about suburbia and environmentalism that are themselves products of the post–World War II era. As any environmental historian would expect, health, ecological, and other natural scientific studies of the period, as well as those extrapolated from the present, have aided this study immensely. So did the contemporary publications and archives familiar to anyone engaged in historical work, especially those illuminating the more regional and local scales of historical experience. In city halls, clerk's offices, and town libraries, in county health, planning, and agriculture departments, in records of homeowner associations, humane societies, wildlife refuges, and individual families, leads turned up for the more original narratives in this book, but also for many others. More unconventionally, extradocumentary evidence punctured many of the assumptions about suburbs and nature prevailing in standard texts about the fifties and sixties.

Oral histories, in particular, shed light on just how people experienced these places on the ground, literally as well as figuratively. Sometimes employed by historians of the suburbs, interviews have found less use in environmental history, even in studies of environmentalism itself. They nevertheless furnish an intimate, individualized antidote to accusations of impersonality and aversion to social conflict that have long dogged the field. More generally, they can illuminate the limits and distortions of those larger and more familiar narratives by which the mass media have ordered our understanding of so many dimensions of our modern era. Conducting interviews, which calls for much time, labor, and listening, can try the patience of a historian in a hurry. Asking semistructured, open-ended questions, as I did, opens the door to abundant digressions, only a few of which proved useful. Establishing shared or larger patterns, as opposed to strictly idiosyncratic variations, requires not just multiple interviews but a studied variety of interviewees.

I relied on what social scientists term "snowballing," conducting subsequent interviews with those suggested by my earliest subjects but making sure to strike a rough balance between men and women. I also sought a more or less representative variety of networks through which to snowball. From early on, I concentrated my interviewing in three contrasting communities within each suburbanizing region: a mass suburb, an upper middle-class suburb, and a suburb that harbored a large minority population (the Amityville area on Long Island and San Gabriel around Los Angeles).

Ultimately, I found no better way of unpacking laypeople's past encounters with a neighborhood ecology than by sitting down and talking with them about their experiences.

Other of the more unusual sources enabling the narrative and analysis of this book lie in what at first glance might seem utterly opposing realms of numbers. Appearing only a couple of times in the final text, digital mapping capabilities provided by Geographic Information Systems (GIS) software nevertheless played a significant role during the early and middle stages of the project. Pairing census information with geography starting in 1960, when all metropolitan counties were fully divvied into tracts, GIS yielded rigorous insight into where a sprawling pattern of housing density turned up when, and how different were its timing and manifestations around New York and Los Angeles, as opposed to Atlanta. In the precise socioeconomic differences between suburban neighborhoods it helped to define, digital mapping richly complemented my understanding of other, more localized evidence I was gathering, including the oral histories. GIS proved indispensable in keeping track of the class and racial implications lurking behind historical phenomenon that, in these times and places, were discussed in class-blind and race-blind ways, from home building to park making, to controlling pollution.

This book's governing conceptions also owe much to the digitalized databases of newspapers and other publications, and to the new understandings of cultural transformation they have suggested. Now appearing in the Appendix, charts of the changing mentions and associations of particular words over time point to the heretofore little studied dynamics of how the language of society such as ours may shift. Cultural historians, if willing to shed their widespread aversion to numbers, may well find a powerful new set of tools here, beyond their usual resort to imagery, anecdotes, and quotes. New questions arise as well. My study suggests that our modern media operates by means of vast and surprisingly rapid swings of vocabulary, from the talk of "suburbia" immediately after World War II to the talk of "environment" in the years just after 1965. The challenge then becomes, How may we understand these shifts, their origins as well as their impacts? Tucked within this main story line of the book are at least the rudimentary suggestions of an answer. When people began speaking of "suburbia" or of "environment," they were responding to changes around them, long since under way. At the same time, those who named or renamed these transformations themselves made history. Hand in hand with linguistic change, awareness could be raised, opposition enhanced, movements stirred.

Interviews

I conducted oral interviews with the people listed below. Their race/ethncity is indicated as follows: W = White, NA = Native American, AA = African American, H = Hispanic/Chicano.

New York City Area

Abrams, Herbert, Levittown, N.Y., February 2, 2001 (W)

Banks, McKinley, and Ballenger, Charles, North Amityville, N.Y.,
  April 28, 1997 (NA, AA)

Berens, Frances, Oyster Bay, N.Y., July 7, 1997 (W)

Botto, Irwin and Cissy, Hicksville, N.Y., March 29, 1999 (W)

Burnett, Eugene, Wyandanch, N.Y., March 19, 1999 (AA)

Burnett, Eugene and Bernice, Wyandanch, N.Y., January 7, 2004 (AA)

Cassano, Louise and Mauro, Levittown, N.Y., July 28, 1999 (W)

Cooley, Arthur, Long Island, N.Y., April 7, 1997 (W)

DellaRatta, Ralph, phone interview, December 10, 1998 (W)

Dengler, Fred, phone interview, February 18, 1999 (W)

Dever, Dinah, phone interview, December 8, 2000 (W)

Godsey, Jack and Betty, Manhasset, N.Y., March 12, 2001

Hicks, Fred, Hicksville, N.Y., December 17, 1998 (W)

Jackson, Alex, Riverhead, N.Y., July 14, 1997 (AA)

Kane, Julian and Muriel, Great Neck, N.Y., April 2005 (W)

Kopchinsky, Harold, Wheatley Heights, N.Y., December 11, 1998 (AA)

Larrequi, William, North Amityville, N.Y., July 27, 1999 (H)

Leftenants, Mary, North Amityville, N.Y., March 30, 1999 (AA)

Levitt, John, Felton, Ga., March 26, 2001 (W)

Levitt, William, Jr., phone interview, March 13, 2001 (W)

McKeown, Michael, Long Island, N.Y, June 14, 1997 (W)

Merrick, James, phone interview, December 8, 1998 (AA)

Mittelman, Ellen and Stanley, phone interview, May 15, 1999 (W)

Paterson, Thomas, Huntington, N.Y., December 18, 1998 (W)

Puleston, Dennis, Bellport, N.Y., September 23, 1996 (W)

Purdy, Seth, Amityville, N.Y., December 4, 1998 (W)

Reed, Eugene, Lindenhurst, N.Y., May 17, 2002 (AA)

Reimers, Richard, Manhasset, N.Y., June 11, 2001 (W)

Reuschle, Frank and Leonie, phone interview, June 28, 1997 (W)

Rowehl, Robert, Mattituck, N.Y., March 29, 1999 (W)

Schnide, Helen, phone interview, December 15, 1998 (W)

Seelinger, Charles, North Babylon, N.Y., July 26, 1999 (W)

Smith, Meta, Syosset, N.Y., March 16, 2001 (W)

Smits, Edward, phone interview, December 14, 1998 (W)

Smoley, Melvin, phone interviews, April 23, 27, 28, 1999 (W)

Spock, Marjorie, Sullivan, Maine, November 23-24, 1996 (W)

Stagg, Richard, phone interview, April 23, 1999 (W)

Turner, John, Cold Spring Harbor, N.Y., May 24, 2002 (W)

Wheeler, Harry and Miriam, phone interviews, December 14, 1998,
     August 18, 2001 (W)

White, Richard, Tucson, Ariz., April 17, 1999 (W)

Worthing, Jerry and Clare, Levittown, N.Y., March 16, 2001 (W)

Wurster, Charles, Old Field, N.Y., November 15, 1996 (W)

Yannacone, Carol, Patchogue, N.Y., August 21, 1996 (W)

Yannacone, Victor, Patchogue, N.Y., August 21, 1996 (W)

Los Angeles Area

Alva, Beatrice "Bea," San Gabriel, Calif., May 20, 1999 (H)

Banks, Charles and Alberta, Pasadena, Calif., June 4, 1999 (AA)

Breslow, Lester, Los Angeles, Calif., October 19, 2006 (W)

Contreras, Manuel and John, Pasadena, Calif., June 3, 1999 (H)

Cordova, Victoria, Duarte, Calif., June 4, 1999 (H)

Cottrell, Sharon, Long Beach, Calif., June 9-17, 2003 (W)

Duncan, Sarah, San Gabriel, Calif., May 22, 2003 (W)

Fantz, John, San Gabriel, Calif., June 9-17, 2003 (W)

Gillespie, Richard, phone interview, June 6, 2003 (W)

Greenwald, Alvin, phone interview, January 12-15, 2005 (W)

Haynes, Charles, Lakewood, Calif., June 5, 1999, (W)

Hillburgh, Bill, Long Beach, Calif., June 9, 1999 (W)

Ishihara, Mary and Ishi, San Gabriel, Calif., June 6, 1999 (A)

Katz, Harold, Lakewood, Calif., June 10, 1999 (W)

Knerr, Richard, and Gillespie, Richard, Arcadia, Calif., June 2, 2003 (W)

Lillard, Louise, North Hollywood, Calif., June 12, 2003 (W)

Lopez, Esmeralda, phone interview, May 21, 2001 (H)

Molina-Leffel, Irma; Hannah, Lee; and Haley, Judy, Lakewood, Calif.,
     June 23, 2003 (H, W, W)

Molina-Leffel, Irma, Lakewood, Calif., June 17, 2003 (H)

Perez, Manuel, Pasadena, Calif., May 23, 2001 (H)

Pinette, David, Arcadia, Calif., May 21, 2001 (W)

Prentice, Cheryl, San Gabriel, Calif., January 11, 2005 (W)

Ruiz, Rosie, Los Angeles, Calif., June 6, 1999 (H)

Rynerson, Bud and Jackie, Lakewood, Calif., June 9, 1999 (W)
Rynerson, Jackie, Lakewood, Calif., October 21, 2006 (W)
Rynerson, Steve, phone interview, February 5, 2009 (W)
Salas, Ernie, San Gabriel, Calif., June 9, 1999, June 12, 2003 (H)
Schnee, Ted and Shirley, Lakewood, Calif., June 10, 1999 (W)
Wagner, Robert and Mickey, Lakewood, Calif., October 21, 2001 (W)
Waldie, Donald, Lakewood, Calif., June 1, 1999 (W)

Acknowledgments

This project, more than a decade in the making, has incurred a mountain of debts that I can only begin to address. Those easiest to thank are the institutions that have offered material support. The genesis of the project goes back to my time at the Federated History Department of the New Jersey Institute of Technology (NJIT) and Rutgers-Newark in the mid-1990s. My position there, as well as generous summer grants, enabled my initial research into the late 1950s lawsuit against DDT. A fellowship at the Rutgers Center for Critical Analysis of Contemporary Culture (CACC) offered me vital time off from teaching to firm up the project's early intellectual footing. On moving to the History Department at Stony Brook University on Long Island in the late 1990s, I gratefully gained the opportunity to teach in, as well as about, the very suburban place I had begun to study. A Mellon Fellowship from the Huntington Library launched the Los Angeles portion of my research, and travel grants from the Historical Society of Southern California permitted vital follow-through. Thanks, too, to the National Humanities Center (NHC), where a fellowship year facilitated the writing of this book's first draft.

Alone in the archives or at my computer during most of my work on this book, I nevertheless enjoyed considerable company—those voices that lingered from many a discussion as well the printed page. Questions raised in the 1990s by Bill Cronon, in publications and in person, helped lay much of the early foundation, including my choice of case studies. Through comments at a 1997 session of the American Society for Environmental History, as well as through their own work, Richard White and Carolyn Merchant molded this book's beginnings. Thanks, as well, to the interdisciplinary groups of scholars I met through my year at the Rutgers CACC, under the leadership of Neil Smith, and during my time at the NHC, which also provided formative food for this book's thoughts. I owe much to the cohort of scholars who over the last decade and more, have sought to "incorporate" or "embody" environmental history. From a 1998 workshop on "Body and Place" in Newark, to the 2002 conference in Madison that gave rise to a special issue of *Osiris*, to the flurry of books, edited volumes, and articles that followed over the last few years, I have learned a great deal from many in this exciting new line of scholarship. I feel obliged especially to single out those collaborators with whom I have worked in the process: Gregg Mitman, Michelle Murphy, Harold Platt, and Chris Rosen. I sought here to apply many of their and others' insights to suburban environmentalism, though I alone am responsible for the results.

Special thanks go to those in the departments in which I have been privileged to work during the many years of this book's composition. At Rutgers-NJIT, a confluence of innovation-minded historians with other scholars harboring lively and far-reaching environmental interests supported an experimentation with new ideas and directions. In Stony Brook's History Department, I found a strong collegial and cooperative culture. Its encouragement and feedback have nourished this project and me in a host of ways. More obliquely, I owe much to my collaboration over nearly a decade with a couple of departments in the United Kingdom. Dialogue with Joseph Melling and Mark Jackson at Exeter University and with Ronnie Johnston, also with Arthur McIvor, at Glasgow-Caledonian, though ostensibly on different topics, has yielded unexpected rewards for this study. Visits there spurred me to think about what my history would look like and mean to someone who was neither an American nor an Americanist. Stony Brook historians, with their foresightful emphasis on thematic and cross-national perspectives, affirmed the importance of such questions. And the search for suitable answers helped make this book writable, inclining me toward what its central thesis has turned out to be.

I thank the many other audiences this work has found within the academy that have challenged my assumptions and propelled my inquiries and arguments along their circuitous way. Among these have been the Princeton Environmental History Reading Group; the Science Studies, History Department, and History of Medicine Colloquia at Stony Brook; the Colloquium in the Department of History and Sociology of Science at the University of Pennsylvania; the Oral History Program at the University of North Carolina (UNC) at Chapel Hill; the Social Science Colloquium at Wake Forest University; the Workshop in the History of Medicine and the Sciences at Yale University; the Conference on City Health at Manchester University, U.K.; the Program on Industrial Environments at the Rutgers Center for Historical Analysis; the Drexel Workshop on Science, Technology, and Society; the History of Public Health Unit at the London School of Hygiene and Tropical Medicine; and sessions at meetings of the American Historical Association, the Organization of American Historians, and the American Society for Environmental History.

Not least of the voices echoing in my head as I have labored over this book were those of my interviewees. Among the many individuals who agreed to sit down and share familial memories with a rank stranger, I am immensely appreciative of their time and their trust. I regret that a single book can only give a glimmer of the richness and breadth of their recollections. I am especially thankful for the help I received from the families whose stories I wound up featuring: on Long Island, the Kanes, the Burnetts, and the Murphys; and around Los Angeles, the Alvas, the Rynersons, and the Lillards. Endeavoring to stay true to what they have told me, I have gravitated away from many scholarly presumptions about suburbs. I can only hope that the resulting history seems closer to what they and other suburban settlers can recognize as their own.

Thanks, too, to the many people who guided and sheltered me in my many travels across New York and to the West Coast. As I visited upward of a hundred libraries and archives, I can only single out the most frequented for thanks among them. Those overseeing the special collections at the Huntington Library, the University of California, Los Angeles, and the Pasadena Historical Society generously steered me through their vast holdings, as did those at Stony Brook University and the Long Island Studies Institute at Hofstra University. A multitude of others helpfully manned the many local, county, and state collections I visited across both these metropolitan regions, from the county archives of Nassau and Los Angeles to the town clerks and librarians in Levittown and Lakewood and Cerritos, Amityville and San Gabriel, Old Field and Beverly Hills. Archivists at the state libraries in Albany and Sacramento as well as the National Archives II in Bethesda also furnished amiable and able guidance. In the course of this project, I learned to use GIS software, benefiting from the assistance of several key helpers, among them Cynthia Dietz, Miriam Dominguez, and Aidan Mallamo. My final use of this kind of information bears the imprint of Anne Knowles's wise counsel.

When it came time to the writing of this work, I first tested the scholarly waters with smaller pieces of text. Thanks to the helpful feedback I received on contributions to edited volumes by Diane Glave and Mark Stoll, and Dianne Harris, also on submissions to the *Radical History Review* and *Osiris*. Toward the middle and latter half of the writing process, my undergraduate students at Stony Brook, especially those in my seminar on "Suburbanism in International Perspective," provided a sounding board for ideas and drafts. Even more valuable have been graduate students, whose insights and sometime assistance, as well as their own work, have helped steer this project; among them are Jon Anzalone, Soraya Baselious, Mithun Bhattacharya, Neil Buffet, Mark Chambers, Jeff Hall, Jeremy Hubbell, Mike Murphy, Steve Patnode, and Gregory Rosenthal. I appreciate those colleagues who read portions of the manuscript at various stages of composition: Jared Farmer, Richard Harris, Tom Klubock, Linda Nash, Elizabeth Pillsbury, Jenny Price, Ellen Spears, David Stradling, Corina Trietel, and Andrew Wiese. A special thanks to Ted Rice for plowing through a version of the whole thing, to Matt Klingle for doing so twice, and to anonymous readers for a variety of publications as well as for the UNC Press.

At the UNC Press, Sian Hunter showed great patience with the project as it took more time than I had imagined and veered in unexpected directions. Thanks to her and a developmental editor for helping trim it to manageable size. I am especially grateful for the care and efficiency with which Mark Simpson-Vos has shepherded the manuscript across the finish line.

FINALLY, MY GRATITUDE GOES OUT TO those many individuals without whom the countless hours spent in archives and at my computer would have been appreciably harder. Among them were Sonia Gonzalez, Barbara Kos, Bob Mohr, Lanzell and Marjorie Powell, James and Winn Rea, and the folks at Bethany Presbyterian, who helped me prioritize. Thanks to those many who I have come to know through homeless and housing and "greening" initiatives, also while coaching in a youth soccer league, who nourished my appreciation of what local ties make possible. Years ago, friends in Kentucky sat through interviews and conversations that figured into my early thinking: John Cumbler, Ralph Schiefferle and Liz Perkins, and Art and Noel Williams. Thanks to Jeff and Laura Scott Sellers for hosting and conversation during my many trips out LA-way; to Randy and Laura Terry Sellers, for all during a year of return to Chapel Hill, and finally to Patrick and Kathryn Firmin Sellers, for the many talks, visits, and distracting jaunts. As for Julia and Phil Sellers, they tolerated so much, helped so much, and were so good-spirited throughout; I hope they are proud of what has come of it all.

For my own nuclear household, this book has been a longtime and sometimes frustrating companion. Nancy has read draft upon draft, even while generously making time and room for me to write. Annie has quite literally grown up with this book, an all-too-silent and truculent sibling. Even while swallowing so much of its author's energy and attention, this final product mirrors, however distantly, our own suburban journey together. As a small measure of recompense, I dedicate this book to them.

Index